A CIRCULAR ECONOMY HANDBOOK

D0218619

PRAISE FOR THE SECOND EDITION

'As the world adopts strategies to address the stress that the planet is under, more organizations are realizing that their knowledge and skills need updating and developing. A key aspect of this new sustainable approach is understanding where stuff comes from, how a business uses it and what happens to stuff after its first life. This is where the circular economy comes in and this book provides a range of knowledge inputs across a number of key sectors and uses business examples that allow any organization to develop new pathways forwards.'
Dr David Peck, Associate Professor, Circular Built Environment and Critical Materials, Delft University of Technology (TU Delft), The Netherlands

'This is a book for everyone in business, or who wants to shape the future of business. The circular economy is the best toolkit we have for future sustainable business and this book leads you through what it is and why so many businesses and governments are getting on board.'
Tom Szaky, Founder and CEO, TerraCycle

'A very good guide, avoiding jargon and bringing concepts to life with clear explanations and concrete examples. It covers everything you need to know about "going circular" and also goes further, reviewing criticisms and setting the bar higher.'
Stephan Sicars, Managing Director, Directorate of Environment and Energy, United Nations Industrial Development Organization (UNIDO)

'Catherine Weetman provides rich insight into the business opportunity of the circular economy. *A Circular Economy Handbook* covers various company cases and frameworks which are of great practical value to those looking for inspiration. It is a great resource for organizations aiming to close the "idea–action gap" to accelerate the transition towards a circular economy!'
Dr Nancy Bocken, Professor in Sustainable Business, Maastricht Sustainability Institute, School of Business and Economics, Maastricht University

'When considering the change of gear from a linear to a circular economy, and the need to accelerate this transition, then this handbook delivers on all levels. A well-versed specialist, Catherine Weetman describes the themes, measurements and outcomes in a non-technical manner shining a light and giving practical guidance to implementing this change.'
Steve Haskew, Strategic Sustainability Executive, Circular Computing

'Every business leader and university should include this book in their programme for the next generation of aspiring professionals. In this latest edition, Catherine Weetman provides even more case studies in the constantly evolving landscape of circular economy developments around the world. A clear and comprehensive must-read for any seasoned or aspiring circular economy or supply chain professional. From electronics to food to fashion, Catherine has considered a wide range of how CE frameworks have been engaged across sectors so in whatever industry your organization resides, there are key takeaways and learnings to help any business transition towards a more circular world. Highly recommended!'
Noreen Kam, Founder and CEO, LUP Global

'The circular economy is smart strategic thinking for profitable and pur-pose-led business. This book presents a catalogue of practical frameworks and inspiring examples for organizations of all sizes and shapes, in every sector, around the world.'
Anna Tari, Founder, Circular Economy Club (CEC)

'Ensuring that the transition to a new economic model takes place under the best possible conditions is no easy task. Thanks to Catherine Weetman and her contributors, this book once again solidifies the foundations and reinforces the credibility of a circular economy helping us to move towards this paradigm shift that we all wish for. This is now your tool to change everything for the better. Use and reuse it, then pass on to others!'
Alexandre Lemille, The Circular Humansphere

'A perfect mix of theory and practical arguments to convince the reader that our future is circular. We must think differently, create new business rules, values and attitudes. With an outstanding compilation of cases, Catherine Weetman demonstrates how to find the right balance between growth, competitive advantage and value creation for all. Essential reading for

political and businesses leaders, in countries like Brazil, that seek knowledge and inspiration to accelerate the transition.'
Beatriz Luz, Founder of Exchange 4 Change Brasil, NEC and Visiting Professor at FIA

'I truly believe that awakening a taste for change – and making it happen – requires a good understanding of the circular economy while being already immersed in its practicality. It is precisely what this unique handbook does, thanks to its collection of content, its structure, and its perspective. Indeed, it provides a wealth of information gathered in one place: a straightforward way to learn fast and get inspired for your circular initiatives. It demonstrates many existing cases and strategies you might apply. You can peruse it in one go, choose a piece of a chapter that applies to your case or read it back and forth. The icing on the cake for this second version? The added chapter about packaging gives an easy-to-follow overview of this complex problem! Expert without falling into jargon, Catherine Weetman makes the Circular Economy attractive to anyone!'
Colienne Regout, CEO, Look4Loops, Canada

'Making the shift towards a circular economy model can be a huge challenge. Catherine Weetman's book is useful to what's needed most in this day and age: getting into action and shifting the existing paradigm. The book offers a range of insights and tools to help you make that shift, and deliver value along the way. Have fun, use it and join, please, our global community of change makers.'
Harald Friedl, Global Adviser, Systems Change and Circular Economy

PRAISE FOR THE FIRST EDITION

bridges from theory to implementation seamlessly. I would recommend it as a 'go-to' reference for anybody looking to learn about, or adopt, circular economy models.'

Steve Smith, former Director, Supply Chain Transformation, Tata Steel Europe

'Introduces the central concepts and ideas for sustainable ways of working in a clear, pragmatic manner. The many practical examples make tangible the supply chain models increasingly required to conserve scarce resources whilst supporting economic growth. Here is a handbook for change that could not be more timely.'

Calum Lewis, Founder and Principal, Green Room Consulting Ltd, and former Senior Director – Demand Planning/Management EMEA, The LEGO Group

'A clearly written and accessible introduction to the development and implementation of circular thinking, with tangible and meaningful examples to help organizations and their partners making the journey towards circularity.'

Dr Matthew Hunt, Director, Environment and Sustainability Consulting, Royal Haskoning DHV

'Catherine Weetman's ambition seems to me to be to set the agenda for businesses and their supply chains in our globalized economy, and her book, *A Circular Economy Handbook for Business and Supply Chains*, does just that. With elegance and flair, this book promises to open people's eyes, rewire their thinking and reset aspirations for what can be achieved by the intelligent application of these ideas. Weetman is a provocative thinker and has put together a book which will help businesses and those who lead them to stay ahead of the process of organizational adaptation and introduce real and much needed change.'

Gerard Chick, former Director of Intelligence, Skanör Group Ltd

'The need for sustainable supply chain management and in particular the management of the closed loop economy (circular economy) is both topical and important. Supply chain practitioners have the challenge to not only learn and understand these new concepts but also utilize a number of tools and techniques to effectively manage their chains. This book provides a comprehensive treatment of topics influencing the circular economy across a variety of sectors and provides valuable guidance for managing supply chains. An abundance of case examples, tools and learning resources within this book will be extremely beneficial to students, academics and practitioners.'

Samir Dani, Professor of Operations Management, and Head of the Marketing, Management and Organisation Group, Keele Business School, Keele University

'This book fills a need by bringing together a wide range of insights and examples about the growing importance of the circular economy and its impact on traditional business models and the supply chain networks with which we are currently familiar. The many practical cases are supported by the very clear structure and the way that the wider context is integrated into the discussion and analysis. The author has a wealth of experience and this is evident throughout the text. This book is a major and timely contribution to improving our understanding of the circular economy and its implications for supply chain and logistics management.'

Michael Browne, Professor of Logistics, School of Business, Economics and Law, University of Gothenburg

'Circular economy is a fast-rising theme among academics and practitioners. This book consists of wide-ranging references and in-depth knowledge, which crystallizes the idea of the circular economy for implementation and research needs.'

Professor Ming K Lim, Professor of Supply Chain and Operations Management, Coventry University

'If you are looking for a comprehensive and practical guide to the supply chain aspects of the circular economy, this book should comfortably meet your needs. It is cleverly structured, highly informative and written in a very engaging style by one of the foremost specialists in the subject.'

Professor Alan McKinnon, Professor of Logistics, Kühne Logistics University

A Circular Economy Handbook

How to build a more resilient, competitive and sustainable business

SECOND EDITION

Catherine Weetman

KoganPage

First published in Great Britain and the United States in 2017 as *A Circular Economy Handbook for Business and Supply Chains* by Kogan Page Limited
Second edition published in 2021

2nd Floor, 45 Gee Street	122 W 27th Street,	4737/23 Ansari Road
London	10th Floor	Daryaganj
EC1V 3RS	New York, NY 10001	New Delhi 110002
United Kingdom	USA	India
www.koganpage.com		

Kogan Page books are printed on paper from sustainable forests.

Hardback	978 1 78966 533 8
Paperback	978 1 78966 531 4
Ebook	978 1 78966 532 1

British Library Cataloguing-in-Publication Data

A CIP record for this book is available from the British Library.

Library of Congress Cataloging-in-Publication Data

Names: Weetman, Catherine, author.
Title: A circular economy handbook : how to build a more resilient,
    competitive and sustainable business / Catherine Weetman.
Other titles: Circular economy handbook for business and supply chains
Description: Second edition. | London, United Kingdom ; New York, NY :
    Kogan Page, 2021. |
Identifiers: LCCN 2020039159 (print) | LCCN 2020039160 (ebook) | ISBN
    9781789665314 (paperback) | ISBN 9781789665338 (hardback) | ISBN
    9781789665321 (ebook)
Subjects: LCSH: Recycling industry. | Business logistics. | Managerial
    economics.
Classification: LCC HD9975.A2 W44 2021 (print) | LCC HD9975.A2 (ebook) |
    DDC 658.7–dc23

Typeset by Hong Kong FIVE Workshop, Hong Kong
Print production managed by Jellyfish
Printed and bound by CPI Group (UK) Ltd, Croydon CR0 4YY

CONTENTS

Online resources to accompany this book can be downloaded from:

www.koganpage.com/CircEcon2

LIST OF FIGURES AND TABLES

LIST OF CASE STUDIES AND SNAPSHOTS – BY SECTOR AND COMPANY NAME

Company	Description	Sector	Chapter
General Electric	3D printing	Aerospace	9
Excess Materials Exchange	a 'dating site' for secondary materials	All	9
Renault	recycling and remanufacturing	Automotive	1
Renault	remanufacturing, reuse and 'cascading'	Automotive	9
bioMASON	microorganisms to grow construction materials	Construction	9
research	bricks from human urine	Construction	9
Calfee Design	renewable inputs	Consumer durables	2
iFixit	knowledge-sharing platform	Consumer durables	8
IKEA	'a positive impact on people and the planet'	Consumer durables	1
IKEA	simplifying reuse	Consumer durables	2
ReTuna	the world's first recycling mall	Consumer durables	3
ShareGrid platform	P2P renting	Consumer durables	3
Apple	safe, recycled, renewable materials	Consumer technology	8
Apple	trade-in	Consumer technology	8
Apple	material recovery robots	Consumer technology	8
Best Buy	keeping electronics in play	Consumer technology	8

Company	Description	Sector	Chapter
Circular Computing	the 'world's first computer remanufacturer'	Consumer technology	8
Dell	recycled and renewable inputs, closed loop process	Consumer technology	8
Electronics companies	reverse supply chains	Consumer technology	13
Environcom	circular service provider	Consumer technology	8
Fairphone	Fairtrade-certified supply chain for gold	Consumer technology	8
Fairphone 2	modular, durable and repairable	Consumer technology	8
GIAB	closing the loop on insurance claims	Consumer technology	8
Homie	pay per use household appliances	Consumer technology	8
iameco	'sustainable, ecological, high performance computers'	Consumer technology	8
Refind Technologies	artificial intelligence for reverse vending	Consumer technology	4
Repair Café	knowledge-sharing pop-ups	Consumer technology	8
Tech Takeback	pop-up events getting end-of-use consumer technology back into the loop	Consumer technology	8
Telefonica UK – O2 Recycle	rewarding recovery flows	Consumer technology	8
Adidas	recycled inputs, 3D printing	Fashion and textiles	2
Ananas Anam	Piñatex™ fabric: renewable inputs	Fashion and textiles	7
ApparelXchange	making it easy to reuse school uniforms	Fashion and textiles	7
Burberry and Elvis & Kresse	luxury products from offcuts	Fashion and textiles	2

Company	Description	Sector	Chapter
circular.fashion	closing the loop with digital identities	Fashion and textiles	7
Clothes Doctor	wardrobe maintenance	Fashion and textiles	7
Dutch aWEARness	leasing and performance contracts for clothes	Fashion and textiles	3
Elvis & Kresse	upcycled inputs	Fashion and textiles	7
Girl Meets Dress	fashion rental and subscriptions	Fashion and textiles	7
Levi Water‹Less	sharing water-efficiency techniques	Fashion and textiles	2
Looptworks	upcycling	Fashion and textiles	7
Patagonia and iFixit	'do it yourself' repairs	Fashion and textiles	12
Petit Pli	inspired by origami	Fashion and textiles	7
ThredUp	clothing exchange platform	Fashion and textiles	7
Tidal Vision	green chemistry and waste = food	Fashion and textiles	7
bio-bean®	energy from waste	Food	6
Espresso Mushroom Company	mushroom growing kits	Food	6
Feedback Global	campaigning to transform the food system	Food	6
Greencup	open loop, cross-sector recycling	Food	6
GRO Holland	growing mushrooms on coffee grounds	Food	6
Milwaukee city	de-icing roads with cheese	Food	2
MyMuesli	bespoke breakfasts	Food	12
Pectcof	coffee cherry – waste = food	Food	2
The Plant	aquaponics and industrial symbiosis	Food	12
Toast Ale	recovered inputs	Food	2

Company	Description	Sector	Chapter
Tomorrow Machine	biodegradable packaging	Food packaging	2
research project	carbon fibre from algae	Industrial	4
Cisco Systems Inc	take-back and recycle programme	Industrial	2
Kalundborg	industrial symbiosis	Industrial	12
Philips	service and performance	Industrial	1
Philips	circular solutions make good business sense	Industrial	9
Rohner	Climatex Lifecycle fabric	Industrial	9
Rype Office	open loop remanufacturing	Industrial	9
Schneider	Circulars 2019 Multinational award-winner	Industrial	9
Herman Miller	design for recyclability	Office furniture	9
Warp IT	reuse platform	Office furniture	9
3D Seed	low-cost, solar-powered kit to recycle PET packaging into 3D printed objects	Packaging	4
Algramo	sharing the savings of bulk distribution	Packaging	10
ARK Reusables	reusable and recyclable food-to-go containers	Packaging	10
Frugalpac	recyclable multi-layer beverage carton	Packaging	10
Garçon Wines	flat wine bottles saving resources, volume, weight and energy	Packaging	10
How2Recycle	taking the guesswork out of recycling	Packaging	10
Loop (by TerraCycle)	making reuse easy and attractive	Packaging	10
Splosh	concentrated refills for household cleaning products	Packaging	10
TerraCycle	recycling hard-to-recycle waste	Packaging	10
Ecovative Design	growing packaging	Packaging; industrial	2
ship dismantling	reverse supply chain and recovery of materials	Transport	12

ABOUT THE AUTHOR

Catherine Weetman

Catherine is an international speaker, workshop facilitator, coach and host of the Circular Economy Podcast. Her consultancy, Rethink Global, helps organizations understand, use and benefit from the circular economy – exploring the 'sweet spot' where strategy, supply chain and sustainability come together.

Catherine has over 25 years' experience in manufacturing, retail and supply chains, and her career spans food, fashion and logistics, including senior roles with Tesco, Kellogg's and DHL Supply Chain.

She is a Visiting Fellow at the University of Huddersfield, a Fellow of the Chartered Institute of Logistics and Transport, and a Fellow of The RSA (Royal Society for the Encouragement of Arts, Manufactures and Commerce). She supports the global non-profit Circular Economy Club as a Mentor and Regional Coordinator for the Tees Valley, UK.

Catherine qualified as an Industrial Engineer and began her career in garment manufacturing, before moving onto logistics solution design, project management, business intelligence and supply chain consulting. Catherine gained an MSc in Logistics and Distribution from Cranfield University and her awards include the Director's Prize for Outstanding Achievement at Cranfield Centre for Logistics and Transportation, and the British Clothing Industries Association Business Fellowship Award.

Catherine says:

I first came across the circular economy back in 2010, when I was struggling to work out how businesses could adopt sustainable strategies. After spending months researching the issues (and getting really depressed about the scale of the problem and lack of solutions), I read about the circular economy in a short book for schools: *Sense and Sustainability* by Ken Webster and Craig Johnson of the Ellen MacArthur Foundation (2009). Suddenly the world looked much brighter, and I wanted to learn more about the circular economy and how it could solve the enormous challenges we face in creating a resilient, healthy, sustainable future. By 2013, I had decided to focus entirely on helping to 'spread the word' on why it is so important for our future, how it is taking shape and how it helps. I believe the circular economy is the best tool we have to underpin profitable, resilient and sustainable business models, and support healthy, equitable societies. My aim is to inspire you to use circular approaches in your own lives and work.

ABOUT THE CONTRIBUTORS

Katie Beverley

Katie is a Senior Research Officer in Ecodesign at PDR, the International Centre for Design Research in Cardiff, Wales. Katie undertakes research, knowledge transfer activities and commercial projects which require the application of design to minimize environmental impact, increase resource efficiency and exploit circular economy opportunities. Katie holds a PhD in chemistry, which proves useful in facilitating discussions between designers, scientists and technologists, and for understanding opportunities for new materials in the circular economy. She has worked with policymakers, educators and businesses (including furniture, automotive, energy storage, electronics, sports equipment, fashion and textiles) both in Wales and internationally.

Jo Conlon

Dr Jo Conlon is a Lecturer in Fashion Business at the University of Manchester. Jo has over 10 years' experience teaching Fashion Business in Higher Education. Prior to this, she worked within the supply chain of Marks & Spencer as a Technical and Sourcing Manager. In 2019, Jo completed a Doctorate in Education (EdD) investigating how digital technologies can reshape fashion business education. Her research centres on the enabling role of digital technologies on knowledge management, learning and change within organizations.

Jo has also received funding for two Knowledge Transfer Partnerships (KTP) projects to implement emerging and enabling technologies. Jo is a Fellow of the Higher Education Academy, a member of the Chartered Management Institute and an Associate of the Textile Institute.

Dr Regina Frei

Dr Regina Frei joined Southampton Business School as Associate Professor of Operations and Supply Chain Management in 2019. She is passionate about sustainable value chains and the circular economy. She has over 40 peer-reviewed publications and 13 research grants. From 2013 to 2019, she was a Senior Lecturer in Manufacturing Engineering and Supply Chain Management at the University of Portsmouth, UK. Previously, she was a Postdoc at Cranfield University and Imperial College London. She holds a PhD in Distributed Robotics from Universidade Nova, Lisbon, Portugal, and an MSc in Micro-Engineering from the Swiss Federal Institute of Technology Lausanne (EPFL), Switzerland. She wrote her MSc thesis at the Royal Institute of Technology (KTH) in Stockholm, Sweden, and did internships with the International Watch Company (IWC) and Schindler Lifts, both in Switzerland.

Richard James MacCowan

Richard is the Founder and Managing Director of the Biomimicry Innovation Lab, and CEO of Smart Stable Limited, an equine technology startup. Alongside this, he is a Visiting Lecturer in Biomimicry and Strategic Product Design at the International Hellenic University. Richard sits on the advisory board of LSW Hotels and Post Harvest Ventures in Uganda.

With a background in human behaviour, real estate development and urban design, Richard has worked across many sectors around the world and given keynote presentations to leading organizations. He is involved with the Global Manufacturing and Industrialization Summit, focusing on new strategies for manufacturing in the Fourth Industrial Revolution.

Richard supports the Circular Economy Club, where he leads the team in York (UK) and mentors startups.

Barry Waddilove

Barry has 30 years' experience working in design and product development with brands and organizations across 25 countries. During 2014 and 2015 he completed extensive research into the role of design in the circular economy, whilst working as a Schmidt MacArthur Fellow with Cranfield University and the Ellen MacArthur Foundation. Barry holds an MDes in Design and Innovation for Sustainability from Cranfield University and is a fellow of the Royal Society for the Encouragement of Arts, Manufactures and Commerce (RSA).

Currently working as Head of Design for Electrolux, North America, Barry is exploring new innovations that meet the company's corporate objective to be circular and climate neutral by 2030.

ACKNOWLEDGEMENTS

Since I wrote the first edition of this book in 2015–16, the circular economy has progressed in leaps and bounds. For this second edition, my challenge was what to leave out, rather than how to find credible examples and evidence-based research. Again, I am grateful to the many people who have inspired me, helped and offered support. I would like to give special thanks to my contributors, including Katie Beverley, Dr Jo Conlon, Dr Regina Frei, Richard James MacCowan and Barry Waddilove; and to those who provided advice, introductions and feedback, including Jo Conlon, Lily Dunn, my colleague Peter Desmond, Alison Jones, Karen Skidmore and the Kogan Page team. Also to Calum Lewis, who provided feedback and suggestions for some of the first edition.

Thank you to everyone who helped with information for case studies and content for the second edition, including Anna Bance of Girl Meets Dress, Rudi Dieleman of Pectcof and Noreen Kam of LUP Global. Also to all my Circular Economy Podcast guests for sharing their 'circular stories': especially to Lucy Antal of Feedback Global, David Bassetti of 3D-Seed, Katie Beverley of PDR, Dr Nancy Bocken of Homie, Izzie Eriksen of ApparelXchange, Adam Fairweather of Smile Plastics, Dr David Greenfield of Tech-Takeback, Jo-Anne Godden of RubyMoon, Tom Harper of Unusual Rigging, Matilda Jarbin of GIAB, Eve Kekeh of Bundlee, Elaine Kerr of International Synergies, Beth Massa of ARK Reusables, Sophie Thomas of Thomas Matthews and Katie Whalen of IIIEE.

I'm grateful to those who provided research, diagrams, charts and other work, including Dr Nancy Bocken, Rhys Charles for his Periodic Table of global end-of-life recycling rates, Dr Fiona Charnley and Dr Mariale Moreno for their Circular Business Model Archetypes, Dr Roland Geyer for his diagram and work on plastic flows, Peter Laybourn of International Synergies, Geoff Kendall of the Future-Fit Foundation, the Ellen MacArthur Foundation for the butterfly diagram, Dr John Mulrow, Erik Assadourian and Dr Victoria Santos for their work on 'degrowth' and 'shrinking', Kate Raworth for the Doughnut, Linda Booth Sweeney for her systems thinking checklist, Katie Whalen, and Kresse Wresling for her 'perfect product' sketch. It has been an honour to share their work, together with other leading thinkers – especially the Circle Economy team, the Ellen MacArthur Foundation, and Walter Stahel.

Over the last five years, I've collected over 600 examples of inspiring businesses, social enterprises, startups, researchers and many others, helping to make history with circular economy innovations. I've also used the Circle-Lab Knowledge Hub, which has over 2,000 case studies from all around the world, and I'm now collaborating with Circle Economy to feed more of my examples into this fantastic free resource.

Thanks to my parents and sisters for their support, and to my friends, especially Lindsay Leonard and Paul Stokes for their regular encouragement and writing advice. To Ken Webster and Craig Johnson of the Ellen MacArthur Foundation for their book *Sense and Sustainability*, which provided an 'aha' moment about the circular economy in 2010, and to Gudrun Freece for her sound advice and sparking the idea for the book's focus. I'm grateful also to those who helped with the case studies for the first edition: Adam Fairweather of Re-worked, Smile Plastics and Innovations Director at Greencup coffee; Dr Carmen Hijosa of Ananas Anam, Dr Greg Lavery, Founder of Rype Office and Director at Lavery/Pennell; Cris Stephenson, Managing Director at Environcom. I'm grateful to Anna Tari and the Circular Economy Club team for providing a free-to-all resource platform and network of like-minded people.

I want to say 'thank you' to my brilliant, generous husband, Mark Jones. Yet again, he has provided boundless encouragement and done far more than his fair share of cooking, dog-walking, and cleaning, along with delivering numerous cups of tea (and pieces of chocolate) to my desk. He also 'tuned in' to the research challenge, flagging up articles and radio programmes. Without his support, this book would not exist.

Lastly, thank you for learning about the circular economy and helping develop smarter ways for business to support society and our living planet. I hope you find inspiration and stories in these pages to help you create better businesses – and a better world.

Introduction

*You never change things by fighting the existing reality. To change
something, build a new model that makes the existing model obsolete.*

R BUCKMINSTER FULLER[1]

In the face of the climate and ecological emergency, the choices we make
matter more than ever. Everything we do – how we work, live, travel and
socialize – can either regenerate our planet and the living systems we depend
on, or destroy it. In just a few centuries we've increased our negative impact
on the earth, its atmosphere, the climate, air, water, soil and nature, to unsustainable levels. We've moved from a world of abundance and limitless
potential to a world of scarcity, constraints and fear.

The circular economy is an essential tool in our survival kit, giving us
smarter ways to design, make and use everything. Instead of using systems
of extraction, pollution and waste that ultimately lead to lost value, we can
design systems to reuse, repair and regenerate, creating value opportunities
for business and society.

A growing body of information focuses on the concept and principles of
the circular economy, highlighting macro-level implications for sectors and
regions. In contrast, this book builds on the underlying principles and theory to examine how it works in the real world. Practical strategies and real
examples for businesses of all shapes and sizes, in every industrial sector,
including lots of startups and small businesses, prove that circular approaches are profitable, resilient and sustainable.

I've focused on what it means for businesses, their customers and supply
chains, using plain language and avoiding jargon, aiming to make it easy to
absorb. I hope to inspire you to use circular approaches in your own lives
and work.

I've included and built on the core concept and elements from leading thinkers and researchers, including the major schools of thought (including Walter Stahel, McDonough and Braungart, Gunter Pauli, the Ellen MacArthur Foundation and Industrial Ecology), business groups, consultancies and eminent scholars.

My career background in manufacturing, retail and the supply chain across food, fashion and FMCG has helped me understand the 'sweet spot' where strategy, supply chain and sustainability come together, to see a wealth of opportunities to design products, services and business models that help us to use our resources, instead of using them up – once they're gone, they're gone. We need to regenerate resources, living systems and societies, instead of creating waste, pollution and destruction.

The book answers questions that come up in conversation with the people that I coach, and at talks and workshops, including:

- What is the circular economy, how did it emerge, and how have the various approaches converged?
- How is it different from 'traditional' business: for product designs, materials, production, supply chains, and for business models?
- Why does it matter – what are the global drivers and trends causing businesses to invest in it and governments to encourage it? How is it better for business and society?
- How is it starting to take shape, in a range of market sectors and businesses of all shapes and sizes?
- How does it change traditional approaches to supply chain strategy and operations?
- How do you create a business case to convince investors and stakeholders, and to make a compelling case for change?
- How should businesses get started on a road map to circularity? Where should they focus first, and how might they measure progress and success?

We will answer these questions, and more, as we investigate what the circular economy means for a range of industry sectors, and along the supply chain. Lots of new business jargon is emerging to describe these 'disruptive innovations' (see Figure 0.1), and we unpack these.

FIGURE 0.1   Buzzwords for a new industrial revolution

Internet of Things   **Artificial Intelligence**   *Shared ownership*
Dematerialization *Biomimicry* Natural capital   **BIG DATA**
Digital Economy   Biological and Technical Nutrients
Up-cycling *Additive Manufacturing*   **Ecodesign**
Closed Loop   **3D printing** *Biorefining* **Design for Disassembly**
Collaborative consumption *Pay As You Go*   Subscriptions
Industrial Ecology *Circular Economy*   *Blue Economy*
Product: Service systems   *Mass customization*   Peer to Peer
Platforms   Reuse   **Cradle to cradle**   Waste=food
Machine learning   Right to repair   **Prosumer**
D4D   Maker Movement   **Remanufacturing**
Systems thinking   *Cooperatives*   Open Sourcing
Permaculture Mobile Apps **Renewable energy** *Resource Efficiency*

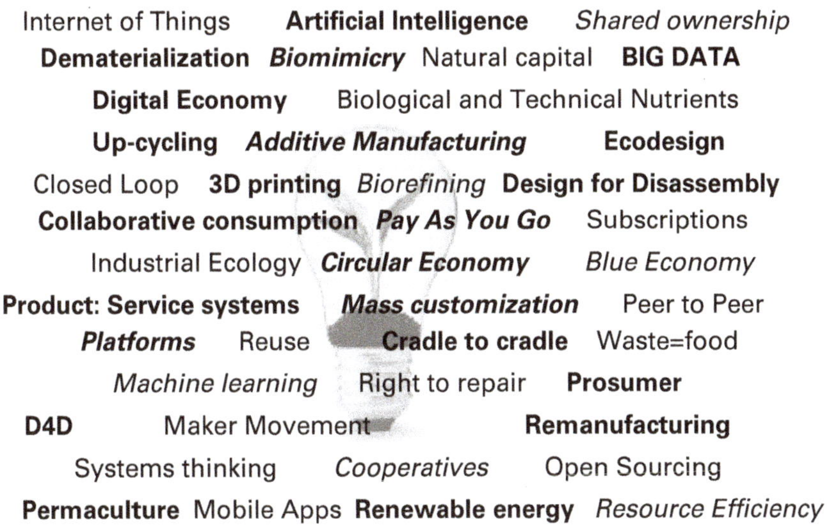

SOURCE: © Catherine Weetman

The second edition

Since writing the first edition in 2015–16, my work in consulting, coaching and speaking meant I continued to collect insightful research and new case studies. When reading through all the notes, examples, journal articles and white papers I'd collected, I realized just how much had changed – this was going to be nearly as big a project as the first edition! Included in the many updates are a new chapter on packaging, major updates to Chapter 3 on business models and a new version of my Circular Economy Framework. The chapter on enablers includes new contributions on biomimicry and ecodesign, plus extra insights on technology such as artificial intelligence and blockchain. Throughout the book, I've added lots of new examples of companies and other organizations putting circular economy principles into practice – 'making it real'.

Global trends signalling a new direction

The next industrial revolution is already under way, with digital technologies transforming products and market sectors. However, there are major challenges, and business leaders have deep concerns about the volatile costs and reliability of access for many resources. Demand is outstripping supply, and we are failing to meet the basic needs of billions of people, with worsening problems of poverty, hunger, access to drinking water and sanitation. Human impact has transformed our planet to such an extent that scientists argue we have entered a new geological epoch – the Anthropocene.[2]

We are the best-informed generation in society – ever. Scientists are discovering more, every day, about how we can conserve, restore and regenerate our world, and how our current materials, methods and models are destroying and depleting it.

Over the last 150 years, as mass manufacturing developed, we have adopted a linear system. We take some materials, make a product and then discard it at the end of its use. This system of 'take, make, waste' (the linear economy) has moved us into 'ecological overshoot'. Each year, the world population is consuming at the level of 1.75 planets.[3] In the past 50 years, we have destroyed or degraded 60 per cent of the earth's ecosystems – our life-support systems.[4] Around the world, we can see the effects of climate change, with flooding, droughts, storms, wildfires, ocean acidification, species extinction and much more. In October 2019, scientists from the Intergovernmental Panel on Climate Change (IPCC) delivered a stark warning: to avoid the catastrophic impacts of climate change, global warming cannot exceed 1.5°C above pre-industrial temperatures. That means we must halve *greenhouse gas (GHG)* emissions by 2030 and reduce them to net-zero by the middle of the century. The circular economy plays a major role in reducing GHG emissions and supporting progress towards the United Nations Sustainable Development Goals (SDGs).

People expect companies to be doing the right things – sourcing ethical, safe materials, making durable, repairable products and providing end-of-life solutions for what they sell. According to Euromonitor International's latest sustainability survey, 54 per cent of global consumers believe ethical purchase decisions will make a difference and one-fifth of the global consumer population prefer to repair damaged items.[5]

How is the circular economy better?

Instead of the 'take, make and waste' approach, the circular economy focuses on circulating resources instead of using them up, and designs waste out of the system. We aim to get more from less, getting more 'use' and value from every product, component and material, and ensuring all 'waste' becomes food – for another industrial process, or for nature – so regenerating future resources and the living systems we depend on. By doing this, we can

FIGURE 0.2   From linear to circular

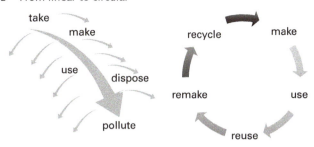

SOURCE: Catherine Weetman

disconnect (or 'decouple') the provision of products and services from resource consumption.

The circular economy is far more ambitious than increased recycling, or 'zero waste to landfill'. It extends the value chain to cover product use and end of life, as well as all the stages of supply, processing, manufacturing, distribution and sales. It means redesigning products, using different raw materials, creating new by-products and recovering value from (previously) waste materials. It may mean selling a service instead of a product, or finding ways to refurbish, repair or remanufacture the product for resale (see Figure 0.2).

This requires radical rethinking for both business strategy and for supply chains, creating collaborative, symbiotic networks that connect within and across industry sectors. Consumers and businesses will expect increased transparency for suppliers and materials, and supply chain teams will source renewable or recycled raw materials and distribute new by-products.

The opportunities are all around us. Half the aluminium produced each year does not make it to the final product, the average European car is utilized for only 2 per cent of the available time, one-third of all food is wasted, and over half of plastics could be mechanically recycled.[6]

The circular economy is not a 'one size fits all' solution, and closing the loop successfully means rethinking the entire process: from farming and mining, through production, to use and post-use, with collaborative approaches throughout the value chain to drive innovation and continuous improvement.

Businesses will develop robust, efficient return loops to recover value and resources from end-of-use products. As the supply chain evolves to include new operations such as remanufacturing or repair and to manage new by-products, partnerships and symbiotic relationships will develop to exchange knowledge and resources.

FIGURE 0.3   Structure of the book

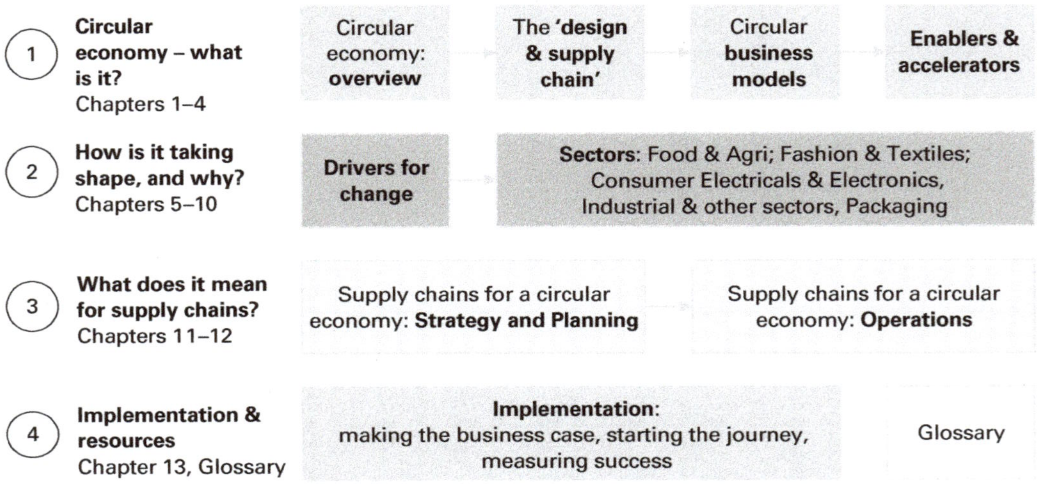

1 | **Circular economy – what is it?** Chapters 1–4

2 | **How is it taking shape, and why?** Chapters 5–10

3 | **What does it mean for supply chains?** Chapters 11–12

4 | **Implementation & resources** Chapter 13, Glossary

Circular economy: **overview**

Drivers for **change**

Supply chains for a circular economy: **Strategy and Planning**

Implementation: making the business case, starting the journey, measuring success

The 'design & supply chain'

Sectors: Food & Agri; Fashion & Textiles; Consumer Electricals & Electronics, Industrial & other sectors, Packaging

Supply chains for a circular economy: **Operations**

Circular **business models**

Enablers & accelerators

Glossary

Success means reframing the way we think about design and rethinking the business model. The focus is on how to find value opportunities – creating, conserving and circulating value – and discovering ways to add value for stakeholders, including customers, suppliers and wider society.

In a circular economy, where waste = food, businesses that focus on keeping their customers for life and developing products that have a 'life of their own' will thrive. Ray Anderson, the founder of Interface, summed it up superbly:[7]

> taking nothing, wasting nothing and doing no harm – and doing very well by doing good, at the expense not of the earth but of less alert competitors.

The book structure

Part One: An overview of the circular economy

We begin with an overview of the circular economy, how it evolved, the main concepts and leading contributors. My circular economy framework 2.0 builds on the common themes from the key schools of thought, and in Chapters 2 to 4, we look at what it means in practical terms for business and in value chains. Chapter 2 looks at the framework's central flow, the 'design and supply chain'; Chapter 3 explores the various business models and their implications; Chapter 4 reviews 'enablers and accelerators', helping create opportunities and incentives for circular approaches.

Part Two: How are businesses adopting circular economy models?

In this Part, we start with the global drivers and trends, including those risks and issues keeping business leaders awake at night. In the next five chapters, we unpack what this means for a range of industry sectors, looking at issues and risks for the 'traditional' supply chain for that sector, followed by practical examples for each element in my circular economy framework.

Part Three: What does this mean for supply chains?

Circular supply chains will evolve to manage an 'ecosystem' with complex choices; aiming for resilience and agility. Chapter 11 focuses on strategy and planning, including network design to suit distributed manufacturing and locally recovered materials. I share my 'eight sustainability principles' for supply chains and show how these can guide decisions and priorities for supply chain redesign. We look at how the supply chain team can develop their own circular initiatives and examine the role of product life-cycle management.

Chapter 12 explores how supply chain operations – including sourcing and procurement, manufacturing, distribution and reverse logistics – need to evolve for a circular economy. We cover remanufacturing, life cycle assessments, technology and other enablers, plus relationships, partnerships and collaboration, and highlight value opportunities in the supply chain itself.

Part Four: Implementation

In Chapter 13, we suggest ways to implement circular economy approaches: whether for an entire business; for a product; or perhaps starting with some aspects of how we design products or processes. How can we create a compelling business case for change and set the strategic direction, involving a wider group of stakeholders to uncover value opportunities? What risks, opportunities and other factors should we consider? What are the common barriers and objections, and how can we overcome these? This chapter includes toolkits and resources to identify opportunities and measure progress and success.

Although I aim to avoid jargon, I recognize that new terms and phrases are emerging and become 'shorthand' – saving time once you are familiar with them. To provide a quick reference for these new words you will see in reports and publications, I include a glossary of terms. In the chapters, **glossary terms** are highlighted in *italics*, generally the first time they appear in each main section within a chapter (unless they are explained within that chapter). A list of all the case examples, organized by industry sector, is included at the early pages of the book.

Numbering: the book uses the following numbering system:

One million = 1,000,000
One billion = 1,000,000,000 = 1,000 million
One trillion = 1,000,000,000,000 = 1,000,000 million (1 million million)

Notes

1   Buckminster Fuller Institute www.bfi.org/ideaindex/projects/2015/greenwave (archived at https://perma.cc/QS4B-LP4G) [accessed 27 December 2019]

2   Lewis SL and Maslin MA (2015) Defining the Anthropocene, *Nature*, **519**, pp 171–80 (11 March 2015)

3   Earth Overshoot Day (2019) Global Footprint Network www.overshootday. org/ (archived at https://perma.cc/7BCA-ANYH) [accessed 14 January 2020]

4   Millennium Ecosystem Assessment (2005) [accessed 8 August 2016] Ecosystems and Human Well-Being: Synthesis [Online] www.millenniumassessment.org/ documents/document.356.aspx.pdf (archived at https://perma.cc/ED8P-BH3K), p 1

5   Euromonitor International Launches New Whitepaper 'How to Become a Sustainable Brand', Euromonitor (9 September 2019) blog.euromonitor.com/ euromonitor-international-launches-new-whitepaper-how-to-become-a-sustainable-brand/ (archived at https://perma.cc/X8HZ-DGQF) [accessed 10 January 2020]

6   Material Economics (2018) The Circular Economy – a Powerful Force for Climate Mitigation. Available from: materialeconomics.com/publications/ the-circular-economy (archived at https://perma.cc/BFS6-TRLA) [accessed 27 December 2019]

7   Anderson, R (1994) included in Lovins, AB (2011) [accessed 10 March 2016] RMI Trustee Ray C Anderson, Rocky Mountain Institute Blog, blog.rmi.org/ GiantPassesRMITrusteeRayCAnderson (archived at https://perma.cc/KZ7Y-APKW)

PART ONE

An overview of the circular economy

1

The circular economy

Every few hundred years in Western history there occurs a sharp transformation. Within a few short decades, society – its world view, its basic values, its social and political structure, its arts, its key institutions – rearranges itself. Fifty years later there is a new world.

PETER F DRUCKER[1]

What is it?

Writing the words quoted above in 1992, respected author and business consultant Peter Drucker continued: 'And the people born then cannot even imagine the world in which their grandparents lived and into which their own parents were born.'

In recent decades, we have transformed the way we live, work and communicate. Society, business and governments are realizing that the 'linear economy' (take, make and discard), which emerged from the early industrial revolutions, is not sustainable – financially, socially or ecologically.

Instead, a new approach, the circular economy, is emerging. Companies will rethink how they design laptops, furniture, sneakers, cars, mobile phones, cleaning products and even jeans. Rather than focusing on how to maximize sales and encourage customers to buy the latest model, companies will develop strategies for continuous value creation and profitable, long-term customer relationships.

Professor Walter Stahel and others paint pictures of the switch from 'ownership' to 'access' in the circular economy.[2] I do not own a mobile phone – instead, I lease it from a company that has designed it to be upgradeable, customizable and easy to repair or remanufacture. I don't buy expensive things for occasional use – instead, I rent them.

Businesses large and small, around the world – established global corporates, and disruptive startups – are rethinking business models and product design. They aim to capitalize on the fantastic opportunities to trade with the rapidly growing 'consumer classes', secure access to future resources, and 'future-proof' their businesses.

We review the issues arising from our traditional 'linear' economy in Part Two and explore the global trends and drivers creating the context for circular approaches in Chapter 5. First, in this chapter, we explore the circular economy in more depth, looking at:

- the background to the circular economy;
- evolution of the concept: the main schools of thought, their principles and how they compare;
- a brief look at some supporting approaches;
- scaling it up: a quick look at the countries, consultancies and companies investing in it;
- a circular economy framework, which we explore in more detail in Chapters 2 to 4.

Instead of leaking value by discarding products and materials after use, the circular economy redesigns products, processes, supply chains and business models to **create, conserve and circulate value**. Creating durable products, and recovering products and materials at end-of-use, enables reuse, repair, remanufacture and recycling. Simple examples include:

- Making orange juice: the 'waste' becomes by-products, with pectin, pulp and zest for food manufacture and essential oils for pharmaceuticals and cosmetics.
- Commercial photocopiers aren't sold now; photocopying is a service with efficient repair networks, together with refurbishing and remanufacturing to enable second and third 'lives' for each machine.

Circular economy approaches regenerate resources and ecosystems, supporting our health and well-being. By converting 'take-make-waste' into 'value loops', thus creating more from less, they decouple resource use from value creation.

Circular economy terminology often categorizes materials into two groups.

- Biological (renewable) nutrients – food, fibres, timber – should be sustainable and renewed to meet or exceed the rate of extraction.

- Technical (finite) nutrients – metals, minerals, fossil fuels – should cycle infinitely. Product design can support effective separation at the end-of-use, for efficient recycling.

This over-simplifies the choices but starts to encourage a different mindset, focusing on material choices and the ease of separation at end-of-use.

Why is the circular economy important?

Why do we need a different approach to business? 'Traditional' industrial processes are a 'linear economy', meaning we take materials, make something, use it and then dispose of it. We could even call it a 'waste economy'!

TAKE, MAKE, WASTE

Modern lifestyles rely on finite resources – metals, minerals and fossil fuels. Our economy also relies on land and water – and we often forget that they are finite too. We dump waste and pollution at every stage of the process, destroying the living systems we depend on, and sometimes harming people. When we discard the product, we waste all those resources – and we waste all the energy, labour and knowledge we invested in the product at every stage in the process.

The linear economy relies on companies striving to sell more: we try to cut costs, try to encourage customers to buy the latest version, or persuade them to buy products with a short life-cycle (eg fashionable clothes). We try to create new 'needs', like antibacterial wipes for your kitchen, bottled water, probiotic yoghurt, or smart speakers.

We extract around 90 billion tons of natural resources, every year, to make what we consume. That's more than 12 tons for every person on the planet. Based on current trends, that number is likely to double by 2050.[3] The systems we've created are shockingly wasteful. The Circularity Gap report says we recover less than 10 per cent of our resources to make them into new products.[4]

We now know we are causing dangerous climate change by burning fossil fuels, using fertilizers and clearing forests, all of which creates greenhouse gas (GHG) emissions. Our world population continues to grow, and people have more money to spend on food, clothing and other stuff. It's great news that people's standards of living are improving, but the downside is that we are creating ever more demand for resources.

FROM DESTRUCTION TO REGENERATION

This system is threatening our future on this planet, with lots of downsides:

- people feel excluded, fearful and exploited;
- businesses face resource scarcity, higher charges on waste and risk to their reputations; and
- we are overloading and depleting nature's living systems.

It's easy to forget that we depend on living systems that provide critical services for us, including pure air, clean water and healthy soils. We are realizing that the way we live and work is destroying nature and pushing the earth's systems towards irreversible tipping points, threatening our ability to survive and thrive.

Governments, businesses large and small, NGOs and consultancies are recognizing these critical problems and risks. They see the potential to re-design the systems that depend on unsustainable consumption and are investing in circular economy approaches. The World Economic Forum, McKinsey, the Ellen MacArthur Foundation, the European Union and many other organizations are helping to accelerate the transition to a circular, resilient and sustainable world.

> Businesses that work on the basis of circular principles are amongst the fastest growing in the economy.
>
> Dr Martin R Stuchtey, McKinsey Center for Business and Environment[5]

Background

As the industrial revolutions scaled up, changing the way many people lived, worked, travelled and communicated, it seemed that resources were uncon-strained. Effectively, we were a relatively small population on a large, boun-tiful planet.

Since the 1950s, agricultural practices have changed in many developed nations, using synthetic fertilizers, chemical pest controls and irrigation to achieve massive increases in crop yields. Alongside this, human population continued its exponential growth path, with increasing numbers of people and levels of consumption. Rachel Carson, in her book *Silent Spring* (1962), raised public awareness of the environment and destruction of wildlife through the widespread use of pesticides.[6] The press condemned her, and the chemical industry even tried to ban the book.

From the 1970s onwards, we began to recognize that many of the resources we rely on for our survival are either finite; or are constrained by

FIGURE 1.1   The great acceleration

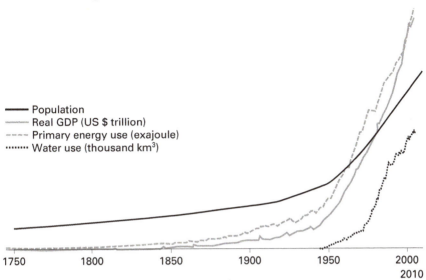

SOURCE: Stockholm Resilience Centre[7]

the speed of regeneration or availability of land in our urban environments. In *Small is Beautiful* (1973), EF Schumacher writes about the need to adopt Buddhist economic principles, understanding 'the essential difference between non-renewable fuels like coal and oil [...], and renewable fuels like wood and water power'.[8] He goes on to explain that 'non-renewable goods should be used only if they are indispensable, and then only with the greatest care and the most meticulous concern for conservation.'

Economist and systems theorist Kenneth Boulding described the issues of open and closed systems in relation to economics and resources.[9] Would growth be limited first by running out of places to store our waste and pollution, or by humanity running out of raw materials to use? Boulding advocated focusing on maintaining our resource stocks and encouraging technological change to reduce production and consumption.

In the 20th century, whilst **population quadrupled**, gross domestic product (GDP) and **consumption increased by a factor of 20**. Many other indicators of consumption and development show the same exponential upward trend from the 1950s, with Figure 1.1 showing some examples. As the effects of this 'great acceleration' became clear, scientists and institutions began to question our 'traditional' ways of making, selling and consuming products. You can see more on the World Economic Forum website.[10]

As we improved techniques for mining, extraction and manufacturing, resource costs declined steadily, despite some short-term increases resulting

FIGURE 1.2   Tipping point

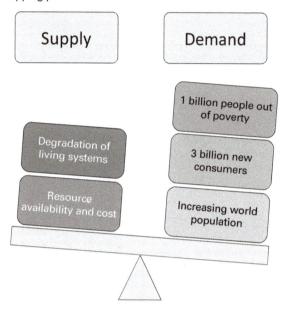

SOURCE: © Catherine Weetman

from wars and geopolitical factors. Over the 20th century, prices halved. As we moved into the 21st century, a tipping point occurred, and the declining trend became a steep upward trajectory, described by consultants McKinsey as a 'century of price declines, reversed in a decade'.[11] We have found, and used, all the 'easy to get at' stuff. Worse still, prices are now volatile, and frequently a shock in one resource flows through to others.

Predictions show a step-change in global demand between 2010 and 2030, as 3 billion new consumers join the 'middle classes', earning enough income to purchase a mobile phone, more processed food and meat, better housing and maybe even to take holidays abroad.

This rapid growth in demand, plus the difficulties of finding cost-effective sources of materials and meeting environmental challenges, puts pressure on the cost of supply. We have serious global challenges of inequality and poverty too, with over 1 billion people lacking secure access to food, water and energy. Figure 1.2 highlights the tipping point we have reached. Increasing pressures of demand, coupled with challenges for supply of resources, and the health of the living systems we depend on for clean air, safe water, food, timber, pollination and medicine, mean we need to rethink our systems. We explore this further in Part Two.

Reports from the United Nations, the European Commission, the OECD, the World Economic Forum and global management consultancies echo the strong warnings published in the Club of Rome's report, *Limits to Growth*, in 1972.[12] They share concerns about overexploitation of important ecosystems and natural resources, an increasingly unstable climate, and pollution of air, water, soil and the earth's atmosphere.

Evolution of the concept: architects, scientists and sailors

In the latter part of the 20th century, leading thinkers developed new concepts for sustainable business models, with systems of recirculation and regeneration of resources being a recurring theme. New terminology appeared in business publications, including *Cradle to Cradle*, *biomimicry*, *ecosystem services*, *design for disassembly*, *industrial ecology* and *resource efficiency*.

First, let's review the different schools of thought, shown in Figure 1.3, looking at how they prioritize different aspects and outcomes, before consolidating them into the circular economy framework used throughout this book.

FIGURE 1.3   Evolution of the circular economy

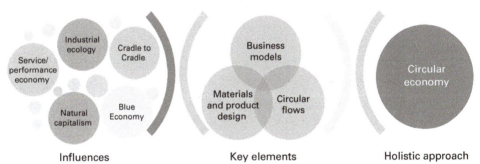

SOURCE: © Catherine Weetman

The performance economy

Swiss architect Walter Stahel is recognized as one of the earliest theorists developing ideas for what is now known as the circular economy. After receiving recognition for his prize-winning paper 'The Product Life Factor' in 1982, he co-founded the Product-Life Institute in Switzerland, a consultancy devoted to developing sustainable strategies and policies.

The Product-Life Institute outlines its main objective as: 'to open new frontiers of economic development towards a Performance Economy (or Functional Service Economy), which focuses on selling performance (services) instead of goods in a circular economy, internalizing all costs (closed loops, Cradle to Cradle).'[13] It goes on to explain that this can be achieved by combining system design, technical and commercial innovation. The focus will be on regional economies, developing business models of remarketing goods (reuse), and extending the product life of goods and components (eg through remanufacturing and upgrading) to create local jobs, increase 'resource husbandry' and prevent waste.

Five 'pillars' support the vision of the sustainable economy and society:

- **Nature conservation:** nature and living systems provide the foundation for human life. We depend on resources 'supplied by the global eco-support system' such as biodiversity, forests, clean air, rivers and oceans. The 'carrying capacity of nature' links to the regional populations and their lifestyles, eg water use, land-use patterns, pollution and waste assimilation.

- **Limiting toxicity:** thus protecting the health and safety of humans and other living species. Examples here include toxic agents such as heavy metals, pesticides, process chemicals and so on. This requires precise measurements (eg in nanograms) and assessment of nature's capacity to absorb and process these toxins.

- **Resource productivity:** with industrialized countries reducing their material use, or 'dematerializing', so other countries can develop. Stahel estimates that we need to reduce resource consumption by a factor of 10, to prevent the threat of a radical change at planetary level and support reduced inequality between nations.

- **Social ecology:** Stahel highlights the importance of peace and human rights, race and gender equality, dignity and democracy, employment and social integration, security and safety.

- **Cultural ecology:** including education and knowledge, ethics, culture, values of 'national heritage' and attitudes towards risk.

Natural capitalism

Natural Capitalism: Creating the Next Industrial Revolution (1999), by Paul Hawken, Amory B Lovins and L Hunter Lovins, describes a blueprint for a new economy.[14] It imagines a new industrial revolution, where environmental and business interests overlap. Companies can simultaneously improve profits, help solve environmental problems and feel positive about their impacts. It sees the key driver for previous industrial revolutions as human productivity, whereas now people and technology are abundant, but natural capital is diminishing.

Natural capital includes both natural resources and ecological systems, providing vital life-support services to all living things. It may be difficult, or impossible, to substitute these services. If we tried to substitute pollination services, provided by bees and butterflies, with hand or robot pollination, we quickly see big questions: how – and how expensive? The authors point out that current business practices typically ignore the value of these services and natural assets, even though this value is increasing in line with their scarcity. Our wasteful use of energy, materials, fibre, soil and water is degrading and depleting natural capital.

Natural capitalism has four principles:[15]

- Increase the **productivity of natural resources**. Innovations can stretch natural resources by 10, or even 100, times further than today. Crucially, the financial savings can help companies to implement the other three principles.

- Use '**biologically inspired**' production models and materials. In closed-loop systems, modelled on nature, every output is either returned to nature as a nutrient (waste = food) or becomes another manufacturing input.

- '**Service and flow**' business models. These deliver value as a continuous flow of services, such as providing illumination instead of selling light bulbs. In these models, providers and customers share objectives and rewards, through resource productivity and product longevity.

- **Reinvest in natural capital** to ensure future prosperity. Using up finite resources means those resources are no longer available. For example, polluting water sources destroys clean water supplies as well as the healthy habitats for fish and other species.

Natural capitalism emphasizes the importance of 'whole system design', using innovative technologies and rethinking 'defective practices' in the way companies allocate capital and governments set policy and taxation.

Industrial ecology

Preserving the materials and energy 'embedded' in a product – raw materials, energy, water and other process aids – is a basic tenet of industrial ecology.[16] It aims to help businesses understand how they use key resources; track material, energy and water flows; and how to account for a product throughout its life-cycle. It aims to change resource use from being implicit to explicit, from the beginning of the cycle to the end-of-use.

A key indicator of a country's environmental impact is what it consumes, rather than what it produces. Although recycling helps reduce energy, preserve resources and reduce environmental impact, we must change what and how we consume. Traditional models of industry – 'take, make and dispose' – should be transformed into 'industrial ecosystems', optimizing consumption of energy and materials, minimizing waste and ensuring that effluents and emissions from one process become the raw materials for another.

Blue Economy

Economist Gunter Pauli's first *Blue Economy* book in 2010 bases its solutions on physics, using nature's systems of cascading nutrients, matter and energy as the ideal model.[17] Gravity is the main source of energy, solar energy is the second renewable fuel and water is the primary solvent. Nature does not need complex, chemical, toxic catalysts, and everything is biodegradable – it is just a matter of time.

The Blue Economy is 'where the best for health and the environment is cheapest and the necessities for life are free thanks to a local system of production and consumption that works with what you have'.[18] Waste does not exist, and any by-product can be the source for a new product. Pauli urges us to question the use of all materials used in production – can you manage without it? Can you do more with less? He reminds us that in nature there is water, air and soil available to all, free and abundant. Sustainable societies 'respond to basic needs with what you have, introducing innovations inspired by nature, generating multiple benefits, including jobs and social capital, offering more with less'.

Pauli believes that our current economic model relies on scarcity as a basis for production and consumption. In contrast, Pauli defines 'wealth' as diversity, the opposite of our industrial standardization. Sustainable business maximizes the use of available material and energy, so reducing the unit price for the consumer. Sustainable business respects local resources, culture and tradition.

Between 2010 and 2013, Pauli published over 100 innovative case examples, aiming to create 100 million jobs and substantial capital value by 2020. All innovations are open-source and published on the Blue Economy website (www.theblueeconomy.org (archived at https://perma.cc/VNM9-6QZU)).

Cradle to Cradle®

Architect William McDonough and Dr Michael Braungart, an environmental scientist, wrote *Cradle to Cradle: Remaking the way we make things* in 2002. They describe the importance of treating materials as biological or technical nutrients and extending the 'use period' for all these materials. McDonough and Braungart encourage a *systems thinking* approach: reframing design to be regenerative and constantly progressing from being 'less bad' to doing 'more good'. They reject the idea that growth is bad for the environment, reminding us that, in nature, growth is good.

Instead of 'eco-efficiency', they aim for 'eco-effectiveness', driving innovation and leadership towards positive goals. They argue that eco-efficient, demand-side approaches may only reduce or minimize damage: eco-efficiency is simply sensible business practice. Eco-effectiveness means setting a design brief to include positive impacts on economic, ecological and social health. The brief should focus on supply-side approaches and include Cradle to Cradle® values and principles. Good design outcomes include fun, beauty and inspiration; and encourage healthy, abundant environmental outcomes.

Their website summarizes the Cradle to Cradle® principles:[19]

- **material health:** value materials as nutrients for safe, continuous cycling;
- **material reutilization:** maintain continuous flows of *biological* and *technical nutrients*;
- **renewable energy:** power all operations with 100 per cent renewable energy;
- **water stewardship:** regard water as a precious resource;
- **social fairness:** celebrate all people and natural systems.

McDonough and Braungart have developed the 'Cradle to Cradle Certified™ Product Standard', managed by the Cradle to Cradle Products Innovation Institute, an open-sourcing, non-profit organization.[20] The standard is a continual improvement process, assessing a product against the five principles listed above, and with a range of achievement levels to support continual improvement.

Ellen MacArthur Foundation

One of the highest-profile organizations promoting the circular economy is the Ellen MacArthur Foundation (EMF), a charity set up by the record-breaking round-the-world sailor, Ellen MacArthur. It works with businesses,

FIGURE 1.4   Ellen MacArthur Foundation systems (butterfly) diagram

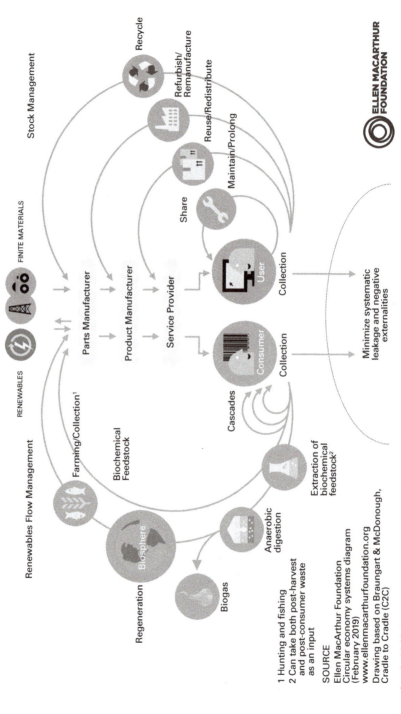

1 Hunting and fishing
2 Can take both post-harvest and post-consumer waste as an input

SOURCE
Ellen MacArthur Foundation
Circular economy systems diagram
(February 2019)
www.ellenmacarthurfoundation.org
Drawing based on Braungart & McDonough,
Cradle to Cradle (C2C)

(Reproduced with kind permission of the Ellen MacArthur Foundation)

governments and education to accelerate the transition to a circular economy, and publishes a wide range of books, papers and videos explaining the concept, principles and benefits. The foundation works closely with consultants McKinsey and with a wide range of global businesses, which form its 'CE100' group.

The first major report in EMF's 'Towards the Circular Economy' series, in 2012, broke new ground, calculating the economic and business opportunities for a restorative, circular model.[21] EMF's circular economy takes its inspiration from nature, where one species' waste is another's food, and the sun provides energy. A circular economy 'cycles valuable materials and products and produces and transports them using renewable energy'.[22]

EMF has three principles for a circular economy:[23]

- **Design out waste and pollution** – what if they were never created in the first place? This includes designing out the negative impacts of economic activity damaging human health and natural systems.

- **Keep products and materials in use** – what if we could build an economy that uses things rather than uses them up? Preserving value means designing for durability, reuse, remanufacturing and recycling, to keep products, components and materials circulating in the economy.

- **Regenerate natural systems** – what if we could not only protect but actively improve the environment? A circular economy avoids the use of non-renewable resources and preserves or enhances renewable ones, for instance by returning valuable nutrients to the soil to support regeneration, or using renewable energy as opposed to relying on fossil fuels.

Figure 1.4 shows EMF's Circular Economy Systems Diagram (the 'butterfly diagram'), with the flows and priorities for circulating renewables (biological materials) and loops for finite (technical) materials.[24]

Building on several schools of thought and influenced by Cradle to Cradle's material cycles, the 'butterfly diagram' is often used to explain the circular economy, with the tightest 'loops' retaining the most value.

If we think about food, we consume it … it can't be 'reused' in its original state. In the 'butterfly diagram', the loops for food and other biological materials include biochemical extraction, biogas, and agricultural regeneration.

We compare the main schools of thought later in this chapter, highlighting the different priorities in their approaches.

Other supporting approaches

Over the past few decades, other schools of thought have developed alongside circular economy approaches, helping to solve specific problems by enriching circular economy solutions:

- **Biomimicry**, as defined by the Biomimicry Institute, is 'an approach to innovation that seeks sustainable solutions to human challenges by emulating nature's time-tested patterns and strategies'.[25]

- **Ecodesign**, or ecological design, developed during the late 1980s as an approach to designing products with special consideration for the environmental impacts during the entire product life-cycle. We look at ecodesign in more detail in Chapter 4.

- **Permaculture** originated in the 1970s, designing ways to mimic natural forest ecosystems, mainly with tree crops, to create perennial agroforestry, or '**perma**nent agri**culture**' systems. It developed into a *system thinking* tool for designing low-input, productive landscapes, enterprises, buildings and communities.

- **The Natural Step** (www.thenaturalstep.org (archived at https://perma.cc/ 6D35-U339)) is a global network of non-profit organizations, focusing on sustainable development using a science-based framework.[26] Its mission is to accelerate the transition to a sustainable society: 'in which individuals, communities, businesses and institutions thrive within nature's limits'. The Natural Step is the basis of the Future-Fit Business Benchmark, which we expand on later in the book.

We see examples of these approaches throughout this book.

Scaling it up: countries, consultancies and companies

Forward-thinking organizations and governments are adopting circular approaches, moving away from our 'take, make, waste' systems towards holistic, regenerative systems. They aim to retain valuable resources, regenerate or at least do no harm to living systems, and balance the needs of humanity with the constraints of our living planet.

China

The first stage of China's circular economy began in 1998, starting with conceptual studies by academics.[27] The second stage included clean production and eco-industrial parks, supported by an increasing government environmental protection department. The third stage, starting in 2006, saw the circular economy presented as an alternative development model. A circular economy 'promotion law' aims to decouple economic growth from resource consumption and pollutants, and to help China leapfrog to a more sustainable economic structure.

European Union (EU)

The EU announced its circular economy action plan, 'Closing the Loop', in December 2015.[28] It sees the transition to a more circular economy as an essential contribution towards a sustainable, low-carbon, resource-efficient economy, generating new and sustainable competitive advantages for Europe. This includes maintaining the value of materials, resources and products in the economy for as long as possible and minimizing waste. By protecting businesses against resource scarcity and price volatility, it creates opportunities for innovative, efficient methods of production and consumption. This includes creating local jobs, opportunities for social integration, saving energy and avoiding irreversible damage from consuming resources faster than the earth's capacity for renewal.

The EU recognizes that businesses and consumers are key in driving the circular economy; and that it must play a fundamental support role. This will include regulatory frameworks and signals on the way forward, with ambitious, broad and concrete actions before 2020. In 2019, the European Commission adopted a comprehensive report on the implementation of the Circular Economy Action Plan, available on its website.[29]

Finland

Finland, aiming to be a pioneer in the circular economy, began work on its national circular economy road map in 2014, publishing the first version in 2016. It wants to 'ensure its success in a world where our economic competitiveness and well-being can no longer rely on the wasteful use of natural resources'.[30]

Japan

Japan, concerned about its limited land and resources, has developed circular economy principles – 'Sound Material Cycle Society' – to support its resilience and self-reliance. Aspects of Japanese culture support this: such as the concept of 'mottainai', meaning it is a shame for something to go to waste without using its full potential. Japan has wide-ranging recycling laws, covering everything from plastic and paper to home appliances and construction materials.[31]

Global consultants, business groups and NGOs

Major global management consultancy McKinsey & Company is a high-profile circular economy advocate. It has published several papers, is knowledge partner to the Ellen MacArthur Foundation (EMF) and provides research and insight for many of the EMF and World Economic Forum (WEF) reports.[32] Another consultancy, PwC, includes 'circular economy solutions' as part of its Sustainability Services, was involved in the RSA Great Recovery project[33] and has published white papers and blogs. Accenture is involved in research programmes, and working with the WEF, Young Global Leaders Forum and others, exploring the transition and transformation required to create a circular economy.[34,35]

New consultancies have emerged to help governments, cities, sectors and individual organizations to understand the opportunities and implement circular economy strategies. In particular, social enterprise Circle Economy and Metabolic (founded in 2012) have contributed to the growing range of white papers and thought leadership articles. In addition, Circle Economy hosts the Circle Lab open-sourced database of circular economy case studies, with over 1,000 worldwide examples by 2019 (see Further Resources at the end of this chapter).

UNITED NATIONS
The United Nations Industrial Development Organization (UNIDO) sees the circular economy as a 'new way of creating value, and ultimately prosperity, through extending product lifespan and relocating waste from the end of the supply chain to the beginning – in effect, using resources more efficiently by using them more than once'.[36] Seeing the circular economy as complementary to the United Nations Sustainable Development Goals, UNIDO projects include resource-efficiency, safe and easily recyclable products with longer lifetimes, and recovery of end-of-use products and materials.

WORLD ECONOMIC FORUM (WEF)
In 2014, the WEF, supported by research and ideas from the Ellen MacArthur Foundation and McKinsey, launched its circular economy 'scaling up'

initiative, 'Project MainStream'. Building on this work, WEF launched its Platform for Accelerating the Circular Economy (PACE) in 2017, as a public–private collaboration.[37] In 2019, the PACE co-chairs were the CEO of Philips, the heads of the Global Environment Facility and UN Environment, supported by the Ellen MacArthur Foundation, the International Resource Panel, Circle Economy and Accenture Strategy.

PACE aims to create systems change at speed and scale by enabling partners to:

- develop blended financing models for circular economy projects, in particular in developing and emerging economies;
- help create and adjust enabling policy frameworks to address specific barriers to advancing the circular economy;
- bring the private and public sector into public–private collaborations to scale impact around circular economy initiatives.

WORLD BUSINESS COUNCIL FOR SUSTAINABLE DEVELOPMENT

The World Business Council for Sustainable Development (WBCSD) says, 'The future of business is circular, and there's no room for waste in it.'[38] It also sees the circular economy as critical to supporting the United Nations Sustainable Development Goals. Its circular economy programme, Factor 10 (referring to a need for a ten-fold improvement in 'eco-efficiency of materials'), aims to 'bring circularity into the heart of business leadership and practice'.

Global businesses getting on board

Leading businesses are also making significant investments in the circular economy, developing ways to gain value from their process and end-of-life waste.

RENAULT: RECYCLING AND REMANUFACTURING

In 2000, Renault began integrating the circular economy into its activities, aiming to 'turn our waste into resources'. Renault tells us that today, over 85 per cent of automotive vehicles are metals and plastics, highlighting the importance of reusing these materials instead of discarding them.

Renault's corporate 'blog', 'Circular economy: re-cycle, re-use, Re-nault!', describes the circular economy as 'the ultimate recycling programme, where ideally nothing goes to waste'.[39] By 2014, the Renault Espace car was 90 per cent recyclable, and all cars in the 2014 range included 30 per cent recycled materials.

By 1999, Renault's circular economy plans included developing mobility services, such as car-pooling, car-sharing and short-term rental, through Renault Mobility. Groupe Renault signed the French Government's Circular Economy Roadmap, which 'focuses on moving towards a 100 per cent plastic recycling rate in France by 2025'.[40]

PHILIPS: SERVICE AND PERFORMANCE[41]

Philips' 2016–2020 strategy sets out 'ambitious targets for the company's solutions, operations and supply chain'. By applying ecodesign and circular economy principles to design solutions, Philips develops new business models and ways of working with customers to 'deliver better health at lower cost and use resources in the most effective way'.

In addition to 'improving the lives of 2.5 billion people each year', its 2020 objectives include 70 per cent of turnover from solutions that meet ecodesign principles, and 15 per cent from circular economy principles:

- carbon-neutral operations;
- recycle 90 per cent of operational waste and send zero waste to landfill;
- sustainable, collaborative approaches with suppliers.

IKEA: 'A POSITIVE IMPACT ON PEOPLE AND THE PLANET'

Speaking at a *Guardian* conference, Steve Howard, IKEA's former Chief Sustainability Officer, said:

> If we look on a global basis, in the West we have probably hit peak stuff. We talk about peak oil. I'd say we've hit peak red meat, peak sugar, peak stuff … peak home furnishings … We will be increasingly building a circular IKEA where you can repair and recycle products.[42]

In the 2018 update to its 2012 People & Planet Positive sustainability strategy,[43] IKEA recognizes its reliance on both natural resources and people. By transforming how it works, from linear to circular, it can 'secure the future of the IKEA business, value chain and the livelihoods of the millions of people that contribute to it'. It sees the three key challenges as climate change, unsustainable consumption and inequality.

By 2030, its ambition is to 'be a circular business built on clean, renewable energy and regenerative resources, de-coupling material use from our growth'. This includes:

- ending its dependency on virgin fossil materials and fuels;
- contributing to a world of clean air, water and improved biodiversity;
- turning waste into resources, sending zero waste to landfill;
- transforming secondary materials into clean and safe resources;
- sourcing and producing renewable and recycled materials with a positive environmental impact;
- set up and promote systems and services to enable a circular economy;
- becoming 'forest positive', promoting sustainable management to eliminate forest degradation and deforestation;
- becoming 'water positive', by leading and developing water stewardship programmes;
- leading regeneration projects on degraded land.[44]

Businesses adopting circular economy approaches are reducing risk, increasing reliance and improving their competitive edge. They're focused on 'doing more good', not just a 'bit less bad', engaging customers, employees and other stakeholders and helping their business be fit for the future.

Throughout the book, we highlight case studies and 'snapshots' covering a range of sectors and geographies, from global 'megabrands' to small businesses, entrepreneurs and social enterprises.

The circular economy: a generic framework

Those early concepts evolved into many 'circular economy' approaches, promoted by governments, NGOs and consultancies. A study by Kircherr, Reike and Hekkert in 2017 found 114 different definitions of a circular economy![45] Generally, they share common principles, as summarized in Figure 1.5.

FIGURE 1.5   Circular economy principles

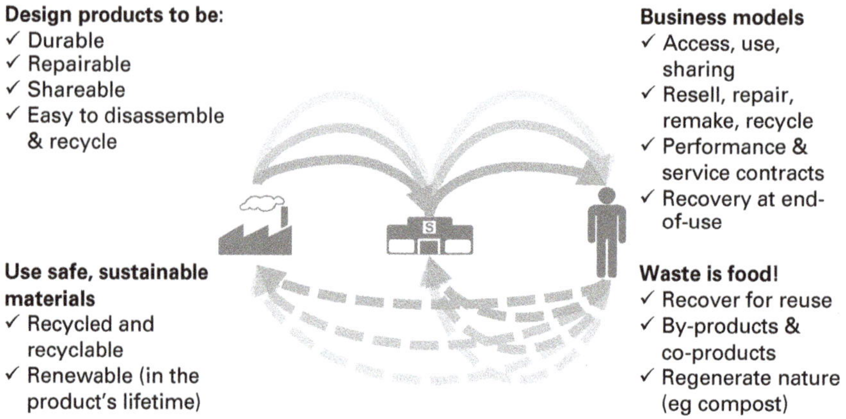

Design products to be:
✓ Durable
✓ Repairable
✓ Shareable
✓ Easy to disassemble & recycle

Business models
✓ Access, use, sharing
✓ Resell, repair, remake, recycle
✓ Performance & service contracts
✓ Recovery at end-of-use

Use safe, sustainable materials
✓ Recycled and recyclable
✓ Renewable (in the product's lifetime)

Waste is food!
✓ Recover for reuse
✓ By-products & co-products
✓ Regenerate nature (eg compost)

SOURCE: © Catherine Weetman

- **Design products and equipment** to be **durable, repairable** and robust, so they stay in use for longer. For the user, the benefit is a better lifetime cost, because robust, repairable products can be rented or shared, therefore more people can use fewer products. Products and resources are more productive: for example, a rented city bike might be in use for 12 hours a day, whereas a 'personal' bike might be used just a couple of times each week. Designs should enable efficient and effective disassembly too, for remanufacturing and recycling.

- **Business models** encourage access and use of products and equipment, instead of ownership. Contracts for service and performance help 'win-win' outcomes for the supplier and customer; and commercial options should encourage recovery of the product, components and materials at the end-of-use. Circular approaches also create markets for new services: for sharing, reselling, reuse, repair, remanufacturing and resource recovery.

- We should use **safe, sustainable materials** that are recycled (and recyclable) or renewable, both for the product and its manufacture.

- **Recover the products, components and materials** at the end of each phase of use, for reselling, repair, remaking or recycling. The aim is to retain the usefulness and value of products and resources, so we can use them as a resource for another industrial process, or they can become food for nature – compost!

Table 1.1 compares the principles of the different schools of thought and aims to outline their different emphases, rather than provide a definitive list

TABLE 1.1 Circular economy approaches – comparisons

Theme	Principle	Blue Economy[ii]	Cradle to Cradle	Circular Economy	Natural Capitalism	Performance Economy[iii]
Design	Biomimicry	**Y**			**Y**	
Design	Diversity	**Y**	y	y		
Design	Systems thinking		y	**Y**	**Y**	y
Conditions	Internalize externalities[i] (policies)			**Y**	y	y
Conditions	Open source	y				
Conditions	Services replace products		**Y**	**Y**	**Y**	**Y**
Flows	Circular flows	y	**Y**	**Y**	y	y
Flows	Prioritize smallest loop			y		y
Flows	Local systems	**Y**				Regional
Living systems	Conserve nature				**Y**	y
Living systems	Regenerate nature		y		y	y
Resources	Limited toxicity					y
Resources	Renewable energy	y	**Y**			y
Resources	Resource productivity		not enough!		esp. natural	y
Resources	Waste = food	y	nutrients	**Y**		y
Resources	Water stewardship		**Y**			
Society	Cultural ecology	y				y
Society	Social ecology	y	social fairness		meet needs	y

KEY: y = included; **Y** = strong emphasis; partial reference

i   *Externalities*: In economics, an externality is the cost or benefit that affects a party who did not choose to incur that cost or benefit.

ii *Blue Economy*: gravity is primary source of energy.

iii *Performance Economy*: Keep technical materials out of biosphere. Jobs linked to resources or energy inputs. Industrial countries' dematerialize', allowing other countries to develop.

FIGURE 1.6   Circular economy loops

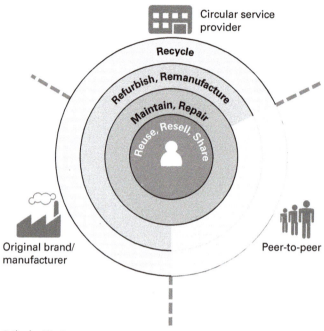

SOURCE: © Catherine Weetman

of the details behind their principles. Some approaches have emphasized 'closing the loop' – meaning recovery of the product, parts or materials, for reuse or for making new products of the same type. In this book, we differentiate between 'closed-loop' and 'open-loop' circular flows, and we examine the differences in Chapter 2.

Looping products, components and materials

EMF and others use loops to highlight the priorities for circular strategies. I have simplified the circular economy loops (see Figure 1.6), with the darker shading highlighting the loops with potential to retain the highest value, and avoid consumption and waste. This image also shows the range of 'actors' involved in the circular economy: the original manufacturer (or brand owner), a circular service provider (dealing with products for a range of brands), or, for the simpler loops, the users themselves.

Most products flow through four typical loops:

- **Reuse, resell and share** – ways to keep the original product in use, such as reselling it, returning it after use for someone else to use it, or sharing it, so more people can use it.

- **Maintain and repair**, to keep the product working efficiently and effectively for longer.

- **Refurbish and remanufacture**, which needs deeper levels of intervention. *Refurbishing* involves cleaning, surface-level repairs and maintenance, perhaps repainting and polishing the product or equipment. Remaking, or *remanufacture*, involves rigorous inspection, repair and replacement of worn materials and components, aiming to make the product as good as new. In the US, legislation means that remanufactured products have the same level of warranty as a 'new' product. In the UK, there is a British Standard BS 8887-2:2009 for remanufacturing terminology.

- **Recycling** is the outermost and least effective loop. Recycling requires lots of energy and may need expensive labour or equipment to sort and separate different materials. There are different 'levels' of recycling too. Ideally, we want to recycle materials to use them again in the same kind of application; and avoid '*downcycling*' them into a lower-grade, lower-value material with inferior functional specifications.

We prioritize the 'tightest' (inner) loops: because they retain more of the value (the materials, energy, water, labour and design input) that we 'embedded' in the product during design, manufacture and the supply chain. It is easy to think about how the loops apply to finite, *technical materials*. However, *biological materials* (food, fibres, timber, etc) and products flow in similar loops, for example in the food sector, in furnishings and textiles.

Circular economy framework

I have blended these approaches into a generic 'circular economy framework', shown in Figure 1.7. The framework includes business models, the 'design and supply chain' (design for durability and recovery, safe and sustainable inputs, process design and recovery flows), enablers and accelerators. We look briefly at each of these here and then explore them in detail in Chapters 2, 3 and 4.

BUSINESS MODELS

Business models and commercial options can encourage and support longer lifetimes, more intense use and successful circulation of the product, parts or materials. These include service models to replace ownership, 'pay per use', lease and hire, sharing and exchange systems. Repairing, manufacturing, recycling or reselling can also form the basis of a business model, and we'll explore these in more detail in Chapter 3.

FIGURE 1.7   Circular Economy Framework 2.0

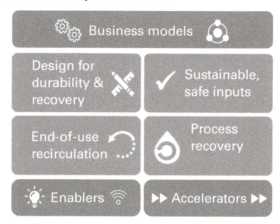

SOURCE: © Catherine Weetman

DESIGN FOR DURABILITY AND RECOVERY

Good design should aim for durability, enabling the product to last longer for its first and subsequent 'lives' (or use cycles) and to be used again. Is it easy to disassemble and repair? The design should enable and encourage circular flows to keep the product, parts and materials circulating at the highest level of usefulness (and hence 'value'), for the longest period. The design should simplify disassembly at the end of each use cycle, giving easy access to future resources.

SAFE AND SUSTAINABLE INPUTS

This means designing the product to use sustainable resources in its *bill of materials*. These should be safe, non-toxic, renewable or recycled, and recyclable. Specifying sustainable materials reduces the risk of future supply shortages, thus improving the long-term security of supply.

PROCESS DESIGN

The manufacturing process aims to to recover resources, including chemicals, additives, water and energy ('nutrients') for future use. We should minimize resource use, both for materials in the product itself and for all the various process inputs we use. We should convert 'waste' – including offcuts, production rejects, end-of-batch excesses and so on – into resources. Can you create or develop by-products and co-products? Could you set up mutually beneficial, or symbiotic, flows to or from other industries?

RECOVERY FLOWS

Here, we aim to recover the product, parts or materials without losing value in the reverse flows, regenerate them, and get them back into circulation. This means setting up effective and efficient circular flows for end-of-use products, components and materials, including:

- resale and reuse options, where the product is resold or rented to another user, perhaps with maintenance and repair to prolong its useful life;

- remanufacturing so that the product matches 'as new' performance for a second life;

- recycling to use the materials or components in another product.

ENABLERS AND ACCELERATORS

'Enablers' and 'accelerators' can support circular approaches, and we examine these in more detail in Chapter 4. **Enablers** include scientific approaches and other ways to think differently, for example: 'green chemistry' to improve material choice or help develop by-products, biomimicry approaches for product design and material selection, open-sourcing and systems thinking. Enablers also include new types of materials and technologies that improve resource utilization or provide information about how a product is used, such as the *Internet of Things, big data, 3D printing, mobile apps* and *sharing platforms*.

Accelerators include legislation, policy levers, *product stewardship* approaches, collaborations and standards. Examples include product *life-cycle assessments*, ethical standards and certifications, and tools to help us understand resource footprints and sustainable sources of materials. Collaborative industry sector initiatives, such as Make Fashion Circular or How2Recycle, can help to accelerate more sustainable, regenerative approaches. Policy and legislation measures include *extended producer responsibility* rules or taxing externalized costs such as pollution and waste, or incentives for repairs, remaking and recycling.

The circular economy approach is supported by approaches based on resource- or eco-efficiency, sustainability, *corporate social responsibility (CSR)*, the *triple bottom line* and so on, but these are not as systems-focused and can probably be classed as encouraging strategies that are 'less bad', rather than 'more good'.

Summary

We have looked at some of the drivers for the circular economy concept and how it evolved, together with a few examples of businesses and organizations investing in it. How should we sum up a circular economy? Here is the European Commission's definition in 2019:

> A circular economy aims to maintain the value of products, materials and resources for as long as possible by returning them into the product cycle at the end of their use, while minimizing the generation of waste. The fewer products we discard, the less materials we extract, the better for our environment. This process starts at the very beginning of a product's lifecycle: smart product design and production processes can help save resources, avoid inefficient waste management and create new business opportunities.[46]

There are wide-ranging **benefits** from 'closing the loop', for business customers and consumers:

- Swapping from finite, potentially risky or under-pressure resources to safe, sustainable materials helps to support **resource security** and price stability.

- Expanding your offer to include repairs, remanufacturing, reselling and sharing can generate **new revenue streams**. Repairable products need supplies of spares, consumables and even special tools. Similarly, new by-products from your recovered waste converts cost into profit.

- Collecting and recovering your own end-of-life products, components and materials 'closes the loop' in your supply chain, helping regenerate future resources. Designing for easy disassembly makes this more **cost-effective**.

- Negotiating contracts for performance can deliver **win-win outcomes** for both customer and supplier. Avoiding waste disposal costs, import tariffs and long-distance, high-inventory supply chains can **save money**.

- Circular, regenerative and win-win strategies can **strengthen and deepen relationships** with suppliers, employees, local communities and shareholders. Circular economy approaches build stronger **brand reputations**, by doing things better and doing better things.

- Many benefits of closing the loop strengthen the core of your business, **reduce risks** and help it become more **resilient**.

Companies like Nike, IKEA and HP and organizations around the world see the circular economy as the best tool we have for **resilient, competitive, sustainable business.**[47]

> And so we call it 'cradle to cradle'. Our goal is very simple. This is what I presented to [President Bush in] the White House. Our goal is a delightfully diverse, safe, healthy and just world, with clean air, clean water, soil and power – economically, equitably, ecologically and elegantly enjoyed, period.
>
> William McDonough (2005)[48]

Further resources

Braungart, M and McDonough, W (2008) *Cradle to Cradle: Remaking the way we make things*, Vintage Books, London

Circle Lab Knowledge Hub: open-source digital platform with over 1,000 case studies and examples, articles, reports, and other resources on the circular economy. www.circle-lab.com/ (archived at https://perma.cc/9NBM-VXG3) [accessed 22 September 2019]

Circular Economy Club: not-for-profit, free to join global network of people and organizations interested and involved in the circular economy www.circulareconomyclub.com/ (archived at https://perma.cc/TER8-7G36) [accessed 22 September 2019]

Ellen MacArthur Foundation (2012) [accessed 15 August 2016] Towards the Circular Economy: Economic and Business Rationale for an Accelerated Transition [Online] https://www.ellenmacarthurfoundation.org/news/towards-the-circular-economy (archived at https://perma.cc/RBN3-HPFE)

Ellen MacArthur Foundation, Resources and Project Mainstream [Online] www.ellenmacarthurfoundation.org (archived at https://perma.cc/897Z-STJN)

European Commission Circular Economy portal ec.europa.eu/environment/circular-economy/index_en.htm (archived at https://perma.cc/MQ2Q-DRQY) [accessed 22 September 2019]

Hawken P, Lovins AB and Lovins HL ([1999] 2010) *Natural Capitalism*, Earthscan, London

Podcast: Circular Economy Podcast, www.circulareconomypodcast.com (archived at https://perma.cc/35XJ-STQ5)

Podcast: Getting in the Loop https://intheloopgame.com/podcasts/ (archived at https://perma.cc/G973-SQ68)

TU Delft with Ellen MacArthur Foundation (2016) [accessed 12 February 2016] CircularX Circular Economy: An Introduction, 1.2 Principles of the Circular Economy [Online] https://courses.edx.org/courses/course-v1:Delftx+CircularX+1T2016/courseware/ (archived at https://perma.cc/JYR9-JRQ9)

World Economic Forum Platform for Accelerating the Circular Economy (PACE) www.weforum.org/projects/circular-economy (archived at https://perma.cc/ 285H-3MBW) [accessed 22 September 2019]

Notes

1 Drucker, PF (1992) The post-capitalist world, *Harvard Business Review*, September–October

2 Stahel, WR (23 Mar 2016) [accessed 1 June 2016] The Circular Economy, Nature News, *Nature Publishing Group* [Online] www.nature.com/news/ the-circular-economy-1.19594 (archived at https://perma.cc/62RW-VW7P)

3 IRP (2017) Assessing global resource use: A systems approach to resource efficiency and pollution reduction [Online] www.resourcepanel.org/reports/ assessing-global-resource-use (archived at https://perma.cc/6BCG-ZGW3)

4 De Wit, M et al, The Circularity Gap Report (2018) [accessed 2 December 2019] Circle Economy www.circle-economy.com/the-circularity-gap-report-our-world-is-only-9-circular/ (archived at https://perma.cc/P3RR-APH8)

5 Ellen MacArthur Foundation, McKinsey Center for Business and Environment (2015) [accessed 28 March 2019] Growth Within: A Circular Economy Vision for a Competitive Europe [Online] www.ellenmacarthurfoundation.org/news/ circular-economy-would-increase-european-competitiveness-and-deliver-better-societal-outcomes-new-study-reveals (archived at https://perma.cc/ VRN3-A5ZM)

6 Carson, R (1962) *Silent Spring*, Houghton Mifflin, Boston

7 Stockholm Resilience Centre [Online] stockholmresilience.org/21/research/ research-news/1-15-2015-new-planetary-dashboard-shows-increasing-human-impact.html/ (archived at https://perma.cc/Z9VP-6VP3)

8 Schumacher, EF (1973) *Small is Beautiful: A Study of Economics as if People Mattered*, Vintage, London, p 44

9 Boulding, EK (1966) [accessed 15 August 2016] The Economics of the Coming Spaceship Earth [Online] www.ub.edu/prometheus21/articulos/obsprometheus/ BOULDING.pdf (archived at https://perma.cc/R2H7-2DBV)

10 WEF (2016) [accessed 18 September 2019] 24 Charts Every Leader Should See, *World Economic Forum* [Online] www.weforum.org/agenda/2015/01/24-charts-every-leader-should-see/ (archived at https://perma.cc/V5LG-URMR)

11 McKinsey Global Institute [accessed 8 June 2015] Rethinking Natural Resource Management, podcast 28 November 2011 [Online] www.mckinsey. com/business-functions/sustainability-and-resource-productivity/our-insights/a-new-era-for-commodities (archived at https://perma.cc/6H3W-HDSX)

12 Meadows, DH, Meadows, DL, Randers, J and Behrens, WW III (1972) *Limits to Growth*, Universe Books, New York

13   Product-Life Institute [accessed 18 September 2019] [Online] product-life.org/ (archived at https://perma.cc/MV66-NDXD)

14   Hawken, P, Lovins, AB and Lovins, LH ([1999] 2010) *Natural Capitalism*, Earthscan, London

15   Lovins, A, Lovins, LH and Hawken P (1999) A road map for natural capitalism, *Harvard Business Review*, May–June, pp 145–58

16   International Society for Industrial Ecology (2015) [accessed 7 February 2016] A Note from the Presidents [Online] is4ie.org/A-Note-from-the-Presidents (archived at https://perma.cc/U7JB-9XP5)

17   The Blue Economy (2016) [accessed 18 September 2019] Principles [Online] www.theblueeconomy.org/Principles.html (archived at https://perma.cc/ RQ6V-C2ZJ)

18   Pauli, G (2009) [accessed 16 February 2016] The Blue Economy: A Report to the Club of Rome, keynote speech [Online] www.worldacademy.org/files/ Blue%20Economy%202009.pdf (archived at https://perma.cc/6WHX-M7VB)

19   MBDC (2016) [accessed 12 February 2016] C2C Framework [Online] www. mbdc.com/cradle-to-cradle/c2c-framework/ (archived at https://perma.cc/ M8YR-WYW2)

20   Cradle to Cradle Products Innovation Institute [accessed 18 February 2016] [Online] www.c2ccertified.org/ (archived at https://perma.cc/MEY3-WQG5)

21   Ellen MacArthur Foundation (2012) [accessed 15 August 2016] Towards the Circular Economy: Economic and Business Rationale for an Accelerated Transition [Online] www.ellenmacarthurfoundation.org/news/towards-the-circular-economy (archived at https://perma.cc/RBN3-HPFE)

22   TU Delft with Ellen MacArthur Foundation (2016) [accessed 12 February 2016] CircularX Circular Economy: An Introduction, 1.2 Principles of the Circular Economy [Online] courses.edx.org/courses/course-v1:Delftx+CircularX+1T2016/courseware/ (archived at https://perma.cc/ JYR9-JRQ9)

23   Ellen MacArthur Foundation, What is the Circular Economy? [accessed 18 September 2019] www.ellenmacarthurfoundation.org/circular-economy/ what-is-the-circular-economy (archived at https://perma.cc/RE8N-7LE8)

24   Ellen MacArthur Association [online] [accessed 23 September 2019] www. ellenmacarthurfoundation.org/circular-economy/infographic (archived at https://perma.cc/N5NQ-U6CJ)

25   Biomimicry Institute [accessed 18 September 2019] What is Biomimicry? [Online] biomimicry.org/what-is-biomimicry/#.VsW6dOahOkV (archived at https://perma.cc/7V65-6JK8)

26   The Natural Step (2016) [accessed 14 February 2016] About Us [Online] www.thenaturalstep.org/about-us/ (archived at https://perma.cc/7QR5-WNNJ)

27   Zhu, D, Director of the Institute of Governance for Sustainable Development at Tongji University in Shanghai, Europe's World (15 June 2014) [accessed 13 February 2016] China's Policies and Instruments for Developing the

Circular Economy [Online] europesworld.org/2014/06/15/chinas-policies-and-instruments-for-developing-the-circular-economy/#.Vr9XGlKhOkU (archived at https://perma.cc/RY2X-99EK)

28 European Commission (2 December 2015) [accessed 13 February 2016] Communication: Closing the Loop: An EU Action Plan for a Circular Economy [Online] eur-lex.europa.eu/legal-content/EN/TXT/?qid=1453384154 337&uri=CELEX:52015DC0614 (archived at https://perma.cc/YV5L-9ES3)

29 European Commission [accessed 18 September 2019] ec.europa.eu/environment/circular-economy/index_en.htm (archived at https://perma.cc/MQ2Q-DRQY)

30 The Critical Move – Finland's Road Map to a Circular Economy 2016–2025 [accessed 22 September 2019] www.sitra.fi/en/projects/critical-move-finnish-road-map-circular-economy-2-0/#challenge (archived at https://perma.cc/5KHZ-3XAH)

31 Cord, DJ, World Circular Economy Forum 2018, Japan and Finland to show off their circular economy at WCEF2018 [accessed 22 September 2019] www.sitra.fi/en/articles/japan-finland-show-off-circular-economy-wcef2018/ (archived at https://perma.cc/YLH6-EKFR)

32 Ellen MacArthur Foundation [accessed 18 February 2016] Research and Insights [Online] www.ellenmacarthurfoundation.org/ce100/the-programme/research-and-insights (archived at https://perma.cc/2J6N-AUJP)

33 PwC (2015–16) [accessed 20 February 2016] Circular Economy Solutions [Online] www.pwc.co.uk/services/sustainability-climate-change/supply-chain/circular-economy-solutions.html (archived at https://perma.cc/BP2G-RLLH)

34 *The Guardian* (13 May 2013) [accessed 13 February 2016] Driving the Circular Economy – Infographic [Online] www.theguardian.com/sustainable-business/driving-circular-economy-infographic (archived at https://perma.cc/WP3T-92EA)

35 Accenture (2014) [accessed 15 August 2016] Circular Advantage: Innovative Business Models and Technologies that Create Value [Online] www.accenture.com/gb-en/insight-circular-advantage-innovative-business-models-value-growth (archived at https://perma.cc/VRB3-4GC3)

36 United Nations Industrial Development Organisation, Circular Economy [Online] [accessed 22 September 2019] www.unido.org/our-focus-cross-cutting-services/circular-economy (archived at https://perma.cc/4MYB-B7QD)

37 World Economic Forum, Platform for Accelerating the Circular Economy [accessed 18 September 2019] www.weforum.org/projects/circular-economy (archived at https://perma.cc/285H-3MBW)

38 WBCSD, Circular Economy [online] [accessed 22 September 2019] www.wbcsd.org/Programs/Circular-Economy (archived at https://perma.cc/GZ9T-T9NT)

39 McEvoy, P (5 June 2014) [accessed 13 February 2016] Groupe Renault, News, Corporate Blog [Online] group.renault.com/en/news/blog-renault/circular-economy-recycle-renault/ (archived at https://perma.cc/A785-DFB7)

40 Groupe Renault, Circular Economy [accessed 19 September 2019] group.renault.com/en/our-commitments/respect-for-the-environment/circular-economy/ (archived at https://perma.cc/F7VZ-XP7X)

41 Koninklijke Philips N.V. [online] [accessed 19 September 2019] www.philips.com/a-w/about/sustainability/our-approach/ambition-2020 (archived at https://perma.cc/NZV5-ZXHK)

42 Farrell, S (18 January 2016) [accessed 13 February 2016] We've Hit Peak Home Furnishings, Says Ikea Boss, *The Guardian* [Online] www.theguardian.com/business/2016/jan/18/weve-hit-peak-home-furnishings-says-ikea-boss-consumerism (archived at https://perma.cc/7HRT-XXPU)

43 IKEA Sustainability Strategy, People and Planet Positive (June 2018) p3 [accessed 19 September 2019] highlights.ikea.com/2018/facts-and-figures/for-a-more-sustainable-future/IKEA-sustainability-strategy-2018-People-and-planet-positive.pdf (archived at https://perma.cc/C2RL-JE3V)

44 IKEA Sustainability Strategy, People and Planet Positive (June 2018) [accessed 19 September 2019] p18 highlights.ikea.com/2018/facts-and-figures/for-a-more-sustainable-future/IKEA-sustainability-strategy-2018-People-and-planet-positive.pdf (archived at https://perma.cc/C2RL-JE3V)

45 Kircherr, Reike and Hekkert (2017) Conceptualizing the Circular Economy: an analysis of 114 definitions, published in Resources, Conservation and Recycling, Elselvier [accessed 28 Mar 2019] www.sciencedirect.com/science/article/pii/S0921344917302835 (archived at https://perma.cc/2XH7-6LZF)

46 European Commission, Eurostat, Circular economy overview [online] [accessed 26 September 2019] ec.europa.eu/eurostat/web/circular-economy (archived at https://perma.cc/Y89R-UN9X)

47 Hower, M (2015) [accessed 26 September 2019] HP, Tetra Pak win big with the circular economy, *Greenbiz*, 24 November [Online] www.greenbiz.com/article/hp-tetra-pak-win-big-circular-economy (archived at https://perma.cc/GLZ3-CD8R)

48 McDonough, W (2005) [accessed 30 September 2019] TED Talk, 14 May 2014 [Online] www.ted.com/talks/william_mcdonough_on_cradle_to_cradle_design (archived at https://perma.cc/U3UC-GTSU)

2

The design and supply chain

Over time, many companies get comfortable doing what they have always done, with a few incremental changes. This kind of incrementalism leads to irrelevance… because change tends to be revolutionary, not evolutionary. It's why we continue to invest for the long term, in our next generation of big bets.

LARRY PAGE, GOOGLE, 2013[1]

In Chapter 1, we saw how the circular economy evolved from converging schools of thought, and we explored the concept of 'looping' materials, with the 'butterfly diagram' and my simpler loops diagram. Next, we begin to look at how companies can incorporate 'circularity' into their products and processes. The circular economy framework in Figure 2.1 shows six blocks (or components), outlining the areas of opportunity.

FIGURE 2.1   Circular Economy Framework 2.0

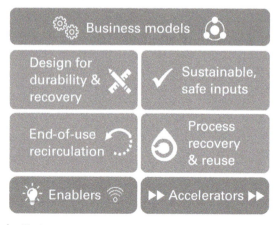

SOURCE: © Catherine Weetman

In the next two chapters, we explore this framework, starting in this chapter with the four components forming the central 'flow' in the framework, covering the 'design and the supply chain'. We review options for successful circular product and process design, material choice, and circular flows to recover the materials and products. Many of these affect supply chain strategies and operations, which we explore in more depth in Part Three. We examine new business models in Chapter 3, then look at enablers and accelerators helping the circular economy in Chapter 4. This chapter includes:

- a quick overview of the **terminology** used in many circular economy reports and toolkits;
- a reminder of the 'loops' in a circular economy and why it is important to prioritize the inner loops;
- exploring the four **design and supply chain** components in my circular economy framework: those points where we can intervene in the existing processes, or value chain, to make it more circular;
- **rethinking** – a brief look using new lenses and taking a 'whole systems design' approach to this design and supply chain, which is key to the success of circular products, processes and business models.

My simple circular supply chain schematic, in Figure 2.2, shows the main flows of materials into and out of a typical manufacturing business. At end-of-use, the product, components and materials stay in the loop, for resale, repair, refurbishing and remaking, or they return to the system for recycling. Waste created along the supply chain – from production waste (offcuts, rejects, effluent, gases, etc) and logistics waste – should be recovered, for reuse in our own process, or as a feedstock for another industrial or natural process. In this chapter, we start to explore some of these new flows and see the opportunities for value creation for the business and its stakeholders.

Circular economy loops

In Chapter 1, we introduced the concept of 'loops' (see Figure 2.3) as options for retaining products and materials in a circular economy. The darker shading in the schematic highlights the loops with the potential to retain the most value. My schematic also shows the range of 'providers' involved in the circular economy: the original manufacturer (or brand owner); a circular service provider (dealing with materials or products for a range of brands or sectors); or, for the simpler loops, the users themselves.

FIGURE 2.2 Simple circular supply chain

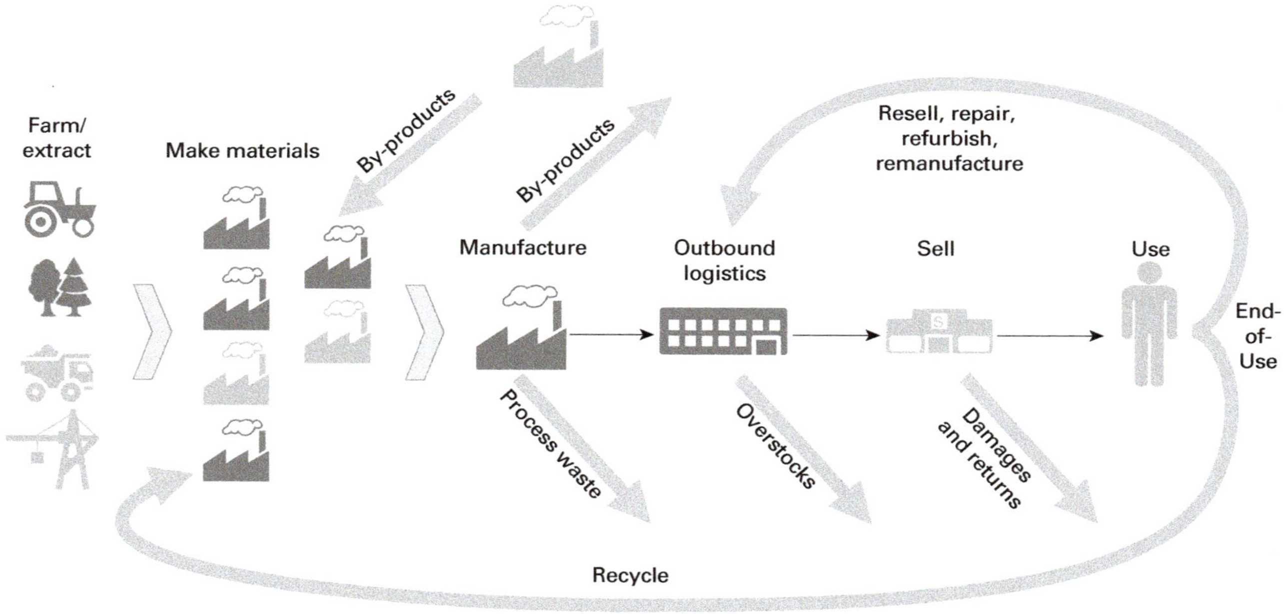

Farm/ extract
Make materials
By-products
By-products
Manufacture
Outbound logistics
Sell
Use
Resell, repair, refurbish, remanufacture
End-of-Use
Process waste
Overstocks
Damages and returns
Recycle

SOURCE: © Catherine Weetman

FIGURE 2.3   Circular economy loops

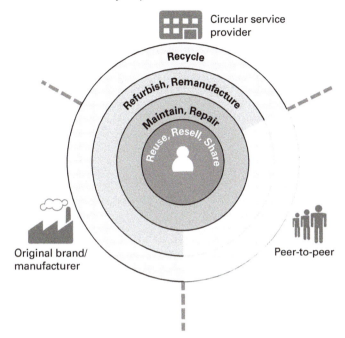

SOURCE: Catherine Weetman

There are four typical loops for products containing technical (finite) materials:

- **Reuse, resell and share** – ways to keep the original product in use, such as reselling it, 'pay as you go' models, or sharing it, so more people have access to it.

- **Maintain and repair**, to keep the product working efficiently and effectively for longer.

- **Refurbish and remanufacture**, which needs deeper levels of intervention. Refurbishing involves cleaning, surface-level repairs and maintenance, perhaps repainting and polishing the product or equipment. Remanufacturing involves rigorous inspection, repair and replacement of worn materials and components, aiming to make the product as good as new.

- **Recycling**, ideally into materials that can be used to make the same product.

We prioritize the 'tightest' (inner) loops because they retain more of the value (the materials, energy, water, labour and design input) that we 'embedded' in the product during design, manufacture and the supply chain.

Recycling is the outermost and least effective loop. Recycling requires lots of energy and may need expensive labour or equipment to sort and separate different materials. Biological materials and products flow in similar loops, for example in the food sector, in furnishings and textiles.

Before we move on to look at the 'design and supply chain' in more detail, first we should define some key terms used throughout the book.

Terminology

The circular economy movement has developed its own terminology, with words like 'circularity', 'nutrients', 'valorization' and so on. While these can serve as a useful shorthand to avoid repeating longer phrases or definitions, they also make it harder to grasp new concepts and findings. In this book, we try to use plain English, and I have created a glossary at the end of the book as a 'ready reference'. Also, glossary terms are highlighted in *italics* the first few times they appear in the book.

Here are a few terms that we use in specific contexts in the book:

Nutrients

Both the Cradle to Cradle approach and the Ellen MacArthur Foundation use the term 'nutrients' to describe materials. This encourages us to consider how to retain the qualities and usefulness of each material as it moves through the system so that it can 'nourish' a new product or process.

Biological nutrients are renewable, living materials from the 'biosphere'. They include foods; plant fibres such as cotton, hemp or kapok; mushrooms, nutshells and fruit skins; timber and other wood products. Animal products and by-products are also biological nutrients – for example, meat, fish, insects, leather, fur, wool, fish skins and shells, animal wastes and so on.

Biological nutrients are generally safe and many are non-toxic (apart from some mushrooms, poisonous plants, venom, etc!). Crucially, they can return to nature at the end of their use, providing food or shelter for living creatures or biodegrading back into the soil.

However, while biological materials are renewable, we must remember that they depend on suitable land, water and supporting ecosystems (for food, protection from predators and so on). Modern industrial processes are undermining ecosystems, and we are overexploiting land through farming, forestry and fishing. We must use biological materials sustainably, ensuring we provide and protect the conditions they need, and that we can regenerate them within the product's lifetime. In other words, if it takes 20 years to grow a tree to make a table, that table should last for at least 20 years.

Technical nutrients are 'finite' materials, mined or extracted from the earth's crust. These include metals, minerals and synthetic chemicals. They also include fossil fuels such as coal, oil and gas, and materials with fossil origins such as oil-based plastics and petrochemicals. Whilst these are formed from biological nutrients, they have formed over thousands or even millions of years and so are not 'renewable' in any practical sense.

Technical nutrients may also degrade over time. Plastics break down first into pieces, or flakes, and eventually into microparticles. Metals like steel will rust when exposed to damp conditions, and chemicals dispersed into soil or water may break down into their constituent parts, or combine with other elements – safely or not.

Thinking about resources and materials as nutrients can help us make sense of the circular economy mantra: 'waste = food'. We'll explore that more later in this chapter. We will also discuss the importance of keeping the technical and biological nutrients separate, so they are easier to separate at the end-of-use.

Closed and open loops

It is also helpful to identify whether materials return to the original business supply chain (closed loop) or disperse to other businesses (open loops). **Closed loops** are a key feature in the *Cradle to Cradle* approach. In this book, closed loops refer to products, components or materials retained or recovered for use again by the same company – either in the same product or process, or in a different product or process.

Examples include recovering excess steel for use in new products, and water recovered and cleaned by the company for its own reuse. That improves our ability to secure our future resources, giving us an incentive to design for repair, disassembly and recovery.

Alternatively, can we keep the materials flowing within the same industrial sector? We can describe these kinds of flows as '**open loop, same sector**'. Could we collaborate with similar companies, with industry suppliers or specialist recyclers? Maybe a specialist supplier could provide 'use' or 'performance' services, such as chemicals as a service.

Examples include specialist metals recyclers involved in processing steel and aluminium from end-of-life cars, or a company that resells or remanufactures products originally made by another company. The Rype Office case study in Chapter 9 is a good example of open-loop remanufacturing.

FIGURE 2.4 The 'rectangle of recovery'

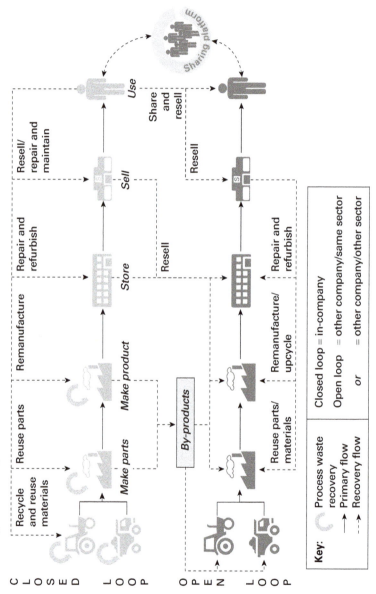

SOURCE: © Catherine Weetman (2015)

Further examples include aluminium beer kegs, 'Dutch trolleys' used in horticulture supply chains, and even recycled paint.

Finally, materials can flow between sectors, making an **open loop, cross-sector** system. This could include by-products created from production waste, such as OrangeFiber (which makes high-quality fabric from unwanted citrus peel) or generic recycled plastics and metals suitable for use in a variety of applications. At British Sugar's factory in Wissington, UK, a wide range of *by-products* flow into civil engineering, farming and energy production.[2] Another example is plastic recycling, where specialist processors deal with mixed plastic waste streams, such as packaging from household waste collections. The resulting recyclate, generally a lower-grade plastic, then flows into a wide range of applications.

The 'rectangle of recovery' in Figure 2.4 helps illustrate the potential open- and closed-loop circular flows.

Materials and other 'ingredients' in the product mix

It is useful to have consistent terms to differentiate between the finished products, plus all the stages of material build-up during the production process: materials, compounds and components. While these are not scientific or commercial definitions, they help clarify aspects of product design and processes:

Materials can be **biological** (harvested from nature) or **technical** (extracted or mined), or mixed, including any processing to refine or clean them ready for use. Technical examples are iron, coal and granite, and biological examples are timber, fish or skimmed milk ('refined' by separating out some of the original milk fat). If combined with other materials, they may become *compounds*.

Compounds consist of two or more ingredients, or elements, chemically united. Some further processing is involved, perhaps using heat or water, or a chemical agent to create the reaction. Examples are metal alloys such as steel or brass, laminated plastics, or mayonnaise (very difficult to separate!).

Components are parts, assemblies or sub-assemblies included in the finished product. They are usually removable in one piece, and have unique identifiers in the *bill of materials*. Examples include a sauce used in a recipe for a takeaway or 'ready meal', an electric motor used in a vacuum cleaner, a circuit board in a laptop computer, or a car dashboard assembly complete with instruments.

Process inputs include energy, water, cleaning products, coatings, dyes and chemicals. These enable, speed up or slow down the manufacturing process; transit packaging, etc. Process inputs are used in the supply chain or in manufacturing, and do not form part of the final product.

Products are the outcome of the process – the item used or consumed by the end-user – consisting of one, several or many materials, compounds and components. We need to consider the context, eg an orange could be a product in its own right, or a material (an ingredient) in another product. The distinction depends on whether further processing occurs, and helps differentiate between the different parts of the supply chain process. Once we extract juice from an orange, the juice becomes a product. In this book, 'products' encompass equipment (eg a heating system) and infrastructure (for example, buildings and bridges).

The design and supply chain

To transition from linear to circular approaches, or to design a new product or service from scratch, where should we start? I find it easiest to think about each main component of the business and its supply chain, and find the points where you can intervene to make circular improvements.

Having introduced the framework in Chapter 1, we now explore the four blocks of the central flow: the 'design and supply chain' (see Figure 2.5). We look at product design, circular inputs, circular processes, and circular (recovery) flows, and we cover business models in Chapter 3.

We'll look at improving products and processes from the perspective of a brand or product manufacturer, rather than for a *circular service provider* (such as a specialist recycler or reseller) – we'll examine how they fit into the system in Chapter 3.

Circular approaches have many benefits: for the company, its customers and other stakeholders. High-quality, durable and repairable products improve customer experience, building trust in the brand, leading to loyal customers (and less marketing expenditure). Long-lasting products may need spare parts and repair services, thus creating new revenue streams:

- Designing products to be **modular** makes repairs simpler and cheaper. Modular products make it easy to develop and offer upgrades, such as new technology, better functionality, or improved efficiency. The Fairphone 2 mobile phone (see Chapter 8) consists of several modules, and if a module needs replacing, the user can swap out any part in a few minutes, needing only a screwdriver.

- **Upgradable** products are a win-win because the customer gets a better product, and the brand keeps the customer's business. The Fairphone 2 is upgradable, too.

FIGURE 2.5 Circular Economy Framework 2.0 – design and supply chain

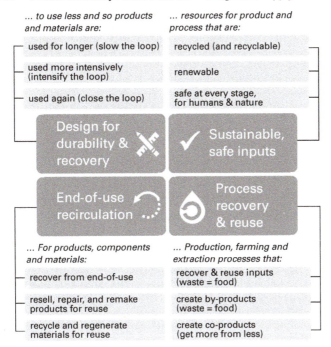

SOURCE: © Catherine Weetman

- Designing products for **repair, remaking and recycling** creates new, profitable activities and reduces the cost of repair, remaking and recovery. These new activities, aimed at keeping products in use, create opportunities for companies to offer added-value services. Longer-lasting products have a higher resale value; they build trust in the brand and open up markets where people can't justify the cost of the brand-new product.

- Specifying **fewer, simpler materials** helps create circular systems too. By avoiding adhesives, bonding, coating and other compounds, it becomes easier and cheaper to reuse the materials, repeatedly.

- Ensuring all materials are **easy to identify**, with standard markings where possible, promotes efficient and effective recycling and reuse.

Design for durability and recovery

We begin with product design, as this influences many other aspects of the system. We want to design products, equipment and infrastructure to get more from less. This means designing them to be durable and repairable, so they stay in use for longer, or are used more intensively. We also want to design them to be remade and eventually recycled.

FIGURE 2.6   Circular Economy Framework 2.0 – design for durability and recovery

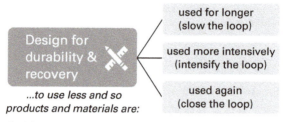

SOURCE: © Catherine Weetman

It is often said that most of a product's impact is determined at the design stage. In *Cradle to Cradle* (2002), McDonough and Braungart argue that designing for **eco-efficiency** (or resource efficiency) 'only works to make the old, destructive system a bit less so'.[3] Appropriate product design enables and encourages a range of circular improvements, helping products last for longer and/or be robust enough to be shared or 'accessed' by many different users. Product design can also reduce waste at end-of-use, and in the manufacturing and supply chain processes.

In addition, product design can influence or restrict the materials used – the *bill of materials*. Product design can encourage the use of renewable or recycled materials, as well as helping or hindering resilience and supply chain agility. Figure 2.6 summarizes the aims: to design to use less, and so the product and materials are used for longer, can be used more intensively, and can be used again (waste = food).

Product design can also support in **narrowing the loop,** to use less. We aim to design out 'leakage', or wasted materials and inputs, at every stage of the process, supply chain and use periods. This is also called *resource efficiency*, or in Cradle-to-Cradle terms, 'eco-efficiency'. We want to use less of each material (whether from recycled, renewable or virgin sources) to reduce the pressure on resources.

We can reduce the use of virgin materials by replacing them with recycled resources or even eliminating the need for the material or component altogether. For packaging, UK cosmetic brand Lush sells soaps in 'naked' packaging, and plastic-free supermarket aisles (and even whole supermarkets) are popping up around Europe.

Other examples include **light-weighting** initiatives for packaging. Similarly, using box-section chassis to produce lighter, stronger cars and 'hollowed out' crank arms for bicycle transmissions all reduce material input and improve performance without compromising the strength. *Additive manufacturing* and *3D printing* can use less material to make stronger, lighter products, by designing structure to provide strength, instead of relying on bulk or expensive bonded materials (see Chapter 4).

We also aim to **simplify the *bill of materials*,** by reducing complexity and using fewer compounds. This can reduce production costs and improve the recovery process, by making it easier to separate those compounds into nutrients at the end of life. Fewer, simpler compounds can reduce energy along the process. Design should avoid mixing biological and technical nutrients, or at least make their separation easy (time, energy, simplicity, cost) at the end-of-use. We should avoid blended materials, for example, polycotton textiles, shoes containing leather and plastics, and so on. For example, a 3D printed shoe uses only one material for both the sole and the upper, and Mud Jeans eliminated the traditional leather label on the waistband of its jeans, to simplify recycling at end-of-use.

DESIGN SO THE PRODUCT AND MATERIALS ARE IN USE FOR LONGER

To keep products in use for longer, we design them to be high quality, robust and easy to maintain and repair, using durable materials.

You might include 'emotional durability': so that the owner will cherish the product, maintain it and even repair it. Take the time to consider local and regional needs, and the consumer trend towards personalization, or 'mass customization'. Using classic shapes, colours and materials can help with this – think about iconic furniture designs, the Roberts radio, VW Beetle, the Mini and so on.

To keep it in use, the product should be easily repairable, enabling straightforward disassembly and swap-out of components for repair and even upgrading. Standardization can reduce the overall parts and materials inventory, especially if deployed across a wide range of products and components – see the Fairphone example in Chapter 8.

DESIGN TO USE THE PRODUCT AND MATERIALS MORE INTENSIVELY

Are there ways to design the product to support sharing, 'pay per use' and other business models so the product is used more intensively? In other words, the product is more productive, and we get more use, or value from the product, its components and materials.

What kind of features might support second and further use cycles? For example, modular, upgradable parts, or a Freepost return label stitched into a garment. We need to make it robust, easy to use, and maybe distinctive to avoid theft – the OV-Fiets rental bikes in the Netherlands are a good design example.

DESIGN TO USE THE PRODUCT AND MATERIALS AGAIN – WASTE = FOOD!

We can design to optimize the product value through several 'use cycles', so we can resell, repair, remake and eventually recycle it. The design can help recovery of components for reuse, remanufacturing or recycling: think about a 'waste = food' approach.

Design for disassembly (D4D) helps separate *technical* and *biological nutrients* for recycling into new inputs. Good design here can reduce labour (or enable mechanization), reducing risk of damage and waste and, ultimately, improve value recovery. Standardization and modular approaches, using screws and fixings that are standard fittings and easy to remove, instead of laminates, bonding, glues, rivets and so on, are all helpful.

Clear labelling of the components and their materials, perhaps including date stamping or quality indicators, can help to streamline sortation and recovery later in the life-cycle. This may support the company's business model or cross-sector recovery processes. Easy-to-identify materials help recovery. For example, the ASTM International Resin Identification Coding System (RIC), set up in 1988, identifies the plastic resin in the product. Symbols, with three arrows forming a triangle, and numbered 1–7 with abbreviated codes for the material (eg 05 PP Polypropylene) are easily recognizable, and help local recycling schemes worldwide to increase successful recycling.

ECOVATIVE DESIGN: GROWING PACKAGING[4]

Ecovative uses mycelium, the root structure of mushrooms, to grow materials that replace plastics.

Developed in 2007, its Mushroom® Packaging is a 'high-performance packaging solution that's cost-competitive with conventional polystyrene foams, yet 100 per cent home compostable'.

The materials are grown in nine days, can be grown into bespoke shapes using custom moulds and are flame-resistant, hydrophobic and biodegradable. You can also purchase Grow-It-Yourself (GIY) kits.

Good product designs can help recover materials, energy and water used to create the materials (eg pesticides, fertilizers and irrigation in agriculture) and in the process. By envisaging the materials, process inputs and end-of-use outputs as 'nutrients', we are more likely to develop circular economy approaches.

FIGURE 2.7   Circular Economy Framework 2.0 – safe, sustainable inputs

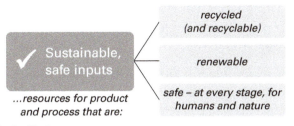

SOURCE: © Catherine Weetman

PRODUCT DESIGN ENABLERS

Design 'enablers', including *ecodesign*, *green chemistry* and *biomimicry*, encourage innovations in material choice and product design. For example, research investigating how spider silk, which is stronger than steel and more elastic than rubber, might be used or synthesized for commercial use.

A systems thinking approach helps identify stakeholders and avoid the 'law of unforeseen consequences'. Designing products to be durable might discourage their replacement with future, more energy- or water-efficient models. Use of modular designs can enable partial upgrades, so a modular car chassis could easily accept a more efficient engine – a few small companies are now retro-fitting electric engines to petrol or diesel cars. We expand on these enablers in Chapter 4.

Safe, sustainable inputs

During the product design phase, we can also experiment with the materials (see Figure 2.7). How can we make these more circular?

Resources and materials, for both the product and the process, should be renewable or recycled, so you can be confident of securing supply over the long term. By switching to abundant, renewable or recycled resources, we are 'closing the loop'. We tend to forget that all material resources have limits:

- Metals, minerals and fossil fuels are finite (technical) resources. Even if the sources seem to be plentiful, issues including trade restrictions and tariffs, plus geopolitics, conflict and natural disasters can all affect supplies.

- Food, fibres, timber and other 'renewable' materials ('biological resources') are also constrained, by the availability of water and suitable land, as well as the risks above. If we choose a renewable material, we must ensure we can source it sustainably and renew it within the intended life-cycle of the product. For example, if we harvest a tree to make five chairs, those chairs should last for as long as it takes a new tree to grow to a harvestable size.

Sustainable inputs also improve the '**resource security**' of the materials. Are there geopolitical risks or economic factors that might restrict future supplies or drive up costs to unaffordable levels? Do you have several sources for key materials, perhaps from different continents? Natural disasters like the Japan tsunami in 2011 disrupted major supply chains for several months. The European Commission publishes a list of critical raw materials (CRMs) with a high supply risk and high economic importance for European industry and value chains. By 2017, the list included 27 materials (see Chapter 9).

Ideally, try to identify alternative materials as well as a range of sources, so that if the material is critical to competitors or to other sectors, you have more options for securing your supplies. Think about both short-term and long-term supply chain disruption, as well as long-term cost trends – perhaps substituting a biological waste for 'technical' materials.

Social and environmental damage from farming, forestry and fishing, mining and material extraction, over-fishing, deforestation, the use of synthetic pesticides, fertilizers from fossil fuels, intensive irrigation in areas or water scarcity and many other issues are highlighting our dependence on unsustainable material sources. I believe it's critical that all the inputs should be safe for humans and living systems, at every stage of the process – however, not all circular economy approaches focus on this.

RECYCLED AND RECYCLABLE INPUTS

We can replace virgin materials with recycled equivalents, by finding ways to recover materials at end-of-use, or collaborating with companies producing by-products or co-products from their own process. Recycled materials may already be available from specialist processors; alternatively, you may be able to work with a recycler or researcher to develop new recycled inputs.

TOAST ALE: RECOVERED INPUTS[5,6]

For bread produced in the UK, 44 per cent is thrown away each year (including 24 million slices of bread by households). Realizing this, Tristram Stuart, founder of food waste campaign charity Feedback, created Toast Ale in 2015, aiming to find a higher-value use for waste bread.

Toast Ale was inspired by the Brussels Beer Project, which created 'Babylone' beer from an ancient Babylonian recipe. Local supermarkets supply their waste bread, which replaces some of the barley in the brewing recipe, typically using 500 kilograms of unused loaves to brew 4,000 litres of ale. Toast Ale launched its first beer in 2016 and has won awards for innovation, sustainability, and for its beer.

ADIDAS OCEAN PLASTIC SHOE: RECYCLED INPUTS, 3D PRINTING[7]

In partnership with Parley for the Oceans, Adidas designed a sports shoe using recycled polyester and gill (fishing) net content, all recovered from plastic waste in the sea (an example of an open-loop, cross-sector flow, between fishing and fashion). The upper is made with ocean plastic content and the midsole is *3D printed* using gill net content and other types of recycled polyamide.

RENEWABLE INPUTS

Are sustainable, renewable materials an option? The ease of renewability is important – how quickly will it re-grow (days or years) and with what level of inputs, such as fertilizers? Sustainability means avoiding land that could grow food crops.

New materials, from abundant, natural sources, are becoming available. Examples include plastics from algae and fish waste, 'leather' from mushrooms, 'silk' from waste citrus peel, and many more. In 2019, Lucy Hughes, 23, a graduate in product design from the University of Sussex, won the UK category of the James Dyson award. She developed a bio-plastic made of organic fish waste that would otherwise end up in landfill, with the potential to replace plastic in everyday packaging. It looks and feels like plastic but is stronger and can be disposed of as food waste.[8]

CALFEE DESIGN: RENEWABLE INPUTS[9,10]

Calfee Design, a high-quality bicycle frame manufacturer in San Francisco, produced its first frame made from bamboo in 2007. Founder Craig Calfee was in Africa in 1984 and noticed first that there was a lot of bamboo; second, people used bikes, which seemed to be in short supply; and third, people needed employment. He began by helping people in Ghana to build their own cargo bikes, using bamboo.

Bamboo is sustainable, smooth and strong, and Calfee says it has 'the best vibration damping for the smoothest ride'. Even better, 'nature provides it in a huge range of tube diameters and wall thicknesses'. Calfee decided to produce the frames to sell in the United States and elsewhere, treating the bamboo to prevent splitting and joining the frame tubes with lugs made of hemp fibre. The resins used are plant-based. A DIY build kit means the home bike-builder doesn't need to learn how to weld!

SAFE, AT EVERY STAGE, FOR HUMANS AND NATURE

We should consider this at every stage of the supply chain, from farming or extraction through production to use, and end-of-use, and adopt the 'precautionary principle', advocated by UNESCO.

Are there toxins or other hazards in the material itself, or used in its extraction or during manufacture? Designers should assess each of the material inputs to ensure the product is safe.

If you cannot ensure its recovery and recycling at the end-of-use, will it biodegrade naturally instead, providing food for nature? Otherwise, will it emit harmful *greenhouse gases (GHG)* such as methane, or degrade into toxic materials or harmful micro-particles?

Process inputs should also prioritize **recycled and renewable inputs** over finite resources. Questions to ask include whether biological process inputs could replace those chemical compounds based on finite materials. How could you replace inputs with potentially harmful effects on the health of humans or other living systems?

In many material specifications, there will be scope to improve (or worsen) the environmental impact of the process. Choosing organically produced food ingredients will reduce the embodied inputs, such as fertilizers, artificial chemicals in pesticides and herbicides, or the use of preventative antibiotics in animal husbandry. Organic production methods emit less pollution, avoiding fertilizer and pesticide run-off, and often replace energy-intensive agricultural machinery with human input.

Process design

We've already mentioned the need to use safe, sustainable materials in the product and the process. We can design circular production processes, too, for 'embedded resources', such as:

- **energy** to power equipment, heat water, dry products, extract dust and fumes, etc;

FIGURE 2.8   Circular Economy Framework 2.0 – process design

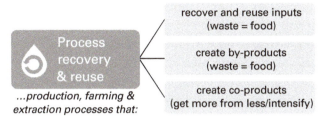

SOURCE: © Catherine Weetman

- **water** to transform, process, dye the materials, and so on, and to rinse excess process chemicals off the product before the next stage;
- **water** for washing materials (eg agricultural products) and packaging before use, and cleaning equipment between production cycles;
- **materials** used during the process (though not listed in the 'contents' of the final product), including dyes, coatings, chemicals and so on.

Recovering energy, water and materials saves money and creates new revenue opportunities. Figure 2.8 shows the goals (similar to those for product design) to ensure 'waste = food' by recovering and recycling those process inputs to use again, creating by-products and co-products to sell. We should also aim to narrow the loop by using less (both materials and process inputs). We may find ways to recycle or reuse process waste, including offcuts, grindings, or sub-standard materials and products. The RealCar project sees Jaguar Land Rover and Novelis recovering aluminium waste from the production line for new products.[11]

RECOVER AND REUSE INPUTS

Here we aim to recover energy, materials, liquids and gases from the process, to be recycled for our own reuse, or to become by-products we can feed into other systems. We aim to recover technical inputs for reuse and to extract the highest value and benefit from biological inputs. Permaculture design principles can help identify 'virtuous circle' opportunities.

Can you create your own **closed loops** and retain the inputs for reuse, or substitute with a more renewable source? Recovering fats from cooking processes to use as energy sources, or making bioenergy from waste food, are common examples. Industrial symbiosis may offer potential open-loop solutions to support this, which we cover later in this chapter.

Recovering **energy from waste** is preferable to it going to landfill or as effluent, but is unlikely to recover the highest value and usefulness – it is *downcycling* rather than *upcycling*. Instead, consider what by-products you might be able to create. High-value chemicals may be embedded in the waste streams, and *biorefining* could extract these, with energy, solids, compost still available in the remaining residue.

Companies are starting to offer chemicals as a service, so the customer buys the performance of the chemicals, and the supplier recovers the used chemicals for refining, potentially extracting contaminating materials that can be refined and turned into by-products. UNIDO's Chemical Leasing Toolkit aims to support companies to develop these services.[12]

CREATE BY-PRODUCTS AND CO-PRODUCTS

Maybe you can recover your own excess, damaged or obsolete products, components and materials. In addition to reducing costs by recovering your own inputs, you could develop new by-products and revenue streams.

BURBERRY AND ELVIS & KRESSE: LUXURY PRODUCTS FROM OFFCUTS[13]

Fashion brand Burberry, criticized for incinerating unsold stock worth around £25 million, created a partnership with sustainable luxury specialists Elvis & Kresse, to transform at least 120 tonnes of leather off-cuts from Burberry production into a range of new luxury accessories and homeware.

Although patterns for leather goods are carefully planned, there are always unusable pieces of high-quality, unused, freshly tanned and dyed leather. Elvis & Kresse transforms these leather fragments into components, first sorting them into size and colour. The cutting process starts after planning which item to make, avoiding excess pieces of any particular shape. The profits are split between charitable causes and furthering Elvis & Kresse's work in reducing and reusing waste, protecting the environment and inspiring craftspeople.

British Sugar, mentioned earlier, is a great example, creating a wide range of by-products and co-products from its production process.[14] These range from topsoil and aggregates to bio-energy and animal feed. There are closed loops (it recycles waste heat and carbon dioxide from manufacture to grow crops in its own on-site hothouses) and open loops to the food sector and other industries.

Earlier, we read about citrus peel, pulp and pips, all produced as a 'waste' from orange juice processed for sale in bottles or cartons. Rather than just sending this to compost, or aiming to recover energy from the waste, we can first extract a range of valuable by-products. Pectin from the pips is a setting agent for jam; we can extract orange essential oils from the peel, for sale to cosmetic or pharmaceutical companies; and fibres can become a thickening agent for processed foods. Even at a smaller scale, we can use the waste more productively – some upmarket hotels use the waste from their freshly squeezed juice to make their own marmalade.

The Ellen MacArthur Foundation defines **industrial symbiosis** as 'a local partnership where partners provide, share and reuse resources to create shared value'.[15] These exchanges will be open loops and could flow to the same industrial sector, or across to a different sector.

In late 2018, the European Union announced a project to develop a 'pre-standard' for industrial symbiosis, aiming to raise awareness, develop standards and promote activity to support the circular economy.[16]

The world's first industrial symbiosis project, the Kalundborg Project in Denmark, began in 1961 (see the case study in Part Three). The UK launched its National Industrial Symbiosis Programme (NISP) in 2003.[17] Regional pilot schemes aimed to create synergistic flows of by-products from one company becoming inputs for another. It demonstrated immediate impacts in reducing virgin resource inputs, carbon emissions and waste to landfill, and in 2005, the UK government invested to extend it across the country. NISP pioneered a facilitated approach to industrial symbiosis, providing ways to share knowledge and ideas across industry sectors. This helps companies to improve resource efficiency and convert surplus materials, water or energy into environmental and financial benefits.

NISP became International Synergies in 2005 and is widely acknowledged for its expertise in devising and managing industrial symbiosis programmes. It works with public and private sector clients, institutions and the research community across five continents.

MILWAUKEE CITY: DE-ICING ROADS WITH CHEESE[18]

Dairies in Wisconsin in the United States donate their waste brine from cheese production to the city authorities, which then use it to de-ice the local roads, saving tens of thousands of dollars each year. An added benefit is that cheese brine has a lower freezing temperature than salt brine, so is effective in a wider range of weather conditions, further reducing the risk of accidents.

> ### PECTCOF: COFFEE CHERRY – WASTE = FOOD[19,20]
>
> Examining the upstream supply chain for coffee reveals a major waste issue when raw ('green') coffee beans are separated from the coffee 'cherry'. Each kilogram of roasted coffee creates an equal amount of waste in the source countries, polluting the environment and leaching acidic compounds into rivers, lakes and soil. The pollution generated from one tonne of green coffee is equivalent to the domestic sewage output of 2,000 households. The chemical formation of the cherry makes it almost impossible for the waste to ferment and oxidize into compost.
>
> Dutch startup Pectcof transforms this waste, using biorefinery concepts with green chemistry and biotechnology. Waste becomes valuable bio-compounds, including food ingredients, biochemical and second-generation biofuels. By 2019, Pectcof had developed technology to further purify the pectine and protein extracts from the cherry, improving the purity of the product. This broadened the range of applications, with testing in confectionery, bakery and soft drink products. It is partnering with industry experts to develop a range of by-products from the process.

USE LESS – AND FEWER, SIMPLER INPUTS

Can you apply resource efficiency principles to the process itself, by looking for inputs not fully utilized, or changing the process to eliminate the need for some inputs?

Let's look at an example from the food sector: processing onions to provide slices for pre-prepared onion rings with batter (for example in takeaway food). Automating this process along a production line presents challenges, needing specialist equipment to hold the onion, remove the stem and base, remove the papery skin, and then slice it into the required thicknesses. There is a high potential for waste, especially if the whole onions have a wide range of sizes – and even shapes. Solutions might include grading the onions into different sizes first, and then resetting the machinery to deal with each size range, finding alternative uses for unsuitable onions (such as onion soup or bases for other recipes), or even working with farmers to find seed varieties likely to produce more uniform results.

A different 'whole system' example of a design to use less is *aquaponics*, farming fish and plants in a mutually beneficial system. Aquaponics systems combine conventional aquaculture (raising aquatic animals such as fish, shellfish, crustaceans or molluscs in tanks) with hydroponics (cultivating plants in water) in a symbiotic environment. In normal aquaculture, fish excretions can build up in the water, increasing toxicity and compromising the health of the fish. In an aquaponics system, water from an aquaculture system flows into a hydroponic system, where bacteria break down the excretions into by-products, including nitrates and nitrites. These by-products can provide nutrition to plants, and the cleaned water recirculates back into the aquaculture system.

LEVI'S® WATER<LESS – SHARING WATER EFFICIENCY TECHNIQUES[21,22]

Global fashion brand Levi's, embarking on a *life-cycle assessment* of its products, found that the product life-cycle uses more than 3,000 litres of water. Levi's® Water<Less collection, launched in 2011, saves up to 96 per cent of water for some products.

By 2019, Levi's® deployed over 20 water-saving finish techniques and publishes its methods to help other companies. It had saved over 3 billion litres and recycled more than 2 billion litres of water. By 2020, its goal is 'for 80 per cent of all Levi's® products to be made using Water<Less® innovations'.

ENABLERS AND ACCELERATORS FOR PROCESS DESIGN

A whole-systems approach helps to safeguard against adverse impacts and the 'law of unforeseen consequences'. While bio-based materials may seem an obvious choice, availability of land and water is limited. Growing crops to produce biochemical or biofuels reduces the land available for human food, for grazing or for forests. The third generation of biofuels improves on this by using 'waste' parts of food crops, such as wheat straw.

Good process design aims to create 'circularity' at every stage along the supply chain. This should include your in-house production methods, as well as the upstream and downstream processes, whether these are in your control or managed by suppliers and partners. The value chain starts with the extraction or harvesting of materials and may have bigger overall impacts than your in-house processes. *Life-cycle assessments* (see Part Three) can help determine the different impacts at each stage, though these can be highly complex and time-consuming. It may be worth considering more speedy and pragmatic ways to gauge likely opportunities for improvement.

FIGURE 2.9   Circular Economy Framework 2.0 – recovery flows

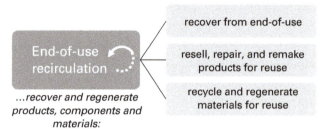

SOURCE: © Catherine Weetman

Recovery flows

The final component in our 'design and supply chain' looks at how to 'close the loop' on the product and materials at the end-of-use, to recover products for reselling, repairing, or remaking; or to recycle and regenerate materials for reuse (see Figure 2.9).

To conserve most value, we prioritize those 'inner loops', enabling reuse of the product, perhaps including maintenance in the field to prolong the in-use lifetime. Alternatively, can you recover the product for refurbishment or remanufacture? Otherwise, can you recover value by 'harvesting' the components, or by recycling the materials?

RECOVER FROM END-OF-USE

Designing systems to recover products and materials helps keep them flowing around the system and thus retain their value for the next cycle. Ideally, we should capture this value for our own business. High-quality, durable products have resale value for another 'use cycle': perhaps by the user (for example on eBay), by a specialist reseller, or by the manufacturer. In Japan, Patagonia's clothing may resell at a *much* higher price than the 'new' version!

Ensuring products and components are kept as intact as possible during recovery minimizes the cost of making them fit for reuse. This is one of the main challenges of recovery systems. Even 'dedicated' recycling streams, such as waste electricals and electronics (WEEE), may involve users 'dumping' their end-of-use items – which could include a phone, a laptop, a TV – or even a washing machine. Products that were in good working order when deposited may be damaged beyond repair by the time they arrive at the processor.

Companies and consortia are developing efficient, effective recovery systems to sort end-of-use products so they can be returned to the highest 'use' level, avoiding mixed-material downcycling. Reverse vending machines and machine learning are now being used to make it easier for users to return end-of-life products (with potential to reward them for the return) and to create automated, effective ways of sorting the products into sub-streams. Plastic bottles, batteries and more can be handled efficiently by these small sorting stations.

RESELL, REPAIR AND REMAKE PRODUCTS FOR REUSE

Having designed or selected products for durability, how can you help keep them in use for longer? You need to consider the 'cost to use' for the customer, whether that is over a longer life-cycle or a value-for-money short-term rental model. Durable products, with 'timeless' design, should depreciate more slowly and have resale opportunities.

You may need systems to maintain the products, ideally on-site to reduce logistics costs and minimize the risk of damage from transit or handling. Can the user repair the products themselves, in situ? The first user may choose to do this, or decide to sell the product to a repairer/reseller, or donate it through a reuse network such as Freecycle, with the product subsequently repaired by a specialist.

Making it easy for users to return products enables you to check for quality, and refurbish and repair where required, to ensure products reflect your brand quality standards and you can resell and create value from them. For cars and motorcycles, many brand dealerships offer pre-used models, often with a limited additional warranty period.

Modular designs make it easier to replace parts or sub-assemblies, without needing specialist tools. How will you help users to diagnose the problem, and guide them to fix it easily? Could you provide easy-to-follow repair instructions or even videos available online? If the repair is too complex or specialized, perhaps requiring diagnostic testing equipment, you may be able to use field engineers who have a rapid response time. Could there be opportunities to provide local repair facilities? Products in near-continuous use should include parts that are easy to 'swap out', so they can quickly return to operational status, with the part repaired off-site. This means they can be repaired using 'scripts', even by logistics providers. Examples include medical equipment, production machinery and bank cash machines.

IKEA: SIMPLIFYING REUSE[23]

IKEA noticed that many of its products were for sale as used items on eBay, and began to worry this could undermine its business. IKEA then realized this was positive, helping the original consumer feel confident they could resell the product in the future, and thus reinforcing the IKEA brand value. The company decided to support resale and reuse by providing easy access to commonly used fixings and fasteners, simplifying replacement if those small parts are lost during disassembly.

Refurbishment and *remanufacture* are options for many products, especially higher-value, perhaps technically-complex designs. This can apply to the whole product, or a component, such as electric motors and alternators (see Renault in Chapter 9). Refurbishment can include repair as well as cosmetic improvements to improve the appearance and functionality of the product. Remanufacturing, explored throughout the book, has a specific definition and a British Standard. Caterpillar and Cummins both have substantial remanufacturing divisions, said to be the most profitable parts of their businesses. John Deere remanufactures its tractor components, Rockwell Automation its electrical equipment, and SKF remanufactures its bearings.[24]

RECYCLE AND REGENERATE MATERIALS FOR REUSE

At the end of each cycle of use, how can you encourage recovery of all the materials? This is especially important when you've changed the product design to use recycled materials – you need to support this pipeline of *secondary materials*, and help convert waste into food for another industrial process. If you can't use the materials in-house, could you encourage and support other recovery methods, for example through sector-wide collaborations? One example is deposit return schemes for glass and plastic bottles. Ideally, recycling avoids downcycling and value loss too.

CISCO SYSTEMS INC: TAKEBACK AND RECYCLE PROGRAM[25]

US multinational Cisco Systems, a leading provider of IT, networking and cybersecurity solutions across the world, offers end-of-life programmes. In the US, Cisco's Takeback and Recycle Program aims to harvest and reuse materials from equipment returned by customers. Products are disassembled and processed, to retrieve materials such as steel, aluminium, copper, plastics, shredded circuit boards, and cables. These materials then return to the relevant market, so they can be made into new products. CISCO US says that over 99 per cent of the electronics sent for processing are recycled.

How can you ensure your product does not end up in landfill, incineration or as pollution in waterways? This is starting to become a reputation risk, especially for single-use plastic packaging or other difficult-to-recycle and problematic materials. Can you offer incentives or collection services to users? An example here is TerraCycle, a circular services provider (covered in more detail in Chapter 10). TerraCycle works with major fast-moving consumer goods (FMCG) brands, manufacturers and retailers, operating programmes to reward communities for returning difficult-to-recycle waste.[26]

Thinking about waste = food, such as compost (food for nature), we should ensure that waste such as packaging is benign, or even beneficial at the end of its use.

TOMORROW MACHINE: BIODEGRADABLE PACKAGING[27]

Swedish design studio Tomorrow Machine specializes in concepts for packaging and food. Questioning whether it is 'reasonable that it takes several years for a milk carton to decompose naturally, when the milk goes sour after a week' sparked ideas for a new design project. This Too Shall Pass is a series of food packages where the packaging and its contents work symbiotically and the packaging has the same short life span as the foods inside. There are three concepts:

- **Oil package:** a caramelized sugar package, also coated with wax, designed for oil-based food.

- **Smoothie package:** formed from water and agar gel (from algae), designed for drinks with a short shelf life, including fresh juice, cream and smoothies.

- **Rice package:** made of biodegradable beeswax, designed for dry goods such as grains and rice. You open this by peeling it like a fruit.

Rethinking supply chains

We've seen how the four central components in my circular economy framework – product design, safe, sustainable materials, process design and recovery flows – form the 'design and supply chain'. Choices and decisions at these points determine whether the product can last longer, be used more intensively, or has value that can be recovered for reuse and regeneration.

You might be able to design-in options, such as a 'menu' of possible materials, to reduce the risk of disruption in case of cost increase or material shortages. Remember that product design and the *bill of materials* drive decisions on sourcing, procurement and logistics, not the other way around.

Our 'design and supply chain' is more complex than a traditional 'linear' supply chain, needing a whole-systems perspective to consider the impact of materials choice, together with product life-extension and post-use options. My 'rectangle of recovery' schematic (see Figure 2.4) shows how materials can flow between the supply chains of companies in different sectors. These could be direct exchanges, as with industrial symbiosis and sales of by-products, or indirectly through collaborative initiatives and circular service providers. When supply chains are circular – with new flows, service networks, more 'touch-points' between the company and the customers, new recovery loops for products and materials – they become multi-dimensional. Circulating products, components and materials and protecting their value (ready for resale, repair, remanufacturing or recycling) means rethinking reverse supply chains and packaging design.

There are broader opportunities to explore, thinking about the ecosystem around your business, and the wider economy, bringing assets, including facilities and machinery, into scope too. Can you share facilities to reduce footprints, investment and energy? Can you find different ways to procure machinery or process aids, perhaps as a service to encourage high performance and continuous improvement from the supplier?

The business ecosystem includes potential collaborative partners. Look upstream and downstream along the supply chain, and work with your suppliers and partners to investigate potential improvements or trade-offs, where a change in one part of the system has greater benefits elsewhere.

Summary

The 'design and supply chain' is fundamental to the circular economy, with major implications for business strategy and future success. It can reduce operating costs; buffer against resource risks (cost and security of supply); help create safer, healthier products; contribute to ecosystem restoration; and create desirable, well-designed and durable products that create, conserve and circulate value for your customers, your business, society and our planet.

The 'design and supply' chain helps you think about all the points where you can intervene in the existing system, to help make it more circular.

FIGURE 2.10   The perfect product

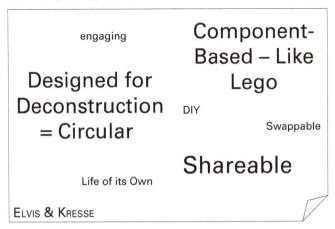

SOURCE: Perfect product features included with permission from Kresse Wesling MBE, Elvis & Kresse

Where can you reduce risk, build resilience, and create new value? Are there opportunities to engage customers and suppliers, to create new market opportunities or develop complementary service offers? Think about the whole value chain – where might you be leaving value 'on the table'? For example, if you create a high-quality, durable product that lasts for longer, can you support resale at the end of the first life, perhaps refurbishing the product to ensure it meets your brand standards? This could be a new revenue stream, as well as engaging you with potential future customers for a new product. Might you need to help the customer understand the cost of ownership, which is potentially cheaper if the product lasts for longer or has attractive resale values?

Kresse Wesling, of Elvis & Kresse (featured earlier and in Chapter 7), gave a detailed design brief for the 'perfect product', shown in Figure 2.10: it should be component-based (like Lego); designed for disassembly and recirculation; can be customized, or upgraded (through 'do it yourself'); and engaging, swappable, shareable and repairable – so it can have a 'life of its own'.

Success means reframing the way we think about design, using the concept of 'nutrients' to focus on the value of every input. Success also means rethinking the business model, and we move on to examine this in Chapter 3. The focus is on how to find value opportunities – creating, conserving and circulating value – and discovering ways to add value for stakeholders. Systems thinking and collaboration can underpin resilience and prosperity.

In a circular economy, where waste = food, businesses that focus on keeping their customers for life and developing products that have a 'life of their own' will find new forms of value, with knowledge exchange, partnerships and symbiotic relationships all helping drive innovation and continuous improvement. Ray Anderson, the founder of Interface, summed it up superbly in the following words that I quoted in the introductory chapter, and which are reiterated here:[28]

> taking nothing, wasting nothing and doing no harm – and doing very well by doing good, at the expense not of the earth but of less alert competitors.

Further resources

Nike Circular Design Guide [Online] www.nikecirculardesign.com (archived at https://perma.cc/943G-P6QM) [accessed 2 November 2019]

Product Design: Ecodesign (2016) Loughborough University, UK [Online] http://ecodesign.lboro.ac.uk/?section=97 (archived at https://perma.cc/CT4Q-ZK7G) [accessed 30 May 2016]

Shedroff, N (2010) Design for Disassembly, excerpt from 'Design is the Problem' [Online] www.atissuejournal.com/2010/03/31/design-for-disassembly/ (archived at https://perma.cc/Q3C7-XKET) [accessed 30 May 2016]

The Centre for Sustainable Design [Online] http://cfsd.org.uk/ (archived at https://perma.cc/UU43-SCC8) [accessed 1 June 2016]

The Circular Design Guide, by IDEO and Ellen MacArthur Foundation www.circulardesignguide.com/ (archived at https://perma.cc/36ZC-JLUR) [accessed 11 November 2019]

Notes

1 Page, L (2013) [accessed 24 February 2016] Alphabet 2013 Founders Letter [Online] abc.xyz/investor/founders-letters/2013/ (archived at https://perma.cc/6R3A-KLP9)

2 British Sugar (2016) [accessed 10 March 2016] How Our Factory Operates [Online]. Website no longer available, but see https://www.britishsugar.co.uk/about-sugar/our-factories (archived at https://perma.cc/63U5-H4GR)

3 McDonough, W and Braungart, M (2002) *Cradle to Cradle: Remaking the way we make things*, North Point Press, New York, p 62

4 Ecovative Design [online] https://ecovativedesign.com (archived at https://perma.cc/X4KA-CJQW) [accessed 23 September 2019]

5 Toast Ale [accessed 3 February 2016] [Online] www.toastale.com/ (archived at https://perma.cc/U4QQ-YAY7)

6 *The Guardian* [accessed 3 February 2016] Five Companies Using Waste Products in Surprising Ways, *The Guardian*, 1 September 2015 [Online]

www.theguardian.com/sustainable-business/origin-green-ireland-partner-zone/2015/sep/01/five-companies-using-waste-products-in-surprising-ways (archived at https://perma.cc/3UBZ-WNM9)

7   Adidas Newstream (8 December 2015) [accessed 21 February 2016] [Online] news.adidas.com/US/Latest-News/adidas-and-Parley-for-the-Oceans-Stop-the-Industry-s-Waiting-Game/s/770e492e-544f-4eda-9b8b-f9e2596569b1 (archived at https://perma.cc/DJ78-JS2B)

8   Smithers, R (2019) Scaling back: graduate invents plastic alternative from fish waste, *The Guardian* (19 September 2019) [online] [accessed 25 September 2019]

9   Calfee Design (2016) History calfeedesign.com/history/ (archived at https://perma.cc/6TEC-96CU) [accessed 21 February 2016]

10 Calfee Design (2016) Bamboo DIY calfeedesign.com/calfee-bamboo-diy-kit/ (archived at https://perma.cc/WYL3-9XCE) [accessed 21 February 2016]

11 Cambridge Institute for Sustainable Leadership, REALCAR project circular economy case study: Collaboration for a closed-loop value chain (2016) [online] www.cisl.cam.ac.uk/resources/low-carbon-transformation-publications/collaboration-for-a-closed-loop-value-chain (archived at https://perma.cc/G4ED-7PKY) [accessed 23 September 2019]

12 Chemical Leasing Toolkit [online] https://chemicalleasing-toolkit.org/ (archived at https://perma.cc/U4CR-2PNY) [accessed 25 September 2019]

13 Wresling, K, An Interview with Burberry (2018) Elvis & Kresse (2 November 2018) www.elvisandkresse.com/blogs/news/interview-burberry-elvis-kresse (archived at https://perma.cc/B57V-Y837) [accessed 9 December 2019]

14 British Sugar [online] www.britishsugar.co.uk\about-sugar\co-products (archived at https://perma.cc/RKP3-JMMH) [accessed 25 September 2019]

15 Ellen MacArthur Foundation (2019) Case Studies: Kalundborg Symbiosis [Online] www.ellenmacarthurfoundation.org/case_studies/kalundborg-symbiosis (archived at https://perma.cc/2U69-5LH7) [accessed 9 December 2019]

16 Interreg Europe [online] www.interregeurope.eu/tris/news/news-article/2676/industrial-symbiosis-european-pre-standard/ (archived at https://perma.cc/K6VV-REQC) [accessed 26 September 2019]

17 National Industrial Symbiosis Programme [accessed 20 February 2016] [Online] www.nispnetwork.com/ (archived at https://perma.cc/XJA7-MFNK)

18 *The Guardian* [accessed 16 September 2015] Five Companies Using Waste Products in Surprising Ways (1 September 2015) [Online] www.theguardian.com/sustainable-business/origin-green-ireland-partner-zone/2015/sep/01/five-companies-using-waste-products-in-surprising-ways?/ (archived at https://perma.cc/ZT5C-UFZL)

19 Pectcof (2016) [accessed 23 February 2016] [Online] pectcof.com (archived at https://perma.cc/FD6P-UMZD)

20 Email to C Weetman from Rudi Dieleman, Pectcof, 26 August 2019

21 Peeters, G, (2010) Levi's: making water less jeans, *The Guardian* (20 Dec 2010) [accessed 24 September 2019] www.theguardian.com/

sustainable-business/levis-water-less-jeans (archived at https://perma.cc/9T7Z-N799)

22 Levi Strauss & Co, Sustainability [online] [Accessed 24 September 2019] www.levi.com/US/en_US/features/sustainability?ab=aboutusLP_sustainability_031918 (archived at https://perma.cc/E7U9-GPW7)

23 Heidenmark Cook, P, Head of Sustainability, IKEA Retail and Expansion, Ikea Group, Rethinking Progress panel discussion, Bradford University (14 April 2015)

24 Le Moigne, R (2018) Making Products Last, *Renewable Matter* 23–24, 2018, p 33 [Online] https://www.oakdenehollins.com/reports/2018/11/16/our-recent-contribution-to-making-products-last (archived at https://perma.cc/RP4E-T3U6) [accessed 30 October 2019]

25 Cisco Systems, Inc. [online] www.cisco.com/c/en/us/about/product-innovation-stewardship/product-recycling/takeback-recycle-program.html (archived at https://perma.cc/9EBG-8LSS) [accessed 26 September 2019]

26 TerraCycle [Online] www.terracycle.com/en-GB/about-terracycle (archived at https://perma.cc/VF6R-VHBZ) [accessed 24 September 2019]

27 Tomorrow Machine [accessed 22 February 2016] [Online] tomorrowmachine.se/ (archived at https://perma.cc/EX3Z-JMGK)

28 Lovins, AB (2011) [accessed 8 September 2020] RMI Trustee Ray C Anderson, Rocky Mountain Institute Blog, https://rmi.org/giantpassesrmitrusteeraycanderson/ (archived at https://perma.cc/Z99M-B5M5)

3

Circular business models

Breaking an old business model is always going to require leaders to follow their instinct. There will always be persuasive reasons not to take a risk. But if you only do what worked in the past, you will wake up one day and find that you've been passed by.

CLAYTON M CHRISTENSEN, PROFESSOR, HARVARD BUSINESS SCHOOL

In Chapter 2, we looked at the 'design and supply chain' elements in my framework (see Figure 3.1), including approaches for designing products and processes, selection of materials and recovery of all those valuable products, components and materials at the end of use. In this chapter, we examine **circular business models** – how do companies design strategies and commercial options to support a shift to a circular economy?

We can think of a business model as a theory, or story, to describe how an organization creates, delivers and captures value. In other words, to create value: what do we think our customers want, and how can we best meet those needs? To capture value: how will we earn revenue and other rewards?

- we begin by asking **why business models are important;**
- review the different **schools of thought on circular business models,** suggested by several consultancies and researchers;
- I suggest grouping these into four **circular business model goals** that summarize the different approaches;
- we look at the need for **strategic alignment** between the chosen business model, the product/service design and the supply chain operations;

FIGURE 3.1   Circular Economy Framework 2.0

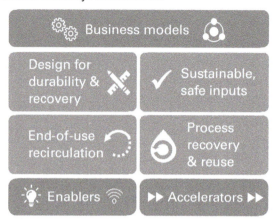

Source: © Catherine Weetman

- examine how a **range of providers** can use circular business models: from private companies to public and community organizations, through to individual people (peer-to-peer);

- look at how companies are rethinking **commercial options** to ensure they capture value from circular approaches like more durable products or resource recovery;

- and we discuss some of the **criticism of the circular economy**, so we can think about designing business and commercial models to avoid unintended consequences.

Why are business models important?

The **purpose** of a business model is critical. A business model can aim to be more circular, and yet succeed in driving more consumption, rather than less. For instance, commentators are criticizing ride-hailing for reducing the cost of personal mobility, and thus increasing the car miles in US cities. The success of Airbnb, making it easier to book non-hotel accommodation, has increased the number of properties available for short-term rent in cities like Barcelona. This has helped drive up rental costs and tourism numbers, thus making it less attractive and affordable for city residents.

We must remember that business is a system, which itself is part of a larger and more complex system that includes a wide range of stakeholders. These stakeholders include customers, employees, suppliers, communities affected by the supply chain, even governments, wider society, and competitors, as well as the business owners (or shareholders).

In the linear, 'take, make, waste' economy, companies want to sell more. They try to persuade us to buy the latest product, to replace the one that's broken or no longer supported, or encourage us to treat clothes, technology, and even furniture as 'fashion', and as such, easy to 'consume' and discard.

However, this wastes precious resources – and wastes our money! The psychology of marketing and fashion is well understood by brands, and is used to convince us to trade up to the next model, to 'keep up with the Joneses', or that wearing those clothes means we can be part of our aspirational 'tribe'. We should question why we want to own stuff that we only use for a few hours each year. For example, cars in Europe are typically idle (ie parked) for 23 hours each day. Why do we want to own it while it depreciates, the performance drops away, or the technology becomes out of date – all of which leave us worse off? One of the earliest examples of planned obsolescence occurred in the early 1900s, when a group of lighting manufacturers formed the Phoebus cartel and redesigned the lightbulb to have a more commercially attractive lifespan. By swapping the carbon filament for tungsten, they altered it to last a few years instead of a few decades.

From consuming to using

The circular economy uses business models that aim to encourage **use** instead of **ownership**, to encourage people to use products for longer, or use them more 'intensively'. What do we mean by 'intensively'? Let's return to our car example (typically used for just one hour each day): an hourly rental system would enable the people to use the car for significantly more hours in a day. Enterprise Car Club has a large fleet of cars and vans spread across an ever-increasing number of UK cities. Vehicles can be reserved for as little as half an hour, a day, or as long as needed, and are collected and returned to designated parking bays. To make this workable, they need to use cars that are robust, durable and easy to drive (and park!).

By improving the 'intensity' of use, society gets more value from less energy and resources. Companies can encourage recovery of the end-of-use product by offering discounts, or guaranteeing a 'buy-back' value. To give another example, cosmetic company Lush gives free products to customers who return their used, recyclable Lush packaging to a Lush store.[1]

Ownership is often retained by the provider, and users pay to rent, pay for access, buy 'performance' of products and equipment, or subscribe to an easily accessible shared service. This creates **new revenue streams and market opportunities** for businesses. Providing access to dedicated or shared services can make the offer more affordable, thus broadening the target market or undercutting competitors. For the provider, there are a number of factors to consider:

- What is the impact on cash flow, and how would this be managed and funded? This might be especially important in transitioning from selling products to providing access.
- What liabilities might arise, and how can these be managed and de-risked? If the provider is maintaining the product, how will it know if something needs fixing? New developments in sensor technologies and the Internet of Things might help with these issues.
- Providing products and equipment with longer design life means designing for the future – might the product include untested materials that turn out to be toxic or dangerous when future research emerges? What are the implications of future product stewardship legislation – might you have to incur costs to deal with unrecyclable or difficult to disassemble products?

Circular business models – schools of thought

The business model is central in helping the shift to 'circularity', and since the first edition of this book, researchers and consultancies continue to examine how the various business models support circular strategies.

Accenture consultants Peter Lacy and Jakob Rutqvist set out 'five new business models for circular growth' in their book *Waste to Wealth* (2015):[2]

- **Circular supply chain.** Provide renewable energy, and bio-based or fully recyclable materials so the same resources can be used again and again.
- **Recovery and recycling.** Recover useful resources or energy from end-of-life products or production waste, thus turning waste disposal costs into revenue.
- **Product life extension.** Prolong the useful life of products and components through resale, repair, remaking and upgrading.
- **Sharing platform.** Increase product utilization by enabling users to use and/or exchange products and services.
- **Product as a service.** Provide access to products and equipment, including contracts for performance, and include incentives so that products last longer and can be maintained, repaired and upgraded.

The ReSOLVE framework, developed by consultants McKinsey,[3] describes 'six ways to bring circular principles to life: ReGenerate, Share, Optimize, Loop, Virtualize and Exchange'. McKinsey has developed a tool based on this framework, to help organizations develop action plans and to calculate their likely costs and benefits. ReSOLVE is included in a toolkit for policy-makers, published by the Ellen MacArthur Foundation, and perhaps fits better into 'getting started' tools, relevant to organizations looking at how best to plan their circular transition and road maps.[4]

Drawing on research and thinking for the new guiding standard, British Standard BS8001:2017, Martin Charter and Stuart McLanaghan conclude there is no 'one-size-fits-all approach' for organizations to deliver circular economy objectives.[5] They suggest six business model categories that can be compatible with circular economic systems, but highlight that these are not exclusive or definitive. Their six categories are:

- on-demand;
- dematerialization;
- product life-cycle extension/reuse;
- recovery of *secondary raw materials*/by-products;
- product as a service/product-service system (PSS);
- sharing economy and collaborative consumption.

Building on the work of early circular economy thinkers – Walter Stahel, Bill McDonough and Michael Braungart – Nancy Bocken and her colleagues (2016)[6] describe two 'fundamental strategies towards the cycling of re-sources':

- **slowing resource loops** – designing long-life products, and/or using service loops like repair and remanufacturing to extend or intensify the utilization of products;
- **closing resource loops** – using recycling to create a loop between post-use and production, thus circulating resources.

Bocken and colleagues argue that these two approaches are distinct from a third approach, which aims to '**narrow resource flows**' by using fewer re-sources for each product (*resource efficiency*). Mariele Moreno, Fiona Charnley and colleagues from Cranfield University (2016)[7] adapt this and categorize business models according to the value flows and primary sources of revenue, as shown in their diagram in Figure 3.2. They suggest that for manufactured products, services (sharing and access) can slow resource

FIGURE 3.2   Circular business model archetypes

Value Flows [1,2]	Primary Source of Revenue	Circular Business Model Archetypes			
		Economic Activities to Close Loops *Stahel* [3]	PSS Business Models *Tukker* [4]	Business model innovations to slow and close resource loops *Bocken et al* [5]	Business models for circular advantage *Accenture* [6]
Slowing resource loops	Profit from increased utilization rate of products, enabling shared use/access/ownership	Reuse and remarket of manufactured goods	Result-oriented services	Access and performance model	Sharing Platform
	Profit from selling access to a product for a specific period of time or 'uses' and retaining material ownership		Use-oriented services	Extending product value	Product as a service
Cycling for longer	Profit from providing maintenance services or sales of refurbished, remanufactured or repaired units	Product-life extension activities for goods	Product-based services	Classic long-life model	Product life extension
	Profit from repeated sales of consumables of services for a long-life product				
	Profit from selling high quality products with a long lifespan at a high price			Encourage sufficiency	
Cascaded uses	Profit from recovering resources/energy out of disposed product of by-products from the same or other company, upcycling or recycling them.	Material efficiency / recycling molecules		Extending resource value	Resource recovery
Narrowing resource flows	Profit from providing renewable energy, bio-based or full recyclable input material to replace single-life-cycle inputs, and use fewer resources from products			Industrial symbiosis	Circular supplies

Services

Manufactured products

Resources

SOURCE: Moreno, M, De los Rios, C, Rowe, Z and Charnley, F (2016) A Conceptual Framework for Circular Design, Centre for Competitive Creative Design (C4D), Cranfield University, published in *Sustainability* 2016, **8**(9), p 937 [Online] https://doi.org/10.3390/su8090937 (archived at https://perma.cc/R2J4-S37L) [accessed 25 March 2020] Value Flows adapted from Bocken et al[1] and the Ellen MacArthur Foundation[2]

1 Bocken, NMP, de Pauw, I, Bakker, C and van der Grinten, B (2016) Product design and business model strategies for a circular economy, *Journal of Industrial and Production Engineering*, **33**, pp 308–20

2 Ellen MacArthur Foundation (2013) Towards the circular economy: Economic and business rationale for an accelerated transition [Online] https://www.ellenmacarthur foundation.org/assets/downloads/publications/Ellen-MacArthur-Foundation-Towards-the-Circular-Economy-vol.1.pdf (archived at https://perma.cc/YE7E-35QN) [accessed 25 June 2016]

3 Stahel, WR (2013) The Business Angel of a Circular Economy – Higher Competitiveness, Higher Resource Security and Material Efficiency. In *A New Dynamic: Effective Business in a Circular Economy*, 1st ed.; Ellen MacArthur Foundation: Cowes, UK, 2013 [Google Scholar]

4 Tukker, A (2015) Product services for a resource-efficient and circular economy – A review, *Journal of Cleaner Production*, **97**, pp 76–91

5 Bocken (2016) (see note 1 above)

6 Lacy, P and Rutqvist, J (2015) *Waste to Wealth: Creating Advantage in a Circular Economy*, Accenture, London

loops, and for products, there are value opportunities from cascaded use (recovery and recycling) and narrowing of resource flows. Cycling for longer offers revenue opportunities for both products and services, through maintenance; sales of refurbished, repaired or remade products; from sales of consumables and servicing for long-life products; or additional profit from selling high-quality durable and premium products.

Geissdoerfer et al (2018)[8] emphasize the importance of a more **intense use** phase as part of the concept of slowing loops. They also add substitution of product use through software and service solutions – 'dematerializing' – which can support the slowing of resource loops and/or narrowing of resource flows.

Summarizing a special edition of the *Journal of Industrial Ecology*, 'Exploring the Circular Economy', researchers Mulrow and Santos (2017)[9] note that many of the journal authors raise the issues of rebound effects and the failure of recycling initiatives to reduce material extraction and its impacts. They cite Bocken et al (2017):[10]

> The basic premises of the CE appear to be closing and slowing loops. Closing loops refers to (postconsumer waste) recycling, slowing is about retention of the product value through maintenance, repair and refurbishment, and remanufacturing, and narrowing loops is about efficiency improvements, a notion that already is commonplace in the linear economy.

Reflecting on the collected observations of the journal authors, Mulrow and Santos suggest that we should add **shrinking loops** to the list of circular economy premises. They highlight the importance of social aspects for solutions like reuse, refurbishment and durability, and note the strong rebound effects of 'virtualization' – providing digital services to replace physical activities. They conclude that industrial ecology experts show 'there are two major gaps in the Circular Economy's relevance for achieving global sustainability. It has not developed language or methods, or necessarily acknowledgement, of the need to **shrink** and **slow** material throughput.'

Circular business models – goals

At the start of this chapter, we reminded ourselves that business is part of a system; and that the purpose of a business is critically important. As Donella Meadows reminds us, the 'least obvious part of the system, its function or purpose, is often the most crucial determinant of the system's behaviour'.[11]

She goes on to explain that 'a change in purpose changes a system pro-foundly, even if every element and interconnection remains the same.'

The work of these researchers – Bocken and team, Geissdoerfer and team, Mulrow and Santos – highlights the need for a clear purpose for circular business models, to ensure we have real 'system value' for all the stakehold-ers: business, society and the living world we all depend on.

Building on their work, I've chosen four goals for circular business mod-els: to slow, intensify, close and narrow the loop. However, if we think about the global issues, of pollution and waste leading to damaged ecosystems, degraded land and contaminated water, plus the critical issues of greenhouse gas levels and air pollution, we can see the need to go further – to design loops and business models for an economy that restores resources, natural systems – and society. We need to go beyond merely closing the loop on resources, by designing regenerative models that restore our damaged eco-systems, clean up pollution and waste and restore health, well-being and prosperity to society. The purpose of circular economy business models should align with those aims. With this in mind, I've expanded 'close the loop' to include regeneration, giving four business model goals (shown in Figure 3.3):

- **Slow the flow** – use the product and materials over a longer period of time, so getting more life out of the same materials.

- **Intensify the loop** – use the product and materials more intensively, more productively – in other words, get more usefulness from the same materials.

- **Close the loop and regenerate** – recover the product and the materials, sort and process them so they can be used again, ideally with the minimum intervention (energy, materials, etc). In addition, regenerate lost materials, regenerate soil, land, water and living systems to provide valuable services and future resources.

- **Narrow the loop** – by reducing material, energy and other resources used at a system level. Clearly, this model can underpin all the others.

Let's explore the four goals in detail.

Slow

For products with a long life that have emotional 'durability' or attachment (a watch, a sofa, everyday clothes), or are in frequent use by the same person or family (a TV, a phone), we can slow down the flow of materials through the system by providing durable, repairable products. Ideally, we should

FIGURE 3.3   Circular business model goals

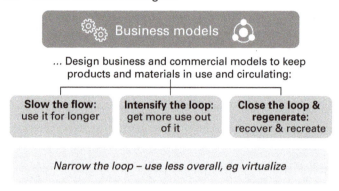

SOURCE: © Catherine Weetman

design our product to be 'timeless', so it doesn't go out of fashion. Ideally, these products should have a lifetime warranty and could be upgraded if there are ways to improve functionality or efficiency.

Manufacturers might ask themselves whether their product lives up to customer expectations. For example, in Europe, the average lifetime of a washing machine has fallen by a third between 2000 and 2010, with a machine now lasting only seven years, according to a report by Green Alliance.[12] Consumers expect them to last 12 years – how many will choose a different brand next time? Research tells us that acquiring a new customer is anywhere from five to 25 times more expensive than retaining an existing one,[13] so underperforming against customers' expectations could be an expensive mistake.

Many people consider reparability as important in deciding what to buy, according to a survey by global repair community iFixit,[14] and 95 per cent of people say that a successful repair makes them more likely to buy more products from that company. Patagonia, with its Ironclad Guarantee and repair services, has also collaborated with iFixit, publishing detailed repair instructions for many of its products onto the iFixit platform.

Those durable, repairable products may also be suitable for reselling by the user, or by specialist retailers. The internet helps reselling businesses connect with both buyers and sellers, and some brand owners have decided to play in both markets: selling – and reselling. Richemont, a Swiss luxury goods brand owner, acquired Watchfinder, a specialist marketplace for luxury watches, in 2018.

By extending the usable lifetime of the product, we can similarly extend the product's replacement cycle and so need fewer products with correspondingly fewer virgin resources and less waste.

There are other benefits to selling a product 'for life'. Companies can generate new profit streams from sales of spares and provision of repair services, to offset production and customer service costs. Loyal customers are likely to buy upgrades and other products from you. Further savings come from spending less on both new product development and disposal of obsolete products and parts.

We might be able to create further value from these more durable products, by finding ways to help them be used more intensively.

Intensify

In this model, we aim to get more from less, making more productive use of the materials and other value 'locked up' in the product or asset. For a wide range of products, equipment and assets, we could extract more value by increasing their utilization. Cars in Europe are typically only in use for one hour in every day, expensive sports equipment might be in use just once a month, farmers may apply chemicals and fertilizers at levels well above what is required. We could encourage people to use the product only when they need to, through **access** systems, or we could encourage people to **share** the facility with others. We could also provide **services** with added-value elements, to encourage customers to utilize the asset and equipment without wanting to own it themselves.

Rachel Botsman (2010)[15] describes 'collaborative consumption' as being supported by three elements: 'product-service systems, collaborative lifestyles and redistribution markets that enable people to pay to access and share goods and services, versus needing to own them outright'. She sees great opportunities for exploiting 'idling capacity', to extract lost value – whether economic, social or environmental – in underutilized assets; and she highlights the power of technology to enable this.

The World Economic Forum (WEF), discussing collaborative consumption, suggests there are 'literally hundreds of ways we can share different kinds of assets: space, skills, stuff and time'.[16] A few examples might include:

- **space:** buildings and infrastructure such as roads, rail and waterways;
- **stuff:** products, materials, equipment;
- **skills:** including knowledge and experience;
- **time (services):** security services, facilities management, healthcare.

The World Economic Forum sees the sharing economy 'enabled and scaled by technology platforms', and providing major benefits to:

- **profit:** through efficient and resilient use of capital and cash, more opportunity for longer-term client relationships and improved feedback on customer needs;
- **people:** through deeper social connections and reduced costs;
- **planet:** through efficient, sustainable resource use and less pollution from waste.

Sharing has become more popular since the 2008 global financial crisis. The subsequent years of recession, austerity measures, unemployment and mortgage foreclosures provided impetus and consumer appetite for many of the 'sharing economy' platforms.

Enabling more people to use fewer products reduces the resources, energy and emissions associated with making the product. However, products used more intensively need to be rugged, robust and easy to maintain and repair. A rented city bike might be in use for 12 hours a day, compared with your personal bike that you use perhaps once a week.

For all the 'intensify' options, ownership tends to remain with the provider, and from the user's perspective, this means you can enjoy the use of the item without having to own it – there is no need to worry about depreciation or how to fund an expensive purchase.

ACCESS

There are a growing number of platforms providing access to services, such as Uber, Angie's List, Upwork and more. They use algorithms to link up providers and users, often taking a fee from each financial transaction. Platforms can also help access assets such as horticultural land and gardens, through initiatives like the landshare movement, which connects people with underused or undermanaged gardens or land with would-be gardeners and smallholders.

Access models are well established, involving systems that enable people to rent assets, products or equipment for a fee, rather than needing to own them outright, thus smoothing cash flow for both customer and supplier. This also removes the need to include the assets on the balance sheet.

Online services and added-value services can make rental a practical option for designer clothes. Girl Meets Dress, based in the UK and launched in 2009, claims to be the world's first online fashion rental service (see Chapter 7).

SHARING

Eckhardt and Bardhi, writing in *Harvard Business Review*, argue that sharing is offered freely: a 'form of social exchange that takes place among people known to each other, without any profit. When "sharing" is market-mediated – when a company is an intermediary between consumers who don't know each other – it is no longer sharing at all.'[17] Eckhardt and Bardhi use the term 'access economy' to describe models such as Zipcar, where 'consumers are paying to access someone else's goods or services for a particular period of time. It is an economic exchange, and consumers are after utilitarian, rather than social, value.'

Some schools of thought (such as the WEF, above) bundle 'sharing models' with those focused on access, such as a pool of cars owned by a company, rather than true sharing of assets owned by the users. In this book, **sharing** means products, items or services owned or provided by non-commercial entities, such as public services, charities, individuals or co-operatives. I've used **access** services when the pool of assets is owned by a business, with the aim of making a profit.

Sharing could be:

- Local government services, providing public transport or public libraries to lend books and music. It could also include bicycles for travelling across the city, such as the paid-for shared services like the London 'Santander bikes' or Paris 'Vélib', but we classify commercial asset pools such as BMW DriveNow as rented or pay as you go, rather than shared.

- Community-based, with a group organizing a shared set of assets or products, or agreeing to share time and skills for an enterprise or project. This might be, for example, the upkeep of a local community hall or sports club, a conservation project, a rural transport service, or shared land.

- Consumer-to-consumer, generally called peer-to-peer (P2P). Examples include car-sharing, lift-sharing or tool-sharing.

Renting or leasing can offer scope for deeper **relationships** between the provider and user, especially if the provider offers aftermarket services, refills or other regular means of contact. However, this depends on the provider's desire to engage with the user and look for opportunities to build trust and loyalty.

SERVICE, PERFORMANCE OR RESULTS

These models extend the access model by including the concept of 'buying performance'. Walter Stahel describes the performance economy as 'taking the principles of the circular economy to the extreme, where we no longer buy goods but simply services'.[18] The value proposition must 'sell' performance rather than ownership, guaranteeing quality and value, preserving value in the 'stock' (ie the product and materials eventually returning to the provider). It needs to be a 'win-win' outcome for both provider and user, with joint objectives and fair allocation of rewards.

The performance model is gaining popularity with organizations in many sectors, with its ability to help strengthen provider–customer relationships; bundle in added-value services to differentiate your company from competitors; and gain valuable intelligence about both your product and how your customer uses it. Rolls-Royce's 'power by the hour' and Philips's 'pay per lux' are well-known examples. A more recent example is RWE, a German utility provider with 24 million customers spread across Europe. It is switching from selling power to providing renewable energy services, integrating and managing grid-connected renewables.[19]

To look at some other general examples:

- **Business to business (B2B):** These include 'shared services' in a multi-occupant office block (maintenance, reception, cafeteria, etc), third-party freight transport and warehousing, and other outsourced services such as call centres. Often performance measures will form part of the commercial agreement. These models are also applicable to public sector organizations.

- **Business to consumer (B2C):** These include a wide range of infrastructure services, such as mobile phone communications, motorway service stations, household waste recovery services, etc.

Generally, the provider retains responsibility for the product, after the customer has finished using it. This provides an incentive to design for recovery and reuse: creating products that are easy to disassemble and reuse or recycle and ensuring materials are safe and non-toxic. This enables the recovery of expensive elements and can avoid the use of materials that cannot be recycled.

This model can foster healthy, long-term and mutually beneficial relationships between the provider and user, though it is critical to ensure that performance measures and commercial agreements meet both parties' objectives. For performance models, provision of knowledge and expertise is a powerful component, with the provider helping the user to use the product or service more effectively (to reduce costs, perform better, etc) and the user providing feedback to help with ongoing product development.

Close and regenerate

For both our 'slow the flow' and 'intensify the loop' approaches, we need to also consider how to recover the value of the products and the materials at the end of use, and ensure we keep them in the system for further cycles of use. 'Closing the loop' on products and materials mean getting them back into the system so they can be used again. We can both create and capture value by closing the loop: to recover, reprocess and regenerate products, components and materials for further use cycles.

Organizations may be involved in one or several elements: from recovering the products, sorting them for processing, preparing products for reuse (everything from inspection, refurbishment and repair to remanufacture) and, if reuse is not possible, recycling them into new materials.

Recovery specialists will retain value and avoid costs by organizing effective and efficient logistics, ensuring products don't get damaged in the recovery process, and having access to a range of reuse opportunities, either directly or through a partnership. It is all too easy to destroy a high proportion of the product's remaining value during the recovery process.

Resource recovery specialists are investing in new technology to recover micro-elements from different waste streams, such as precious metals from road-sweepings (from car catalytic converters), micro-nutrients from food waste and sewage, and researchers are investigating how to convert human urine into fertilizer.[20]

Getting the product, components or materials back into use may involve partnering with 'circular service providers' – organizations specializing in repair, refurbishment, remanufacturing or recycling. Alternatively, brands and manufacturers may decide to do this themselves, developing and protecting the intellectual property for their inspection and remediation processes – and providing a strong incentive to design the product to optimize later disassembly and reuse.

Remanufacturing can open up new markets, especially where your brand has a great reputation for quality, but is expensive compared with the lower-quality competition. Rype Office makes beautiful, high-quality remanufactured furniture for typically less than half the cost of new (see Chapter 9).

In the US, remanufactured products have a warranty equivalent to (or better than) a new one, giving the buyer confidence. More companies are developing highly profitable remanufacturing solutions, with Dell, Caterpillar and Cummins as big-brand examples.

Our least preferred recovery strategy is **recycling**, as this uses most energy and resources. A report by Green Alliance[21] found that for mobile phones, the value of the recyclate is only 0.24 per cent of the original product value, whereas a reused iPhone retains almost half its original value.

As I argued earlier, we need to go further than recovery and recycling if we are to provide for the well-being of our future population – we need to **regenerate** natural systems, such as soil, water, forests, peatlands and wetlands, and all the biodiversity these systems support. Regenerative agricultural approaches are gaining traction in the US and across Europe, with more research on 'no-till' and the benefits of 'mob grazing', based on how animal herds behave in the wild. Companies are starting to see the value of helping restore and protect the land and living systems their supply chains depend on. Nestlé has worked with organizations like the non-profit Earthworm Foundation, developing its Rurality and Landscapes programme to help smallholder farmers preserve and regenerate their land.[22]

Innovations like Ecovative (mentioned in Chapter 2), using mycelium to 'grow' packaging and other products from waste straw, could also be viewed as regenerative. Researchers are investigating other ways to create new valuable materials from biological waste, with reports in 2017 that waste from the agri-food industry was used to develop biomaterials that act as matrices to regenerate bone and cartilage tissues, highly relevant to the treatment of age-related diseases.

In addition, we should apply the 'regeneration' lens to finite materials – looking at how we could recover and regenerate materials currently 'lost' from the economic system. An example is *urban mining*, where landfill and dumps are 'mined' to find and recover valuable materials like metals (read more about urban mining in Part Two).

To sum up the new way of thinking about end-of-use products and materials, we can adopt the mindset of Walter Stahel, mentioned in Chapter 1, so that 'the goods of today become the resources of tomorrow at yesterday's prices'.[23]

Narrow

We can also use strategies that 'narrow the loop', reducing the materials, energy and other resources needed to make and deliver the product itself. These strategies include using less material to make a physical product, reducing the resources consumed in the production process, or swapping physical materials for 'virtual' approaches – called *dematerialization* by some schools of thought.

We might take the view that using less isn't a compelling strategy – but it could help a company be more competitive than its peers. In addition, it could enhance its reputation and brand value by reducing or avoiding the use of scarce or under-pressure resources. As well as reducing the cost, it can reduce the dependency on material inputs.

By adopting the mindset of 'zero waste' for the supply chain processes, we can encourage new ideas for by-products and co-products too, creating more value and resilience for the organization. Fashion brand Burberry works with Elvis & Kresse to repurpose offcuts from leather and other textiles into high-quality furnishings and personal products (see Chapter 2).

Replacing physical products with digital or 'virtual' ones can have a big impact on resource use. When reviewing the 'whole-system' impacts of these, we should remember the energy needed to run the software, store the data and so on – in 2019, many of these systems are still reliant on finite fossil fuels. Product ranges and entire company business models have been transformed from physical objects to virtual ones – photographic films, videotapes, answering machines and much more – although there is a 'retro' movement trying to bring back esoteric objects like vinyl records.

Designing products to be multifunctional can also reduce resource use, and create disruptive innovations. When writing the first edition of this book, 'smartphones' were relatively new, and yet now, most people wouldn't consider owning a camera, a personal dictating machine, a personal music player and so on.

However, while it is fundamentally important that we reduce our footprint and reliance on scarce resources, 'narrowing' the loop is not enough.

Capturing system value

Companies may choose to focus on one of these circular business model goals – rethinking their product or service offerings to narrow, slow, intensify, close and regenerate the loop – or to incorporate several of the goals. BMW, for example, makes high-quality cars that should have a good resale value, so they can be kept in use for a longer lifetime – slowing the flow. BMW has also developed a 'pay per use' system, DriveNow – intensifying the flow. BMW is investing in remanufacturing and closed-loop recycling too, and is highly likely to be narrowing the loop through resource-efficiency measures.[24]

We need to ensure we capture the value we created in the product or service design so that we avoid 'leaving the value on the table' for someone else.

FIGURE 3.4   Strategic alignment: business models, product design and supply chains

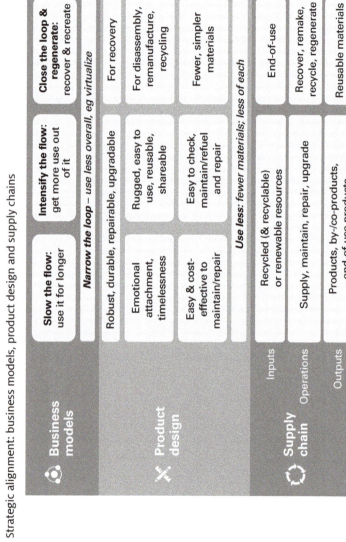

	Slow the flow: use it for longer	Intensify the flow: get more use out of it	Close the loop & regenerate: recover & recreate
Business models			
	Narrow the loop – use less overall, eg virtualize		
Product design	Robust, durable, repairable, upgradable		For recovery
	Emotional attachment, timelessness	Rugged, easy to use, reusable, shareable	For disassembly, remanufacture, recycling
	Easy & cost-effective to maintain/repair	Easy to check, maintain/refuel and repair	Fewer, simpler materials
	Use less: fewer materials; less of each		
Supply chain Inputs	Recycled (& recyclable) or renewable resources		End-of-use
Operations	Supply, maintain, repair, upgrade		Recover, remake, recycle, regenerate
Outputs	Products, by-/co-products, end-of-use products		Reusable materials

SOURCE: © Catherine Weetman

Strategic alignment

In Chapter 2, we examined the 'design and supply chain', looking at product design, material choices, manufacturing processes and recovery flows. While these intervention points all enable the product value chain to become more circular, a supportive business model can amplify the circular benefits.

A company might start its transition to circularity with ideas for a new product or service, or look to improve an existing offer by redesigning its supply chain to recover value from end-of-life items, or by redesigning its business model. Whatever the starting point, we must remember that the business is part of a bigger system. Considering this system can help us think about the wider implications of our proposed changes, and what else we can alter to support the desired outcome.

Figure 3.4 shows how the circular business model goals align with product design and supply chain components, with areas of overlap between strategies for slowing and intensifying. To capture the optimal value, we need to consider the whole business system – including the impact on suppliers, strategic supply chain partners, customers and employees.

For example, if you create a product that is durable and so has a solid end-of-use value (benefiting the user), can you capture value at this point? Could you offer a take-back option (rewarding the user) or support peer-to-peer resale markets through platform software, verification of authenticity and so on? If you plan to recover the product, might the product need processing to make it ready for another cycle of use – with refurbishing and even remanufacturing required? Designing the product with this in mind can vastly improve the profitability of remaking and resale.

Providers – private, public and peer-to-peer

Chapter 2 described the different groups of providers involved in the circular economy: the original manufacturer (or brand owner); a circular service provider (dealing with products for a range of brands); or, for the simpler loops, the users themselves (see Figure 2.3 in Chapter 2).

In thinking about the 'design and supply chain' and circular business models, it is easy to envisage how it works from the perspective of the manufacturer, or brand. However, we can also see that the circular economy offers a wide range of opportunities for new business models: for organizations providing circular services involving products from a single brand or manufacturer, from several, or for one or several industry sectors. Table 3.1

TABLE 3.1 Business model variations for different providers

Circular Business Model	Slow Use it for longer	Intensify Get more from less	Close Recover &/or process to use again	Regenerate Restore lost and damaged resources	Narrow* Use less resources
Design ethos	High quality, rugged, repairable	Rugged, easy to use & maintain	Ease of recovery, disassembly, remanufacture and recycling	Regenerate/purify ecosystems, recover lost resources	To use less of each material in the supply chain and in-use
Brand/ original equipment manufacturer (OEM)	• Premium product, lifetime warranty	• Enable access to product through PAYG or services	• Exchange value for returned product/ materials	• Ecosystem restoration • Urban mining • Water purification	• Dematerialize • More efficient design • Waste=resource, eg by-products
Circular service provider (CSP)	• Reseller • Restoration/ upgrades eg electric car conversions	• Brokerage • PAYG or services • Digital platform	• Recycler • Remanufacturer • Reverse logistics provider	*As Brand/OEM*	• Use secondary materials
Community or public service	• Repair support	• Libraries • Shared assets, eg landshare	• Public service recycling; Reuse charities	• Community composting, water purifying	• Community purchase schemes
Peer-to-peer (P2P)	• Reselling and donating	• Share time & assets, eg ride/car share	• Exchange value for returned product/ materials	• Rewilding, tree-planting, composting, etc	• Buy less

(P R O V I D E R)

* Narrowing the loop: resource efficiency supports the circular economy, but is not itself a circular model. Dematerialization could be circular, but care is required for (eg) energy usage.

summarizes the various options across the business model goals for each group of providers.

Brands and manufacturers

We have already seen examples for brands and original equipment manufacturers (OEMs). They may choose to control or operate all the circular elements themselves, perhaps to control the intellectual property associated with the product or service, or to manage all the 'touch-points' with the customer and so on. Alternatively, they may decide to outsource some or all of the circular activities to a specialist 'circular service provider'.

Circular service providers

Creating value from waste is not new, but technology and the potential to add value is now opening up new markets and specialist opportunities. This could involve recovering the product or materials, through effective logistics networks, through reverse vending machines and so on – or it might involve processing the product, components or materials so they can have another cycle of use. Katherine Whalen and team at IIIEE, Lund University, talk about 'gap exploiters' – 'third-party firms that create value through the re-utilization of existing products' by slowing down the throughput of products in the system.[25]

The business models for these circular service providers (CSPs) focus on circular flows: closing and regenerating the loop, including resource recovery, remanufacturing, and recycling. These providers are in the ideal position to capitalize on new markets for recycled materials, for better-value refurbished or remanufactured products, or to provide solutions that take advantage of new product stewardship legislation or waste disposal taxes.

They may also offer services designed to keep the product and components 'in the loop', offering maintenance, repairs, and resale services. Specialist consultancies and designers are also focusing on the circular economy and may build their business models around improving circularity for others.

REFILL AND MAINTAIN

A wide range of businesses provide support services to products or assets already in use, often helping to prolong their life-cycles. Examples include vending machine service companies, providing refill services and resolving breakdowns (product blockages, etc), and specialist maintenance and repair companies such as windscreen repairs, electrical equipment repairs, shoe cobblers or liquid fuel suppliers maintaining fuel pumps. Specialists that calibrate and maintain high-value medical equipment, industrial fans and extraction systems, or production equipment, may bundle-in procurement and stock-holding services for a 'full service' offer.

RESELL AND REUSE

These businesses specialize in buying and selling already-used products or assets. Again, these models are already familiar to us: for example, used car dealerships, antique furniture shops, vintage fashion boutiques, reclaimed construction materials, and so on. Access to the internet now helps them to reach a bigger audience, without needing to advertise in specialist magazines or be limited to 'passing trade'.

A company may offer office or house clearance services, buying the entire contents of the building after a company liquidation or the death of the householder. It may resell some categories of products itself (eg antique furniture, office desks) and sell other categories to resellers or recyclers dealing specifically with those products or materials. The business chooses what to process and what to sell, based on its experience and knowledge of the product or material concerned, the local market conditions, the volume of flows and critical mass needed for investment in specialist processing equipment, the price variance versus new, and so on.

REMANUFACTURE

These businesses provide specialized manufacturing services to return a 'used product to at least its original performance with a warranty that is equivalent to or better than that of the newly manufactured product'.[26] Operations include dismantling, restoring and replacing materials and components, plus testing the parts and the product against the original design specifications, to ensure that post-remanufacture performance is at least as good as the original performance specifications. Nextant Aerospace, in the US, remanufactures aircraft originally made by other manufacturers, and Rype Office (in Chapter 9) remanufactures high-quality office furniture. We look at remanufacturing in more detail later in the book, examining its increasing popularity, challenges, opportunities and supply chain impacts.

RECOVERY AND RECYCLING

Here the business purpose is to recover products or resources in order to reprocess them itself (recycling, remanufacturing, etc) and/or to resell to specialists for further reprocessing. A waste recycling company may specialize in (say) plastics recycling, and separate out any 'contaminants' such as metal and paper for selling on to other specialist recyclers. Recycling has often been a profitable activity and, more recently, companies such as Sita and Veolia have invested in research and technology to find new ways of recovering valuable recyclate from mixed-waste streams. Veolia Environmental Services used to describe itself as a waste management and recycling company, and in 2018, it became more ambitious (and circular), with a 'resourcing the world' mission.[27] Walter Stahel suggests that the entire waste management industry needs to move in that direction: 'the challenge ... is to shift the thinking behind its activities from zero-value waste to highest-value preservation, and move its revenue base up the value preservation chain.'[28]

Public services and community groups

Public sector services play a vital role in the circular economy, especially in providing ways to intensify the use of products and resources. Everything from roads and bridges, healthcare, emergency services, shared housing, schools and community sports facilities can be used more productively than services dedicated to private companies or small groups of users.

We should also mention other groups, such as social and community enterprises. These may be set up as non-profit-making ventures or cooperatives, and can use any of the business models, including 'sell'. Examples include recycling of plastic, such as The Plastic Bank, and ReTuna in Sweden.

RETUNA – THE WORLD'S FIRST RECYCLING MALL[29,30]

The mall, located next to the recycling centre in Eskilstuna, a small riverside city 70 miles west of Stockholm, Sweden, opened in 2015. Visitors bring and sort waste materials, and drop off reusable toys, furniture, clothes, decorative items, and electronic devices in the mall's depot.

Depot staff perform an initial culling of what is usable, and distribute these items to the recycling shops in the mall. Shop staff perform a second culling, choosing what they want to repair, fix up, convert, refine – and ultimately sell.

ReTuna also offers adult education courses focused on design-based recycling. The mall quickly gained popularity, with sales of 2.5 million Swedish krona in 2015 (about $275,000) increasing to 10.2 million SEK ($1.12 million) in 2017.

Another social enterprise, ApparelXchange in Scotland, aims to make it easy to reuse school uniforms. Donated uniforms are sorted, quality checked and cleaned, and then resold through retail and online outlets (see Chapter 7).

Peer-to-peer

We looked at some of the options for circular flows between individual people earlier. Informal sharing is still common, and informal reuse or resource exchanges are popping up too. OLIO, in the UK, is a free app connecting neighbours with each other and with local shops, meaning they can share surplus food and other items, avoiding waste. Digital platforms can act as a marketplace, using algorithms to match users and providers. These platforms might be operated by commercial or non-profit organizations.

SHAREGRID PLATFORM: P2P RENTING[31]

ShareGrid, a P2P photographic and filmmaking marketplace, began in Los Angeles in 2013. By 2019, it listed over 12,000 active members and equipment valued at over US$600 million. It verifies members and provides insurance as part of the transaction, helping to overcome concerns about loss or damage to expensive equipment. People listing equipment can 'meet' local, pre-screened photographers, and approve requests to rent. Rentals are secured using several identification credentials. Peer reviews and public profiles of each member help to build trust, and renters must provide liability cover, which can be purchased through the site.

Commercial options

The business model tells the story of how we plan to create value for our customer, how we deliver it to them, and how we capture value for our own organization. It includes a range of different elements, including how we earn revenue and other ways of funding our activities. Capturing value means thinking about the commercial options – contracts, ownership, whether you expect payment in advance/on delivery/over a 'use period', and other scenarios – and how they best support the business model aims.

How can we best capture the value opportunities from shifting to a circular strategy? Deciding to offer more durable products that are designed for ease of repair, upgrade and end-of-use recovery means we can capture

FIGURE 3.5   Commercial options

SOURCE: © Catherine Weetman

value by recovering those end-of-use products and components. But if we've sold the product to the customer, how do we ensure we get the product back into our own supply chain several years later? Commercial models that encourage, or enforce, recovery help us get access to that value, rather than 'leaving value on the table' for a competitor, or a specialist reseller, remanufacturer or recycler.

In this durable products scenario, options could include:

- leasing the product to the customer;
- providing a bundle of services that include the product, such as repairs and upgrades;
- providing a subscription service so the customer can swap to a newer version when appropriate;
- or even selling the product, and providing an incentive for the customer to return it at the end-of-use – such as a discount off a new product, or a guaranteed buy-back value.

Figure 3.5 shows the seven commercial options typically found in the circular economy.

Generally, circular economy advocates see a need to move away from traditional 'ownership' and transactional models, in which a company makes a product and sells it to a customer. Instead, they focus on 'use', or access – providing the benefit of the product to the customer.

We've seen that circular business models seek to keep goods and materials flowing in cycles, and recovering those resources for reuse can be beneficial. When resource costs are highly volatile and on upward long-term trends, it makes good business sense to retain ownership of goods, thus securing access to future resources. The company can choose whether to remanufacture components, entire products, or to recover materials to recycle into new resources.

However, ownership models can still be a valid choice for goods that increase in value (housing, 'collectibles', art), rather than depreciate over their useful lives, or where the customer decides they are likely to keep the product for longer than the assumption in the contract. For example, if I'm thinking of buying a laptop and there is a lease or subscription option, I need to decide how soon I will want to have a new laptop. If I think I'm likely to keep it for five years, and writing the purchase cost off over five years is cheaper than the three-year lease option, I may decide to buy the laptop.

A downside of ownership is the lack of incentive – for both the provider and user – to recirculate the product when it's reached the end of its useful life. In many countries, surveys tell us that households own several no-longer-in-use computers, and phones, with many people put off recycling by worries about the security risk of sending the product to a recycler or reseller.

Circular economy commercial options tend to fit one of these categories:

- **Sell and resell:** ownership of the product or asset transfers from buyer to seller for an agreed price.

- **Contract or lease:** the supplier and customer agree a legal contract to include the use of the product, equipment or asset for a specific time period. Often, this includes added-value services such as maintenance or provision of consumable items, to help extend the usable lifetime of the product. Contracts will usually stipulate what happens to the product at the end of the contract, for example return to the provider. Leasing generally includes only the provision of the assets or products, not the cost of maintenance or value-added services. These additional services may be offered by the same provider – the 'lessor' – but charged separately on a 'time and materials' basis, and the provider may use the lease terms to prevent maintenance by other parties. Examples include many products, buildings and facilities, or infrastructure such as pipelines or telecommunication masts.

At the end of the lease, the asset rights return to the provider, though there may be a clause to allow the user (the 'lessee') to commit to a further rental period or purchase the asset at a reduced cost. The provider does, however, have a strong incentive to provide a durable, reliable and high-performing item, to improve the prospect of future repeat business, and enhance the brand reputation.

DUTCH AWEARNESS – LEASING AND PERFORMANCE CONTRACTS FOR CLOTHES[32]

In textiles, Dutch aWEARness operates a closed-loop manufacturing process for its workwear production by using recyclable polyester fabric. A leasing model retains ownership of the materials and customers pay for the performance of the clothes over an agreed number of years. This system uses 95 per cent less water and 64 per cent less energy, and produces 73 per cent fewer carbon emissions per garment during production than standard cotton. At the end of each 'life', the products are recycled back into new clothing, with no loss of quality.

- Use, pay as you go/pay per use or rent: the user pays a fee for temporary use of the product or service. Renting tends to be time-specific (eg one hour, one day) whereas pay as you go/pay per use often involves metered charges – eg for a cellphone: paying for call time or messages.

Renting models are relevant to both 'linear' and circular economy approaches. Renting tools and equipment is common in business-to-business sub-sectors, especially where complex, fast-developing or expensive technology is involved. It is starting to expand into other sectors, such as consumer equipment, computers, gardening equipment, power tools and so on. In early 2016, the most prominent new rental services provided accommodation, car-sharing, taxi-type services or lift-sharing.

Rental platforms often take a sizeable cut of the transaction fee (eg Airbnb takes 9–15 per cent) and rely on reciprocal reviews and ratings to build credibility and trust. The software features also help build trust, with many of the service platforms using Facebook to allow people to see whether

TABLE 3.2 Commercial options for circular business models

Commercial model	Description	Circular Business Model Archetype				Examples (italics = generic)
		Slow	Intensify	Close & regenerate		
Selling	Transfer ownership of the product or asset to the customer for a fee	✓				*Housing, furniture, clothes, food*
Reselling	Connect buyers and sellers and facilitate their transactions, charging fees for successful transaction			✓		eBay, *resource exchanges*
Contract, Lease	Make high-margin, high-cost products affordable through contracts which may included added-value services. Ownership of the product generally stays with provider	✓				*Property, medical scanners, document management services, chemical leasing*
Use, Rent	Enable access to part of a product or service, enjoying many of the benefits of full ownership at a fraction of the price		✓			WeWork, *timeshare properties*
Pay-As-You-Go	Enable access to metered services, with fees based on actual usage rates		✓			Amazon Web Services, BMW DriveNow
Subscription	Charge the customer a subscription fee to gain access to a product or service		✓			Nike Adverturers, Vigga baby clothes, *Fashion subscriptions*
Sharing	Allow other people to use your products or services, generally on the basis of trust and implied reciprocation instead of fees		✓			*lift-sharing, tool-sharing*
Service and Results	Sell the service the product performs, may include contracts based on performance outcomes		✓			Rolls Royce areo engines, Philips 'pay per lux', *Software as a Service*
Recovery & Exchange	Recover end-of-use products, components and materials for reuse, remanufacture, recycling. Pay a fee or provide other benefit to user (eg reduce their disposal costs)			✓		WR Yuma (discount on next purchase when returning old sunglasses)

they have friends in common, or use PayPal to reduce the likelihood of payment fraud. Uber says its review system means drivers with poor ratings get less work (and so drop out of the system) and badly behaved passengers will find it difficult to obtain a ride.

- **Subscription:** the user pays a regular fee, which allows use of a product or service. Subscription models are common for products that have frequent upgrades, such as phones and software, and are starting to emerge for clothing that people might quickly grow out of (toddler or maternity wear), or for which they might want to have access to lots of choices (eg fashion subscriptions – see more in Chapter 7).

- **Share:** products, assets or services, owned by individuals or in community/public sector organizations (eg local government) are made available for other people to use, with or without a fee. Obvious examples are public transport, public car parks, public libraries, water fountains and so on. Peer-to-peer sharing could be informal (we lend power tools to our neighbours) or more organized, such as lift-sharing.

- **Results and performance:** the supplier and customer agree their criteria for the performance, or outcome (result) required, and agree fees and other commercial terms that depend on those criteria being met. This commercial mechanism is obviously integral to the performance business model. Approaches could involve bundling in 'total cost of ownership' features such as energy, desired outcomes for the user (for example dyeing of textiles to an agreed depth of colour, colour-fastness, etc).

- **Recovery and exchange:** at the end of the first use cycle, ownership transfers from the user to a provider or third party (individuals, companies, charities, etc). There may be value in the products or materials themselves in the open market, or the user may even be willing to pay the provider to take the product or materials away – especially if, otherwise, the user would have to pay a disposal cost (to send to landfill for example). This is sometimes referred to as *negative value*.

Table 3.2 summarizes these commercial options and shows how they align with the circular business model goals of slow, intensify, close and regenerate.

Criticisms and issues

The 'rebound' effect, mentioned earlier in this chapter, reminds us that circular is not necessarily sustainable and better for society. Companies can make use of circular approaches and yet still be putting toxic chemicals or unrecyclable materials into the market. They can design a perfect circular product, and still be exploiting workers along the supply chain. They can be making recyclable products with very little chance of those products being recovered and recycled.

Mike Berners-Lee, in his book *There is No Planet B* (2019),[33] explains the rebound effect using the example of buying a more efficient (eg electric) car. It saves fuel and carbon emissions, but over the long term, those savings might be lost in a number of ways:

- you drive further each year;
- you can afford to live further away from work in a larger property that needs more heating;
- you spend the fuel savings on other things that have a higher carbon footprint;
- fuel stations adjust to the drop in demand, lower their prices and sell more to others;
- car manufacturers change their marketing approach to sell their less efficient cars to others;
- the oil industry adjusts its strategy to sell to other industries and countries;
- and so on.

Trevor Zink and Roland Geyer, in their paper 'Circular Economy Rebound',[34] highlight the dangers of strategies that result in an increase in net environmental impact, resulting in 'circular economy backfire'. In addition to the electric car example above, we can think of the ride-hailing apps that increase car miles by luring people away from walking, cycling and public transport.

To avoid rebound, they argue that the circular economy must actually draw the user away from primary production (and resource extraction) so that 'secondary goods' must actually substitute for primary goods. (**Note:** 'primary production' means the initial production of the brand-new product, whereas 'secondary production' is some form of refurbishment, remanufacturing and so on.) They warn that this is a 'substantial hurdle given that the two primary tools that a marketer might use to draw away customers – lowering prices or finding niche markets – are off-limits in order for the circular economy to avoid rebound'.

Erik Assadourian and John Mulrow[35] make the case for a 'marriage between **degrowth** and the circular economy'. They argue that shrinking our demand for both materials and energy is essential if we are to have an economy that functions within the earth's limits (see the section on planetary boundaries in Chapter 5). They worry, like Zink and Geyer, that some consultants and governments see the circular economy as a way of continuing to fuel growth, by avoiding the constraints of finite resources.

Assadourian and Mulrow argue the need for a circular economy with a much smaller throughput, 'spiralling down' as we get better at recirculating and using fewer products and materials together with less water and energy – a 'spiral economy'. Their article includes other suggestions for how to achieve this aim of 'one planet living', where we regenerate land, water, resources and ecosystems and can thrive and prosper within the means of our planet.

ETHICAL CONCERNS

There are other issues to consider. Whilst the rise of 'collaborative consumption' and sharing models provides economic benefits and enables individuals to earn money from underused assets or convert spare time into income, there is a range of concerns, including **legalities, insurance, ethics and exploitation**. Sub-letting properties on Airbnb may be prohibited under the lease terms, for example, and tax collectors are becoming interested in the profits from eBay and sharing schemes. Governments are moving to clarify or update regulations and close loopholes, accepting that these forms of commerce are likely to expand further.

The 'gig' economy aspect of some of the service and 'pay as you go' models is causing concern. The gig economy describes models that separate a traditional company 'job' into individual tasks or 'gigs' that independent workers are paid to do. For example, Uber pays drivers for single taxi journeys rather than employing them and paying a salary. There are concerns that the new form of the gig economy has all the same issues of temporary labour models that make it difficult to plan working hours, rely on a regular wage or even to offer your services to more than one employer. In the United States, Oregon advised that Uber drivers should be classified as employees rather than independent contractors, thus entitling them to a minimum wage and safe working conditions.

Summary

We've defined business models as describing how an organization creates, delivers and captures value. Businesses are systems in themselves and are also part of a much wider system. As systems-thinker Donella Meadows reminds us, the purpose of a business model is likely to be the most important driver of the system behaviour.

Growing pressure from society, shareholders and governments is encouraging companies to explore sustainable strategies, fit for a future with a global population of 10 billion or more. Organizations are trying to decouple resource use from revenue and profit streams, finding ways to do more with less. They want to provide for the needs of the growing 'consumer class' and build more resilient, sustainable businesses. They also want to strengthen relationships with partners, suppliers and, crucially, with customers – getting to know more about future needs and staying 'front of mind', rather than relying on ever-more expensive marketing in the competition for people's attention.

We looked at how various schools of thought are framing the business models appropriate for a circular economy, and reviewed the four goals I've chosen to summarize circular business models: to slow, intensify, close and regenerate, and narrow the loop. We then looked at the strategic alignment between these four goals; the approach to designing products and services; and the inputs, operations and outputs of the supply chain.

A range of actors can use circular economy approaches, and we looked at how these business models would be relevant to several different groups of 'providers': brands and manufacturing businesses, circular service providers, public sector organizations, non-profits and communities, and individual people too.

Designing business models for a circular economy requires different thinking and unconventional approaches. It means challenging accepted commercial mechanisms and retaining ownership of the product throughout its (longer) life-cycle, taking responsibility for performance, finding new ways to create value and deepen customer relationships, researching sustainable materials and embracing new technology.

It's worth reminding ourselves that we are using up resources faster than they can be regenerated, with the Footprint Network estimating the global ecological footprint at 1.6 planets.[36] Critics of the circular economy are concerned that it is being deployed to drive growth and potentially increasing consumption – not 'bending the curve' on our exponential growth in resource use, land-use change, emissions and more. Even though we know that being sustainable and closing the loop on materials is not enough, it feels as though regeneration is lacking attention. Instead, we need to 'raise the bar' even higher, aiming for regenerative models that restore our damaged ecosystems, clean up pollution and waste, and restore health, well-being and prosperity to society.

Business models should underpin a circular economy that manages, preserves and regenerates resources, working within the earth's limits to support a healthy, prosperous society – creating, conserving and circulating value. A circular, regenerative business means resilience, profitability and sustainability: a better business, and a better world.

Further resources

Bocken et al (2019) A Review and Evaluation of Circular Business Model Innovation Tools, *Sustainability*, **11**, 2210; doi:10.3390/su11082210 [accessed 20 October 2019]

Botsman, R and Rogers, R (nd) *What's Mine is Yours: The Rise of Collaborative Consumption* [Online] http://rachelbotsman.com/ (archived at https://perma.cc/F8NW-P6HP) [accessed 5 March 2016]

Ellen MacArthur Foundation (2015) *Delivering the Circular Economy: A toolkit for policymakers* [Online] www.ellenmacarthurfoundation.org/publications/delivering-the-circular-economy-a-toolkit-for-policymakers (archived at https://perma.cc/ML7Y-PELD) [accessed 11 October 2019]

The Product-Life Institute [Online] http://product-life.org/en/node (archived at https://perma.cc/HD3G-3A97) [accessed 1 June 2016]

Notes

1 Lush Handmade Cosmetics Ltd, 10 Things You Should Know About Lush Packaging [Online] www.lushusa.com/story?cid=article_10-things-lush-packaging (archived at https://perma.cc/RAS4-T7MV) [accessed 12 October 2019]

2 Lacy, P and Rutqvist, J (2015) *Waste to Wealth*, Palgrave Macmillan, Basingstoke

3 Rossé, M, Shiran, Y, Stuchtey, M (2015) Closing the Loop: Getting Started on the Circular Journey, Corporate Forum (8 October) [Online] www.corporateecoforum.com/closing-the-loop-getting-started-on-the-circular-journey/ (archived at https://perma.cc/5NDH-WE2B) [accessed 27 September 2019]

4 Ellen MacArthur Foundation (2015) Delivering the circular economy: a toolkit for policymakers [Online] www.ellenmacarthurfoundation.org/publications/

delivering-the-circular-economy-a-toolkit-for-policymakers (archived at https://perma.cc/ML7Y-PELD) [accessed 11 October 2019]

5   Charter, M and McLanaghan, S (2019) Business Models for a Circular Economy, *Designing for a Circular Economy*, Routledge

6   Bocken, NMP, de Pauw, I, Bakker, C and van der Grinten, B (2016) Product design and business model strategies for a circular economy, *Journal of Industrial and Production Engineering*, **33** (5), pp 308–320, dx.doi.org/10.108 0/21681015.2016.1172124 (archived at https://perma.cc/J3VW-VBZP) [accessed 2 October 2019]

7   Moreno M, De los Rios C, Rowe Z and Charnley F (2016) A Conceptual Framework for Circular Design, *Sustainability*, **8** (9), p 937. https://doi.org/10.3390/su8090937 [accessed 21 November 2019]

8   Geissdoerfer, M, Morioka, SN, de Carvalho, MM and Evans, S (2018) Business models and supply chains for the circular economy, *Journal for Cleaner Production*, **190**, pp 712–721 www.researchgate.net/publication/324617908_ Business_models_and_supply_chains_for_the_circular_economy (archived at https://perma.cc/5DVC-UUWM) [accessed 2 October 2019]

9   Mulrow, J and Santos, V (2017) Discard Studies [Online] discardstudies. com/2017/11/13/moving-the-circular-economy-beyond-alchemy/ (archived at https://perma.cc/K7M7-C36C) [accessed 10 October 2019]

10 Bocken NMP, Ritala, P and Huotari, P (2017) The circular economy: exploring the introduction of the concept among S&P 500 firms, *Journal of Industrial Ecology*, **21** (3) [Online] onlinelibrary.wiley.com/doi/pdf/10.1111/jiec.12605 (archived at https://perma.cc/B786-JV2L) (archived at https://perma.cc/ B786-JV2L) [accessed 11 October 2019]

11 Meadows, DH, edited by Wright, D (2008) *Thinking in Systems: A Primer*, Sustainability Institute, Chelsea Green Publishing

12 Benton, D and Coats, E (2016) *Better products by design: ensuring high standards for UK consumers*, Green Alliance, 9 November [Online] www.green-alliance.org.uk/ecodesign_products.php (archived at https://perma.cc/T2RS-C8ZE) [accessed 19 October 2019]

13 Gallo, M (2014) The value of keeping the right customers, *Harvard Business Review*, 29 October [Online] hbr.org/2014/10/the-value-of-keeping-the-right-customers (archived at https://perma.cc/25ZF-KKWB) [accessed 19 October 2019]

14 Bluff, J (2013) iFixit community survey: the results are in, 1 May [Online] www.ifixit.com/News/ifixit-community-survey-the-results-are-in (archived at https://perma.cc/GU2T-2EK8) [accessed 19 October 2019]

15 Botsman, R (2010) *Evolution of Theories: Collaborative Consumption* [Online] rachelbotsman.com/thinking/ [accessed 5 March 2016]

16 World Economic Forum (2014) *Towards the Circular Economy: Accelerating the Scale-Up Across Global Supply Chains* [Online] www3.weforum.org/docs/WEF_ENV_TowardsCircularEconomy_Report_2014.pdf (archived at https://perma.cc/X435-X4G3) [accessed 18 October 2019]

17 Eckhardt, GM and Bardhi, F (2015) The sharing economy isn't about sharing at all, *Harvard Business Review*, 28 January [Online] hbr.org/2015/01/the-sharing-economy-isnt-about-sharing-at-all (archived at https://perma.cc/T99K-JVDE) [accessed 4 March 2016]

18 Stahel, W (2013) The circular economy: interview with Walter Stahel by Daan Elffers, *Making It Magazine*, 28 June [Online] www.makingitmagazine.net (archived at https://perma.cc/3LFU-5AQE) [accessed 4 March 2016]

19 SustainAbility (Feb 2014) Model Behavior: 20 Business Models Innovations for Sustainability, p 20 [Online] www.sustainability.com/library/model-behavior#.V7Uu6KKK2kU (archived at https://perma.cc/NB5H-H5P2) [accessed 15 August 2016]

20 Yalin, L (2019) Wastewater is an asset – it contains nutrients, energy and precious metals, and scientists are learning how to recover them, *The Conversation*, 19 March [Online] theconversation.com/wastewater-is-an-asset-it-contains-nutrients-energy-and-precious-metals-and-scientists-are-learning-how-to-recover-them-113264 (archived at https://perma.cc/33QG-YPEL) [accessed 20 October 2019]

21 Benton, D and Hazell, J (2013) Resource resilient UK, *Green Alliance* [Online] https://www.green-alliance.org.uk/page_816.php (archived at https://perma.cc/JNC4-SFWL) [accessed 20 October 2019]

22 Earthworm (2019) Nestlé says yes to restoring forests and regenerating soils, *News*, 13 September [Online] www.earthworm.org/news-stories/nestl%C3%A9-says-yes-to-restoring-forests-and-regenerating-soils (archived at https://perma.cc/S33Y-NFY8) [accessed 20 October 2019]

23 Stahel, WR (23 March 2016) The circular economy, *Nature News*, Nature Publishing Group [Online] www.nature.com/news/the-circular-economy-1.19594 (archived at https://perma.cc/SMG7-HZZK) [accessed 15 August 2016]

24 May, P (2019) BMW accelerates into the circular economy, *GreenBiz*, 4 October [Online] www.greenbiz.com/article/bmw-accelerates-circular-economy (archived at https://perma.cc/RR75-2FDW) [accessed 21 October 2019]

25 Whalen KA, Milios L and Nussholz J (2018) Bridging the gap: barriers and potential for scaling reuse practices in the Swedish ICT sector, *Resources, Conservation and Recycling*, **135**, pp 123–131 [Online] lup.lub.lu.se/record/2783e403-5f84-4568-9dc1-02a56f5ff (archived at https://perma.cc/7WRQ-L6KW) [accessed 21 November 2019]

26 Centre for Remanufacturing and Reuse (2016) *What is Remanufacturing?* [Online] www.remanufacturing.org.uk/what-is-remanufacturing.php (archived at https://perma.cc/Q5WU-5EJM) [accessed 23 October 2019]

27 Veolia Group (2018) 2018 Integrated Report [Online] www.veolia.com/en/2018-integrated-report (archived at https://perma.cc/4JH7-8YUJ) [accessed 21 October 2019]

28 Stahel, W (2015) Interviewed by Maxine Perella, *Ahead of the Curve* [Online] www.recyclingwasteworld.co.uk/interviews/ahead-of-the-curve/83796/ (archived at https://perma.cc/9DGC-XS95) [accessed 26 February 2016]

29 Retuna website www.retuna.se (archived at https://perma.cc/G8SE-W7Q3) [accessed 10 January 2019]

30 Savage, M (2018) This Swedish mall is the world's first ever secondhand shopping center, *Huffington Post*, 28 November [Online] www.huffingtonpost.co.uk/entry/recycled-mall-sweden-retuna_n_5bfd0762e4b0eb6d931346b3?guccounter=1 (archived at https://perma.cc/5XK5-VVMJ) [accessed 10 January 2019]

31 ShareGrid https://www.sharegrid.com/ (archived at https://perma.cc/TVV8-U8W6) [accessed 10 May 2016]

32 Earley, K (2014) Dutch aWEARness creating the first circular supply chain for textiles, *Sustainable Brands* [Online] www.sustainablebrands.com/read/defining-the-next-economy/dutch-awearness-creating-the-first-circular-supply-chain-for-textiles (archived at https://perma.cc/4U3T-G5W9) [accessed 23 October 2019]

33 Berners-Lee, M (2019) *There is No Planet B: A Handbook for the Make or Break Years*, Cambridge University Press, Cambridge, p 207

34 Zink, T and Geyer, R (2017) Circular Economy Rebound, *Journal of Industrial Ecology*, **21**, pp 593–602 onlinelibrary.wiley.com/doi/full/10.1111/jiec.12545 (archived at https://perma.cc/23NY-M4FS) [accessed 1 October 2019]

35 Assadourian, E and Mulrow, J (2018) 'Til sustainability do you part: arranging a marriage between degrowth and the circular economy, *Resilience* [Online] www.resilience.org/stories/2018-10-03/til-sustainability-do-you-part-arranging-a-marriage-between-degrowth-and-the-circular-economy/ (archived at https://perma.cc/5YWR-DC8R) [accessed 3 October 2019]

36 Global Footprint Network, Living Planet Report 2018 [Online] www.footprintnetwork.org/living-planet-report/ (archived at https://perma.cc/25WS-HT6Q) [accessed 3 October 2019]

4

Enablers and accelerators

The social dynamics of human history, even more than that of biological evolution, illustrate the fundamental principle of ecological evolution – that everything depends on everything else.

KENNETH E BOULDING, ECONOMIST, EDUCATOR, POET, SYSTEMS SCIENTIST AND PHILOSOPHER[1]

In Chapters 2 and 3, we looked at how organizations are incorporating the circular economy into their strategies and business models, with products, services and supply chains to support different ways of delivering value to customers, suppliers, internal stakeholders and wider society.

In this chapter, we cover the 'enablers' and 'accelerators' providing further support for circular economy strategies. **Enablers** (shown in Figure 4.1) help to:

- **'Think differently'** to develop circular strategies and processes, aiming to unlock new ways of creating and capturing value along the value chain. New approaches to design, systems thinking, and green chemistry can unlock existing problems in more circular ways.

- Use **new materials** to replace finite sources with renewable or recycled alternatives, to avoid toxic chemicals, and to improve product functionality.

- Adopt new **technology,** including the *Internet of Things*, artificial intelligence and much more, to improve effectiveness or help capture more of the value.

Accelerators tend to be external factors, influencing choices or promoting more effective circulation. These include collaborations, independent

FIGURE 4.1   Circular Economy Framework 2.0 – enablers

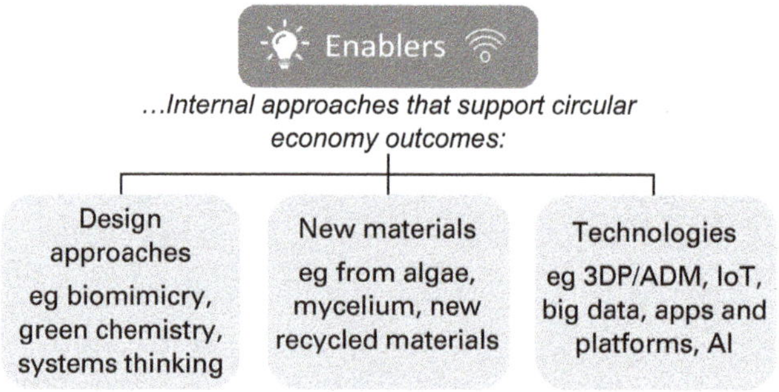

Source: © Catherine Weetman

assessments and certification, financial support, government policy and legislation.

Enablers: thinking differently

Designing new business models, products, services and materials is challenging. Established companies are threatened by 'disruptive' startups: unencumbered by an established way of doing things, by their investments in expensive facilities and processes, or by cultural resistance to change.

Whether you start with small, incremental changes to product design, creating by-products, or choosing different materials, the overall implications (and the business case) need careful planning. You may aim for large-scale innovations, with more potential for unforeseen consequences. Considering the whole system – and all its links, actors and feedback loops – can avoid pitfalls and create innovative solutions. In this section, we look at some ways of 'thinking differently' that support circular economy approaches.

Systems thinking[2]

Systems thinking includes a range of methods and approaches (referred to as 'pluralism') to help solve problems. It helps us to understand how business models and services might work and to examine different factors influencing the effectiveness of our intended model.

In *Thinking in Systems*, Donella Meadows begins by explaining that a system is an 'interconnected set of elements that is coherently organized in a way that achieves something'. She goes on to highlight that a system must be formed of three types of things: **elements**, **interconnections** and a function, or **purpose**. The earth is a system, as is the solar system, and the galaxy – so we can see that systems can be embedded in other systems, which in turn are embedded in other systems.

She uses the example of a football team, a system with:

- **elements** including the players, the coach, a field, a ball, etc;
- **interconnections** including the rules, the coach's strategy, communications between the players, and not forgetting the laws of physics that govern the motions of the ball and the players;
- a **purpose** – that could be to win games, to have fun, get exercise, win sponsorship, attract fans – or all of those.

Meadows highlights a core insight of systems theory – that once we notice the relationship between structure and behaviour, we can start to understand how systems work, what causes them to produce poor results, and how to 'shift them into better behaviour patterns'. Each of us consists of systems: our digestive system, our immune, circulatory and nervous systems. We are surrounded by systems too: schools, hospitals, factories, cities, the economy – and living systems, such as animals and trees (which are part of a larger forest system).

Systems have stocks and flows (inflows and outflows), and some have feedback loops:

- causing stocks to maintain their level – stabilizing loops;
- causing stocks to grow or decline – reinforcing loops.

Meadows believed we live in times where our world is more crowded, messy, interconnected and interdependent than ever before, and a world that is changing more rapidly. The more ways we have of seeing the world, the better. Using systems thinking as a 'lens' to view our world, and everything in it, allows us to reclaim our intuitive understanding of whole systems – we become better at understanding parts, seeing interconnections, asking 'what-if' questions about possible changes, and 'being creative and courageous about system redesign'.

In the *Systems Thinking Playbook* (2010),[3] Linda Booth Sweeney and Dennis Meadows define a systems thinker as someone who:

- sees the whole picture;
- changes perspectives to see new leverage points in complex systems;
- looks for interdependencies;
- considers how mental models create our futures;

- 'goes wide' (uses peripheral vision) to see complex cause and effect relationships;
- finds where unanticipated consequences occur;
- focuses on structure, not blame;
- holds the tension of paradox and controversy without trying to resolve it too quickly;
- makes systems visible through causal maps and computer models;
- seeks out stocks and accumulations and the time delays and inertia they can create;
- watches for 'win-lose' mindsets, knowing they usually make matters worse in situations of high interdependence;
- sees oneself as part of, not outside of, the system.

For more on systems thinking, see Further Resources in this chapter.

Biomimicry
Contribution by Richard James MacCowan

'Look deep into nature then you will understand everything better,' said Albert Einstein. Biomimicry, or biomimetics, looks to the natural world to find solutions to overcome our technical challenges.

We could consider Earth as a giant research and development lab: in action since life first began nearly 4 billion years ago and evolving millions of species. By investigating how functions and processes have evolved, modern-day designers and engineers are developing new technologies and solutions based on the principles that prosper in the natural world today. From engineering and design to business and IT, developers are increasingly looking to nature for answers. Biomimicry is a design philosophy, rooted in science, with creativity at its core.

Civilizations have been looking to nature for unique solutions to problems for thousands of years. Still, it's only since the mid-20th century that this approach has started to become mainstream, helped by our greater understanding of the natural world, and increases in technology to explore the systems and processes in greater detail.

Through geological processes, over millions (even billions) of years, everything will be recycled. Nature looks at greenhouse gases, such as atmospheric carbon, as a feedstock, a raw material. Trees, plants and huge structures like coral reefs are all created from carbon. But our take, make, waste systems are set up as if everything can be regenerated over a few of our human generations. The circular economy aim – to reduce, reuse, recycle and recover – can be more easily realized if we learn from the multifunctional systems found in the natural world.

As a species, humans use energy to overcome problems. In contrast, in the natural world, it is predominantly about how material and structure is used. When we manufacture stuff, we like to heat, beat or treat it into submission. In contrast, nature uses structure and shape to overcome a problem. Our methods often rely on heavy elements, whereas in the natural world, the lighter elements dominate. In nature, we find that many different species have solved problems in similar ways. Think of the problem of travel to cover long distances for food or winter habitats, and to escape predators – solved by insects and pterosaurs, birds, mammals and even reptiles. We call this convergent evolution, as seen in the development of smartphones, cars, houses and much more.

A well-known biomimicry example is the Velcro hook and loop fastener. In 1941, a Swiss engineer noticed how burdock seeds stuck to the coat of his dog via small hooks. After developing the idea over many years, he finally patented it in 1955.

For product design ideas, we can think about sharks. Over millions of years, they have evolved to have a cartilaginous skeleton and skin made of tooth-like dermal denticles which reduce drag through the water. Sharks have inspired many companies and products: antibacterial materials found in healthcare and contact lenses, to aviation companies like Airbus, looking to reduce drag (air resistance) on planes.

Shark skin also inspired Sharklet Technologies to create new forms of materials. A materials scientist, aiming to stop barnacles growing on ship hulls, observed that Galapagos sharks have diamond-shaped denticles with millions of tiny ribs that repel microbial activity. After many prototypes, the team developed a working solution that resisted 85 per cent of green algae compared with smooth surfaces. Unlike other anti-fouling coatings, this doesn't use chemicals. The medical industry now uses this same technology to repel bacteria, in catheters, tubes, wound dressings and contact lenses.

Rheon Labs, a UK-based technology company, produces highly strain-rate sensitive polymers that stiffen momentarily while absorbing energy for impact protection in both industry and sports applications. This is based on the concept of rheology, which is the force applied to a material (stress) and the change in its shape (strain). Combined with bespoke geometries, and computational generative design techniques, this allows them to create the materials for bespoke needs of the user and save material in the manufacturing process.

Nature can self-repair, too – think of skin cuts and blisters. Now, self-repairing materials are emerging for aircraft and buildings, to revolutionize the way we travel and live.

Biomimicry also helps us develop better processes to conserve our natural assets. Take the baleen filter in the mouths of baleen whales, such as humpback, grey or blue whales. These whales feed by scooping up large amounts of water containing krill, fish and other small prey. They force the water out past these filters and capture the remnants as food. Baleen Filters, an Australian-based water filtration company, has developed separation and self-cleaning technology based on these baleen processes. This enables the technology to remove nearly 100 per cent of visible material with virtually no downtime, using less water in the process. The technology uses 4 per cent of the standard filtration technologies, resulting in smaller carbon footprint.

Nature holds many secrets which we are only just beginning to unlock. Biomimicry design and innovation means we can tap into the strategies and adaptations that have enabled successful species to evolve, survive, thrive and adapt for millions of years.

Ecodesign
Contribution by Katie Beverley

Industrial ecologists Thomas Graedel and Braden Allenby (1995)[4] tell us that 80 per cent of a product's environmental impacts are determined during the design phase, so we can see that design is an essential tool to support the transition to a circular economy. It can increase product resource-efficiency throughout the life-cycle, increase the likelihood of consumers choosing circular products over the alternatives, help businesses develop services, and help governments to design policies that meet the needs of all stakeholders.

Ecodesign aims to minimize the overall environmental impact of a product or service. It encourages innovative design solutions that consider the entire life-cycle, from extraction or harvesting of raw materials, through production, distribution and use, all the way to end-of-use recycling, 'repair-ability' and disposal. Ecodesign is an approach, rather than a label or certification for certain products. Using a holistic approach, it aims for 'environmental, social and economic benefits as well as aesthetically appealing and durable design' and 'promotes behavioural change in producers and consumers towards product-service systems and self-sufficiency'.[5] Applying ecodesign helps companies to:

- design products that are both necessary, and emotionally and physically durable;
- use fewer materials and resources, and choose those with the minimum environmental impact;
- produce the least waste and pollution possible;
- reduce the ecological impacts in distribution and the supply chain;
- design to make reuse and recycling easier.

Ecodesign can help us to narrow, slow, intensify and close the loop, furthering all our circular economy aims. We can slow the rate of resource consumption by designing products and components so that they use the minimum possible material to fulfil their function, can be made with the lowest possible production energy, and do not rely on consumables.

We can reduce demand on virgin raw materials and boost markets for secondary raw materials, by choosing materials that are recycled or derived from by-products that would otherwise be wasted. We can reduce waste at end-of-life, by selecting renewable and recyclable materials (and by this, we mean truly recyclable – where a route to recycling is readily available and there is a market for the recyclate) and using colours and finishes that do not affect recyclability.

Design for disassembly strategies (minimizing the number of different materials used in a product, reducing the time, tools and equipment needed to take it apart and avoiding the permanent joining of non-similar materials) can facilitate material recovery at the end-of-life. Design for disassembly can also support remanufacture, upgrade and reuse of components, and this is becoming increasingly important as changes to European legislation aim to make repairability and life extension easier. Meanwhile, the ecodesigner's most powerful tool – life-cycle assessment – helps to ensure that proposed changes do not simply shift the resource burden elsewhere in the product life-cycle.

Arguably, however, designers can contribute most to the circular economy transition when they go beyond incremental technological innovation of existing products and look for opportunities to change how consumer needs are met. 'Slowing the flow' requires changes to consumer behaviour – for example, recognizing the value in circular products, keeping products for longer, engaging simultaneously with products and services, and shifting from ownership to access.

At the product level, incorporating **user-centred design** (a design approach that involves users from product conception to realization) into the ecodesign process can lower the risk when bringing a novel circular product to market.

At the service level, applying a service design process – where designers engage with multiple stakeholders to understand their needs and incorporate them into the service offer – can ensure that circular products and services work synergistically to change behaviour across the value network.

The value of engaging users in the design process doesn't end there; the more designers understand consumers, the better they become at understanding what happens to products when they leave the factory gates. The use and end-of-life phases are widely regarded as a bit of a 'black hole' in life-cycle assessment and can lead to large uncertainties in determining resource-efficiency and circularity.

This process of involving users throughout the design process incorporates some aspects of systems thinking, in that it considers how a product or service fits into the day-to-day behaviours of users and influences the user ecosystem. However, this still sets the designer as the external 'problem-solver', rather than a creative stakeholder in the system. In systems design for a circular economy, designers take on more of a role as a facilitator, providing an environment where different stakeholder views are combined to create a shared vision of a circular future that forms the framework for new policies, business models, services and products. This systems-based approach is well placed to support policymaking. For example, in Zero Waste Scotland's 'Design for a Circular Economy' Action Plan, designers facilitated multidisciplinary groups to discuss circular economy needs, conflicts and co-create policy objectives.

User engagement can turn circular behaviour from possibility to probability and provide high-quality information on in-use impacts that can in turn feed back into the ecodesign process to improve decision-making – a circular design process! A growing number of designers are combining eco-, user-centred and service design processes to design, develop and deliver innovative circular solutions.

Frugal innovation

Highlighted back in 2010 in *The Economist*, **frugal innovation** is often described as the art of doing more with less. It might involve reducing the complexity and cost of a product, and it could include removing non-essential features; or may radically redesign a previously expensive product to both simplify it and make it affordable for lots more people. The business model may rely on high volume to offset tiny profit margins, or finding novel distribution channels.

Radjou and Prabhu, writing in *Harvard Business Review* (2014),[6] describe frugal innovation as 'a disruptive growth strategy that aims to create significantly more business and social value while drastically reducing the use of scarce resources such as energy, capital and time'. It rejects designs that are complex, resource-intensive and expensive to produce, instead 'creating meaningful products and services that integrate four core attributes ... affordability, simplicity, quality and sustainability. Frugal innovation is not just about doing more with less but about doing better with less.' It is a normal approach in resource-constrained regions, where limitations of money or materials focus design in different ways and result in innovative solutions. For example, in rural India, where there is no electricity, a potter came up with the idea of a clay fridge for storing food, using water to provide thermal cooling. Now famous, his Mitticool fridge system has spread all over the country.

Green chemistry

Green, or sustainable, chemistry supports circular economy principles:

- for low-carbon, cleaner, sustainable and renewable inputs and processes;
- and for products and materials to be 'nutrients' at the end of use – safely recovered, reused or recycled; to safely create energy or to biodegrade as 'food' for nature.

It originated in the 1960s, becoming a formal scientific field in the 1990s and shares some objectives with green engineering. Green chemistry is a philosophy as well as a science and aims to find innovative, scientific solutions to real-world environmental problems.

In contrast to waste treatment and 'remediation' (cleaning up) of pollution, green chemistry 'keeps the hazardous materials out of the environment in the first place'. It also aims for a chemist's version of resource efficiency – 'atom economy' – 'so that the final product contains the maximum proportion of the starting materials. Waste few or no atoms.'[7] A 'green chemist' aims to use feedstocks that are renewable and inherently safe, to use the least inputs with the fewest process steps, and ensure the end-of-life material is benign (to both human and environmental health) or can be reclaimed safely.

Enablers: technology[8,9]

Alec Ross, author of *The Industries of the Future*, tells us that the key raw material of the Agricultural Revolution was 'land', in the Industrial Revolution it was 'iron' and for the Industrial Age, it is 'data'.[10] By June 2019, the internet reached over 58 per cent of the world's population, 4.5 billion people.[11] In Chapter 3, we noted the need for trust in sharing models and peer-to-peer rental, and how some platforms use social media to tap into existing social connections. Chapter 3 also highlighted the accelerating dissipation of technology: until the late 'noughties', most of us had not heard about smartphones, 'wearables', or the Internet of Things – now they are widespread. Amazon, Bitcoin, Uber and many more are disrupting their sectors. The CEO of technology company ARM described '[micro] chips for 20 cents that have got more computer power in them than put a man on the moon'.[12] Technology to help us connect with each other is advancing rapidly, in both reach and capabilities:

- Mobile phone use is still growing, driven mainly by developing countries. By early 2019, over 5 billion people had mobile phones, up 2 per cent on the previous year. The speed of growth is slowing, but the industry expects the number of unique mobile subscribers to reach 5.9 billion by 2025, equivalent to 71 per cent of the world's population.

- Mobile internet is expected to grow from around 3.25 billion in 2018 to 5 billion users by 2025.

- Almost 3.5 billion people use social media, with more than a million new users joining every day in 2018.

Digital technologies have already transformed some sectors. Music, photography and increasingly print is stored as digital files, often in 'the cloud' rather than on your own computer – or even accessed 'on-demand' from sharing sites:

- Digital **platforms**, for both traditional employment and freelance assignments, help people learn, find work or sell 'stuff'. Consumers can be '*prosumers*': sell on eBay and Etsy, rent out a room on Airbnb, and lend each other money through Zopa and PayPal.

- Smartphones are now capable of **scanning and recognizing text and codes** (such as QR codes) and making automated payments.

- 'Smart speakers' and other devices can be **controlled by voice**.

- Hacking, copying, open sourcing and free education all make intellectual property harder to protect.

These advances are transforming business and the wider economy, creating new digital markets and being deployed for key business functions: for example in sourcing and procurement, certification and supply chain transparency, and for more effective use of assets and resources.

Additive manufacturing and 3D printing

Additive manufacturing, invented in the 1980s, is evolving from its main use as a prototyping tool in niche sectors. The range of available materials is broadening rapidly, and businesses of all sizes (and consumers) are 3D printing a growing range of products.

Additive manufacturing covers a wide range of materials and technologies,[13] using 'heat, light, binders of pressure to build up materials layer by layer according to a computer-aided design (CAD) file'.[14] The term emphasizes its key difference to traditional, or 'subtractive' manufacturing technologies, involving removal or reduction of parts of the original material to create the desired shape. The technologies include fused deposition modelling (FDM), direct ink writing, matrix composites, stereolithography (SLA), digital light processing and 3D printing (3DP). In this book, we use **3D printing (3DP)** as shorthand for all the additive manufacturing technologies and processes.

3D printed structures with enhanced strength or flexibility, the nature of the process itself and the range of materials all have great potential to improve resource efficiency and support circular economy models.

Designers think differently to exploit the potential of 3DP, making objects in a single process instead of designing multiple parts or components that then need to fit together. The 3DP component is often stronger and lighter than the multi-part component.

Building up the product or component from micro-particles of powder or liquid, in a similar way to nature's 'manufacturing' process for fibres and polymers, can revolutionize both the manufacturing process and the possibilities for the end product. Simpler, renewable, safer and more natural materials are both better for health (of humans and living systems) and for recyclability at end-of-use. Using recycled materials creates scope for local closed loops. We can 'make-on-demand' instead of 'make-for-stock'.

Designs begin with a 3D computer drawing, or by scanning an existing object in 3D and sending the resulting file to the printer. By using the internet, 3DP can take place wherever the materials are available, so that objects are made close to the end-user, and printed on-demand.

We can 'make-on-demand' instead of 'make-for-stock'. 3DP can reduce waste: both in manufacture (by being additive instead of subtractive) and at the recovery stage through enabling the use of simpler, more easily recycled materials. The 'additive' nature of the process enables highly efficient use of materials, with very little wasted.

An expanding **range of materials** already includes metals and metal alloys, ceramics, matrix composites of metals or ceramics, cement, modelling clays, thermoplastics, rubber and photopolymers. New materials, using recycled or biomaterials, including plastics and resins, help 3DP to support the circular economy.

KEY SECTORS

By 2019, there was significant progress, with 3D Innovations reporting that the 'automobile, aerospace and dental industries have been utilizing 3D printings' customization ability for years now, but other industries are also starting to take notice'.[15]

A report by McKinsey Global Institute estimated the potential economic impact of 3DP at US$550 billion a year by 2025.[16] Companies are creating concept designs, enabling rapid prototyping, making the finished product or even the machine tools to reduce set-up costs and time for mass production processes. Developments include components to replace complex sub-assemblies such as batteries, transistors and LEDs, and 3DP circuit boards are now a 'do it yourself' option:

- Printing with metals is developing, with metal additive manufactured aeroplane seats weighing in at 50 per cent lighter than the existing model.

- Printing speeds are increasing: researchers reduced the impact of vibrations during printing (a cause of poor quality) whilst doubling the printing speed, whilst MIT developed a desktop printer capable of printing at 10 times the speed of currently available printers.

MASS PRODUCTION VERSUS 3D PRINTING

In traditional manufacturing, production lines are set up to achieve the high volumes of throughput necessary to offset the costs of setting up the process, designing and procuring machine tools, fine-tuning the process to minimize rejects and so on. Most manufacture today still uses the mass production approach adopted by Henry Ford in the early 1900s, needing manual labour, high investments, centralized inventory, lots of stock and long-distance transport. In contrast, 3DP uses powder or liquid, with no waste. There is no tooling or assembly, and set-up costs are low – whether you make one object or thousands, the production cost per item varies little. The printed objects can be of almost any shape, and the range of materials is expanding fast. The 3DP process reduces material types and the need for cutting, so reducing waste.

Companies are seeing 3DP as a way to achieve a fast, agile and efficient supply chain, with rapid prototyping and trialling of potential new products giving them incredible speed-to-market.

MASS CUSTOMIZATION AND 'BESPOKE' DESIGNS

Companies of all sizes and hobbyists are also using 3DP to create personalized or bespoke product designs – 'mass customization'. On the face of it, customization seems counter-intuitive to circular economy aims – but it has the potential to create emotional durability and thus support longer product lifetimes.

Karl Lagerfeld, of fashion design house Chanel, created a 3DP version of the brand's iconic suit in 2015; a high-heeled shoe was created with a 3Doodler pen; designers are creating all manner of clothes using 3DP technologies. Both Nike and Adidas have invested in 3DP to create customizable products and experiment with the design freedoms enabled by 3D approaches. In 2013, they announced its use in rapid prototyping, reducing development times for new products.[17] Nike launched a football shoe with a lightweight contoured 3D printed plate to help performance.[18]

SPARE PARTS

The 'repairer' movement is using 3DP to make spare parts at home, to repair anything from a washing machine to a car; American TV host Jay Leno bought a 3D printer to keep his collection of vintage cars going. The potential here is enormous; rather than holding stocks of spare parts, you download the 3D drawing from the internet and find a provider to print the part locally. You could print parts for obsolete products, perhaps by scanning the existing part and creating the design from that. Aftermarket service organizations can print spare parts locally, and then ship to a remote stocking point for a field engineer to collect just before their site visit. This may change logistics infrastructures, away from large central warehouses to much smaller local facilities with manufacturing capabilities.

The spare parts scenario has fantastic potential for many sectors, transforming maintenance repairs and operations (MRO). Rather than holding expensive inventories of spare parts for production equipment – 'just in case' – instead, we can print parts on-site, or order them from a specialist local printer as required. We return to this in Part Three.

CONSUMERS AND MICRO-BUSINESSES

Consumers are using 3DP too, either for hobbies or to become *prosumers*. Search the internet for 'furniture' and '3D printing' and many examples appear, especially for decorative items such as chairs, lamps, coffee tables and ornamental sculptures. The relatively low cost of 3DP technology helps designers and small companies to create something different and desirable. There is even a 'self-replicating manufacturing machine': RepRap (short for 'replicating rapid prototyper') is a free (no licence or download charges) desktop 3D printer, capable of printing plastic objects.[19]

3D printing can also help raise awareness of, and potentially resolve problems associated with, single-use plastics.

3D SEED – LOW-COST, SOLAR-POWERED KIT TO RECYCLE PET PACKAGING INTO 3D PRINTED OBJECTS [20]

3D Seed sets up projects to allow communities and businesses to grind up everyday plastic waste, such as PET bottles, and then to 3D print it into small objects. Users can download designs from open-source sites like 'Thingiverse', or create their own 3D designs – thus learning new design skills and seeing waste plastic as a valuable resource. The equipment uses very little energy and can run on solar power.

Although we know that recycling plastic into toys and gifts is not the answer to our problems with waste plastic, initiatives like 3D Seed are a great way to help people understand how waste can become a valuable resource, and to help people develop the skills to make their own designs.

In 2019, an engineer at De Montfort University in the UK developed a prosthetic limb socket made from recycled plastic bottles.[21] Prototypes of the design, believed to be the first of its kind made from recycled plastic, cost around £10 to produce instead of an average of £5,000 – perhaps another example of frugal innovation. They were successfully trialled with two patients in India, and are comfortable and durable.

ISSUES WITH 3DP

Unfortunately, 3DP is not a perfect tool in our circular economy 'toolbox', with a number of issues to resolve, including intellectual property rights and material choices. The music industry experienced problems with copyright infringements when 'sharing' sites such as Napster took off, and there are similar issues for copyright and patent infringement when existing product designs are scanned and then printed by a third party.

Current materials are also causing concerns. Earlier, we saw that 3DP relies on finite resources such as metals, oil-based plastics and resins. These are often mixed-material compounds that may be extremely difficult to separate at end-of-life and are potentially toxic. There are other health concerns too – including a report by Wadhwani (2015) highlighting studies on 'ultrafine particle (UFP) and other emissions from desktop 3D printers', advising caution in indoor environments without adequate ventilation.[22] A study found encouraging developments in the use of recycled materials, and 3D printable thermoplastics from squid DNA and filament from seaweed.

Biomimicry is helpful for design, learning from the way nature uses structure to provide strength, flexibility, resilience or lighter weight. Using a single material (as nature does) can create products that are recyclable at the end of use. New materials include developments with pine resin and cellulose. Garmulewicz reminds us that biomimicry principles can help us to substitute nanostructure for toxic chemical additives, to 'revolutionize the potential to cycle materials'.[23]

Digital platforms and applications

Software – for example, platforms for interaction and exchanges between participants, and mobile 'apps' on smartphones, computers, smartwatches, etc – is already transforming how we use and 'consume'. Digital technology and sharing platforms mean that instead of owning a collection of music CDs or film DVDs, you 'stream' entertainment on demand, often free of charge. Algorithms make the platforms highly effective at matching supply and demand, and often the slightly better algorithm will 'corner the market'. Uber's algorithm finds the nearest available driver and aggregates data to spot changes in regional demand in order to bring in more drivers or to change the pricing. A higher price can either divert demand to other forms of transport, and/or attract more drivers into the pool – you might have planned an evening off, but if the fee increases by enough, you might decide to work instead.

Connection to GPS location information, to social network sites, the exchange of images, the ability to read barcodes or quick response (QR) codes, and other innovative features all help to broaden the potential of these technologies. If you want to rent a car, you can quickly see the nearest available one and can leave it in a convenient car park at the end of the rental period, making it immediately available for the next user. If you want to share a lift or expensive equipment, social media can establish trust through your connections.

There are issues and concerns with this platform model. Controlling the matching of supply and demand means both provider and user are reliant on the platform, and this allows some operators to use zero-hours contracts (the 'gig economy') to lower their supply costs. Platform operators may use differential (or 'surge') pricing to increase prices in times of high demand, which can be seen as exploitative but can also encourage more providers into the marketplace to meet that short-term demand. In addition, the requirement to publish your GPS location, and allow face-recognition, access to your social media accounts, proof of identity and so on, allows the operator (and in some countries, the government) to monitor your activity closely – with the potential to limit your freedom to use the services provided by the platform.

The Internet of Things and intelligent assets

The *Internet of Things (IoT)* refers to interrelated computing devices (machines, sensors, devices, wearable objects, etc) that have unique identifiers (UIDs) and are able to transfer data over a network without needing human interaction.

Intelligent assets are physical objects that can sense, record and send information about their status, condition, their surroundings and so on. These objects may be connected in the IoT, or not part of a network: instead, they hold their information for interrogation, downloads, etc, on request, or when triggered.

The Internet of Services, meanwhile, refers to the platforms and applications that connect users to providers, such as smartphone apps, exchange platforms and so on.

The Internet of Things (IoT) or 'intelligent assets' have scope to extend the lifetimes of asset and product, reduce their in-use consumption, and help with their effective recovery at end-of-use. This connectivity between devices and physical infrastructure is referred to as the Internet of Things or the 'industrial internet', and the technology enabling the connections is known as 'machine to machine' (M2M). IoT has great potential to reduce energy use and improve time- and resource-efficiency across many sectors. The benefits, including improved reliability and performance of infrastructure, machinery, vehicles, etc, are especially relevant to agriculture, energy, transportation and the built environment.

We are already seeing both the IoT and intelligent assets in our homes, allowing control of temperatures, entertainment, security devices and more. The fifth generation of mobile internet connectivity, 5G, with its increased bandwidth, will enable IoT devices to collect and transfer even more data, bringing further benefits.

A report from GSMA in 2018 sees the early industrial developments as being still in their infancy, with great potential for buildings, cities and enterprises. It predicts growth from 7.5 billion connections in 2017 to over 25 billion by 2025.[24]

The network of connections includes actuators and low-cost sensors, collecting data, monitoring conditions and activities, making decisions and optimizing processes. Organizations can track energy usage minute by minute, use 'big data' analytics to predict energy supply peaks and troughs, and help users reschedule energy-intensive processes when supply is more abundant (and cheaper). Asset and product status, location, flows, ownership or custody, patterns of activity and much more can be tracked, analysed and acted upon. Objects can be controlled and configured remotely, such as household heating controls from your smartphone using the Hive or Tado apps.

General Motors' OnStar system allows vehicle owners to control their car locks, flash the lights and request roadside assistance through an app, and has automated collision response, with built-in sensors automatically connecting an OnStar adviser to the vehicle. A touch-button can trigger crisis support or alert emergency services.

Precision farming can connect different data sources, including in-soil sensors and drones to survey crop growth and conditions at a detailed level within a field. iCropTrak provides mobile farm management and agriculture decision tools, with GIS software, 'that make farmers of every size more efficient at growing safe food for the growing population, being more profitable, while continuing to preserve and maximize natural resources'.[25]

General Electric (GE) and Philips are using the IoT to connect their products and provide revenue-earning services to customers, including safety, security and navigation services.[26] GE launched its 'Predictivity' line of services to industrial customers in 2012 and generated revenues of US$290 billion within a year. In 2019, GE offers the Predix Platform: a scalable, asset-centric data foundation connecting data, providing event management, analytics, and processing for industrial applications. Connection and data monitoring are important in making Philips' 'pay per lux' lighting service cost-effective for users. Philips connects the lights to a management service, monitors it remotely and provides maintenance when required.

Artificial intelligence

Artificial intelligence is the broader concept of machines being able to carry out tasks in a way that we would consider 'smart', performing cognitive functions in a similar way to humans – for example, finding information, reasoning and decision-making. Crucially, these machines should be capable of learning – otherwise, it is 'old-fashioned' computer programming and human-decided algorithms. 'Smart speakers' or 'virtual assistants', including Siri and Alexa, are a couple of examples, and another is the Nest 'learning thermostat', owned by Google and Amazon's transactional AI, learning to predict what we're interested in buying based on our online behaviour.

REFIND TECHNOLOGIES – ARTIFICIAL INTELLIGENCE FOR REVERSE VENDING[27,28]

Refind Technologies, in Sweden, provides intelligent sorting and grading solutions using machine vision and learning, developing solutions mainly for used electronics. Refind uses cameras and machine learning software to teach systems to recognize items based on their looks. These systems can grade and sort used products, enabling producers, retailers and recyclers to 'squeeze out as much value as possible from used and returned electronics, batteries, lamps or other complex products that otherwise would have been dumped or treated inefficiently'.

Its first solution, in 2014, was a reverse vending machine, tested in stores around Oslo, and said to be the first of its kind worldwide. Customers could return all types of household batteries and receive a discount coupon, worth one krone per battery, that could be used when buying new batteries.

A report from the Ellen MacArthur Foundation and Google sees AI playing an important role in the shift to the circular economy (see Further Resources for this chapter), including:

- helping to design new products, components and materials, especially through rapid prototyping and testing and iterative design processes;
- operating circular business models such as asset-sharing and product-as-a-service, especially managing fluctuating supply and demand, predictive maintenance and decision-making about the next use cycle for returned products;
- optimizing reverse logistics, sorting and recycling infrastructure, to help close the loop.

Asset tracking

Assets can be tracked using the IoT and sensor technology, or by simpler technologies such as 'smart labels', radio frequency identification (RFID) tags, QR codes and so on. Understanding more about how a product is used, which parts are durable, which are not and where it has been, provides valuable feedback to improve the designs, the materials, and examine the benefits of being involved in reuse models.

Autonomous technology

Autonomous technology machines act independently of humans. The IoT supports the development of autonomous vehicles, such as drones, parcel (ro)bots and self-driving cars. These also require 'machine vision', sensors, actuators and artificial intelligence. Although we see news headlines about near-misses between drones and aircraft and hear concerns about taxi driver employment versus self-driving cars, autonomous technology can support the circular economy. Using a logistics example, delivery routes are generally constrained by maximum legal driving shifts and to allow drivers to return to their home base. Driverless vehicles provide scope for greatly increased productivity, through increased vehicle fill and reduced empty miles. Major truck manufacturers are already trialling autonomy and 'platooning'. Waymo (owned by Google's parent company Alphabet) completed a trial of autonomous taxis in 2019, in California, moving over 6,000 people in the first month.

Drones can make lightweight deliveries without using roads, reducing investment for new roads in fast-expanding cities and avoiding congestion delays. A report for the World Economic Forum estimated that drone technology could reduce last-mile delivery costs by 25 per cent and emissions by up to 90 per cent.[29]

Big data

Big data is distinct from 'business intelligence'. Business intelligence creates statistics from data with high information density to measure things, detect trends, analyse behaviour, etc.

Oracle uses Gartner's definition: big data is data that contains greater variety arriving in increasing volumes and with ever-higher velocity. This is known as the three Vs.[30] Big data generally does not 'ask why', and instead simply detects patterns, looking for regressions, non-linear relationships and causal effects. It can often be a low-cost by-product of digital interaction.

There is a wide **variety** of data types and sources, providing scope for a deeper or wider range of insights. Big data uses text, images, audio, video and completes missing pieces through data fusion. Data is generated and processed at high **velocity** and is often available in real time. Data shows a high degree of **variability**, with inconsistencies, together with **veracity** or quality variations with the potential to affect accuracy of analysis.

For the circular economy, big data enables analysis and information on energy use, asset utilization and flows of materials, all helping with 'smart designs' to improve responsiveness, optimize efficiency and reduce structural waste. Connected devices – the IoT – will provide much of this valuable data.

Blockchain

Blockchain uses shared databases (digital ledgers) to record and verify information without the need to centralize it. Data is recorded in these shared databases by a network, or chain of devices ('nodes'). These nodes independently timestamp the data and verify that it matches the data placed by other nodes. After the data is verified, the new data can be recorded in the database – in other words, a new 'block' has been added to the 'chain'. The encryption and decentralization of data is what makes it more secure.

Matthew Hooper, writing for IBM in 2018,[31] tells us that blockchain has the potential to transform traditional business models, for global supply chains, financial services, healthcare, government and many other industries. He sees benefits including greater transparency, enhanced security, improved traceability, increased efficiency and speed of transactions, and reduced costs.

From a circular economy and sustainability perspective, the potential for greater trust and transparency in complex supply chains is already proving useful. It can track and prove provenance for materials and components in every sector. Blockchain is already used to manage data and battery storage capabilities for small-scale renewable energy projects, making the grid more flexible and efficient and so lowering the overall cost of energy supply.

Cloud computing

Cloud computing, or cloud technology, provides computer services on demand, using the internet or through a network. It allows access to a shared pool of computing resources, enabling users to configure, store and process data in third-party data centres. Economies of scale create savings once a critical mass is reached. In addition, data centres can be located away from the company operations in cooler regions, thus reducing energy costs to cool the computer servers. In addition to being an 'on-demand' service itself, cloud computing can facilitate other shared or on-demand services.

Technology – issues and concerns

There are widespread ethical and safety concerns, including the risk of privacy and security breaches. There have been many serious security breaches of both business and government technology, such as hacking into control systems, websites and communication networks. Machine-connected control systems for energy-generating plants (including nuclear) have been a concern after hackers shut down a major European steel plant. Researchers in the United States identified 25 vulnerabilities that hackers could use to crash or seize control of servers in US power plants.

There are widespread concerns about AI, particularly ethical risks and allowing the power of AI to be controlled by private companies. Technology expert Julia Bossman, writing for the World Economic Forum in 2016,[32] draws our attention to concerns around the loss of jobs, distribution of wealth, guarding against mistakes, the potential for AI bias, such as sexism and racism, keeping AI secure, and not forgetting the risk of unintended consequences.

Drones have already been involved in near-misses with aircraft in the UK, and have temporarily shut airports down. Although autonomous vehicles combined with 'machine vision' have potential to improve road safety, there are concerns about the risk of collisions, and decision-making too – should the control system keep the driver safe instead of swerving to avoid a pedestrian? These concerns were heightened after one of Uber's autonomous test vehicles hit and killed an Arizona pedestrian in 2018. Hacking is another concern, with onboard car systems already being hacked, just to prove it is possible.

Enablers: new materials

Technological advances continue apace, both in materials and in the ways we can transform them: from abundant, natural resources; using living organisms to 'grow' materials; and creating new materials from bio-based waste.

Investment in research and development is producing new materials from abundant natural resources too, including dyes and textiles from algae, lightweight products from fungi, and innovations for cellulosic and lignin fibres (from wood), for example, to make a transparent and flexible computer screen, as a carbon-fibre replacement or as a renewable 3D printing feedstock. So rather than waiting millions of years for plants and trees to become oil, why not just use the tree itself, and plant a replacement for each one you harvest?

We should be careful not to use or displace food crops. Using non-edible parts of the plant (rice straw and hemp fibre), or finding plants that will grow in poor soils and difficult conditions – maybe even on building roofs – is a better option.

ABUNDANT NATURAL MATERIALS – CARBON FIBRE FROM ALGAE[33]

In autumn 2019, a research team in Germany developed a process that created carbon fibres from algae oil. Carbon fibre made using this method uses far less energy (and so creates far fewer carbon emissions) than using concrete or steel – but there are other benefits for carbon reduction. Algae absorb CO_2, 'locking it in' to the raw material and so storing atmospheric carbon whilst the material is intact.

Biochemical and **biorefining** processes are developing rapidly, and are aligned with circular economy principles. The International Energy Agency (IEA) defines biorefining as 'the sustainable processing of biomass into a spectrum of:

- bio-based products: chemicals, materials, human food and animal feed;
- bioenergy: fuels, power and/or heat.'[34]

Using waste from the food and agricultural supply chain can have substantial benefits, creating valuable by-products as well as reducing the costs, pollution and emissions of disposal. In 2019, Lucy Hughes, 23, a graduate in product design from the University of Sussex, won the UK category of the James Dyson award.[35] She developed a bio-plastic made of organic fish waste that would otherwise end up in landfill, with the potential to replace plastic in everyday packaging. It looks and feels like plastic but is stronger and can be disposed of as food waste.

Combining reuse of waste with fungi means we can 'grow' products. Ecovative, an early innovator, use moulds and agricultural waste such as straw and adding mycelium spores to grow objects that are light and strong, and at the end of life can safely be returned to nature (see Chapters 2 and 3 for more on Ecovative).

Other developments mean we can use less of each material, or to avoid bonding and alloys. **Graphene,** discovered in 2004 in the UK, is a revolutionary new two-dimensional material with extraordinary properties. It is about 100 times stronger than the equivalent thickness of the strongest steel, conducts heat and electricity efficiently and is nearly transparent. **Nanotechnology** is another transformative development, with enormous benefits but concerns about its health risks. Wikipedia lists a wide range of existing applications, including infusing bandages with silver nanoparticles to heal cuts faster, and clothing infused to keep people cooler and last longer. Researchers have discovered issues, such as bacteriostatic silver nanoparticles – used in socks to reduce foot odour – released when washing the socks. Once flushed into the waste-water stream, these particles could damage natural bacteria ecosystems, farms and waste treatment processes.

These and other technologies are developing at pace and disseminating rapidly. Companies of all sizes, across many sectors and geographies, are seeing their potential and looking at how to best use them for both immediate and longer-term competitive gains.

Accelerators

A range of **external** factors provide conditions for circular economy models to thrive, including collaboration, life-cycle assessment, certification, financial support, policies, legislation and product stewardship approaches (see Figure 4.2).

FIGURE 4.2   Circular Economy Framework 2.0 – accelerators

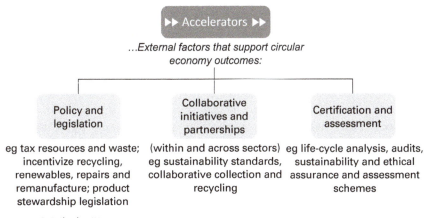

Source: © Catherine Weetman

Collaboration

Collaboration can open up new possibilities, share knowledge and find ways to align visions and objectives. Successful collaborations benefit all partners and can include economic, social and environmental shared value. They can extend across geographic and sector boundaries, and may be led by one company, be a sector-wide initiative, or even cross-sector. They can include companies, their suppliers, research organizations and governments. Collaborations might focus on a sector or a value chain, or aim to further knowledge-sharing on a topic.

Research indicates that companies working more collaboratively with their supply chains achieve 15 per cent increases in annual revenue.[36] The research examines offshore manufacturing, agriculture, mining, quarrying and utilities, identifying two areas for major value opportunities:

- **Vertical collaboration:** by optimizing supplier–customer activities across the supply chain. These include demand planning and fulfilment levels, product innovation, recirculating and reusing waste, risk reduction and improved confidence in future investments.

- **Horizontal collaboration:** integrating the activities of multiple suppliers to improve scale. This includes investments that benefit a group of suppliers, sharing best practice, sharing transport and logistics, or purchasing deals for a group of suppliers.

Collaboration can involve exchanging knowledge or resources – the 'space, stuff, skills and services' in the sharing models. Collaboration goes further than sharing resources, by sharing aims and objectives and often giving something up to achieve a greater impact – for instance, sharing some confidential information with a supplier to help design a more effective material. A simple example is the industry-standard mobile phone charger, finally adopted after years of every phone manufacturer using its own design of charging plug and connection (see more about this in Part Three).

There are movements towards industry standards for materials, supplier ethics or environmental procurement, perhaps sharing previously confidential information with competitors, in order to improve the sector's prospects or reduce future risks. Sometimes these collaborations aim to reduce the need for regulation through self-policing rather than government control (and consequential costs of inspection and intervention).

One example is the Bioplastic Feedstock Alliance (BFA) set up in 2013, with Coca-Cola, Danone, Ford, Heinz, Nestlé, Nike, Procter & Gamble, Unilever and World Wildlife Fund (WWF) among the founding members.

BFA members 'are all committed to using informed science and critical thinking to help guide the responsible selection of feedstocks for biobased plastics ... to encourage a more sustainable flow of materials, helping to create lasting value for present and future generations'.[37] BFA focuses on guiding the responsible selection and harvesting of feedstocks – such as sugar cane, corn, bulrush and switchgrass – used to make plastics from agricultural materials.

Companies are also collaborating with campaign organizations and NGOs (non-government organizations). The combination of independent research and potential for culture change within the company can help accelerate changes.

Life-cycle assessment and certification

A life-cycle assessment (LCA) is 'a cradle-to-grave approach for assessing industrial systems that evaluates all stages of a product's life. It provides a comprehensive view of the environmental aspects of the product or process', including ethical practices and material provenance.[38] We look at the LCA process in more detail in Chapter 12. Many companies embarking on these have found them to be extremely detailed, time-consuming and costly, often needing cooperation and commitment from a wide range of suppliers. One approach is to focus on key materials, carbon or water as a starting point. Some companies are choosing to work with sector groups, aiming to share information and develop a richer, more accurate 'crowdsourced' assessment.

Collaborative examples include a Scotch whisky LCA.[39] It covers all the processes from cereal growing, use of raw materials and manufacturing, to transporting the packaged product to customers. It measures impacts for 'climate change, water use and land use' together with 'environmental effects of emissions to air, land and water'.[40]

The Sustainable Apparel Coalition, the Sustainable Packaging Coalition and other collaborative organizations are helping companies work with their supply chain partners and with their competitors, to share knowledge and agree on standard approaches to improve sustainability. The Ellen MacArthur Foundation is supporting many collaborative projects to further the circular economy, including the Food Initiative, Make Fashion Circular, the New Plastics Economy, the World Economic Forum Platform for Accelerating the Circular Economy (PACE) and, of course, the CE100. Circle Economy, an employee cooperative consultancy, also manages a number of programmes, covering areas such as the built environment, circular textiles, circular finance and circular cities. The OECD also has an initiative: the Circular Economy in Cities and Regions.

Certifications help set standards for ethical, environmental, animal welfare or product ingredients. There are many, both local and global, across all industry sectors. Some almost compete with each other, charging for certification of the product or company, perhaps partially offset by the promise of marketing benefits. The Rainforest Alliance, Fairtrade, Forest Stewardship Council, organic certifications and many others are helping consumers and companies to make informed choices about their purchases.

Finance for the circular economy

Circular economy commercial models have financial implications for providers, especially for cash flow. Financial support may be useful, especially to help transition from product sales to product-as-a-service. Rental and performance-based services provide regular income over a longer period, but mean an initial downturn in cash flow for established companies. New companies may need higher levels of 'pre-financing' (capital) to set up and become stable. There may be new legal issues about product ownership, collateral and so on.

DLL Group, a subsidiary of Rabobank Group, describes itself as a financial partner delivering 'original, integrated financial solutions to support the asset life-cycle from leasing, vendor and commercial finance to remarketing'.[41] ING Bank highlights the scope for banks to work with their clients, looking at how to build circular business models that include clear incentives for the end-user as well as the provider.[42] It suggests rethinking business cases around value captured from extending product life (instead of the common practice of writing assets down to zero over a nominal period), and collaborating with equity providers and crowdfunding platforms to provide more flexible financing. It suggests that banks can act as a 'launching customer' by adopting circular sourcing and procurement practices to stimulate demand for IT, office buildings and furniture, energy and so on.

Policy, legislation and product stewardship

Governments are becoming more aware of adverse impacts and costs created by our systems of production, use and end-of-use. These impacts, or 'externalities', are directly linked to the product or process but are not included in the scope of responsibility for the producer or user. Well-publicized examples include the impact of sugar on obesity, heart disease, diabetes and tooth decay; the impact of *greenhouse gas (GHG)* emissions on climate change; particulates from diesel on air quality and lung and heart disease; and lots more.

Governments have options for preventing the impact or recovering costs to deal with the problem. The UK think-tank Chatham House suggests several approaches for 'smart regulations':[43]

- fiscal measures, taxes and incentives to price in the externalities associated with resource use, waste and pollution and encourage owners to put materials and assets back into circulation;
- end-of-life regulations, such as those in the EU, Japan and South Korea, aiming to improve rates of remanufacturing and reuse;
- 'top runner' standards, setting minimum performance standards that tighten over time. These encourage innovation and remove inefficient or problematic goods from the market;
- public procurement standards for public sector agencies and government departments. This can help create or expand markets for more sustainable goods;
- public support for innovation, setting policies to encourage private sector investment;
- addressing legal frameworks, to review the legal implications of collaborative and cooperative initiatives, including antitrust frameworks and data protection.

'Product stewardship' and 'extended producer responsibility' both aim to encourage producers to take responsibility for the entire life-cycle of the product, from production, through use, and at end-of-use.

- **Extended producer responsibility (EPR)** is a mandatory requirement for the manufacturer to be responsible for its product, including packaging and end-of-use management.
- **Product stewardship** can be either voluntary or required by law, and involves the manufacturer plus a wider group of stakeholders, including suppliers, retailers and consumers.

Examples in the EU include the Waste Electrical and Electronic Equipment (WEEE) Directive, the End of Life Vehicle Directive (ELV), and the Packaging Waste Directive. Japan, mindful of scarce natural resources, implemented

FIGURE 4.3   Accelerating the circular economy – seed, support, share, set direction

Approach	Examples			
Communication, research, knowledge-share	Circle Scan: Amsterdam, Bilbao, Brussels, Glasgow[1]	Resource Solutions Network (RISN), Phoenix, USA[2]	Circular Procurement Guide, MVO Netherlands	C40 Cities Initiative
Collaboration	Circular Peterborough Commitment[1]	ReCirc Singapore[2]	UrbanWINS waste management, EU (8 cities)[2]	FORCE valuechain partnerships, EU (4 cities)[2]
Procurement & policy	Green Demolition bylaw, Vancouver[1]	Circular Contracting, Apeldoorn, NL[1,2]	Western Cape Industrial Symbiosis Program WISP[2]	LWARB CE Route Map, London[2]
Platform/resource exchange	Share Peterborough[1]	Austin, USA[2]	Gothenburg & Eskilstuna, Sweden[1]	ReUse Center, Ann Arbor, USA
Funds & incubators	Green & Digital Demo Program, Vancouver[1]	[Re]Verse Pitch Competition, Austin, USA[1]	Meermaker Fund, Haarlemmermeer, NL[1]	LWARB, London[2] Paris & Co, France[2]
Innovation & market development	Park 20|20 Haarlemmermeer, NL	Circular Buiksloterdam, Amsterdam[1]	Biogas from organic waste, Oslo[1]	Cambie Street Bridge Heat Recovery, Vancouver[1]
	Derelict buildings as resources, Lolland, NL[2]	Upcycled brick modules Resource Rows, Copenhagen[2]	Rainwater harvesting, Resource Rows, Copenhagen[2]	ReTuna, Eskilstuna, Sweden[2]
Hubs, campus, facilities	RDM Campus, Rotterdam[2]	Blue City, Rotterdam	Baltimore Community Toolbank, USA[1]	

1. Lindner et al (2017) *Circular Economy in Cities around the World*
2. WEF & PwC (2018) *White Paper Circular Economy in Cities*

the Law for the Promotion of Efficient Utilization of Resources, aiming to minimize producer and consumer waste. Every buyer of a new vehicle pays a recycling charge at the time of purchase, and this money is retained until the vehicle is disposed of at end-of-life. Impressive results include only 5 per cent of waste going to landfill, 98 per cent of metals recycled and 89 per cent of materials recovered from WEEE.[44] Recovered materials are generally inputs for manufacturing the same kind of products, closing the loop, and helping to buffer the technology sector against raw material costs.

Policies should also aim to avoid increasing consumption, for example with the 'rebound effect' if something becomes more affordable through circular approaches (see criticisms of the circular economy in Chapter 3).

Cities around the world are supporting circular economy initiatives, perhaps offering funds or helping join providers and users together. Reviewing a number of initiatives and reports in 2019, I found examples of cities helping to seed startups, support initiatives, share knowledge and set the direction for the circular economy – see Figure 4.3. I grouped the examples into these categories:

- **communication, research, knowledge-share** – raise awareness, help generate ideas, fledge startups from research projects, provide research for business or community projects;

- **collaboration** – create opportunities for business or communities; work with other cities to share knowledge, scale successful initiatives, share best practice;

- **procurement and policy** – create market opportunities through circular procurement in local government, support take-up through incentives and stewardship policies, lobby for national policy support;

- **platform/resource exchange** – encourage 'waste = food' and industrial symbiosis, support new circular systems, eg reuse, repair, remake, recycle;

- **funds and incubators** – support innovative new business and community initiatives;

- **innovation and market development** – direct involvement and support of circular projects, raise awareness and showcase benefits, accelerate take-up, help scaling-up to achieve 'minimum viable market';

- **hubs, campus, facilities** – support fledgling businesses and entrepreneurs, knowledge-sharing, communicate the city's innovation support and as a 'good place to invest'.

Summary

Organizations are gaining from collaborative approaches, either vertically with suppliers and customers, or horizontally with competitors or industry peer groups. Companies are investing in information about their materials and sources of supply, aiming to de-risk and inform future product designs. Legislative approaches are coming into focus as governments and NGOs become aware of the increasing costs and adverse impacts of 'externalities'. All this affects supply chains, changing sourcing and procurement, focusing on control of products in use and at end-of-use, or collaborating to share knowledge and facilities with partners worldwide.

Organizations are deploying a wide range of internal 'enablers' to develop their circular economy business models, products and services. These include ways to think differently, such as systems thinking, biomimicry and green chemistry, plus technologies ranging from 3DP, through 'big data' to the IoT. 3DP can revolutionize product design, material choice, the manufacturing process, reusability of the product, and can decentralize the supply chain, removing inventory and logistics links. The IoT can transform product longevity and reliability, reducing maintenance and breakdown costs and providing valuable information to both provider and user. Platforms and 'apps' provide real impetus to the sharing and renting models, with scope to gain vast improvements in resource-efficiency and shift consumer preferences from ownership to access. These enablers are not limited to circular economy initiatives and can transform the effectiveness of both the business and its supply chain.

Technology and digital innovations offer enormous potential to support the circular economy. The speed of change is accelerating, though, and companies need to invest ahead of their disruptive competitors:

> We learned this from the consumer internet world: by the time it's obvious, it's too late. What that means is, now is the time to act. That you've got to realize we're in the first two minutes of a soccer match; by halftime it's too late.
>
> Bill Ruh, CEO of GE Digital, USA[45]

Further resources

Artificial Intelligence and the Circular Economy (2019) Ellen MacArthur Foundation and Google, 23 January [Online] www.ellenmacarthurfoundation.org/publications/artificial-intelligence-and-the-circular-economy (archived at https://perma.cc/365H-8VGD) [accessed 26 October 2019]

Ask Nature (from the Biomimicry Institute) asknature.org/ (archived at https://perma.cc/AVG3-WNTN) [accessed 29 October 2019]

Biomimicry Institute [Online] biomimicry.org/ (archived at https://perma.cc/C9T3-4SW6)

Ecodesign strategy wheel (Lifecycle Design Strategies) by TU Delft (1997) wikid.io.tudelft.nl/WikID/index.php/EcoDesign_strategy_wheel (archived at https://perma.cc/9YUT-8DEU) [accessed 8 November 2019]

European Commission Ecodesign portal (2019) ec.europa.eu/growth/industry/sustainability/ecodesign_en (archived at https://perma.cc/28ZV-CJ4C) [accessed 8 November 2019]

Intelligent Assets: Unlocking the circular economy potential (2016) Ellen MacArthur Foundation and World Economic Forum, 8 February [Online] www.ellenmacarthurfoundation.org/publications/intelligent-assets (archived at https://perma.cc/RJN5-VT5J) [accessed 26 October 2019]

International Standards Organization (2011) Environmental management systems – Guidelines for incorporating ecodesign, ISO 14006:2011. www.iso.org/standard/43241.html (archived at https://perma.cc/ZG5Q-LK6M) [accessed 8 November 2019]

Leyla Acaroglu on systems thinking – www.leylaacaroglu.com/writing-by-leyla//tools-for-systems-thinkers-the-6-fundamental-concepts-of-systems-thinking (archived at https://perma.cc/VXF5-SRZB) and www.disruptdesign.co/blog/the-3-main-systems-at-play-in-the-world-are (archived at https://perma.cc/2J6E-GF3U) [accessed 10 October 2019]

Meadows, DH, *Leverage Points: Places to Intervene in a System* donellameadows.org/archives/leverage-points-places-to-intervene-in-a-system/ (archived at https://perma.cc/6G3Q-QV8B) [accessed 19 November 2019]

Meadows, DH (2008) *Thinking in Systems: A Primer*, Sustainability Institute, UK

Sweeney, LB and Meadows, D (1995) *The Systems Thinking Playbook*, Chelsea Green Publishing

The Systems Thinker thesystemsthinker.com/ (archived at https://perma.cc/MDE6-9CM9) [accessed 19 November 2019]

World Economic Forum with Accenture (2016) Digital Transformation of Industries [Online] reports.weforum.org/digital-transformation-of-industries/wp-content/blogs.dir/94/mp/files/pages/files/digital-enterprise-narrative-final-january-2016.pdf (archived at https://perma.cc/7BZG-NXDX) [accessed 29 May 2016]

Notes

1 Boulding, KE (1978) *Ecodynamics: A new theory of societal evolution*, Sage Publications, Thousand Oaks, CA

2 Meadows, D (2008) *Thinking in Systems: A primer*, The Sustainability Institute, United States, pp 1–7

3 Sweeney, LB and Meadows, D (1995) *The Systems Thinking Playbook*, Chelsea Green Publishing, p 2. Included with the kind permission of Linda Booth Sweeney.

4 Graedel, TE and Allenby, BR (1995) *Industrial Ecology*, Prentice Hall College Division, New York

5 About Ecodesign (2019) Ecodesigncircle https://www.ecodesigncircle.eu/about-ecodesign (archived at https://perma.cc/3JH2-R62P) [accessed 30 September 2019]

6 Radjou, N and Prabhu, J (28 Nov 2014) [accessed 5 March 2016] 4 CEOs who are making frugal innovation work, *Harvard Business Review* [Online] hbr.org/2014/11/4-ceos-who-are-making-frugal-innovation-work (archived at https://perma.cc/FG8M-DEBF)

7 United States Environmental Protection Agency (2015) [accessed 3 March 2016] [Online] www.epa.gov/greenchemistry/basics-green-chemistry (archived at https://perma.cc/CEA2-LVH8)

8 The Mobile Economy 2018 (2018) GSM Association [Online] https://www.gsma.com/mobileeconomy/wp-content/uploads/2018/05/The-Mobile-Economy-2018.pdf (archived at https://perma.cc/W4KP-7773) [accessed 26 October 2019]

9 Picardo, E (2019) 10 of the world's top companies are American, *Investopedia* (30 May) [Online] https://www.investopedia.com/articles/active-trading/111115/why-all-worlds-top-10-companies-are-american.asp (archived at https://perma.cc/B3RZ-3CNY) [accessed 26 October 2019]

10 Ross, A, Author of *Industries of the Future*, interviewed in Start the Week, BBC Radio 4 [Online] www.bbc.co.uk/programmes/b0713zf1 (archived at https://perma.cc/QQ8K-2YPX) [accessed 22 February 2015]

11 Internet World Stats [Online] www.internetworldstats.com/emarketing.htm (archived at https://perma.cc/WXW9-PEKL) [accessed 1 March 2016]

12 Ruddick, G (2016) Arm's £14bn secret, *The Guardian*, 27 February, p 38

13 Wikipedia (2016) 3D printing, processes [Online] https://en.wikipedia.org/wiki/3D_printing (archived at https://perma.cc/6KXW-SNPD) [accessed 2 March 2016]

14 Garmulewicz, A (14 Aug 2015) 3D Printing and the Circular Economy [Online] [accessed 3 March 2016]. Website no longer available.

15 3D printing trends to watch for in 2019, *3D Innovations* (6 December 2018) https://3d-innovations.com/blog/3d-printing-trends-2019/ (archived at https://perma.cc/5WZH-4JD6) [accessed 27 October 2019]

16 Cohen, D, Sergeant, M, and Somers, K (Jan 2014) 3-D printing takes shape, *McKinsey Quarterly*, p 2 [Online] http://www.mckinsey.com/business-functions/operations/our-insights/3-d-printing-takes-shape (archived at https://perma.cc/Y34A-NERU) [accessed 15 August 2016]

17 Helsel, S (11 June 2013) New rapid stamping ground for Nike & Adidas, *Inside 3D Printing* [Online] inside3dprinting.com/new-rapid-stamping-ground-for-nike-adidas/ (archived at https://perma.cc/KZ8L-VCFH) [accessed 2 March 2016]

18 Nike News (24 February 2013) [Online] news.nike.com/news/nike-debuts-first-ever-football-cleat-built-using-3d-printing-technology (archived at https://perma.cc/VK3N-8ZDK) [accessed 2 March 2016]

19 RepRap [Online] reprap.org/wiki/RepRap (archived at https://perma.cc/MY64-EKRR) [accessed 2 March 2016]

20 David Bassetti (2019) Episode 8, Circular Economy Podcast (6 October 2019) https://www.rethinkglobal.info/episode-12-david-bassetti-of-3d-seed/ (archived at https://perma.cc/3SZK-VWRT)

21 Prosthetic limbs from plastic bottles, *Positive News*, **99**, Oct–Dec 2019, p 14 [Online] www.positive.news (archived at https://perma.cc/3WDA-CPYD)

22 Wadhwani, A (26 June 2015) [accessed 2 March 2016] How sustainable is 3D printing, *Triple Pundit* [Online] www.triplepundit.com/2015/06/sustainable-3d-printing/ (archived at https://perma.cc/5R6L-ERSU)

23 Garmulewicz, A, 3D Printed Materials and the Circular Economy, ThinkDIF Festival, Ellen MacArthur Foundation [Online] thinkdif.co/emf-stages/3d-printed-materials-and-the-circular-economy (archived at https://perma.cc/7VR9-NURG) [accessed 27 October 2014]

24 The Mobile Economy 2018, GSM Association [Online] https://www.gsma.com/mobileeconomy/wp-content/uploads/2018/05/The-Mobile-Economy-2018.pdf (archived at https://perma.cc/W4KP-7773) (archived at https://perma.cc/6AFA-VNR4) [accessed 27 October 2019]

25 Cogent3D (2015) iCropTrak, About Us [Online] www.icroptrak.com/about-us (archived at https://perma.cc/9ATB-PCMR) [accessed 13 March 2016]

26 Gunnarsson, F et al (2014) *The Internet of Things: Are organizations ready for a multi-trillion dollar prize?*, CapGemini Consulting [Online] www.capgemini.com/resources/internet-of-things (archived at https://perma.cc/QWG2-LY67) [accessed 15 August 2016]

27 Getting in the Loop podcast (2019) How artificial intelligence can help create a more circular economy with Johanna Reimers, Episode 014 [Online] https://intheloopgame.com/podcast/014/ (archived at https://perma.cc/HK98-D39C) [accessed 1 September 2019]

28 Reimers, J (2017) The world's first reverse vending machine for batteries is launched in Norway, *Refind Technologies*, Blog, 24 April [Online] https://www.refind.se/worlds-first-reverse-vending-machine-for-batteries (archived at https://perma.cc/X4QG-UU5S) [accessed 1 September 2019]

29 World Economic Forum with Accenture (2016) Digital Transformation of Industries [Online] reports.weforum.org/digital-transformation-of-industries/wp-content/blogs.dir/94/mp/files/pages/files/digital-enterprise-narrative-final-january-2016.pdf (archived at https://perma.cc/7BZG-NXDX) [accessed 29 May 2016]

30 The Definition of Big Data, Oracle [Online] https://www.oracle.com/big-data/guide/what-is-big-data.html (archived at https://perma.cc/3MVK-J93U) [accessed 28 October 2019]

31 Hooper, M (2018) Top five blockchain benefits transforming your industry, *Blockchain Development*, IBM, 22 February [Online] https://www.ibm.com/blogs/blockchain/2018/02/top-five-blockchain-benefits-transforming-your-industry (archived at https://perma.cc/DJ5H-WWB5) [accessed 26 October 2019]

32 Bossman, J (2016) Top 9 ethical issues in artificial intelligence, *Global Agenda*, World Economic Forum (21 Oct) [Online] https://www.weforum.org/agenda/2016/10/top-10-ethical-issues-in-artificial-intelligence/ [accessed 28 October 2019]

33 Kennedy, S (2019) Researchers turn algae into a material as hard as steel, *Yale Climate Connections* (15 October) [Online] https://www.yaleclimateconnections.org/2019/10/researchers-turn-algae-into-a-material-as-hard-as-steel/ (archived at https://perma.cc/EXN8-RE4P) [accessed 22 October 2019]

34 International Energy Agency (2016) [Online] www.iea-bioenergy.task42-biorefineries.com/en/ieabiorefinery/Activities-1.htm (archived at https://perma.cc/8ZXN-GDL2) [accessed 7 March 2016]

35 Smithers, R (2019) Scaling back: graduate invents plastic alternative from fish waste, *The Guardian* (19 September) [Online] https://www.theguardian.com/world/2019/sep/19/scaling-back-graduate-invents-plastic-alternative-from-fish-waste (archived at https://perma.cc/7DZ7-JFGD) [accessed 25 September 2019]

36 Lavery, G et al (2013) *The Next Manufacturing Revolution: Non-labour resource productivity and its potential for UK manufacturing*, p 125 [Online] https://www.ifm.eng.cam.ac.uk/uploads/Resources/Next-Manufacturing-Revolution-full-report.pdf (archived at https://perma.cc/2AXN-62U7) [accessed 15 August 2016]

37 Bioplastic Feedstock Alliance (2016) [Online] bioplasticfeedstockalliance.org/who-we-are/ [accessed 25 March 2016]

38 United States Environmental Protection Agency (2006) *Lifecycle Assessment Principles and Practices Glossary* [Online] www.epa.gov/sustainability/glossary-sustainable-manufacturing-terms (archived at https://perma.cc/62AZ-XJN2) [accessed 29 May 2006]

39 Scotch Whisky Association (2008) [Online] www.scotch-whisky.org.uk/
media/12908/lifecycleassessment.pdf (archived at https://perma.cc/3SX2-
E5NA) [accessed 5 March 2016]

40 Gandy, S and Hinton, S (2018) Whisky by-products in renewable energy,
ClimateXchange, February [Online] https://www.climatexchange.org.uk/
research/projects/whisky-by-products-in-renewable-energy/ (archived at
https://perma.cc/2VJX-W3P5) [accessed 28 October 2019]

41 DLL Group (2016) [Online] www.dllgroup.com/gb/en-gb/about-us (archived
at https://perma.cc/MD35-T8S6) [accessed 29 May 2016]

42 ING Economics Department (May 2015) *Rethinking Finance in a Circular
Economy*, pp 5–8 [Online] www.ing.com/web/file?uuid=94261282-eed1-40b4-
9d98-b333009aeca0&owner=b03bc017-e0db-4b5d-abbf-
003b12934429&contentid=34276 (archived at https://perma.cc/
N2U5-YNWU) [accessed 15 August 2016]

43 Preston, F (2012) *A Global Redesign? Shaping the circular economy*, Chatham
House, UK [Online] www.chathamhouse.org/sites/files/chathamhouse/public/
Research/Energy,%20Environment%20and%20Development/bp0312_
preston.pdf (archived at https://perma.cc/FDZ3-G7HA) [accessed 15 August
2016]

44 World Economic Forum (2014) *Towards the Circular Economy: Accelerating
the scale-up across global supply chains*, p 26 [Online] www.weforum.org/
global-challenges/projects/circular-economy/ (archived at https://perma.cc/
4EDG-LV6V) [accessed 28 February 2016]

45 World Economic Forum with Accenture (2016) *Digital Transformation of
Industries*, p 14 [Online] reports.weforum.org/digital-transformation-of-
industries/wp-content/blogs.dir/94/mp/files/pages/files/digital-enterprise-
narrative-final-january-2016.pdf (archived at https://perma.cc/7BZG-NXDX)
[accessed 29 May 2016]

PART TWO

How are businesses adopting circular economy models?

5

Drivers for change

Anyone who believes exponential growth can go on forever in a finite world is either a madman or an economist.
KENNETH BOULDING, ECONOMIST, SYSTEMS SCIENTIST AND PHILOSOPHER, ADDRESSING THE US CONGRESS (1973)[1]

Startups, small businesses, social enterprises and major global corporates are seeing opportunities from circular approaches: rethinking products, processes and business models. Here, we look at the factors driving this, with:

- a quick overview of our **industrial economy**, including world trade and population growth, leading to:
- wide-ranging developments transforming agriculture and industry, plus a global stocktake of technical, energy, water and biological resources, and issues of demand exceeding supply;
- a '**great acceleration**' of human impact on the earth, leading scientists to conclude we have entered a new geological era, the **Anthropocene**;
- **risk and uncertainty**;
- **global trends and drivers**;
- and finally, how the circular economy helps us find **opportunities from these challenges.**

Our industrial economy

The first industrial revolution began in Britain in the 1700s, centred on textiles, iron and coal, together with water transport. Next came steam power and later the internal combustion engine and electrical power. In the

FIGURE 5.1   World trade growth

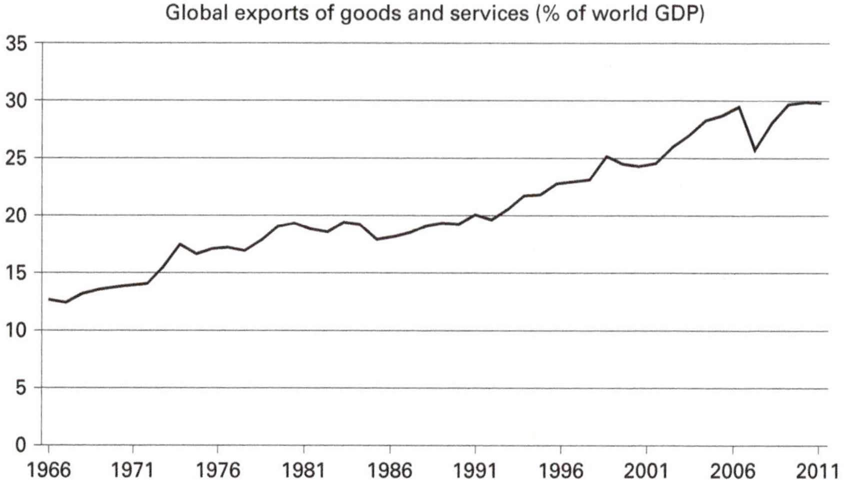

Global exports of goods and services (% of world GDP)

SOURCE: World Bank national accounts data, and OECD national accounts data files

late 1800s, the telegraph provided the first means of rapid overseas communications.

The first major impacts from **world trade**, in the 1600s, came with exchanges of plants, animals and diseases between Europe and the United States. Inter-trading between nations grew steadily, from 8 per cent in 1913 to over 12 per cent by 1966. In the mid-1990s, the World Trade Organization (WTO) was formed, and supported trade negotiations. Global trading expanded, and companies switched production to regions where the labour cost was low. Business focused on labour productivity, not resource productivity. Global trade continued to increase, with a dip after the 2008–09 global financial crash, as shown in Figure 5.1. By 2013, the World Bank estimates show it had reached almost 30 per cent of global GDP.

The agricultural '**green revolution**' began after the Second World War; and since the 1960s there has been a near doubling of crop yields, with vastly decreased labour inputs and reduced costs. This growth in productivity came from developing new crop varieties, combined with a fourfold increase in fertilizer use, a doubling of land under irrigation and a massive increase in pesticide use.[2] Modern industrialized, chemical-based agriculture requires substantial amounts of fossil energy to power farm machinery and produce fertilizers and pesticides.[3] In 1940, 2.3 calories (kcal) of fossil fuel could provide one calorie of food, whereas nowadays it needs as much as 10 kcal of fuel to put 1 kcal on our plates – a quadrupling of energy inputs. The

FIGURE 5.2   A growing population

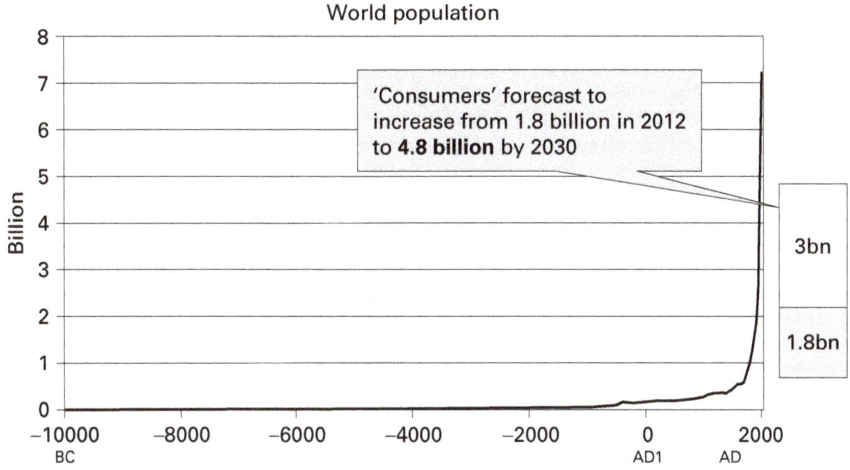

World population

'Consumers' forecast to increase from 1.8 billion in 2012 to **4.8 billion** by 2030

3bn

1.8bn

SOURCE: US Census International[4]

Food and Agriculture Organization (FAO) estimates that unsustainable land management practices mean that one-third of all soils worldwide are degraded.[5]

Human population has grown exponentially. Figure 5.2 shows the trend: from about 4 million people about 12,000 years ago when we began to evolve from hunter-gatherers to farmers, increasing to 3 billion by 1960. It then took only 40 years to double, reaching 6 billion in the year 2000. Despite falling fertility, the UN predicts a global population of 9.7 billion people by 2050, more than trebling in less than a century. More than half the global population lives in urban areas, and the UN expects this to increase to two-thirds by 2050.[6] The UN report looks at the increase in 'mega-cities', with at least 10 million inhabitants. In 1990, there were 10 mega-cities worldwide, increasing to 28 by 2014 and projected to increase to 41 by 2030. This puts further pressure on land use and requires construction of new homes and infrastructure, including water and sewage pipelines, railways and roads, and provision of energy and other services.

Adding further pressure, over the next 20 years, 3 billion people will move from 'subsistence' to 'consumers', as their income increases to over US$5,000 per year – all aspiring to the living standards of people in developed economies – more meat, processed food, more consumer goods. The vast majority of these new consumers are in Asia-Pacific regions, so countries like China are concerned to secure key food resources for their increasingly affluent population.

Climate change

In October 2018, the IPCC (Intergovernmental Panel on Climate Change) warned that 'we are already seeing the consequences of 1°C of global warming through more extreme weather, rising sea levels and diminishing Arctic sea ice, among other changes.'[7] The Paris Agreement adopted by 195 nations at the COP21, in December 2015, included the aim of strengthening the global response to the threat of climate change by 'holding the increase in the global average temperature to well below 2°C above pre-industrial levels and pursuing efforts to limit the temperature increase to 1.5°C above pre-industrial levels.' The report points out that 'limiting global warming to 1.5°C compared with 2°C would reduce challenging impacts on ecosystems, human health and well-being, making it easier to achieve the United Nations Sustainable Development Goals'. However, limiting global warming to 1.5°C would require 'rapid and far-reaching' transitions in land, energy, industry, buildings, transport, and cities. Global net human-caused emissions of carbon dioxide (CO_2) would need to fall by about 45 per cent from 2010 levels by 2030, reaching 'net zero' around 2050.

Ecological footprint

It is easy to forget that the earth provides everything we need to survive and prosper. We take our 'technical resources' (metals, minerals, oil, etc) from the earth's crust and grow 'biological materials' (food, fibres, timber, etc) with nature's help. We depend on nature for our fresh air, clean water and healthy soil, and the complex living systems that 'clean up' after us. So if we assess the stocks of these, how do they match up to current (and future) demand?

The WWF Living Planet Report (2018)[8] warns that our ecological footprint – a measure of human consumption of natural resources – has increased by about 190 per cent over the last 50 years. Threats to nature and living systems include habitat loss and degradation, overexploitation, climate change, pollution and invasive species. Population sizes of vertebrate species have declined by 60 per cent between 1970 and 2014, and freshwater species have declined dramatically. Marine and freshwater ecosystems face 'huge pressures', and since 1950, almost 6 billion tonnes of fish and invertebrates have been taken from the earth's oceans. Plastic pollution has been detected in all major marine environments around the world.

If the whole world lived as we do in the EU, we would need four planets. A country can exceed its biocapacity: by harvesting natural resources faster than they can regenerate, drawing on resources that have accumulated over time, or by importing products (using the biocapacity of other nations). It can use the 'global commons', releasing carbon emissions into the global atmosphere. We come back to this later in the chapter, with Earth Overshoot Day. Clearly, not all countries can exceed their capacity!

Resources: technical

Resource extraction increased twelvefold between 1900 and 2015, as global material use grew from 26.7 billion tonnes in 1970 to 90 billion in 2017, almost tripling in less than four decades. The International Resource Panel predicts it will double again by 2050, reaching 170–184 billion tonnes.[9]

Mining metals, minerals, oil and gas is becoming more expensive, and geopolitics is an increasing concern; the EU lists 20 metals and minerals as critical in terms of security of supply. China supplies around 95 per cent of the *rare earth elements* and restricts their exports. Renewable energy technologies, batteries, fibre-optics and high-tech products include rare earth elements. The British Geological Institute publishes a 'supply risk index', ranking elements according to reserves, cost or difficulty of extraction, and geopolitical risks.[10] China is the main source for 12 of the top 15 by level of risk, which includes platinum, used in electrodes and catalytic converters, strontium used in optics, and thorium, considered a potentially safer nuclear fuel.

Modern industry also uses a massive number of 'novel compounds': new compounds, containing elements that either cannot be separated at the end of the product's life or require intensive energy input to enable separation and recycling. There are 30,000–70,000 chemicals in everyday use, most of which are not tested for their effects on health.

Resources: energy

The 'peak oil' concept – that the rate of new discoveries each year is now declining – was topical around 2010, with many analysts believing we had reached or passed the peak. Annual discoveries of oil worldwide reached a peak in 1964, and since 1981, the world has consumed more oil each year than it has discovered. By around 2007, the world was using around four barrels of oil for every single new barrel discovered.[11]

'Net energy' is the relationship between energy expended to extract and process a fuel, and the resulting energy available for use. Fossil fuels are becoming increasingly difficult to extract and refine; we have found and used all the easy stuff, so less **net** energy is inevitable. Both nuclear energy and renewables require energy to set up, and in the case of nuclear, to deal with waste. Worldwide, there is growing pressure to speed up a switch to renewable energy and leave fossil fuels 'in the ground'. Research by the Carbon Tracker Initiative in 2013 shows that to reduce the risk of carbon emissions tipping us into the dangerous scenario of more than 2 degrees centigrade of global warming, we can burn less than one-third of known fossil fuel reserves.[12] We need a zero-carbon approach to manufacturing and the supply chain.

Resources: water

Water appears on risk registers of governments, *non-government organizations (NGOs)* and companies worldwide. The average daily drinking requirement per person, worldwide, is 2–4 litres. However, to produce one person's daily food needs 2,000–4,000 litres. That seems incredibly high until we examine the water footprints for a Western diet, for example, 2,500 litres for a kilogram of rice, over 15,000 litres for a kilogram of beef, and even 170 litres for a pint of beer. On average, it takes 1 litre of water to produce each calorie we eat. Chapter 6 examines water footprints in more detail.

Global water usage has increased at more than double the rate of population growth in the last century, and goes on growing as demands from farming, industry and domestic usage all increase. Water scarcity is now a major issue. Water tables in parts of China, India, West Asia, the former Soviet Union and the United States are dropping. Many regions worldwide extract water for irrigation faster than rainfall can replenish it, including 60 per cent of the European cities with more than 100,000 people.

Resources: biological

Across the world, we have converted almost 30 per cent of forests, grasslands, wetlands and other vegetation types into agricultural land or urban areas.[13] This affects both water flows and biogeochemical cycling of carbon, nitrogen, phosphorus and other important elements, and is a driving force for major reductions in biodiversity.[14] **Forests** are vital for climate regulation. Although forest loss has slowed recently, 129 million hectares were lost between 1990 and 2015, as land is cleared for palm oil, soybeans (to feed humans, and animals for meat), and other cash crops.[15]

A special IPCC report, on climate change and land, 'shows that better land management can contribute to tackling climate change, but is not the only solution'.[16] Agriculture, forestry and other types of land use account for 23 per cent of human greenhouse gas emissions. At the same time, natural land processes absorb carbon dioxide equivalent to almost a third of carbon dioxide emissions from fossil fuels and industry. The report warns there are limits to how we can use land to address climate change, for instance through growing crops for energy and planting forests to draw down carbon. **Bioenergy** needs to be 'carefully managed to avoid risks to food security, biodiversity and land degradation'.

About 500 million people live in areas affected by **desertification**. These areas, together with drylands, are 'also more vulnerable to climate change and extreme events including drought, heatwaves, and dust storms, with an increasing global population providing further pressure'. The report points out that new understandings show 'an increase in risks from dryland water scarcity, fire damage, permafrost degradation and food system instability, even for global warming of around 1.5°C', and that at 2°C of global warming, 'very high risks related to permafrost degradation and food system instability are identified'.

Living systems feed us, protect us, heal us, clean our habitats and provide the air we breathe. Living systems are the 'income' derived from a healthy environment – our 'natural capital'. They provide us with clean air and water, climate stabilization, rainfall, productive oceans and freshwater, fertile soils, watersheds. They also process our waste – natural and industrial, from air, soil and water. Figure 5.3 highlights human impacts on the geosphere, biosphere and atmosphere. We are overloading nature with chemicals it either cannot deal with or cannot process at the rate we require. Human impact is degrading and destroying other species too. As we saw earlier, biodiversity is declining, and we are causing the sixth great species extinction, with vertebrates lost at a rate far higher than in previous mass extinctions.

Welcome to the Anthropocene

The Holocene epoch began approximately 10,000 years ago (about 8000 BC) with the end of the last glacial period. It includes the growth and impacts of humanity worldwide, including development of major civilizations, transition from hunter-gathering to farming and, close to the end of that era, the Industrial Age.

FIGURE 5.3   Supply chain impacts

Raw materials   Manufacture   Store   Sell   Use

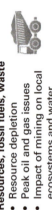

Returns

Deforestation and land use change
- CO_2 impact on climate regulation
- Ecosystem destruction
- Biodiversity loss

Soil
- Soil degradation requires oil and mineral inputs to replace nutrients
- Chemical residues including nitrogen and phosphorus
- Desertification in key growing areas eg California

Oceans and water
- Depletion of ground-water sources
- Pollution of freshwater
- Water scarcity issues
- Overfishing depletes marine species
- Acidification impacting on coral and marine habitat

Greenhouse gas emissions
- Climate disruption – droughts and floods, weather pattern change
- Emissions > ocean acidification
- Air quality impact on health

Resources, fossil fuels, waste
- Resource depletion
- Peak oil and gas issues
- Impact of mining on local ecosystems and water
- Waste versus food security

Scientists have analysed the earth's temperature back through time, using ice-core data covering the last 800 millennia, showing ice ages and periods warmer than today. Data for the last 100,000 years shows the Holocene as incredibly stable compared with all those previous peaks and troughs. It is the only period in known history with such incredible stability of temperature, thus providing perfect conditions for the exponential growth of human population: 'a safe operating space for humanity'.[17]

Leading scientists conclude that **human activity**, including our global economic system, '**is now the prime driver of change in the earth system** – the sum of our planet's interacting physical, chemical, biological and human processes'.[18] Analysis by the Stockholm Resilience Centre provides a range of 'planetary dashboard' indicators covering socioeconomic and earth system trends, charting human activity over the Industrial Age (from 1750 to 2010) together with subsequent changes in the earth system, including greenhouse gas levels, deforestation, biodiversity loss and ocean acidification.[19] Man-made materials, such as plastics and concrete, together with the fallout from nuclear weapons, are leaving a **geological footprint on the planet**. These indicators of humanity's impact are central to discussions proposing that we have entered a new epoch, the Anthropocene.

The 'great acceleration'

These 24 global indicators follow a similar trend to the increasing world population, all showing exponential growth (Figure 5.4 shows just a few of these). Some, including species extinction, loss of rainforest, and fishery exploitation, have become crises. The 'profound transformation of the earth's environment'[20] accelerated sharply during the second half of the 20th century, as economic activity increased by a factor of nearly 10 and the world's population became more interconnected, with global trade and information flows. This sharp increase is the '**great acceleration**'.

We manage nearly all of the earth's land and have domesticated half of the total land surface. Very little pristine coastline still exists, and most of the world's fisheries are overexploited or fully exploited. Greenhouse gases, reactive gases and aerosol particles have significantly changed the atmosphere over the last century. A sixth great extinction is under way, affecting all other forms of living species – and this is the first such event 'caused by another species – Homo Sapiens'.

> We have got our foot on the accelerator, driving towards the abyss.
> Ban Ki-moon, Secretary-General of the United Nations, speech to World
> Climate Conference in 2009[21]

FIGURE 5.4   The great acceleration

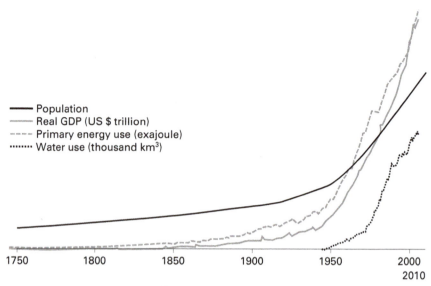

SOURCE: Stockholm Resilience Centre[22]

Planetary boundaries

In 2009, a group of leading earth system scientists worked together at the Stockholm Resilience Centre to develop the concept of planetary boundaries. They identified nine natural processes, including the freshwater cycle, climate regulation and the nitrogen cycle, all critical for keeping the planet in the stable state we need. Under too much pressure from human activity, any one of these processes could be pushed into abrupt and potentially irreversible change. To avoid that, the scientists proposed a set of boundaries below each of their danger zones (such as a limit of 350 parts per million of carbon dioxide in the atmosphere to prevent dangerous climate change) – with the area within the boundaries defined as 'a safe operating space for humanity'.

An updated report (2015) finds that 'four of nine planetary boundaries have now been crossed as a result of human activity: [...] **climate change, loss of biosphere integrity, land-system change, altered biogeochemical cycles (phosphorus and nitrogen)**'.[23] Two of the boundaries – climate change and biosphere integrity – are defined as 'core boundaries', and 'significantly altering either of these core boundaries would drive the earth system into a new state'.

Demand exceeding supply

Food, water and energy are dependent on biodiversity and ecosystems; and are core to our survival. We have issues of poverty and inequality to over-come. Figures from 2015 show that almost 1 billion people suffer from hunger; nearly 800 million people (over 10 per cent of the global popula-tion) are living without a clean water supply; 1.4 billion people lack access to a reliable electricity supply; 2.7 billion rely on traditional sources of bio-energy such as wood for their heating and cooking.

Each year, Earth Overshoot Day is calculated by the Global Footprint Network.[24] It marks the date on which we have used up all the regenerative resources for that year. In 2019, it was 29 July – so the next day, 30 July, we started to consume more ecological resources and services than our planet can regenerate in a year. We maintain the deficit by 'liquidating stocks of ecological resources and accumulating waste, primarily carbon dioxide in the atmosphere'. Each year, Earth Overshoot Day occurs earlier in the year, and there are calculations for the overshoot date if the whole world lived like a particular country. For 2019, the worst scenario would be if we all lived like the people of Qatar (11 February), Luxembourg (16 February) or the United Arab Emirates (8 March). The best-performing countries are Iraq (7 December), Ecuador (14 December) and Indonesia (18 December). Even the best-performing countries still use up all their ecological resources and services before the end of the year.

Unrelenting pressure on **natural resources** (including land and water), driven by supply and demand imbalances, mean we have reached a tipping point. Environmental reports and risk indices, generally upward price trends (whether driven by real costs or speculation and hedging) and volatility of prices, all underline this. Those reliant on materials, energy and water are concerned about input costs, and security of access to those critical re-sources. Aiming to grow by selling more requires new thinking, focusing more on how to use resources more effectively, and recover those resources for future reuse.

Structural waste

Companies and governments are becoming more aware of 'structural waste', a term for poor asset utilization. Often, this structural waste has existed for decades, but competition and drives for more sustainable outcomes are put-ting it in the spotlight. In addition, new technologies mean that we can make radical improvements.

Structural waste examples include transport (mentioned earlier), with cars typically parked up for 23 hours in every day and the woeful inefficiency of the internal combustion engine – only around 1 per cent of the fuel is used to move the people in the car! In the food system, about one-third of all food produced is lost or wasted in the supply chain or by consumers; and up to 70 per cent of fertilizer applied to fields not taken up by the crops.[25] Cities could realize benefits from reducing structural waste, such as ride-sharing or provision of free bicycles to improve the capacity of roads and public transport and reduce pollution. However, there is also the risk of the **rebound effect** undermining these benefits – if 'ride-sharing' (eg Uber) is cheap, people may choose to use that instead of public transport.

Forward-thinking organizations are developing strategies to help de-risk their operating models, improve access to markets, eliminate structural waste to improve their competitive edge, and develop business 'ecosystems' to build a network of partnerships and resources supporting agile, resilient value chains for future prosperity.

Cost volatility and long-term trends

The MGI Commodity Price Index shows prices, in real terms (so without inflation), for a basket of commodities.[26] McKinsey points out that a century of price declines, as we became efficient at mining and farming, was reversed in just a decade. The turning point happened after the global financial crisis in 2008, and since then, volatility of prices has become a major concern for many governments and companies. Security of supply is also a worry – if resources are not available locally, will you be able to access them? Organizations in China and the United States are already buying land where key resources are located.

Externalities

Among the many undesirable side effects of our linear, capitalist economy, there are *externalities*: companies send pollutants from the manufacturing process – such as effluent, emissions or solid wastes – into local water basins, soils or the atmosphere. Often, *ecosystems* have to clean up these pollutants: living systems such as plants, trees and other living organisms. Man-made materials, or 'novel' compounds, can be difficult for nature to process: taking decades or even centuries to break down, and with a risk that chemicals and toxins may destroy those living systems in the process. The costs of these externalities tend to be obscured and may end up being paid for by consumers, other businesses and taxpayers – household sewage

FIGURE 5.5   Global resource extraction and sources

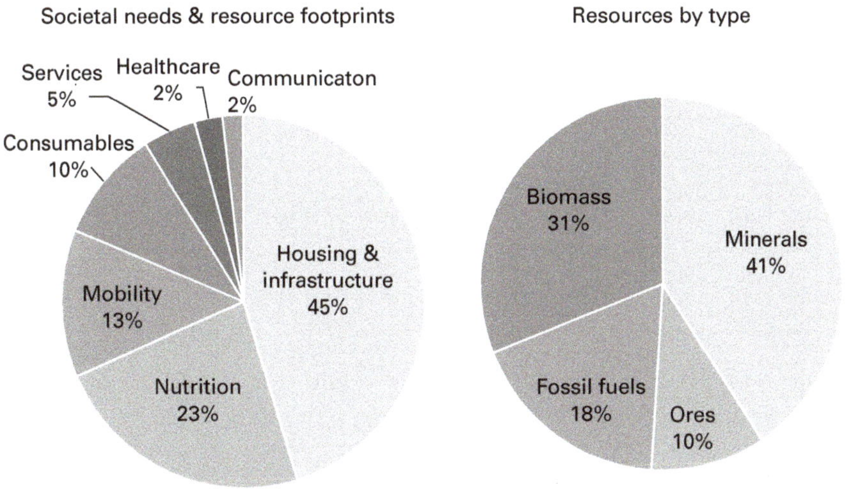

Societal needs & resource footprints

Resources by type

Services 5% — Healthcare 2% — Communicaton 2%
Consumables 10%
Housing & infrastructure 45%
Mobility 13%
Nutrition 23%

Biomass 31%
Minerals 41%
Fossil fuels 18%
Ores 10%

Resources in Gigatonnes (billion tonnes) for 2015 – total 92.6 G tonnes.
SOURCE: Circle Economy, *Circularity Gap Report* (2018)

costs, healthcare costs, insurance for flood risks and so on. Governments are beginning to use legislation and taxation to recover costs and force businesses to clean up industrial processes.

Our balanced scorecard

Our industrial, linear economy – take, make and discard – is now undermining resource availability and security. Circle Economy's Circularity Gap Report (2018)[27] highlights that the linear economy, with its 'toxic cocktail of negative consequences', has created a 'resource-constrained world with high-impact megatrends of rapid population growth and widespread urbanization'. From the Industrial Revolution of the 1700s, humans have become a 'geological force', leading to human-caused climate change and mass extinction of species. Burning fossil fuels, deforestation, industrial agriculture, pollution of soil, water, air and the earth's atmosphere, together with a still-growing population, expanding urbanization and increasing consumption of products and services has led us to a crisis point.

The report calculates that global resource flows are only 9.1 per cent circular, with just 8.4 billion tonnes of materials cycled each year as part of the 92.8 billion tonnes entering the global economy. Figure 5.5 shows the global material footprints of the six key societal needs from the Circularity Gap Report, satisfied by four resource groups (minerals, metal ores, fossil fuels and biomass).[28]

Building on the supply chain impacts shown earlier in Figure 5.4, we could use a balanced scorecard approach to measure our impact. In Chapter 1, we looked briefly at the Natural Step, a global non-profit network aiming to accelerate the transition to a sustainable society. The Natural Step approach describes four 'system conditions' for a sustainable society, in which nature is not subject to systematically increasing:[29]

- 'concentrations of substances from the earth's crust' (such as heavy metals and carbon from fossil fuels);
- 'concentrations of substances produced by society' (eg antibiotics, volatile organic compounds);
- 'degradation by physical means' (including land degradation, deforestation, desertification and draining of water sources).

The fourth condition relates to people: 'and in that society, there are no structural obstacles to people's health, influence, competence, impartiality and meaning'. Scoring our linear systems might result in a scorecard like the one shown in Figure 5.6.

Risk and uncertainty

Companies and governments are facing challenging, complex issues of risk and uncertainty. Resource 'security' – protecting your ability to access the resource – is becoming a key issue for governments and companies.

The World Economic Forum publishes a global risks report each year, and the 2018–19 report highlighted extreme weather events, failure of climate change mitigation and adaptation, and natural disasters as the three highest risks in terms of both likelihood and impact.[30] The report splits the risks into five categories, but many of them impact more than one category, as I show in Figure 5.7.

Governments are moving to protect their citizens against some of these risks by legislating or prosecuting for pollution and emissions, taxing the use of water, banning toxic pesticides or restricting exports of key commodities. Some organizations, such as the Organization of the Petroleum Exporting Countries (OPEC), aim to restrict the supply of critical resources in order to protect their future profits.

These risks, combined with the trends highlighted earlier, create high levels of uncertainty for organizations. Can we secure the resources we need, at a cost that enables us to operate profitably? Are our suppliers, partners

FIGURE 5.6   Natural Step system conditions – scorecard

Natural Step criteria	Supply chain stage				
	Raw materials	Manufacture	Logistics and sales	Use	End-of-life
Scarce materials taken from the earth	⬇	⬊	⬇	⬊	⬆
Man-made toxic and persistent chemicals	⬊	⬇	⬊	⬈	⬈
Destruction and pollution of nature	⬈	⬇	⬊	⬈	⬈
Work and/or use conditions	⬊	⬊	⬈	⬈	⬊

Key:	Good	Quite good	Quite bad	Bad	Don't know
	Positive impacts, no concerns	Positive or neutral impacts, few concerns	Negative or neutral impacts, many concerns	Negative impacts, widespread /major concerns	Not enough information
	⬆	⬈	⬊	⬇	?

SOURCE: Adapted from Streamlined Life Cycle Assessment (based on Natural Step System Conditions), Sustainable Wealth Creation, 2007, with kind permission of Forum for the Future

and markets likely to face disruptions from war, trade conflicts, extreme weather events or financial problems? What about trade tariffs and geopolitical risks? How can we future-proof our business by reducing our exposure to these risks?

Looking at those risks from the World Economic Forum reminds us that natural disasters, drought, flood and, more recently, cyber-crime, can disrupt supply chains for several months. In Chapter 2, we mentioned the European Commission's list of Critical Raw Materials (CRMs): raw materials assessed as having a high supply risk and significant economic importance for European industry and value chains. By 2017, the list included 27 raw materials.

FIGURE 5.7   Global risks

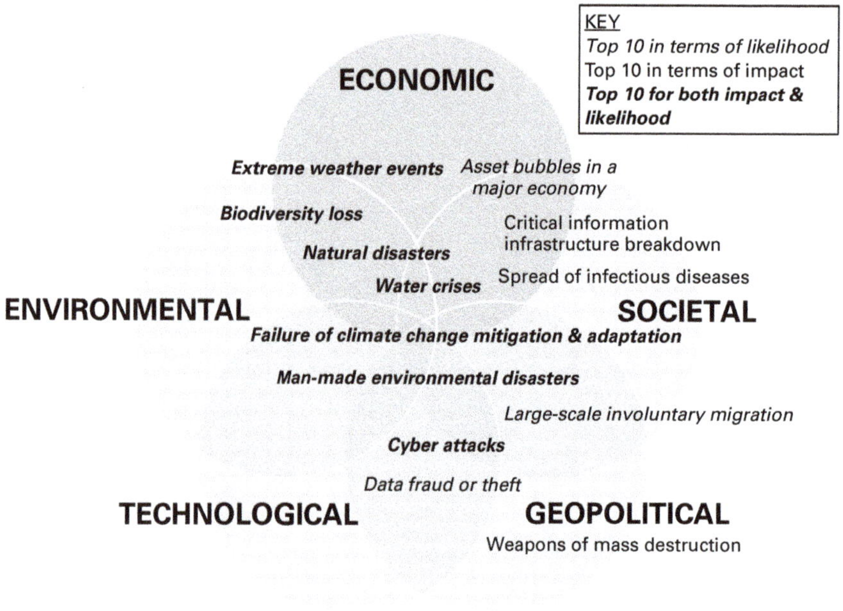

KEY
Top 10 in terms of likelihood
Top 10 in terms of impact
Top 10 for both impact & likelihood

ECONOMIC

Extreme weather events   *Asset bubbles in a major economy*

Biodiversity loss   Critical information infrastructure breakdown

Natural disasters

Water crises   Spread of infectious diseases

ENVIRONMENTAL   **SOCIETAL**

Failure of climate change mitigation & adaptation

Man-made environmental disasters

Large-scale involuntary migration

Cyber attacks

Data fraud or theft

TECHNOLOGICAL   **GEOPOLITICAL**

Weapons of mass destruction

SOURCE: Adapted from World Economic Forum Global Risks Report 2019

Linear risk

Authors from Circle Economy and other consultancies, in an essay on linear risks (2018),[31] explain that traditionally, *externalities* are largely absent from corporate risk profiles and financial statements. Companies are not rewarded for positive impacts like job creation, provision of education and healthcare for staff, or for environmental improvements. However, nor are companies penalized for 'negative societal impacts – like generating or incinerating waste, depletion of scarce resources, noise and air pollution, or degrading ecosystems'.

The authors note a growing trend for companies to internalize externalities, driven by factors ranging from increased regulations and shareholder actions to market dynamics that are disrupting historic patterns of supply and demand. They highlight four 'linear business practices', with business strategies that:

- use non-renewable resources;
- focus on selling new products with short lifetimes;
- avoid collaboration and partnerships, instead, controlling knowledge;
- lack innovation or adaptation to evolving market conditions.

The essay includes a linear risk matrix, mapping the four linear practices against risk factors from the Open Risk Manual: market and trade-related; operational; business including socio, economic and political factors; legal risks including regulations, standards, lawsuits, etc.

Reputational risk

The business context is changing too – organizations are recognizing that business exists as a sub-set of our living world, and of society – not the other way around! Brand value and the 'licence to operate' should depend on responsible approaches to the use of resources. Organizations are improving their approaches to procurement, processing, manufacturing and end-of-use for the product, ensuring that these 'do no harm' to communities and living systems. Brands are powerful and can drive sales growth. However, both consumers and NGOs are starting to expose ethical and environmental issues. Information travels fast, destroying trust and reputation almost overnight. The internet and social networks connect people with like-minded peers, with fast and easy access to information. Organized campaigns from NGOs and consumer groups publicize environmental or ethical concerns.

Issues related to 'conflict minerals' have emerged, along with legislation and guidelines. The Fairphone supply chain for gold (see Chapter 8) highlights the risks for land use, labour exploitation, criminality and pollution risks in the mining of precious metals.

Global trends and drivers

The structure of our society is changing. In the 18th century, we moved from rural to industrial societies, but in the 21st century, we are becoming a 'networked' society, able to connect with each other, around the world. Millions of us can share information and trade directly with people and businesses in other countries. We can be either consumers or *prosumers*.

Scientific advances are gaining a deeper understanding of nature's complex systems and how much we can learn from them. *Biomimicry, green chemistry* and earth systems science, coupled with discoveries of new materials and fantastic technology inventions, can transform the way we make, use and reuse things. Knowledge, new developments and frugal innovation can bring a new age of prosperity, enabling the Anthropocene to be a positive era.

As we have seen, companies and governments are facing increasingly complex external factors, affecting business success, supply chain resilience, consumer behaviour and economic or political conditions. In Chapter 13, we discuss the 'PESTLE' (political, economic, social, technological, legal and environmental) model as a way to review the external factors driving change.

Global demographics and power shifts

The continued rise of **urban populations,** with 50 per cent of the world population already living in urban areas (set to be over 60 per cent by 2030), increases the critical mass available for effective asset-sharing and recovery services. Asset-sharing models can access a larger group of potential customers, so are more likely to be able to gain publicity and take-up, avoiding the slow starts that may hamper entrepreneurial enterprises. Both forward and reverse logistics flows can be cheaper and faster in urban areas, with reduced distances and increased density of drops and collections.

There are **regional imbalances** in global population growth, with the developing economies (generally in the southern hemisphere) increasing faster than the industrialized economies in the north. As these emerging markets develop, both as producers and consumers, the sources, flows and stocks of financial wealth are shifting accordingly. These countries tend to have a higher proportion of younger people, all aspiring to have jobs and lifestyles just like the ones they see in the media.

Global **economic growth** has shifted to these emerging markets, and **political power** is shifting too. Many developed countries are heavily reliant on resources or trade from the emerging markets. It could be rare earth minerals from China, beef from Brazil, or gas from Russia, or it could be imported food and textiles from Africa – you may depend on the resource itself, or the low cost of sourcing from that region. Geopolitics and nationalism are creating trade tensions, with tariffs and restrictions causing concerns for governments and businesses.

This **competition for resources,** combined with increasing awareness of environmental and climate issues, is transforming the behaviour of companies and their customers. Values, attitudes, motivations and priorities all are changing, sometimes rapidly.

Inequality and social divisions are a concern in many countries. 'Rising income and wealth disparity' ranked fourth in respondents' list of underlying trends in the World Economic Forum's Global Risks Perception Survey in 2018.[32]

Technology advances

Economist Jeremy Rifkin points out that when new communication technologies converge with energy innovations, fundamental economic change occurs.[33]

Technology developments have lowered the barriers to entry for fast-moving companies, disrupting long-established business models and giving access to new markets and 'connected consumers'. Rapid switches to new technologies, such as electric vehicles with lithium batteries, can suddenly mean demand for a resource outstrips the available supply.

Digital and other technologies continue to advance rapidly, with innovations that even early in the 21st century seemed to belong to the realms of science fiction: Google glasses, smartphones, augmented reality, cloud computing and so on. Across many products, dissipation speed is increasing and product life-cycles are shortening. It took 75 years for the telephone to connect 50 million people, nearly 40 years for the first radios to reach 50 million users, 13 years for televisions, but only 4 years for the internet to reach that number.

Software, cloud storage, geo-mapping and mobile internet combine to enable high-functionality 'apps', linking people with nearby assets (for example, cars to rent) or spaces (such as car parking). We discussed these 'enablers' in Chapter 4.

Technology for new materials, such as graphene, and new biorefining processes helped by *green chemistry* and *biomimicry* design are all helping to create new possibilities for how we make, use and reuse things.

Consumer behaviour

Euromonitor notes that values are changing: 'conscious consumption has replaced conspicuous consumption and is at the heart of changing values and priorities. Gone are the days of ownership as a status symbol.'[34] For decades, advertising has encouraged ownership of ever more 'stuff', trying to establish dissatisfaction with what we have now in order to persuade us that we need a better, newer or extra product in our lives. Companies drive desire for a new product by creating the perception that it will improve our status – but that status is cheaper to attain if you rent the product, instead of buying it. You might rent luxury clothes; or a limousine for a big celebration. Walter Stahel suggests that ownership is only worthwhile if the asset appreciates. The psychology of ownership is changing.

Consumers, especially 'millennials', increasingly prefer **'access' over ownership**. This may be a temporary trend, fuelled by reduced earnings and lack of stable employment, but it is a helpful enabler for the circular economy. A survey by PwC found that 19 per cent of the adult population in the United States had 'engaged in a sharing economy transaction', with 72 per cent seeing themselves as a consumer in the sharing economy in the next two years.[35] Those most excited about the concept are middle-income households, those with children at home, or those aged 18–24. Asked about the value of ownership, 7 per cent agreed that 'access is the new ownership' and 43 per cent that ownership 'feels like a burden'.

Writing about the **sharing economy** for the World Economic Forum's Global Agenda in early 2019, April Rinne predicts that a growing middle class will drive the sharing economy in the near future.[36]

Looking back on the previous decade's 'explosive growth', she notes that in 2009 only a handful of 'sharing platforms' existed, including Zipcar, BlaBlaCar and Couchsurfing, with Airbnb and Uber launching around the same time. (We should note that Rinne includes 'pay as you go' services in her definition of the sharing economy, and highlights the risk of 'sharewashing' with companies using the term, even though there is no sharing involved.)

She sees sharing as having moved on from being a 'millennial preference' to a part of modern society, with 'access over ownership' made ever easier by digital and mobile technologies. However, we should also note that even those high-profile companies raising billions of dollars from their IPOs have yet to make a profit. There are other issues, with criticisms about their pricing strategies and reliance on the 'gig economy' for flexibility and low costs.

Rinne sees continuing challenges for policymakers, pointing out that no city has 'figured it out' or developed an integrated strategy for sharing – though in 2018 over 40 cities collaborated to publish 'a declaration of common principles and commitments for sharing cities'.[37]

Even with vast arrays of similar products to choose from, demand for bespoke or customizable products – **'mass customization'** – is making inroads into the mass production norm of the 20th century. Consumers are looking to personalize their products or choose elements from a menu of options. This is especially relevant for cars, computers, fitted kitchens and other 'status' products.

Consumers can also become *prosumers*, selling to each other or turning their hobby into earnings, all helped by the 'maker' movement and 'repair' cafés and clubs. You can now rent out spare rooms on Airbnb; become a trader on eBay; or be a freelance 'outworker', making products at home.

Knowledge and information are more accessible. The concept of intellectual property, and the ability to own (and earn money from) ideas and patents, is giving way to *open sourcing*.

Business-to-business (B2B) procurement is seeing increasing pressure for transparency and evidence of sustainable, ethical and responsible practices at every tier in the supply chain. Blockchain, big data and e-procurement systems are helping companies to have more visibility, more choice and more trust in their suppliers. We will look at this in more detail in Part Three.

Shareholders versus stakeholders

Society and governments are seeing the downsides of our capitalist, market economy with its emphasis on maximizing **shareholder value**. Criticisms – including focusing on short-term profits instead of long-term value, high levels of executive pay, slowing productivity – drive a growing distrust of big corporations.

The Future-Fit Foundation, a UK Charity developing free tools to help businesses become 'future-fit', reminds us that 'our global economy is failing society in three **critical ways**:

- Environment – we are disrupting and degrading Earth's natural processes and depleting the resources which humanity and all other life depends upon

- Society – the basic needs of billions of people around the world are not being met, while the gap between the haves and have-nots grows

- Business – business has the power to address these challenges, but today's markets are doing little to encourage, recognize and reward bold action.'[38]

It criticizes shareholder value for prioritizing financial returns above everything else, meaning 'companies privatize gains and externalize losses'. **Shared value**, a strategy developed by Mark Kramer and Michael Porter in 2011, is 'not social responsibility, philanthropy, or sustainability, but a new way for companies to achieve economic success'.[39] However, the Future-Fit Foundation argues that in shared value approaches, business still comes first, as 'negative impacts are not sufficiently internalized, or are justified by "doing good" elsewhere'. Instead, the Future-Fit Foundation advocates **system value**, in which business 'in no way hinders – and ideally contributes to – society's progress toward future-fitness'.

From challenges to opportunities

Circular economy strategies, as we will see throughout this book, offer a wide range of opportunities, with new services, new markets and benefits for society. Even recycling, our least preferred strategy, can significantly reduce greenhouse gas emissions. Circle Economy reports that, on average, the carbon footprint (CO_2e) of products produced from recycled resources is almost 1.4 tonnes lower per tonne of product, compared with those produced from virgin resources.[40] In other words, the energy used to reprocess the recycled materials far outweighs the use of virgin materials.

Some circular economy schools of thought also focus on better social outcomes, and there is a growing movement towards solutions that are both circular *and* sustainable – environmentally, socially and financially.

We need to be ambitious and aim high. Today – with depleted resources, degenerated soil, heavy levels of pollution and waste, and ecosystem destruction – 'sustainability' is not enough. As we noted in Chapter 3, we need to both shrink our economy and **recover and regenerate** technical and biological resources. Instead of thinking about 'reducing' extraction and waste, we should aim to 'eliminate', and to 'regenerate resources *and* nature'.

The circular economy plays a fundamental role in reducing *GHG* emissions and drawing down carbon, especially for the 67 per cent of global GHG related to material management.[41] By offering a new economic model with strategies that keep products and their materials in circulation, we can extract more value from them, at the same time reducing our footprint on the earth. Reselling, repairing, remaking and recycling means we avoid waste, pollution and degradation of land, water, air and atmosphere. We can design systems that regenerate instead of plundering and destroying.

Historians will struggle to understand why we did not react – it is time to put this at the top of our agendas. We face the end of cheap energy, plus the overexploitation of both finite and renewable resources, resulting in increasing costs, and growing population and consumption – plus significant risk from degradation of living systems. The linear economy, with products and materials flowing mainly in one direction, is wasteful of both resources and value opportunities. Systems fit for the future will cycle materials and products: sourcing renewable or recycled materials, managing flows of by-products and creating closed loops to recover valuable resources. We need fundamental changes in traditional business models. 'Business as usual' is not an option.

The real act of discovery consists not in finding new lands, but in seeing with new eyes.

Marcel Proust

Further resources

Aiming Higher [Online] WWF Living Planet Report 2018, wwf.panda.org/ knowledge_hub/all_publications/living_planet_report_2018/ (archived at https:// perma.cc/X25A-PEZF) [accessed 15 November 2019]

De Wit, M et al (2018) *The Circularity Gap Report: an analysis of the circular state of the global economy*, Circle Economy, January [Online] www.circle-economy.com/the-circularity-gap-report-our-world-is-only-9-circular/ (archived at https://perma.cc/B8J2-8PWF) [accessed 22 November 2019]

Steffen, W (2015) *Planetary Boundaries 2.0: New and improved*, Stockholm Resilience Centre [Online] stockholmresilience.org/21/research/research-news/1-15-2015-planetary-boundaries-2.0---new-and-improved.html (archived at https://perma.cc/SRS7-AJUN) [accessed 27 March 2016]

Notes

1 Boulding, K (1973) [accessed 8 June 2015] Energy Reorganization Act of 1973: Hearings, Ninety-Third Congress, First Session, on H.R. 11510, United States, Congress House, p 248 [Online] en.wikiquote.org/wiki/Kenneth_ Boulding (archived at https://perma.cc/UA4Y-BA4H)

2 Ellen MacArthur Foundation (2013) Towards the Circular Economy, Report, 2, p 22

3 Wertime, SF (2010) [accessed 26 March 2016] Energy Use in the US & Global Agri-Food Systems: Implications for Sustainable Agriculture, The Oildrum [Online] www.theoildrum.com/node/6575 (archived at https://perma.cc/ NWV5-L7DC)

4 Kharas, H (2010), *The Emerging Middle Class in Developing Countries*, OECD Development Centre, Working Paper No. 285, January, http://www.oecd.org/social/poverty/44457738.pdf (archived at https://perma.cc/ FMB6-XCQL)

5 FAO (4 December 2014) [accessed 26 March 2016] Nothing dirty here: FAO kicks off International Year of Soils 2015, *UN FAO* [Online] www.fao.org/ news/story/en/item/270812/icode/ (archived at https://perma.cc/5X5G-4C7S)

6 United Nations (10 Jul 2014) [accessed 31 May 2016] *World's Population Increasingly Urban With More Than Half Living in Urban Areas* [Online] www.un.org/en/development/desa/news/population/world-urbanization-prospects-2014.html (archived at https://perma.cc/CMD5-SSE5)

7 Summary for Policymakers of IPCC Special Report on Global Warming of 1.5°C approved by governments, Press Release, IPCC, (8 October 2018) [Online] www.ipcc.ch/sr15/ (archived at https://perma.cc/26A9-3K8E) [accessed 23 November 2019]

8 WWF (2018) [accessed 15 November 2019] *Living Planet Report 2018: Aiming higher* [Online] wwf.panda.org/knowledge_hub/all_publications/ living_planet_report_2018/ (archived at https://perma.cc/X25A-PEZF)

9 Bringezu, S et al (2017) *Assessing Global Resource Use: A systems approach to resource efficiency and pollution reduction*, Report of the International Resource Panel, United Nations Environment Programme, Nairobi, Kenya

10 British Geological Survey (2016) [accessed 23 November 2019] *Risk List 2015: An update to the Supply Risk Index for Elements or Element Groups that are of Economic Value* [Online] www.bgs.ac.uk/mineralsuk/statistics/ riskList.html (archived at https://perma.cc/Q9T9-R4MJ)

11 Webster, K and Johnson, C (2008) *Sense and Sustainability: Educating for a circular economy*, TerraPreta, Skipton, p 57

12 Carbon Tracker Initiative (2013) [accessed 29 May 2016] *Unburnable Carbon: Wasted capital and stranded assets*, Carbon Tracker and Grantham Research Institute on Climate Change [Online] http://www.lse.ac.uk/GranthamInstitute/ wp-content/uploads/2014/02/PB-unburnable-carbon-2013-wasted-capital-stranded-assets.pdf (archived at https://perma.cc/LY2A-5VS2)

13 WBCSD (2008) [accessed 15 August 2016] *Sustainable Consumption Facts and Trends*, p 10 [Online] http://www.wbcsd.org/pages/edocument/ edocumentdetails.aspx?id=142 (archived at https://perma.cc/5B5N-54UV)

14 Stockholm Resilience Centre (22 January 2015) [accessed 26 March 2016] *The Nine Planetary Boundaries: Land use* [Online] www.stockholmresilience.org/ 21/research/research-programmes/planetary-boundaries/planetary-boundaries/ about-the-research/the-nine-planetary-boundaries.html (archived at https://perma.cc/N5GY-Q6NY)

15 *The Guardian* (20 September 2015) [accessed 26 March 2016] Rate of global forest loss halved [Online] www.theguardian.com/environment/2015/sep/07/ rate-of-global-forest-loss-halved-says-un (archived at https://perma.cc/ NFM8-WMXM)

16 Land is a Critical Resource, IPCC report says (2019) [accessed 22 November 2019] *News Release*, The Intergovernmental Panel on Climate Change (IPCC), 8 August [Online] www.ipcc.ch/2019/08/08/land-is-a-critical-resource_srccl/ (archived at https://perma.cc/7A9Y-CGPL)

17 Rockstrom, J et al (2009) [accessed 27 March 2016] A safe operating space for humanity, *Nature*, 24 September [Online] www.scribd.com/doc/296173520/ rockstrom-2009-A-safe-operating-space-for-humanity (archived at https://perma.cc/732C-PT2W)

18 Welcome to the Anthropocene (2016) [accessed 27 March 2016] *The Great Acceleration* [Online] www.anthropocene.info/great-acceleration.php (archived at https://perma.cc/H5XB-RETG)

19 Stockholm Resilience Centre (2015) [accessed 27 March 2016] *New Planetary Dashboard Shows Increasing Human Impact* [Online] http://stockholmresilience.org/research/research-news/2015-01-15-new-planetary-dashboard-shows-increasing-human-impact.html (archived at https://perma.cc/7RCN-94AA)

20 Steffen, W et al (2004) *Global Change and the Earth System: A planet under pressure*, Springer, Berlin, p 6

21 Ki-moon, B (2009) *Speech to World Climate Conference-3*, Secretary-General Ban Ki-moon, Geneva (Switzerland), 3 September, UN News

22 Stockholm Resilience Centre [Online] http://stockholmresilience.org/21/research/research-news/1-15-2015-new-planetary-dashboard-shows-increasing-human-impact.html/ (archived at https://perma.cc/95JJ-46BM)

23 Steffen, W (2015) [accessed 27 March 2016] *Planetary Boundaries 2.0: New and improved*, Stockholm Resilience Centre [Online] stockholmresilience.org/21/research/research-news/1-15-2015-planetary-boundaries-2.0---new-and-improved.html (archived at https://perma.cc/SRS7-AJUN)

24 Earth Overshoot Day (2019) [accessed 22 November 2019] [Online] www.overshootday.org/ (archived at https://perma.cc/UE62-BC8J)

25 Ellen MacArthur Foundation (2015) [accessed 21 November 2019] *Growth Within: A circular economy vision for a competitive Europe* [Online] www.ellenmacarthurfoundation.org/publications/growth-within-a-circular-economy-vision-for-a-competitive-europe (archived at https://perma.cc/5CFG-48CV)

26 McKinsey Global Institute (2016) [accessed 27 March 2016] *Interactive Commodity Price Index* [Online] www.mckinsey.com/business-functions/sustainability-and-resource-productivity/our-insights/resource-revolution-tracking-global-commodity-markets (archived at https://perma.cc/7GAA-27DM)

27 De Wit, M et al (2018) [accessed 22 November 2019] *The Circularity Gap Report: An analysis of the circular state of the global economy*, Circle Economy [Online] www.circle-economy.com/the-circularity-gap-report-our-world-is-only-9-circular/ (archived at https://perma.cc/B8J2-8PWF)

28 De Wit, M et al (2018) [accessed 22 November 2019] *The Circularity Gap Report: An analysis of the circular state of the global economy*, Circle Economy [Online] www.circle-economy.com/the-circularity-gap-report-our-world-is-only-9-circular/ (archived at https://perma.cc/B8J2-8PWF)

29 The Natural Step (2016) [accessed 29 May 2016] *The Framework: 4 basic system rules* [Online] www.thenaturalstep.org/our-approach/ (archived at https://perma.cc/449Y-JLWH)

30 World Economic Forum (2019) [accessed 10 October 2019] *Global Risks Perception Survey 2018–19* [Online] www.weforum.org/reports/the-global-risks-report-2019 (archived at https://perma.cc/KWD4-DGSH)

31 Circle Economy, PGGM, KPMG, EBRD, and WBCSD (2018) [accessed 21 November 2019] *Linear Risks* [Online] www.circle-economy.com/report/linear-risks-how-business-as-usual-is-a-threat-to-companies-and-investors/ (archived at https://perma.cc/3DKX-MLBS)

32 World Economic Forum (2019) [accessed 10 October 2019] *Global Risks Perception Survey 2018–19* [Online] www.weforum.org/reports/the-global-risks-report-2019 (archived at https://perma.cc/KWD4-DGSH)

33 Rifkin, J (2011) [accessed 15 August 2016] *The Third Industrial Revolution: How lateral power is transforming energy, the economy, and the world,* Palgrave Macmillan, Basingstoke [Online] www.thethirdindustrialrevolution.com/ (archived at https://perma.cc/4AE8-WKT6)

34 Boumphrey, S (2019) [accessed 11 October 2019] 5 drivers shaping megatrends, *Euromonitor International,* 20 August [Online] blog.euromonitor.com/5-drivers-to-understand-megatrends/ (archived at https://perma.cc/KJB8-HMQA)

35 PwC (2015) [accessed 7 March 2016] *Consumer Intelligence Series: The sharing economy* [Online] www.pwc.com/us/en/industry/entertainment-media/publications/consumer-intelligence-series/sharing-economy.html (archived at https://perma.cc/XDM5-ESHK)

36 Rinne, A (2019) [accessed 11 October 2019] World Economic Forum [Online] https://www.weforum.org/agenda/2019/01/sharing-economy (archived at https://perma.cc/M5LV-XV77)

37 Sharing Cities Action Task Force [accessed 11 October 2019] [Online] http://www.sharingcitiesaction.net/declaration/ (archived at https://perma.cc/XVF9-BV64)

38 Future-Fit Foundation, *What You Need to Know* [accessed 11 October 2019] [Online] https://futurefitbusiness.org/what-you-need-to-know/ (archived at https://perma.cc/JX5M-8MZ2)

39 Porter, ME and Kramer, M (2011) [accessed 11 October 2019] Creating shared value, *Harvard Business Review* [Online] www.sharedvalue.org/about-shared-value (archived at https://perma.cc/GVU6-9WNP)

40 De Wit, M et al (2018) The Circularity Gap Report: an analysis of the circular state of the global economy, Circle Economy (January 2018). Available from: www.circle-economy.com/the-circularity-gap-report-our-world-is-only-9-circular/ (archived at https://perma.cc/B8J2-8PWF) [accessed 22 November 2019]

41 De Wit, M et al (2018) [accessed 22 November 2019] *The Circularity Gap Report: An analysis of the circular state of the global economy,* Circle Economy, January [Online] www.circle-economy.com/the-circularity-gap-report-our-world-is-only-9-circular/ (archived at https://perma.cc/B8J2-8PWF)

6

Food and agriculture

We don't grow tomatoes just because it feels good ... We do it because we think we can make a return on the investment. It's a good example of how sustainability can be used to drive a business forward.

DR MARK CARR, GROUP CHIEF EXECUTIVE, AB SUGAR (2014)[1]

As the food sector includes such a wide variety of sub-sectors, I decided to explore one with an apparently simple ingredient: coffee. We start by looking at the overall food system, including a selection of circular economy developments, then move on to the coffee sub-sector. We will cover:

- a quick global overview;
- major issues, including business models, water, energy and other resources;
- what a balanced scorecard might include;
- circular economy developments, including business models, product designs, safe and sustainable inputs, process design and recovery flows;
- enablers and accelerators for circular approaches;
- the coffee sub-sector: challenges, examples and case studies for circular economy developments, with supply chain implications;
- a summary, reflecting on the serious challenges ahead.

Background and global trends

The World Bank values the food and agricultural industry at around US$7.8 trillion, or 10 per cent of global GDP.[2] Spending on food varies widely,

FIGURE 6.1   Global exports of crops and livestock

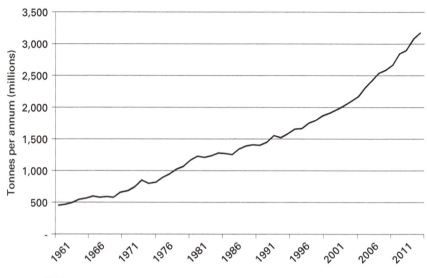

SOURCE: FAOStat

accounting for around 13 per cent of household income in the United States (and less than is spent on housing and transportation), but taking the biggest share of household income in Asia, at 23 per cent.

Agriculture, directly or indirectly, employs around 2 billion people, over a quarter of the global population,[3] with up to 60 per cent of agricultural workers living in poverty.[4] Some of the largest global companies are food and beverage producers, including well-known names such as Associated British Foods, Coca-Cola, Danone, General Mills, Kellogg, Mondelez International (previously Kraft Foods), Nestlé, Pepsico and Unilever. Together, these companies generate revenue of US$400 billion each year and employ millions of people in their supply chains.[5]

Vertical integration in agriculture is increasing, with major corporations supplying seeds, pesticides and livestock pharmaceuticals. Since 2015, the 'Big Six' agrochemical/seed firms have become a 'Big Four', estimated to control over 60 per cent of global proprietary seed sales.[6] Dow and DuPont merged, Chemchina acquired Syngenta, and Bayer acquired Monsanto, selling Bayer's seed divisions to BASF to satisfy antitrust regulators.

Growth in **world trade** of crops and livestock has grown steadily (see Figure 6.1). However, these exchanges of crops, livestock and other biological nutrients increase the risk of transferring pests, diseases and invasive species around the world, threatening the health of both humans and other living species. The FAO lists avian influenza; locust and other insect infestations; wheat, cassava, maize and banana diseases; foodborne pathogens and mycotoxins as 'examples of threats to the human food chain that may impact human health, food security, livelihoods, national economies and global markets'.[7]

Issues

In Chapter 5, we noted that the agricultural 'green revolution' had increased crop yields, helping reduce hunger and malnutrition and creating opportunities for food producers across the world. Despite this, some might argue we have the least efficient food supply system ever. It is another linear system: take, make, waste … and pollute.

Mike Berners-Lee highlights the inefficiencies in the food system (shown in Figure 6.2):[8] around the world, **we grow 9,750 kcal, per person, every day**, of which 5,940 kcal are edible by humans and 3,810 kcal are grass and pasture. We send **1,740 kcal of human-edible crops into the meat and dairy supply chain**, meaning we feed 5,550 kcal of crops to animals every day (3,810 + 1,740). However, after animals have eaten that 5,550 kcal, **meat and dairy products** provide only 590 kcal of food back into the human food system, as animal energy losses use up 4,960 kcal (heat and methane). We **save seeds** (130 kcal worth) for the next crops, we use 810 kcal as **biofuels**, and 740 kcal is wasted in the supply chain. This leaves 3,110 kcal available for eating: of which 580 kcal is lost in processing and household waste, 180 kcal are consumed as **dietary excesses**, and the final **2,350 kcal is what we need for healthy eating** – just 24 per cent of the calories grown. Berners-Lee's analysis shows a similar pattern for protein, too.

Of more than 50,000 edible plant species in the world, only a few hundred contribute significantly to food supplies. Just 15 crop plants provide 90 per cent of the world's food energy intake, with three – rice, maize and wheat – making up two-thirds of this.[9] Those three form the staple diet of over 4 billion people, meaning we lack resilience – pests and diseases, plus poor harvests (likely to increase with climate disruption) all threaten food security. We should note that sugar cane is the world's largest crop by production quantity, though also used for biofuel.

Agriculture produces more than enough food to feed everyone on the planet, yet the FAO (2019)[10] reports that after a decade of steady decline, the number of people suffering from hunger in the world has slowly increased for several years in a row. Over **820 million people** go to bed **hungry** every night, and one-third of food is wasted. Food insecurity is more widespread – altogether, the FAO estimates that over 2 billion people do not have

FIGURE 6.2   Food choices – calories grown versus calories required for healthy living

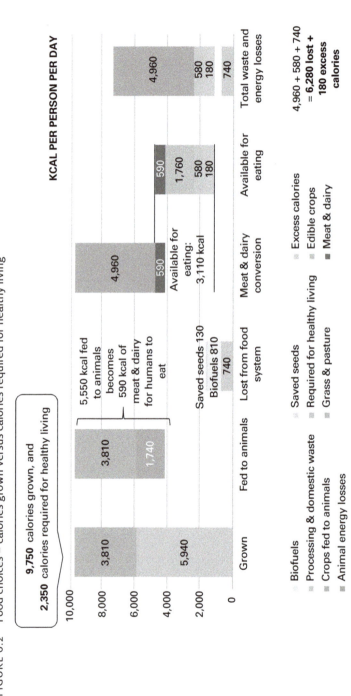

SOURCE: Berners-Lee (2019)[11]

FIGURE 6.3   Agriculture's environmental footprint 2019

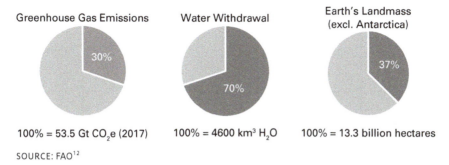

Greenhouse Gas Emissions   Water Withdrawal   Earth's Landmass (excl. Antarctica)

30%   70%   37%

100% = 53.5 Gt CO_2e (2017)   100% = 4600 km³ H_2O 100% = 13.3 billion hectares

SOURCE: FAO[12]

regular access to safe, nutritious and sufficient food, including 8 per cent of the population in Northern America and Europe.

Diet-related ill-health is a major problem, with more than 2 billion adults overweight, of whom over one-third are obese. In 2018, an estimated 40 million children under five were overweight. In 2016, 131 million children 5–9 years old, and 207 million adolescents were overweight. Diet-related illness includes heart disease, diabetes, tooth decay and gum disease. The EAT-Lancet commission (2019)[13] reports that current dietary trends, combined with projected population growth, 'will exacerbate risks to people and planet. The global burden of non-communicable diseases is predicted to worsen and the effects of food production on greenhouse-gas emissions, nitrogen and phosphorus pollution, biodiversity loss, and water and land use will reduce the stability of the Earth system.'

Oxfam calculates the 'calories needed by that 13 per cent of the world population [going hungry] equate to just 3 per cent of global food supply': roughly one-tenth of the food wasted each year across global supply chains.[14]

Global agriculture has a major **environmental impact**, occupying 37 per cent of the earth's landmass, using 70 per cent of global water withdrawals in 2010 and (with the food system) producing around one-third of *greenhouse gas* emissions (GHG), as shown in Figure 6.3.[15]

Business models and consumption

In industrialized countries, the food system encourages consumption of processed foods, year-round availability of fruits and vegetables, and addictive sugars, flavours and additives. According to campaign organization FoodPrint, the 'cheap grains that have led to proliferation of a high-sugar, high-fat, meat-rich diet around the world have created a massive public

FIGURE 6.4   World consumption of meat and dairy

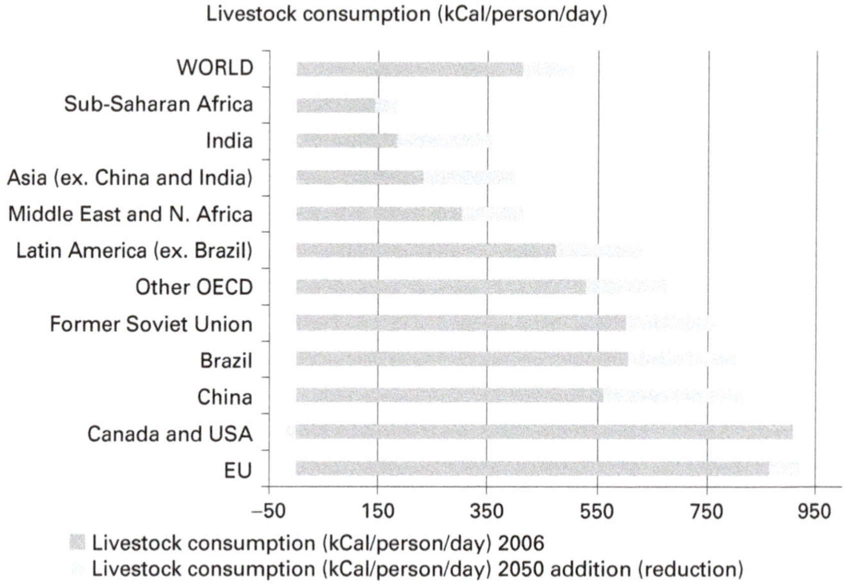

Livestock consumption (kCal/person/day)

-50	150	350	550	750	950

■ Livestock consumption (kCal/person/day) 2006
Livestock consumption (kCal/person/day) 2050 addition (reduction)

SOURCE: Ranganathan (2013)[16]

health crisis as heart disease, a diet-related disease, has become the leading cause of death in the US, with diabetes also in the top ten.'[17]

In earlier chapters, we saw forecasts for the increasing consumer population, expected to be around 9.7 billion people by 2050, with much of this increase in Asia and Africa. As people in developing economies increase their spending power, they tend to eat more meat, more dairy and more processed food, adopting 'Western' diets. World Resources Institute forecasts for 2050, in Figure 6.4, show consumption of calories from livestock (meat and dairy) increasing by 94 per cent in India, 46 per cent in China, 37 per cent in the Middle East and Africa and 29 per cent in Sub-Saharan Africa.[18]

Resources: energy

Undermining the benefits of modern industrialized agriculture is the heavy reliance on fossil energy needed to power farm machinery and produce fertilizers and pesticides.

Estimates show that modern agriculture uses 10 calories of fossil fuel to put a single calorie on our plates. That figure excludes agriculture's share of transport and emissions from food manufacturers. Analysis shows that the food production and supply chain system accounts for about 30 per cent of total global energy consumption,[19] and a similar level of global GHG emissions.

Majot and Kuyek, writing in *The Guardian* (2017),[20] report that 'the top 20 meat and dairy companies emitted more greenhouse gases in 2016 than all of Germany, Europe's biggest climate polluter by far. If these companies were a country, they would be the world's seventh largest greenhouse gas emitter.' They point out that just three meat companies – JBS, Cargill and Tyson – are estimated to have emitted more greenhouse gases in 2016 than France, and nearly as much as some of the biggest oil companies such as Exxon, BP and Shell.

Resources: water

Global water usage has grown at more than double the rate of population growth in the last century, and goes on growing to meet increasing demands from farming, industry and domestic users.

Figure 6.1 showed the breakdown of global water usage, with irrigation for crops (fibres, tobacco, biofuels, etc, as well as food) at 70 per cent. Our average daily drinking requirement is 2–4 litres, but to produce the daily food for each person needs 2,000–4,000 litres of water. **Water footprints** for a range of food products, shown in Figure 6.5, highlight the water impacts of livestock (often due to irrigation of crops grown for feed, such as soy and corn).

Water scarcity is now a major issue, with 1.7 billion people living in water-stressed countries in 2015. The UN expects this to rise to two-thirds of world population by 2025.[21] Major companies have faced production issues and lawsuits over water in recent years, including Nestlé and Anheuser-Busch in the United States, and Coca-Cola in India and the United States.

Resources: technical

Modern agriculture depends on artificial inputs from finite materials, such as oil-based fertilizers, plus nitrogen and phosphorus (with concerns that both are nearing the peak of their supply too), and some artificial 'enhancers' such as pesticides, herbicides, etc. Use of **chemical inputs** in agriculture is increasing, as industrial farming approaches replace smallholder methods. Farmers may use a range of artificial 'enhancers', often synthetic compounds, including fertilizers, insecticides, pesticides, fungicides, herbicides. These leave residues on the crop (which we then eat), in the soil, their run-off

FIGURE 6.5   Food water footprints

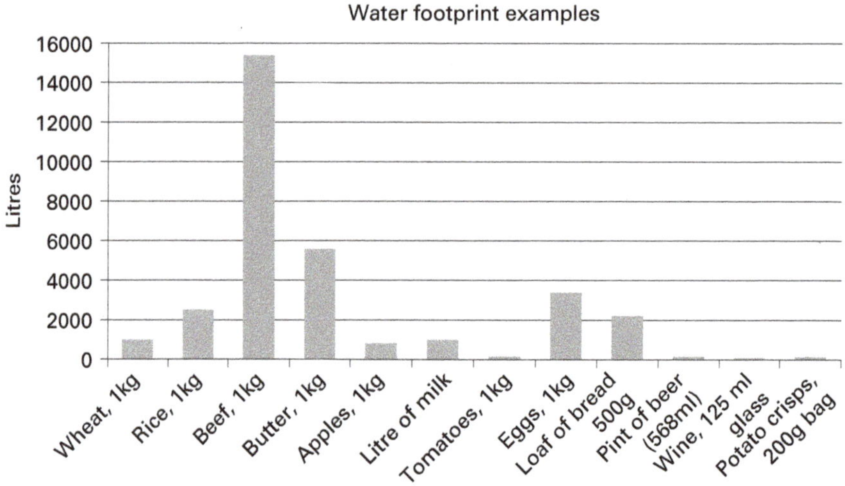

enters freshwater supplies, and adds to the pollution levels in the air – all affecting the health of plants, birds, fish and animals. In Chapter 5, we noted that 30,000–70,000 chemicals are in everyday use, most of which are not tested for their effects on health.

Pollutants in the run-off from soil, including nitrogen and phosphorus from **artificial fertilizers**, cause both eutrophication and increased toxicity of water. This harms animal and fish populations as well as human health through contamination of irrigation and drinking water. Eutrophication is the effects of added natural or artificial nutrients to water in aquatic systems, associated with wide swings in dissolved oxygen concentrations and frequent algal blooms. Industrial fertilizer contributes to GHG emissions, releasing carbon dioxide, and nitrates are transformed into nitrous oxide, also a potent greenhouse gas.

Resources: biological

How we use the **agricultural land** is interesting – crops grown to feed people directly currently take up just 4 per cent of the earth's available land surface, whilst crops to feed cattle, sheep, pigs and chickens account for 30 per cent – seven times as much. Figure 6.6, adapted from an infographic by consultancy BestFootForward, illustrates the 'foodprint' for the types of food eaten in the UK, and again the main contributor is meat.

Croplands and pasture occupy roughly half the global land not covered by ice, water or desert. Continued expansion of cropland and pastures is the

FIGURE 6.6   UK 'foodprint'

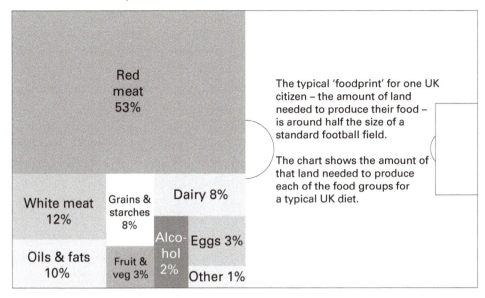

SOURCE: BestFootForward (2011)[22]

main source of **ecosystem degradation** and **biodiversity loss.** Conversion of forests, savannas and peatlands to agriculture accounts for around 11 per cent of global GHG emissions. Cropland and pasture expanded by roughly 500 million hectares between 1962 and 2006, equivalent to roughly 60 per cent of the area of the United States.[23]

The FAO (2014) estimates that '**a third of all soils are degraded,** due to erosion, compaction, soil sealing, salinization, soil organic matter and nutrient depletion, acidification, pollution and other processes caused by unsustainable land management practices'.[24] It warned that 'unless new approaches are adopted the global amount of arable and productive land per person will in 2050 be only one-fourth of the level in 1960'. Healthy soils are essential for our survival, providing food, fuel, fibre and medical products. Soil supports ecosystems, including the carbon cycle, storing and filtering water, and improving resilience to floods and droughts. Nutrient depletion is also a concern, with indications of deficiencies in both macro and micronutrients. Farmers often pay for chemicals and fertilizers, to compensate for the loss of ecological services previously provided, free of charge, by soil. Alternatives such as organic farming and genetically modified organism (GMO) crops still depend on some inputs, and most modern farmers plough (or till) the soil, again contributing to degradation.

Agriculture is responsible for about 80 per cent of **global deforestation**. As Henriette Walz of the Rainforest Alliance highlights, the global outcry in 2019, after news of devastating fires in the Amazon, illustrates how deforestation has global ramifications.[25] Commodity production – for palm oil, soy, timber, and beef, plus cocoa and coffee – is a major driver of this. Clearing forest to grow crops harms local people and wildlife and destroys critical carbon sinks that the world needs to slow climate change.

Other issues include **animal welfare and disease**, and **species extinction** is threatening many insects and pollinators, creating yet more risk. The UN IPBES published a special report in 2019, warning that 1 million species were now at risk, and that 'human-induced changes are creating conditions for fast biological evolution – so rapid that its effects can be seen in only a few years or even more quickly'.[26] It reports that:

> [the] rate of global change in nature during the past 50 years is unprecedented in human history. The direct drivers of change in nature with the largest global impact have been (starting with those with most impact): changes in land and sea use; direct exploitation of organisms; climate change; pollution; and invasion of alien species.

Balanced scorecard

These are examples of *externalities* being funded by society, with rising costs of national health schemes, private and corporate health insurance, lost employment days and so on.

The **food–water–energy nexus**, shown in Figure 6.7, is worrying companies, governments and NGOs.[27] Water crises, energy price shocks and food crises have featured regularly in the World Economic Forum Global Risks Landscape since 2009. The three resources are interlinked: water is a major input for growing crops in the fields and along the entire agri-food supply chain. We use energy to produce and distribute water and food, to pump water from groundwater or surface water sources, to power tractors and irrigation machinery, and to process and transport agricultural goods. A whole-systems approach is vital to assess outlooks for all three elements, and further complexities arise with other key sectors depending on water and energy.

Global food companies share a wide range of concerns, with Nestlé's 'materiality matrix' listing food security, climate change, water stewardship, food safety, human rights, business ethics and others as major concerns.[28] NGOs are campaigning for improvements: Oxfam publishes its 'Behind the

FIGURE 6.7   Food–water–energy nexus

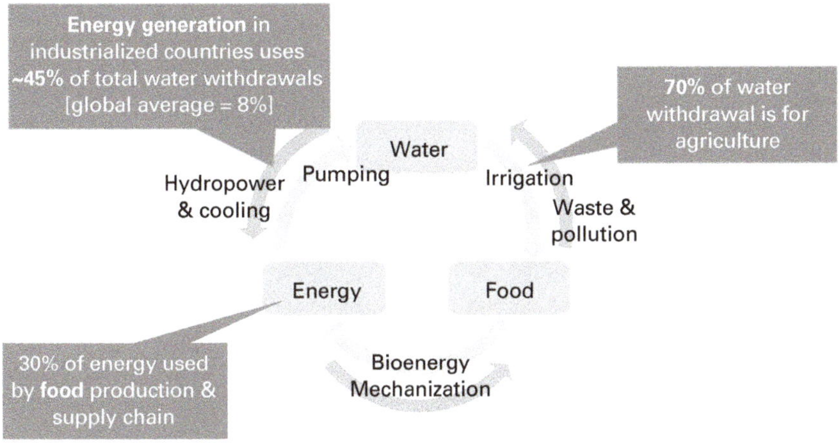

Energy generation in industrialized countries uses ~45% of total water withdrawals [global average = 8%]

70% of water withdrawal is for agriculture

Water

Hydropower & cooling   Pumping   Irrigation

Waste & pollution

Energy   Food

30% of energy used by food production & supply chain

Bioenergy Mechanization

SOURCE: WWF Living Planet Report, 2014

Brands' scorecard for the top 10 global food and beverage brands, covering a range of sustainability indicators and encouraging consumers to take action. Table 6.1 outlines criticisms of the food supply chain, using the Natural Step system conditions for a 'baseline assessment'.[29]

Food security covers availability (both quantity and quality) and access. For many countries, this affects malnutrition, hunger, poverty, and even civil wars and migration. For the UK, it is more an issue of imbalances of trade. The UK produces only about three-quarters of its indigenous foods, importing the rest, so effectively 'offshoring' its water footprint, energy use and GHG emissions.[30] WRAP reports that eight of the top 10 UK food import countries are prone to drought. Countries and companies, concerned about food security, are acquiring both food producers and land, aiming to secure their own future supplies. Oxfam calculates that land acquired between 2000 and 2010 could feed 1 billion people and that much of it is either left idle as speculators wait for values to increase, or it is used to grow crops, often biofuels, for export.[31]

There is **structural waste** all along the supply chain. In farming, only 5 per cent of applied fertilizer provides nutrition to humans, and up to 70 per cent of fertilizer is not utilized by crops; instead, it leaks into the soils, causing water pollution, eutrophication and releasing GHG emissions.[32]

Previous FAO reports estimated that one-third of total food production is lost each year between farm and fork. That figure is in the process of being replaced with two separate SDG indicators, to provide more clarity:

TABLE 6.1   Natural Step system conditions – food supply chain issues

System condition	Supply chain stage				
	Raw materials	Manufacture	Logistics and sales	Use	End-of-life
Scarce materials taken from the earth	Oil-based fertilizers, phosphate, chemical pesticides, irrigation	Energy from fossil fuels, water use	Energy use and plastic packaging	Energy and water	Energy use for waste transport and processing
Man-made toxic and persistent chemicals	Agri inputs pesticides etc, toxins, pollution to soil, water, air	Processing inputs, E numbers, chemicals, cleaning chemicals	Particulates from eg diesel, many issues with air and sea freight and refrigeration		GHG emissions incl. methane from decomposition of food waste in landfill
Destruction and pollution of nature	Pesticides, chemical and nutrient run-off, animal welfare	Concerns re effluent and pollution to air	Shipping and road freight pollution	Effluent from cleaning chemicals	Landfill or incineration, pollution and toxins from packaging and chemical food additives
Work and/or use conditions	Child labour, safety, slavery, pollution affecting communities, fair conditions and prices for growers	Child labour, safety, slavery, pollution affecting communities	Working conditions and pay, traffic congestion	Chemical additives, sugar, salt etc	

SOURCE: Adapted from Streamlined Life Cycle Assessment (based on Natural Step System Conditions), Sustainable Wealth Creation, 2007, with kind permission of Forum for the Future

FIGURE 6.8   Global food loss, by region

Percentage of Food Loss

Percentage of Food Loss

SOURCE: FAO (2019)[33]

- The Food Loss Index is calculated by the FAO and provides new estimates for part of the supply chain, from post-harvest up to (but not including) retail.

- The Food Waste Index, calculated by UNEP, measures food waste at retail and consumption levels, and is forthcoming.

Figure 6.8 shows the percentage of food lost, for each global region, excluding retail. In the UK, almost half the total food discarded, around 7 million tonnes, comes from homes. A typical UK family throws away around £700 of food each year,[34] and we could have eaten more than half of this. In addition to the food losses, we waste all the embedded water, energy, fertilizer and other inputs too. Manufacturers and retailers are engaging with consumers to help reduce retail and consumer waste levels, and the FAO has a toolkit with suggested actions at each stage of the supply chain.

Returning to the population growth and increased food needs from the beginning of this chapter, the World Resources Institute (WRI) estimates that **global crop production** will need to **increase by 70 per cent**, from 9,500 trillion calories in 2009 to 16,000 trillion calories by 2050.[35] This includes crops for direct human consumption, animal feed, seeds, biofuels and industrial use. Reducing food waste will only partially close the gap. The WRI estimates that halving the food losses would produce around 1,400 trillion calories.

FIGURE 6.9 Supply chain impacts

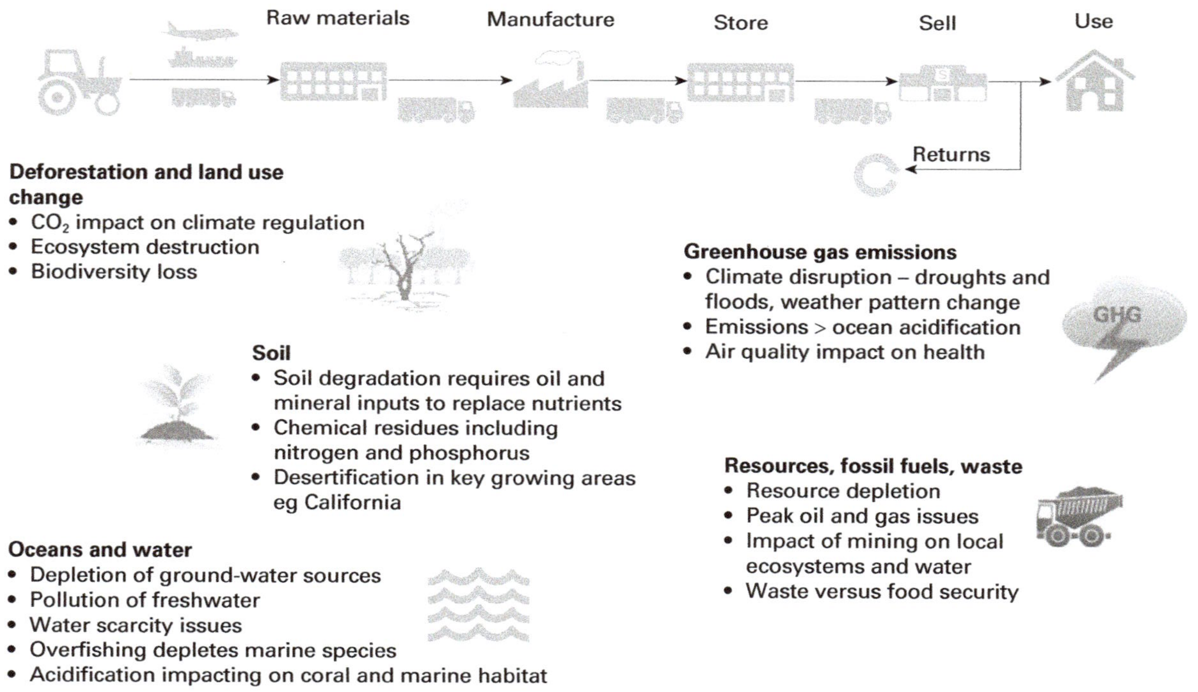

Raw materials   Manufacture   Store   Sell   Use

Returns

GHG

Deforestation and land use change
- CO$_2$ impact on climate regulation
- Ecosystem destruction
- Biodiversity loss

Soil
- Soil degradation requires oil and mineral inputs to replace nutrients
- Chemical residues including nitrogen and phosphorus
- Desertification in key growing areas eg California

Oceans and water
- Depletion of ground-water sources
- Pollution of freshwater
- Water scarcity issues
- Overfishing depletes marine species
- Acidification impacting on coral and marine habitat

Greenhouse gas emissions
- Climate disruption – droughts and floods, weather pattern change
- Emissions > ocean acidification
- Air quality impact on health

Resources, fossil fuels, waste
- Resource depletion
- Peak oil and gas issues
- Impact of mining on local ecosystems and water
- Waste versus food security

SOURCE: © Catherine Weetman

Competition for land use is another challenge, with some governments planning to produce more biofuels for transport. Producing 10 per cent of all transport fuels from biofuels by 2050 would use around one-third of global crop production, but produce only 2 per cent of global energy and increase the food gap to around 100 per cent. The WRI calculates that 'eliminating the use of crop-based biofuels for transportation would close the food gap by around 14 per cent'.

We can see the wide range of impacts on living systems, many of which are interconnected, in Figure 6.9. It is difficult to see how more industrialization and intensification could provide the answer. 'New technologies' such as genetic modification could mean more vertical integration, with a few global corporations gaining control of the entire supply chain, locking farmers into the supply of ever more complex and expensive seeds.

Circular economy developments

Global food companies and startups are innovating all along the supply chain, developing new foods, better ways to preserve and extend shelf life, and finding ways to extract value from waste. The circular economy framework in Figure 6.10 reminds us of the wide range of opportunities for the food sector, especially for circular inputs, product and process design. We will look at examples of these throughout this section.

Business models

Increasing levels of vegan, vegetarian and 'flexitarian' diets have spurred innovation in meat substitutes. Some are plant-based, whereas others aim to 'grow' meat in laboratory conditions. Plant-based diets offer benefits for the environment, and for the business – longer shelf life, fewer food safety risks and cheaper ingredients with broader supply bases can all reduce costs.

Businesses based entirely on circular flows are emerging too. In the United States, Imperfect buys misshapen produce (rejected by retailers) direct from farmers and sells it at a 30–50 per cent discount to subscribers. FoPo makes food powder from fruits that are near expiry, or just ugly, as a food ingredient for baking and ice cream, preserving the nutrients, aroma and flavours.

Companies are creating products with ingredients recycled from other processes. In the UK, Snact makes fruit snacks from surplus produce, rejected for being too big, small, ugly, or simply too abundant. Rubies in the Rubble uses surplus produce to make chutney, with ingredients that 'pass

FIGURE 6.10   Circular Economy Framework 2.0

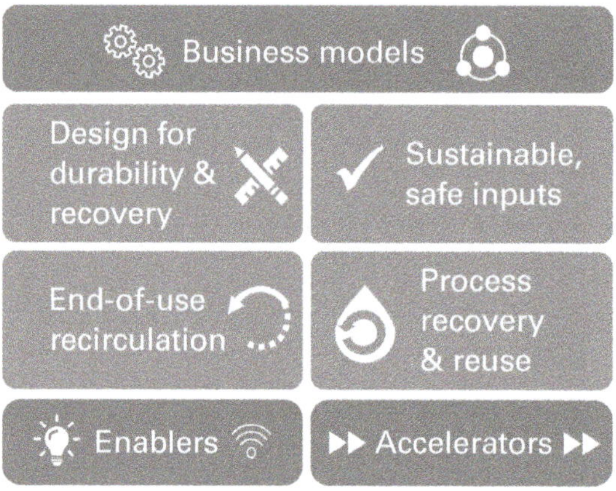

SOURCE: © Catherine Weetman

the taste test, not a beauty contest'.[36] Toast Ale, covered in Chapter 2, uses waste bread to replace some of the ingredients in beer.

Business models can focus on reducing waste or even eliminating packaging. Original Unverpackt, 'Germany's first zero-waste supermarket', stocks all food in bulk and allows customers to buy the exact quantity of food they need, using their own containers. Forgetting a container just means borrowing multi-use containers or using recycled paper bags. Many more examples of circular packaging approaches are covered in Chapter 10.

AgriProtein points out that since the 'Triassic period, nature's 125,000 species of flies have broken down, recycled and cleaned up waste using the world's most up-to-date antibiotics that they naturally produce', and that flies and their larvae are natural foods for many fish, birds and mammals.[37] It produces high-protein feed ingredients for farmed animals, fish and pets, plus soil conditioners, using fly larvae fed on existing organic waste. EnviroFlight in the United States uses waste from breweries, ethanol production and pre-consumer food waste as a feedstock for Black Soldier Fly larvae, which bioconvert it into a high-protein, low-fat feedstuff for omnivorous fish species, poultry and pigs.

Researchers are developing insect-based foods and ingredients for humans too. Flexitarian, plant-based diets, seasonal food and local supply chains can all contribute to circular food systems, helping reduce energy and waste and provide healthier diets.

At the end of the process, circular services providers around the world are creating energy and other by-products from food waste, especially fats, and this is becoming more effective as technology develops.

Design for durability and recovery

We might think that resource-efficiency is already a priority in food manufacture, but waste can occur in surprising ways. Odd-shaped vegetables may not be easy for machines to peel and chop, leading to wastage. Different stages of ripeness in a batch of fresh ingredients can also pose challenges. It may be possible to find seed varieties that fit the requirements, otherwise you could look at collaborations and co-products to make use of the rejected inputs: fruit leathers, ready meals, chutneys and jams can use peelings and 'imperfect' specimens.

The concept of designing food products to be slower, or more intense, may seem challenging, but portion size and packaging can ensure food stays fresh and retains its nutrients, and information on the label can help people understand how to store the food. Fermented foods are growing in popularity, and offer nutritional benefits as well as having long shelf lives.

Thinking about how to ensure 'waste = food' is more straightforward. This could be suggesting recipes to the consumer, using plant parts often wasted, such as vegetable stalks, or fermenting foods (sourdough bread, pickles, yoghurt, etc) to improve longevity and provide additional micronutrients simultaneously.

Safe, sustainable inputs

Whilst all food ingredients appear to be renewable, meat and dairy put more pressure on resources than crops. Plant-based diets are becoming more popular in many industrial economies, though food producers are using this to market ready meals, convenience and 'ultra-processed foods'. In San Francisco, startup Hampton Creek aims to disrupt the food industry by replacing egg ingredients with plants, starting with egg-free 'mayo' (in the United States 'mayonnaise' must contain eggs) made from yellow peas, and cookies.[38] Note that this isn't circular, though!

Restaurants and food producers are more conscious of aiming for zero waste and creating new ways to use peelings, stalks, misshapen produce, and more.

Circular food systems should be using sustainable, safe ingredients – not those causing deforestation, needing chemical inputs and pesticides, or relying on irrigation. Locally produced, in-season produce has a smaller supply-chain footprint too.

Process design

Even **organic farming** is energy-intensive, with ploughing and cultivation to grow and harvest annual crops. Alternatives, with growing interest worldwide, are *permaculture* and agro-forestry systems – moving away from monoculture and designing 'forest gardens' to produce food, fibres and timber on a self-supporting basis, with designs seeking to provide water and nutrients without using labour or fossil fuels. Deeper understandings of the complexity of soil, the functions of mycorrhizas (fungal associations between plant roots and beneficial fungi, which effectively extend the root area of plant systems) and the damage caused by compaction and tilling, are opening up different approaches.

Farmers are learning about 'holistic' and **'regenerative' farming** and **'no-till'** approaches to optimize yields, labour and inputs. Rotational grazing allows pastures to regenerate more quickly, and diverse grass, herb and plant mixes provide healthier diets and reduce the need for vaccines and antibiotics. No-till methods reduce soil compaction, increase biodiversity and micronutrients, and improve water retention and soil health. The 4p1000 Initiative says that regenerating soil could significantly contribute to carbon drawdown – achieved through an annual growth rate of 0.4 per cent (4 per 1,000) in the soil carbon stocks, in the first 30–40 cm of soil.[39]

Different ways of farming are developing. Foodchain, in the United States, is an example of indoor **aquaponics**, claiming to use less than 10 per cent of the water required in conventional agriculture. **Underground farming** uses LED lighting to grow food indoors in cities. Zero Carbon Food cultivates herbs and vegetables in abandoned railway tunnels underneath London, using sealed clean-room environments, hydroponic irrigation systems and sourcing energy from green suppliers.[40] It sells all its produce within the M25 to maximize freshness.

Companies are recovering value from both ingredients and process inputs. Examples of cascaded use include the orange-peel examples, mentioned in Chapter 2. Dairy producers Arla Food Ingredients and Danone create new protein products using whey from the yoghurt process. A study estimated that fish, beer and whisky waste and by-products could benefit the Scottish economy by up to £800 million.[41]

In the circular economy, end-of-use products should become compost (ie food for nature), or be available for reuse. For food, thinking at a molecular level can help identify ways to recover value. What useful chemical elements can we extract from waste flows to become valuable by-products? The remaining waste can continue into energy conversion, compost and so on.

Horizon Proteins is developing processes to recover and reuse protein and energy from fermentation and distillery by-products, for use as a sustainable and nutritious food for farmed salmon.

British Sugar is reputed to generate 25 per cent of its revenue from co-products, created from the waste streams of sugar production. It sells topsoil for landscaping, aggregate for building, animal feeds, chemicals for the cosmetics industry, horticulture, bioethanol fuels, liquefied CO_2 for soft drinks and electricity to the national grid.[42]

FEEDBACK GLOBAL: CAMPAIGNING TO TRANSFORM THE FOOD SYSTEM[43]

Charity Feedback Global reports that systemic overproduction means that 'throughout the supply chain, food is discarded because it does not meet the aesthetic requirements of supermarkets.' An estimated 65 per cent of mangos in Senegal are wasted every year (88,000 tonnes), mostly as a result of cosmetic specifications. Leaving large volumes of rejected fruit in the field increased the prevalence of fruit fly, leading to further losses. In Peru, onion producers said they 'regularly waste 8.5 per cent of their crop in a "good year" and up to 60 per cent in a bad year, because of the shape, size and colour of their products'.

In the UK, organizations like FareShare and Company Shop aim to recover food whilst it remains edible and nutritious, diverting it to food banks or for sale at a lower cost. Company Shop, founded in the 1970s, reports that it is 'the UK's largest redistributor of surplus products', using a network of staff shops, 'click and collect' and standalone stores, to prevent over 30,000 tonnes of food waste each year.[44]

Recovery flows

Legislation and taxes can encourage 'zero waste to landfill' approaches. Adverse publicity on food waste highlights issues of inequality and poverty, and the ethical problems of throwing away vast quantities of still edible food whilst people are queuing at food banks or suffering hunger and mal-nutrition. **Reuse** for food and drink products is somewhat counterintuitive – but a supply chain should be agile enough to reroute product before its shelf life expires, such as into foodbanks or catering.

FIGURE 6.11   Digital solutions for food waste

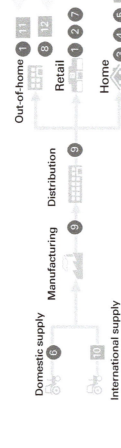

Redistribute excess
1. FoodCloud (Ireland & UK)
2. No Food Waste (India)
3. Olio (UK)
4. Unsung (US)
5. Yo No Desperdicio (Spain)
6. Agribay (UK)
7. Plan Zheroes (UK)
8. Karma (Sweden, Paris, London)
9. Spoiler Alert (US)

Reducing waste/improving process
10. Cheetah (West Africa)
11. MintScraps (US and Thailand)
12. Winnow (Europe, UAE, Asia, Australia)
13. Wise Up on Waste (Europe) – Unilever

Alert for expiring/short dated
14. 11th Hour (Singapore)
15. NoFoodWasted (The Netherlands)
16. Too Good To Go (Europe & US)

Domestic supply
Manufacturing   Distribution
International supply

Out-of-home
Retail
Home

Companies also use processed food waste, including manufacturing waste or out-of-code stock, to create animal food – however, given the issues with sugar in human diets, this might not be a sensible solution.

Energy from waste should be our last strategy, once we have extracted all other value from end-of-life food products. Sometimes, food safety regulations mean it is the only option. International Synergies helped a UK meat processor to comply with new Animal Byproducts Regulations by using its meat and bone meal (MBM) and blood meal outputs as inputs to the cement and pet food industries. MBM, a product previously sent to landfill, is ideal as a fuel source due to its high calorific value, and the combustion of MBM generated significant quantities of calcium salts, a raw material replacement.[45]

Enablers

Green chemistry and **biorefining** and other approaches are developing new **by-products** and extracting value from waste, for example for food or – as for the orange essential oils example in Chapter 2 – as high-value inputs for cosmetics, pharmaceuticals and other sectors. AgriDust is an organic feedstock for 3D printing, consisting of around two-thirds food waste plus a potato starch binder.[46] This material could replace plastic in short-lived products like packaging or plant pots.

Ellen MacArthur Foundation's Urban Biocycles report (2017)[47] notes that biorefineries could become an integral component of urban waste management infrastructure, using organic waste materials to manufacture many of the materials derived from fossil-fuel-based oil and petrochemical feedstocks. Techniques including thermal treatment, biological processes and enzymatic conversions can transform organic material into valuable chemicals and products.

Digital platforms enable rapid notification and exchange of available resources, with Spoiler Alert (developed at MIT in the United States) helping food manufacturers, wholesale distributors, and grocery retailers manage unsold inventory more effectively. Big data, geo-location and mobile apps are all helping reduce food waste across the retail, restaurant and food-to-go sectors, as well as in the home. Figure 6.11 shows some of these solutions, many highlighted by *The Guardian* in 2017.[48] Many aim to match and connect providers with users, enabling redistribution of excess food, often without charge. Agribay, in the US, focuses on farm waste, whilst Olio (UK), Unsung (UK) and Yo-No-Desperdicio (Spain) help people share excess food with neighbours. No Food Waste (India) and Plan Zheroes (UK) help retailers, and Food Cloud (UK and Ireland) helps retail and out-of-home outlets and supports 9,500 charitable groups.

Some apps target redistribution of food that's nearing the end of its shelf life at out-of-home outlets, such as 11th Hour (Singapore), No Food Wasted (Netherlands) and Too Good To Go (Europe and US). Other organizations have developed technology and algorithms to improve production and buying processes. Cheetah, in West Africa, 'crowd-sources' information on poor road conditions, inadequate refrigeration, corruption and other obstacles that delay fresh produce on its route to market. Winnow (UK) helps restaurants measure, analyse and reduce food waste, Wise Up on Waste (Europe) is a data collection and analysis tool from Unilever, and MintScraps (US and Thailand) is a software-as-a-service (SaaS) platform allowing restaurants to monitor and reduce their waste. Meanwhile, Karma (Sweden, Paris, London) is a platform for restaurants and cafés to upload information about excess food, so people can collect it at a reduced price.

Other technology developments can help reduce resource use and waste, including robots to apply targeted chemical applications – just for those plants with a problem, and even robots that recognize and remove specific weeds. Drones, geo-mapping and big data are all being used to help with crop and irrigation planning and to identify problems with disease and nutrition. Precision agriculture and knowledge-sharing can help farmers understand more about what is happening and how to improve it, without blanket applications of fertilizer, chemicals and water, 'just in case'.

Accelerators

To improve food safety and security, shorter and more transparent supply chains can enhance trust and react more effectively if problems arise. Food fraud has existed for centuries and continues across many products. As an example, the UK manages to consume 1,800 tonnes of Manuka honey from only the 1,500 tonnes produced in New Zealand each year.[49] **Certifying organizations** control organic and biodynamic standards, and animal welfare standards, as well as ethical standards. There are specialist groups such as the Sustainable Restaurant Association, the Ethical Tea Partnership and many more. However, some have been criticized for weak standards, and even corruption. Certification can encourage producers to use more sustainable methods, and can include supporting resources such as training, advice, benchmarking, digital tools and so on.

Collaboration between companies can help circularity too. Chapter 2 outlined the National Industrial Symbiosis Project (NISP) initiative in the

UK, linking companies to turn waste into a resource flow. Examples for food **symbiosis** include pastry waste from Apetito, routed into Andigestion's anaerobic digestion plant to generate electricity.[50]

Governments are beginning to set **policies** to improve the food system, focusing on healthy diets with sugar taxes, restricting marketing of un-healthy foods, or reducing food waste (Italy, France and South Korea all have policies restricting disposal of food waste).

Coffee sub-sector

As an example of circular approaches for food, let's examine what is happening with coffee, now the second most traded commodity on the planet (after oil),[51] with 8.6 million tonnes in 2015.[52] Consumption is around 1.6 billion cups of coffee a day worldwide,[53] and Scandinavian countries top the 'league table' for per capita consumption. In the UK, the number of coffee shops quadrupled between 2001 and 2011.[54]

The **coffee supply chain** is complex, with around 100 million people involved in growing coffee worldwide; 70 per cent of growers are small-holders, and third-world farmers receive only 10 per cent of the final retail price.[55] There are ethical concerns that 'coffee production has been linked to slavery and child labour, and many of the beans you buy are grown in countries that under-regulate use of chemicals and pesticides'.[56]

In response to growing worldwide demand, farming and production methods have changed. Traditionally, coffee was cultivated under a shaded canopy of trees. This agroforestry approach prevents topsoil erosion, elimi-nates the need for chemicals and provides beneficial ecosystem habitats and biodiversity. In the 1970s, farmers were encouraged to replace their old, 'inefficient' methods with new, more intense systems, growing coffee in sunny plantations, with tillage and fertilizer input. This, together with growth in demand, means that in Central America alone, 2.5 million acres of **forest were cleared** for coffee farming.[57] In Colombia, Central America, the Caribbean and Mexico, over 40 per cent of the coffee area has been converted to 'sun coffee', with a further 25 per cent in conversion by 2016.

Coffee has a significant **water footprint**, needing an average of 140 litres to make one cup, mostly in irrigation for sun-grown crops and the early stages of production.[58] Development of wet-mill processing, as farming switched to sun crops, meant significant consumption and waste of water, 'often 10,000 m^3 per ton of green coffee ... the pollution load in the waste-water from the wet milling of coffee can be 30 to 40 times greater than the one found in urban sewage'.[59]

The end of the process produces **waste coffee grounds**, with one gram of coffee generating 0.91 grams of waste, producing around 8 million tonnes of waste coffee grounds each year.[60] If sent to landfill, one tonne of coffee waste can produce around 14 tonnes of CO_2.[61]

Circular economy developments

The coffee value chain can improve circular input flows by returning to **agroforestry** (shade-grown) coffee, reducing reliance on artificial inputs and optimizing yields through sharing best practice and minimizing waste. For packaging, bio-based materials are being developed for coffee machine 'pods' and for takeaway cups.

Examples of **process design** improvements tend to focus on the upstream supply chain, with resource-efficiency and closed-loop (on-farm) value recovery. Wet-mill processing separates the coffee bean (the seed) from the cherry (outer part of the fruit). Chapter 2 outlined how Pectcof creates value from waste coffee cherries, creating a range of by-products and detoxifying the waste stream. The Energy from Coffee Wastewater project, in Central America, is installing biodigesters on coffee farms, converting the wastewater into biogas that can then power machinery or stoves for drying the coffee bean.[62]

Nestlé finds that farmers typically use 60 per cent more water than necessary for irrigation during the dry season. Whilst 'big agriculture' is investing in drones, big data and other technologies for resource-efficiency and yield increases, small-scale farmers can benefit from simpler **water-saving** solutions. Nestlé launched a programme in Vietnam providing low-cost, easy-to-use tools for farmers. Examples include inverting plastic bottles to observe soil condensation levels, and using an easily calibrated empty can to measure rainfall.[63]

Researchers are developing **new products** from the phytonutrients in the coffee plant, currently lost through factory farming and industrial processing. Coffeeberry® produces patented ingredients from handpicked coffee, used to create nutrient-rich powders, granules and extracts. An ex-Starbucks engineer set up CF Global to mill the coffee cherry, producing a nutritious ingredient for bakery products. KonaRed in Hawaii uses local coffee cherries to make antioxidant-rich juices, and in the United States, Replere infuses coffee cherries as a raw ingredient for skincare products.

CASE STUDY: GREENCUP – OPEN-LOOP, CROSS-SECTOR RECYCLING[64]

Jeremy Knight founded Greencup in 2004, quickly became 'obsessed with coffee waste', and decided to find a way to recycle coffee grounds. A project with Imperial College London created a fertilizer using a mix of 2–3 per cent coffee pellets to soil, with no added chemicals. The organic coffee pellets are rich in nutrients, including immediately available potassium, magnesium and nitrogen, with some of the nitrogen slowly released over time.

Designer Adam Fairweather, innovations director at Greencup, on discovering that only 18–22 per cent of the coffee bean ends up in the finished drink, began searching for a way to unlock more value by creating new materials from the coffee grounds. Fairweather, also a partner at Smile Plastics and founder of Re-worked, worked on ways to create socially engaging, value-added products from coffee waste:

- In 2010, Smile Plastics helped Greencup's customer Google recycle its coffee waste into furniture designed by Re-worked, using a material made with over 60 per cent used coffee grounds.

- A collaboration between Re-Worked and Italian coffee machine company SanRemo created a very neat loop. The cover panels of the SanRemo Verde coffee machine use a material made from 70 per cent coffee grounds plus other natural components, and the steam knobs and 'portafilter' handles are made from recycled wooden pallets.[65]

- A further collaboration, with Fairtrade-registered goldsmith Rosalie McMillan resulted in her Java Ore collection.[66] This combines another coffee-ground material, Çurface, with gold and sterling silver to create a wide range of jewellery.

Supply chain and circular processes

Greencup provides a 'full service' to its customers, supplying coffee machines and organic Fairtrade coffee beans, training baristas, and collecting the waste coffee grounds. The in-house 'Greencup Fleet' collects each container of waste grounds when making the next delivery, leaving a clean container with the customer. Returned waste is consolidated before despatch to the fertilizer plant.

Greencup and a partner company operate specialist composting and biomass conversion facilities, creating biochar and other raw ingredients, plus blending and bagging the fertilizer, then sold through many garden centres throughout the UK.[67]

Coffee grounds: creating value for other sectors

Researchers and startups are finding ways to create value from waste grounds.

GRO HOLLAND: GROWING MUSHROOMS ON COFFEE GROUNDS

GRO Holland uses coffee grounds from restaurant chains as a base on which to grow mushrooms. No other new raw materials are needed for the production, so providing a closed nutrient loop for the restaurants.[68] The project inspiration is the Ten Foundation, which teaches orphans in Zimbabwe how to grow their own food on organic waste materials.[69] GRO (Green Recycled Organics) set up a *closed-loop* partnership with two foodservice chains, and can now grow 2,000 kilos of oyster mushrooms each week. Logistics is a closed loop too, with vehicles delivering the mushrooms and returning with the next batch of used coffee grounds.

ESPRESSO MUSHROOM COMPANY: MUSHROOM-GROWING KITS

In 2011, the Espresso Mushroom Company started in the UK, and now supplies restaurants and greengrocers locally and online. It also sells 'Kitchen Gardens', mushroom-growing kits using coffee grounds from 100 espressos and mushroom 'spawn' (seeds), then grown for a month before delivery. Customers water for a couple of weeks and then harvest around 350 grams of mushrooms.[70]

Companies have found ways to convert waste coffee grounds into firewood substitutes too – though we should note that energy-from-waste should be the final stage in the circular economy: after we have extracted all other valuable nutrients, chemicals, fibres, etc, from the product. Examples include the Java-Log® Firelog[71] and bio-bean® in the UK.

BIO-BEAN®: ENERGY FROM WASTE[72]

In 2013, a student found research supporting his theory that used coffee grounds contain oil and so could be a fuel source. He went on to develop coffee-derived biomass pellets and launched bio-bean®, with coffee collection services across the UK. It built the world's first industrial-scale coffee recycling factory two years later and in 2016, bio-bean® launched a consumer product, Coffee Logs.

bio-bean® says 'spent coffee grounds still retain up to a third of the volatile aroma and flavour compounds as contained in fresh roasted beans' and in 2019, it plans to sell its first natural flavouring ingredient into the food and beverage industry. Its product development team is working on more products, ranging from dyes and pigments to bioplastics and cosmetics.

Companies are developing new materials, including textiles. Singtex Industrial Company in Taiwan has patented a process to make S.Café®, a viscose-like material, from waste coffee grounds.[73] Virus makes sports clothing, using Coffee Charcoal™ infused yarn as a performance fabric. C2Renew created a wire filament for 3D printers, Wound Up, using a composite of recycled coffee grounds that can make products, including cups. Scientists in South Korea have found that coffee beans have the potential for **energy storage and capture** of methane, a GHG.[74] The researchers are hopeful that methane from used coffee beans could become a clean energy fuel for cars. Menicon's fermentation technology converts coffee grounds from Starbucks stores in Tokyo into feed for dairy cows.

Accelerators using **collaborative** initiatives include Fairtrade, the Rainforest Alliance and company initiatives. Nestlé set up its Ecolaboration project in 2009, aiming to improve the sustainability of its Nespresso coffee capsule system. Nestlé encourages its employees to suggest ideas for the project, through its MyEcolaboration initiative.[75] It aims to increase sourcing of coffee from sustainable and Rainforest Alliance certified farms, triple the capacity to recycle used capsules to 75 per cent, and reduce the carbon footprint for a cup of Nespresso by 20 per cent.

Supply chain implications

Circular flows in the coffee supply chain are already feeding by-products into many different sectors, as shown in Figure 6.12. *Open loops*, whether into other food companies or to wider sectors, will involve challenges of forecasting supply and demand, logistics for new product formats, and managing irregular or unpredictable volumes. *Closed loops*, recovering energy and water on farms and in factories, are more straightforward.

We can see that by-product and recovery loops require new flows, different materials and locations, potentially fluctuating volumes, and other complications. The supply chain is the key to unlocking access to the value

FIGURE 6.12   Circular economy supply chain for coffee

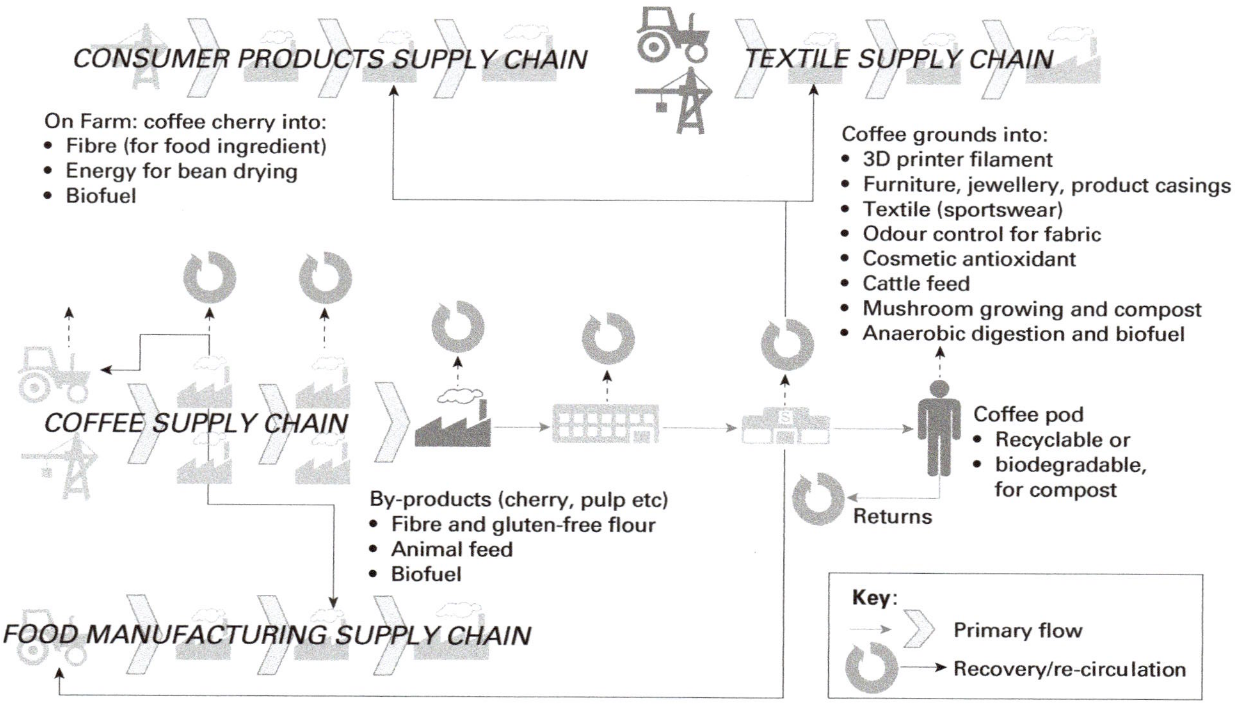

CONSUMER PRODUCTS SUPPLY CHAIN

TEXTILE SUPPLY CHAIN

Coffee grounds into:
- 3D printer filament
- Furniture, jewellery, product casings
- Textile (sportswear)
- Odour control for fabric
- Cosmetic antioxidant
- Cattle feed
- Mushroom growing and compost
- Anaerobic digestion and biofuel

On Farm: coffee cherry into:
- Fibre (for food ingredient)
- Energy for bean drying
- Biofuel

By-products (cherry, pulp etc)
- Fibre and gluten-free flour
- Animal feed
- Biofuel

COFFEE SUPPLY CHAIN

FOOD MANUFACTURING SUPPLY CHAIN

Coffee pod
- Recyclable or biodegradable, for compost

Returns

Key:
- Primary flow
- Recovery/re-circulation

SOURCE: © Catherine Weetman

potential in these new flows. Finding new sales channels for by-products may be challenging, especially for the early stages with erratic volumes and difficult-to-forecast supplies.

Summary

There are many conflicting issues facing food and agriculture, as farmers, producers, governments and NGOs develop plans to reduce hunger, protect and regenerate our living systems and improve our food supply systems to feed our increasing population. The current systems present enormous challenges. Processing food, aiming to provide convenient, tasty and good-value food for the consumer, combined with a profit for the food company, often conflicts with more sustainable approaches to agriculture, production and retailing. At every stage, water, energy, added ingredients (natural or synthetic) and inputs increase our demands on finite resources, often without improving human nutrition and health.

We have seen that agriculture has a heavy footprint, for water, land degradation, deforestation and climate. Global GHG emissions in 2030 need to be approximately 55 per cent lower than in 2017 to put the world on a least-cost pathway to limiting global warming to 1.5°C.[76]

Dietary health is a major issue. Campaigns for sugar taxes are gaining ground, recognizing that sugar is addictive and causes immense harm to health, including diabetes, obesity and tooth decay. Overweight people are at more risk of cardiovascular disease, osteoarthritis and various cancers. The EAT-Lancet Commission (2019)[77] reports that healthy diets 'consist of a diversity of plant-based foods, low amounts of animal source foods, unsaturated rather than saturated fats, and small amounts of refined grains, highly processed foods, and added sugars'. This requires major shifts, including over 50 per cent reduction in global consumption of unhealthy foods, such as red meat and sugar, together with a doubling in consumption of healthy foods, such as nuts, fruits, vegetables, and legumes (though these will differ by region). These changes are likely to benefit human health, averting over 10 million deaths per year, a reduction of around 20 per cent.

Regenerative farming, agro-forestry and avoiding intensively farmed meat can reduce the systemic overload on land, water and biodiversity. A 'flexitarian' diet, based on local and seasonal foods, safe, sustainable ingredients, together with circular approaches creating value from what we used to consider as waste, can all help. However, a sustainable agriculture and food supply chain seems at odds with the business models of many companies.

As Ulrike Sapiro, Director of Sustainability for Coca-Cola Western Europe (2016), says:

> Achieving a circular economy will require us to make some big changes to the way we are doing things … [these] may make us feel uncomfortable and may be met by resistance, but I think we can, and have to, overcome them.[78]

Further resources

Feedback Global – food waste campaign charity: feedbackglobal.org

Food and Agriculture Organization of the United Nations – Status of the World's Soil Resources: 'A reference document on the status of global soil resources with a strong regional assessment on soil change. It provides a description and a ranking of 10 major soil threats that endanger ecosystem functions, goods and services globally and in each region separately.' It includes descriptions of 'direct and indirect pressures on soils and ways and means to combat soil degradation at all levels'. [Online] http://www.fao.org/publications/en/ (archived at https://perma.cc/6D8K-U3DK)

Oxfam International [accessed 1 June 2016] Behind the Brands campaign [Online] https://www.oxfam.org/en/campaigns/behind-brands (archived at https://perma.cc/7P43-PE99)

United Nations Water, Food and Energy Nexus [accessed 27 March 2016] [Online] www.unwater.org/topics/water-food-and-energy-nexus/en/ (archived at https://perma.cc/4Y53-TDYZ)

Water Footprint Network [Online] http://waterfootprint.org/en/ (archived at https://perma.cc/2EGD-W69W)

Willett, W, Rockström, J et al (2019) [accessed 24 November 2019] *Food in the Anthropocene: the EAT–Lancet Commission on healthy diets from sustainable food systems* [Online] www.thelancet.com/commissions/EAT (archived at https://perma.cc/D7UP-HUFE)

Notes

1 Circular Economy Business Forum (2014) [accessed 25 May 2016] *British Sugar: the UK's Largest Producer of Sugar … and Speciality Salad Tomatoes* [Online] www.cebf.co.uk/british-sugar.html (archived at https://perma.cc/98VK-UZ6U)

2 Plunkett (2016) [accessed 28 March 2016] *Plunkett's Food Industry Almanac Market Research* [Online] www.plunkettresearch.com/industries/food-beverage-grocery-market-research/ (archived at https://perma.cc/H648-S6HB)

3 Ranganathan, J (3 December 2013) [accessed 28 March 2016] Global food challenge explained in 18 graphics, *World Resources Institute* [Online] www.wri.org/blog/2013/12/global-food-challenge-explained-18-graphics (archived at https://perma.cc/3XF5-KW62)

4 Oxfam (26 February 2015) [accessed 25 May 2016] *Behind the Brands: Food justice and the 'Big 10' food and beverage companies*, Briefing Paper 166 [Online] www.oxfam.org/en/file/bp166-behind-brands-260213-en2pdf (archived at https://perma.cc/M966-YK7X)

5 Oxfam (26 February 2015) [accessed 25 May 2016] *Behind the Brands: Food justice and the 'Big 10' food and beverage companies*, Briefing Paper 166 [Online] www.oxfam.org/en/file/bp166-behind-brands-260213-en2pdf (archived at https://perma.cc/M966-YK7X)

6 Howard, PH (2018) [accessed 24 November 2019] *Global Seed Industry Changes Since 2013*, 31 December [Online] philhoward.net/2018/12/31/global-seed-industry-changes-since-2013/

7 FAO (2016) [accessed 27 May 2016] *Food Chain Crisis* [Online] www.fao.org/food-chain-crisis/en/ (archived at https://perma.cc/Y6LA-W9XP)

8 Berners-Lee, M (2019) *There is No Planet B: A Handbook for the Make or Break Years*, Cambridge University Press, Cambridge, pp 12–15

9 FAO (2019) [accessed 24 November 2019] *Staple Foods: What do people eat?* [Online] www.fao.org/3/u8480e/U8480E07.htm (archived at https://perma.cc/TQ8H-EEYH)

10 FAO, IFAD, UNICEF, WFP and WHO (2019) [accessed 24 November 2019] *The State of Food Security and Nutrition in the World 2019: Safeguarding against economic slowdowns and downturns*, FAO, Rome [Online] http://www.fao.org/3/ca5162en/ca5162en.pdf (archived at https://perma.cc/U4VC-BZ3M)

11 Berners-Lee, M (2019) *There is No Planet B: A Handbook for the Make or Break Years*, Cambridge University Press, Cambridge, pp 12–15

12 FAO (2019) *World Food and Agriculture – Statistical pocketbook 2019*, FAO, Rome [Online] www.fao.org/publications/card/en/c/CA6463EN (archived at https://perma.cc/N7KA-C4DY) and UN Environment (2018) Emissions Gap Report 2018 https://www.unenvironment.org/resources/emissions-gap-report-2018 (archived at https://perma.cc/2LRU-GJGU)

13 Willett, W, Rockström, J et al (2019) [accessed 24 November 2019] *Food in the Anthropocene: the EAT-Lancet Commission on healthy diets from sustainable food systems* [Online] www.thelancet.com/commissions/EAT (archived at https://perma.cc/D7UP-HUFE)

14 Raworth, K (2012) The doughnut can help Rio+20 see sustainable development in the round, *The Guardian*, 16 June [Online] https://www.theguardian.com/global-development/poverty-matters/2012/jun/16/doughnut-rio20-sustainable-development (archived at https://perma.cc/NQ3E-BQ8C)

15 Ranganathan, J (3 December 2013) [accessed 28 March 2016] Global food challenge explained in 18 graphics, *World Resources Institute* [Online] www.wri.org/blog/2013/12/global-food-challenge-explained-18-graphics (archived at https://perma.cc/3XF5-KW62)

16 Ranganathan, J (3 December 2013) [accessed 28 March 2016] Global food challenge explained in 18 graphics, *World Resources Institute* [Online] www.wri.org/blog/2013/12/global-food-challenge-explained-18-graphics (archived at https://perma.cc/3XF5-KW62)

17 FoodPrint (2019) [accessed 24 November 2019] *Sustainable Agriculture vs. Industrial Agriculture* [Online] foodprint.org/issues/sustainable-agriculture-vs-industrial-agriculture/ (archived at https://perma.cc/2QFV-JZFV)

18 Ranganathan, J (3 December 2013) [accessed 28 March 2016] Global food challenge explained in 18 graphics, *World Resources Institute* [Online] www.wri.org/blog/2013/12/global-food-challenge-explained-18-graphics (archived at https://perma.cc/3XF5-KW62)

19 UN Water (2014) [accessed 28 March 2016] *The Food, Water and Energy Nexus* [Online] www.unwater.org/topics/water-food-and-energy-nexus/en/ (archived at https://perma.cc/4Y53-TDYZ)

20 Majot, J and Kuyek, D (2017) [accessed 24 November 2019] Big meat and big dairy's climate emissions put Exxon Mobil to shame, *The Guardian*, 7 November [Online] www.theguardian.com/commentisfree/2017/nov/07/big-meat-big-dairy-carbon-emmissions-exxon- (archived at https://perma.cc/LGX2-E56Z)

21 UN Water (8 September 2015) [accessed 2 April 2016] *Water and Sustainable Development* [Online] www.un.org/waterforlifedecade/water_and_sustainable_development.shtml (archived at https://perma.cc/F444-X8DC)

22 BestFootForward (2011) [Online] http://anthesisgroup.com/how-much-land-does-it-take-to-feed-the-uk/ (archived at https://perma.cc/43VH-GEBR). Best Foot Forward's foodprint tool is based on UK data showing kilograms of food groups used per person per year from the UN Food and Agriculture Organization

23 Searchinger, T et al (December 2013) [accessed 2 April 2016] Creating a sustainable food future: interim findings, *World Resources Institute* [Online] www.wri.org/publication/creating-sustainable-food-future-interim-findings (archived at https://perma.cc/RN4K-PP5P)

24 FAO (4 December 2014) [accessed 26 March 2016] Nothing dirty here: FAO kicks off international year of soils 2015, *UN FAO* [Online] www.fao.org/news/story/en/item/270812/icode/ (archived at https://perma.cc/5A2W-8VSB)

25 Walz, H (2019) [accessed 24 November 2019] Agriculture and deforestation, *The Ecologist*, 27 September [Online] https://theecologist.org/2019/sep/27/agriculture-and-deforestation (archived at https://perma.cc/4AKR-SKRW)

26 IPBES (2019) [accessed 25 November 2019] Summary for policymakers of the global assessment report on biodiversity and ecosystem services of the Intergovernmental Science-Policy Platform on Biodiversity and Ecosystem

Service [Online] ipbes.net/system/tdf/ipbes_global_assessment_report_
summary_for_policymakers.pdf?file=1&type=node&id=35329 (archived at
https://perma.cc/VS8J-LKAK)

27 FAO (2014) [accessed 27 March 2016] *Water, Food and Energy Nexus*
    [Online] www.unwater.org/topics/water-food-and-energy-nexus/en/ (archived
    at https://perma.cc/4Y53-TDYZ)

28 Nestlé (2014) [accessed 15 August 2016] *Nestlé in Society – Creating shared
    value and meeting our commitments 2014*, p 16 [Online] http://www.nestle.
    com/asset-library/Documents/Library/Documents/Corporate_Social_
    Responsibility/Nestle-in-Society-Summary-Report-2014-EN.pdf (archived at
    https://perma.cc/YH8D-CTF8)

29 The Natural Step (2016) [accessed 26 May 2016] [Online]
    www.thenaturalstep.org/our-approach/ (archived at https://perma.cc/L38B-99CP)

30 House of Commons Environment [accessed 1 April 2016] Food and Rural
    Affairs Committee, Food security: Second Report of Session 2014–15 [Online]
    www.publications.parliament.uk/pa/cm201415/cmselect/cmenvfru/243/243.pdf
    (archived at https://perma.cc/KZ4L-SF48)

31 Oxfam (October 2012) [accessed 15 August 2016] *Our Land, Our Lives*,
    Briefing Note, p 2 [Online] http://www.oxfam.org/sites/www.oxfam.org/files/
    bn-land-lives-freeze-041012-en_1.pdf (archived at https://perma.cc/46Z2-
    XVTS)

32 Ellen MacArthur Foundation, SUN, McKinsey (June 2015) [accessed 15
    August 2016] *Growth Within: A circular economy vision for a competitive
    Europe*, p 19 [Online] https://www.ellenmacarthurfoundation.org/publications/
    growth-within-a-circular-economy-vision-for-a-competitive-europe (archived at
    https://perma.cc/KR92-8MBM)

33 FAO (2019) *State of Food and Agriculture 2019* [Online] http://www.fao.org/
    state-of-food-agriculture/en/ (archived at https://perma.cc/SF3U-72RK)

34 WRAP (2016) [accessed 2 April 2016] Food Waste Statistics, *Love Food
    Hate Waste* [Online] www.lovefoodhatewaste.com/node/2472 (archived at
    https://perma.cc/P9RS-56FY)

35 Ranganathan, J (3 December 2013) [accessed 28 March 2016] Global food
    challenge explained in 18 graphics, *World Resources Institute* [Online]
    www.wri.org/blog/2013/12/global-food-challenge-explained-18-graphics
    (archived at https://perma.cc/3XF5-KW62)

36 Rubies in the Rubble [accessed 1 April 2016] [Online] www.rubiesintherubble.
    com/ (archived at https://perma.cc/6QBR-QLQT)

37 AgriProtein (2019) [accessed 25 November 2019] [Online] agriprotein.com/
    about-us/

38 Neate, R (2015) Crazy recipe for success: egg-free egg, *The Guardian*,
    21 March

39 Welcome to the '4 per 1000' Initiative (2019) [accessed 24 November 2019]
    [Online] www.4p1000.org/ (archived at https://perma.cc/8S2N-S88X)

40 Zero Carbon Food Ltd (2016) [accessed 1 April 2016] [Online] www.zerocarbonfood.co.uk/about-us/ (archived at https://perma.cc/6NMG-FWS2)

41 Zero Waste Scotland (2016) [accessed 2 April 2016] *Sector Study on Beer, Whisky and Fish* [Online] www.zerowastescotland.org.uk/ BeerWhiskyFish#sthash.ogn3kOCw.dpuf (archived at https://perma.cc/ U4E9-BSJ4)

42 British Sugar (2019) [accessed 26 November 2019] [Online] www.britishsugar. co.uk/about-sugar/co-products (archived at https://perma.cc/SXH7-FRPB)

43 Colbert, E (2017) [accessed 24 November 2019] *Causes of Food Waste in International Supply Chains*, Feedback Global [Online] feedbackglobal.org/ wp-content/uploads/2017/05/Causes-of-food-waste-in-international-supply-chains_Feedback.pdf (archived at https://perma.cc/PQ5W-9CBQ)

44 Company Shop Ltd (2016) [accessed 1 April 2016] [Online] https://www.companyshopgroup.co.uk/ (archived at https://perma.cc/MF8N-9D8D)

45 Email from Peter Laybourn, International Synergies Ltd, 2 October 2019

46 Till, J (8 April 2015) [accessed 2 April 2016] Biodegradable planters and bowls with AgriDust, *Packaging Insider* [Online] thepackaginginsider.com/ biodegradable-planters-bowls-agridust/#s0SRTej5DUFyCh3o.99 (archived at https://perma.cc/RB52-F4TD)

47 Ellen MacArthur Foundation (March 2017) [accessed 24 November 2019] *Urban Biocycles* [Online] www.ellenmacarthurfoundation.org/assets/ downloads/publications/Urban-Biocycles_EllenMacArthurFoundation_ 21-06-2017.pdf (archived at https://perma.cc/4CDU-57ZA)

48 Wong, K (2017) [accessed 24 November 2019] Tackling food waste around the world: our top 10 apps, *The Guardian*, 6 February [Online] www.theguardian.com/sustainable-business/2017/feb/06/food-waste-apps-global-technology-leftovers-landfill (archived at https://perma.cc/52VV-C79N)

49 Firn, D (2016) From honey to milk, how fraud enters the food supply chain, *The Review, Financial Times*, 10 March, p 14

50 WRAP (2010) [accessed 31 March 2016] [Online] www.wrap.org.uk/content/ information-sheet-apetito-waste-prevention-boosts-business-efficiency (archived at https://perma.cc/S7ML-KDTZ)

51 EDIE.net (22 February 2016) [accessed 11 March 2016] *Green Beans: 5 sustainable coffee innovations* [Online] www.edie.net/library/Green-beans-5-sustainable-coffee-innovations/6689 (archived at https://perma.cc/9U8A-77CN)

52 International Coffee Organization (29 February 2016) [accessed 11 March 2016] *The Current State of the Global Coffee Trade* [Online] www.ico.org/ monthly_coffee_trade_stats.asp (archived at https://perma.cc/FC25-DG7U)

53 EDIE.net (22 February 2016) [accessed 11 March 2016] *Green Beans: 5 sustainable coffee innovations* [Online] www.edie.net/library/Green-beans-5-sustainable-coffee-innovations/6689 (archived at https://perma.cc/9U8A-77CN)

54 Blacksell, G (4 October 2011) [accessed 11 March 2016] How green is your coffee? *The Guardian* [Online] www.theguardian.com/environment/2011/oct/04/green-coffee (archived at https://perma.cc/BT8F-K2HY)

55 Blacksell, G (4 October 2011) [accessed 11 March 2016] How green is your coffee? *The Guardian* [Online] www.theguardian.com/environment/2011/oct/04/green-coffee (archived at https://perma.cc/BT8F-K2HY)

56 The World Counts (2016) [accessed 11 March 2016] *World Coffee Consumption Statistics* [Online] www.theworldcounts.com/counters/world_food_consumption_statistics/world_coffee_consumption_statistics (archived at https://perma.cc/4YTX-5HJZ)

57 The World Counts (2016) [accessed 11 March 2016] *World Coffee Consumption Statistics* [Online] www.theworldcounts.com/counters/world_food_consumption_statistics/world_coffee_consumption_statistics (archived at https://perma.cc/4YTX-5HJZ)

58 Chapagain, AK and Hoekstra AY (2007) The water footprint of coffee and tea consumption in the Netherlands, *Ecological Economics*, **64**, pp 109–18

59 Kubota, L (8 July 2013) [accessed 31 March 2016] *The Use of Water in Processing: Treatment, conservation, and impacts on quality* [Online] www.scaa.org/chronicle/2013/07/08/the-use-of-water-in-processing-treatment-conservation-and-impacts-on-quality/ (archived at https://perma.cc/PB8C-X5ZC)

60 Dugmore, T (2014) [accessed 1 April 2016] *The Business of Food Waste*, Centre for European Policy Studies [Online] www.ceps.eu/sites/default/files/u153872/Tom%20Dugmore%20%20The%20Business%20of%20Food%20Waste.pdf (archived at https://perma.cc/C9WH-88XK)

61 EDIE.net (22 February 2016) [accessed 11 March 2016] *Green Beans: 5 sustainable coffee innovations* [Online] www.edie.net/library/Green-beans-5-sustainable-coffee-innovations/6689 (archived at https://perma.cc/9U8A-77CN)

62 EDIE.net (22 February 2016) [accessed 11 March 2016] *Green Beans: 5 sustainable coffee innovations* [Online] www.edie.net/library/Green-beans-5-sustainable-coffee-innovations/6689 (archived at https://perma.cc/9U8A-77CN)

63 EDIE.net (22 February 2016) [accessed 11 March 2016] *Green Beans: 5 sustainable coffee innovations* [Online] www.edie.net/library/Green-beans-5-sustainable-coffee-innovations/6689 (archived at https://perma.cc/9U8A-77CN)

64 Good News Network [accessed 11 March 2016] *Check Out the Surprising Products Being Made From Coffee Grounds* [Online] www.goodnewsnetwork.org/surprising-products-made-from-coffee-grounds/ (archived at https://perma.cc/5YS3-WUTV)

65 SanRemo UK (2016) [accessed 11 March 2016] *Verde TCS* [Online] www.sanremouk.com (archived at https://perma.cc/NP2W-VJHR)

66 McMillan, R (2016) [accessed 11 March 2016] [Online] www.rosaliemcmillan. com/collection/ (archived at https://perma.cc/E93U-5EYL)

67 Fairweather, A (2 April 2016) emails to C Weetman

68 GRO Holland [accessed 11 March 2016] [Online] www.rabobank.com/en/ about-rabobank/in-society/sustainability/circular-economy-challenge/ tomatenvel-in-autodashboard.html (archived at https://perma.cc/QCN9-RFC8)

69 Food Valley Update (4 January 2016) [accessed 31 March 2016] *News* [Online] www.foodvalleyupdate.com/news/from-coffee-grounds-to-vegetarian- oyster-mushroom-snack/ (archived at https://perma.cc/P6LX-NBH5)

70 Donovan, L (26 September 2013) [accessed 1 April 2016] Word of Mouth, *The Telegraph* [Online] www.telegraph.co.uk/foodanddrink/10333559/ Word-of-mouth-The-Espresso-Mushroom-Company.html (archived at https://perma.cc/Y6X3-SANY)

71 Riordan T (2003) [accessed 31 March 2016] Patents: a fireplace log made of recycled coffee grounds burns brighter and hotter than sawdust logs, *New York Times*, 13 October [Online] www.nytimes.com/2003/10/13/business/patents- fireplace-log-made-recycled-coffee-grounds-burns-brighter-hotter-than.html (archived at https://perma.cc/9G37-CWRG)

72 bio-bean (2019) [accessed 24 November 2019] [Online] www.bio-bean.com/ (archived at https://perma.cc/JK8R-96KK)

73 Singtex (2019) [accessed 25 November 2019] [Online] www.singtex.com/ en-global/technology/fabrics_info/scafe (archived at https://perma.cc/7A7S-QXDZ)

74 EDIE.net (22 February 2016) [accessed 11 March 2016] *Green Beans: 5 sustainable coffee innovations* [Online] www.edie.net/library/Green-beans-5- sustainable-coffee-innovations/6689 (archived at https://perma.cc/9U8A-77CN)

75 Nestlé Nespresso [accessed 31 March 2016] [Online] www.nespresso.com/ ecolaboration/gb/en/article/7/1736/about-ecolaboration-trade.html (archived at https://perma.cc/HZ9W-8C8T)

76 IPCC (2018) [accessed 24 November 2019] *UN Environment Emissions Gap Report 2018* [Online] www.ipcc.ch/site/assets/uploads/2018/12/UNEP-1.pdf (archived at https://perma.cc/3GJU-5RZT)

77 Willett, W, Rockström, J et al (2019) [accessed 24 November 2019] *Food in the Anthropocene: the EAT–Lancet Commission on healthy diets from sustainable food systems* [Online] www.thelancet.com/commissions/EAT (archived at https://perma.cc/D7UP-HUFE)

78 Sapiro, U (18 March 2016) [accessed 27 May 2016] *The Circular Economy: What does it mean to Coca-Cola's Director of Sustainability?* [Online] www.coca-cola.co.uk/blog/the-circular-economy-what-does-it-mean-to-coca- colas-director-of-sustainability (archived at https://perma.cc/YDL8-LMC8)

7

Fashion and textiles

Be part of the solution rather than part of the problem, and you can sleep at night.

YVON CHOUINARD, PATAGONIA (2015)[1]

The fashion industry is a typical 'linear economy', with most business models dependent on increasing consumption (and thus disposal). In this chapter, we cover:

- a background, with recent history and global trends, and an overview of the process;
- issues and challenges in the traditional fashion supply chain, including business models and resources and a 'balanced scorecard';
- circular economy developments, including business models, sustainable inputs, product design, process design and recovery flows;
- then we summarize, and look at what's next.

Background and global trends

Until roughly the mid-19th century, clothing was 'bespoke', often requiring fitting, and largely produced by local tailors and 'seamstresses'. The world wars saw factories set up to make uniforms and other textiles. Sewing machines and the industrial revolution gradually changed the nature of clothing, enabling mass production and standard sizes. In the 1980s, World Trade Organization agreements led to phasing out of quotas and tariffs,[2] and clothing production moved around the world, as clothing brands and major retailers found new low-cost manufacturing countries to help them compete on price and speed to market.

'Fast fashion' emerged in the 1990s, as manufacturers developed 'quick response' methods. According to Burgen, the retailer Zara 'can get a new design made up and distributed in a week, and it launches about 12,000 new designs every year'.[3] Critics say that 'fast fashion' has now become 'throwaway fashion', with relatively cheap clothing marketed as something to wear on a few occasions, before discarding it to make way for new items.

Clothing production doubled, from around 50 billion items a year in 2000 to over 100 billion by 2015, outstripping global GDP growth, and with a total value of US$1.3 trillion.[4] That equates to a global average of 14 garments per person, and consumption in the United States is around 50 garments per person.[5]

Clothing and textiles represent around 7 per cent of total world exports, and the market is growing at around 2.5 per cent each year. Around one-third of sales are in the United States, one-third in Western Europe and one-quarter in Asia. Sales are growing fastest in Brazil, China, India, Mexico and Russia, far outstripping sales in developed economies such as the US and the UK. Major players include H&M, Zara (parent Inditex), Adidas, Nike, Gap, Levi Strauss, LVMH and TJX. Sales are through retail outlets, catalogues and online, with the online channel growing rapidly.

Apparel production has low barriers to entry, and new suppliers can set up quickly with little investment. Often, supply chains extend across countries and even continents, and companies may subcontract to others to avoid turning away orders from important customers. The end customer may not be aware of the subcontracting, and overall there are many issues with **lack of transparency**: which suppliers are involved; the provenance of materials; the employment conditions of the workers; the efficiency and environmental standards of production. **Employment** estimates vary, with Fashion United (2015)[6] estimating 75 million worldwide for the garment industry, and the Ellen MacArthur Foundation (EMF, 2017)[7] reporting a figure of 300 million all along the clothing value chain. EMF notes that cotton production alone accounts for almost 7 per cent of all employment in some low-income countries. Indications show that around three-quarters of garment workers are female.

To make textiles, fibres are spun or extruded into yarns, then knitted or woven into fabrics. The first commercial man-made fibre was artificial silk, using natural cellulosics (from bark, wood or plants), produced in France in 1892.[8] Other cellulosics and acetates followed; a scientist at DuPont developed nylon in the 1930s; polyester was developed in the mid-20th century.

Textile uses include clothing for fashion or workwear, upholstery, household linens, carpets and so on:

FIGURE 7.1   Textile fibre production, by type of fibre

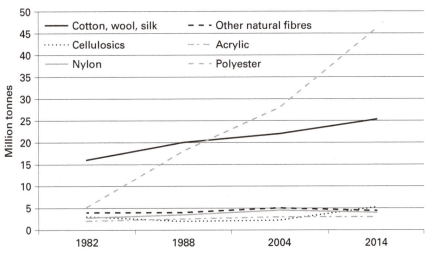

SOURCE: Fiber Source, Fiber World, The Fiber Year, Textiles Intelligence, Textile Basics

- Man-made fibres including polyester, nylon and acrylic now account for well over half the tonnage of all textiles produced, and polyester quantities increased by a factor of eight between 1979 and 2014.

- Cotton accounts for around 85 per cent of the natural fibres used worldwide, and up to 30 per cent of total fibre production. In 2015, 26 million metric tonnes of cotton was produced globally, much of it for the apparel industry, with organic cotton making up less than 1 per cent of this.[9]

Figure 7.1 shows the growth of fibre production and the contribution of major fibre types.

Figure 7.2 outlines **typical processes in the fashion supply chain,** starting with fibre production, then yarn or thread spinning, followed by textile manufacture, dyeing and finishing, then final garment production. Big retailers and global fashion brands decide what to produce, where from, and at what price. The fragmented nature of these supply chains means that suppliers and manufacturers have little influence, so are effectively competing with other countries to produce the cheapest, fastest products at the appropriate quality.

Issues

A UK survey of fashion purchasing habits for women found that the majority did not know how long they intended to keep their new purchases, and

FIGURE 7.2   Fashion supply chain

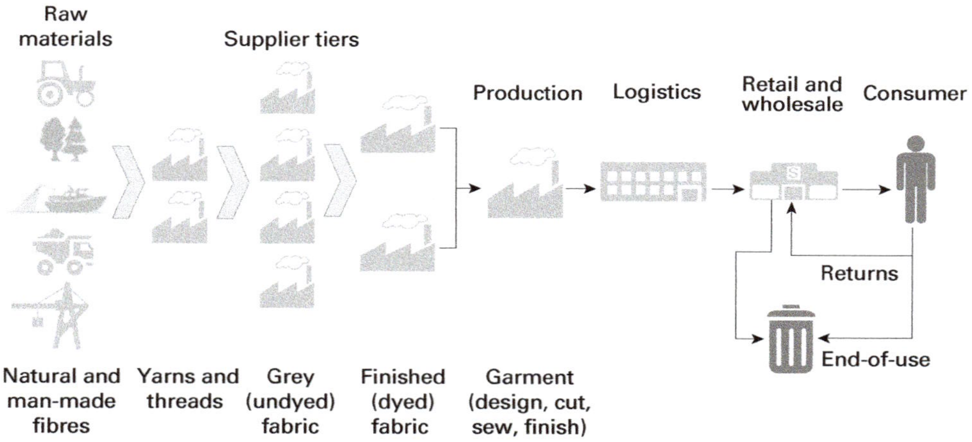

Raw materials		Supplier tiers				Production	Logistics	Retail and wholesale	Consumer

Natural and man-made fibres | Yarns and threads | Grey (undyed) fabric | Finished (dyed) fabric | Garment (design, cut, sew, finish) | | |

Returns

End-of-use

SOURCE: © Catherine Weetman

that when cheaper items became stained or damaged they were more likely to dispose of them than to clean or repair them.[10] In the UK, the average lifetime of clothing is 3.3 years.[11]

The average US citizen throws away over 30 kilograms of clothing and textiles each year.[12] The United States generates 11.5 billion kilos of post-consumer textile waste each year, with only 15 per cent recycled and the remainder going to landfill.

On top of discarded clothes from post-consumer use, there is also the issue of unsold products and customer returns, especially from online sales. Returns of 30 per cent are common for fashion online retailers, with customers often choosing more than one size or colour and then returning the items not required. With 'fast fashion', the time taken for return, receipt and processing might miss the window of opportunity for restocking and selling the item at, or close to, its original price.

Business models and consumption

'Fast fashion', with rapid changes in product ranges, heavy marketing activity and ever-cheaper prices, encourages people in developed economies to purchase more clothes each year. Some clothing is now so cheap that it has become a single-use item, especially for fashion-conscious young people who may decide not to wear a new item after they've posted a 'selfie' on social media. *The Observer* (2018)[13] reported that online brand Boohoo had nearly 500 dresses available for less than £5, and that rival Asos had 250 dresses and over 2,000 tops on sale for less than £10.

Product design

A garment typically consists of several component parts. There may be 'body fabrics' (an outer layer plus linings), as well as additional waddings, interlinings and trim fabrics. Other components include the thread to sew the pieces together, plus fasteners such as buttons, zips or toggles. All components can be made from natural or man-made materials or blends of the two. Local specialisms in manufacturing mean that components for a garment may come from more than one continent. In addition, retailers or brands may source the same garment from two separate locations, providing flexibility to respond to sales fluctuations through a more local manufacturer. Packaging, potentially including hangers, tickets for price/size/brand information and wrapping, is added during garment production or closer to the point of sale.

Resources: materials

Textile raw materials are usually categorized as either natural (plant or animal) or man-made (synthetic or regenerated cellulosic):

- **Natural fibres** from plants and animals include cotton, flax, hemp, sisal angora, cashmere, wool, and silk.

- **Man-made fibres** from **cellulosics sources** such as trees and other plants include viscose, rayon, TENCEL® lyocell and modal.

- **Man-made fibres** from **synthetic polymers** (often by-products of petroleum) include polyester, polyamide (nylon) and acrylic.

When comparing footprints and production methods, we should note that natural does not necessarily mean 'good', and man-made mean 'bad'. Made-By publishes an environmental benchmark for fibres, used by some leading brands. It classifies fibres based on *GHG*, human toxicity, eco-toxicity, plus energy, water and land use.[14] There are five classifications, with recycled wool, recycled cotton, organic hemp and flax, and mechanically recycled polyester or nylon in Class A (the best), compared with conventional cotton, rayon and viscose in Class E (the worst).

    Cotton, accounting for around one-third of fibres used in textiles, is the most important non-food agricultural commodity worldwide, and is 'particularly vulnerable to pests if no protection methodology is employed'.[15] In India, cotton accounts for over half of all **pesticides** used each year, despite occupying only 5 per cent of cropland. Hardly any global production is organic, and even **genetically modified** (GM) cotton requires pesticide use. The Better Cotton Initiative explains that 'one large class of GM cotton plants has a gene implanted that creates Bacillus thuringiensis (Bt), a toxin found in nature, which provides "built-in" protection from certain insect categories'. The Environmental Justice Foundation (EJF) produced a report with the Pesticide Action Network highlighting the impacts of chemicals used in cotton farming worldwide:[16]

- Cotton accounts for 16 per cent (US$2 billion-worth) of global insecticide releases, more than any other type of crop. Around 40 per cent of this is toxic enough for the World Health Organization to classify them as hazardous to human health.

- Aldicarb, common in cotton farming, is highly toxic to humans, with just one drop absorbed through the skin being enough to kill an adult. Aldicarb is used across 26 countries in 2003, and with almost 1 million kilos applied to cotton grown in the United States.

- 1–3 per cent of farm workers worldwide suffer from acute pesticide poisoning, with at least 1 million requiring hospital treatment each year. EJF cites joint research from the Food and Agriculture Organization of the United Nations (FAO), the United Nations Environment Programme (UNEP) and the World Health Organization (WHO), and estimates that 25–77 million agricultural workers are affected.

In 1988, after opening a new store in Boston and stocking the shelves with lots of cotton sportswear, Patagonia employees were complaining of headaches. Patagonia closed the store and investigated – a chemical engineer found the employees were breathing in formaldehyde fumes. Patagonia started asking questions, finding that most '100 per cent pure cotton' clothing is typically only 73 per cent cotton. In other words, over a quarter of the fabric consists of chemicals, including formaldehyde (a toxin), applied to stop wrinkling and shrinkage.[17]

Other natural fabric sources include **fur, fleeces and skins** from a wide range of animals. Leather has many sustainability issues, particularly with non-vegetable tanning methods. Wool, cashmere and silk all have ethical concerns, even so-called 'ethical silk', etc. There is more interest in cruelty-free textiles and leathers, and an increasing popularity of **vegan apparel**, defined by PETA as containing 'no leather, fur, wool, skin, exotic skins or any other animal-derived fabric'.

Man-made cellulosic fabrics include viscose and rayon. Viscose is a wood-based fibre and only a tiny minority is made using closed-loop production processes like Tencel (Lyocell and Modal). The remainder is criticized as 'dirty viscose' because of the chemicals used and released.

Synthetic fabrics may have significant environmental and human health risks too. Polyester, a plastic made from crude oil, is linked to carcinogenic and endocrine-disrupting effects.[18] Polyester is highly flammable and so is often treated with flame-retardants, exposing workers, consumers and living systems to more toxins. In use, and when washed, polyester sheds plastic microfibres. Fashion United (2018)[19] reports that each cycle of a washing machine can release more than 700,000 plastic fibres into the environment, which can end up in rivers and oceans, absorbing toxic chemicals and entering the food chain. Both virgin and recycled polyester contribute to microplastics pollution. Polyester is not biodegradable, meaning it could take from 20 to 200 years to degrade – into more microfibres.

MANUFACTURING – CHEMICAL INPUTS AND EFFLUENTS

Hazardous substances affect the health of textile workers **and** those wearing the clothes, and escape into the environment too. Over 8,000 synthetic chemicals are used in textile production globally, and 17–20 per cent of industry-caused water pollution is estimated to be caused by textile dyeing and treatment.[20] Environmental charity Greenpeace tested a range of clothing for toxic chemicals and dyes,[21] purchasing over 140 items of clothing from 20 global fashion brands, in 29 countries worldwide, all from authorized retailers. Analysis showed high levels of toxic phthalates in four garments, and carcinogenic amines from the use of azo dyes in two garments. NPEs (nonylphenol ethoxylates) were found in 89 garments, almost two-thirds of those tested, and a similar proportion to an earlier investigation in 2011.

Major brands, including Gap, H&M and Adidas, have begun collaborating to develop processes with zero-discharge of hazardous chemicals, aiming for 'widespread implementation of sustainable chemistry and best practices in the textile and footwear industry to protect consumers, workers and the environment'.[22]

Resources: energy

To produce 60 billion kilograms of fabric uses an estimated 1,000 billion kWh of electricity.[23] McKinsey (2016),[24] noting that countries with large fabric- and apparel-making industries rely mainly on fossil fuels for energy production, estimate that making 1 kilogram of fabric generates an average of 23 kilograms of greenhouse gases. The authors estimate that washing and drying 1 kilogram of clothing over its entire life-cycle, using typical methods, creates 11 kilograms of greenhouse gases. Analyses of the 'carbon footprint' or GHG emissions of fashion products often conclude that 'in-use' GHG emissions are the most significant portion of the whole. The example in Figure 7.3 shows 37 per cent of emissions arising in-use, compared with 44 per cent for the manufacturing processes.

Resources: water

The 60 billion kilograms of fabric in the energy example above also uses 6–9 trillion litres of water.[25] Cotton plantations tend to be heavily irrigated, affecting water availability for other farming needs and for domestic and industrial needs. Analysis of the water footprint for C&A's supply chain by source country revealed a wide range.[26] India had the highest use, at over 9,000 cubic metres per tonne of seed cotton. The global average was 4,000

FIGURE 7.3   Example life-cycle GHG emissions for jeans

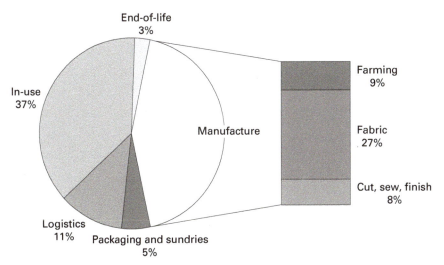

Emissions by phase in life-cycle – kg CO_2e

SOURCE: Levi Strauss[27]

cubic metres of water. However, river basins in some of the key source regions were water-stressed for several months each year. The report highlighted the key river basins affected by water scarcity and looked at the share of the C&A blue water footprint (surface and groundwater sources) attributed to each basin. The report found four high-priority river basins (all with more than six months of moderate to high scarcity each year), affecting six source countries, shown in Table 7.1.

TABLE 7.1   Water footprint versus water scarcity

Basin	C&A source countries	Share of C&A supply chain Blue WF located in the basin	Months of year with basin under moderate to severe scarcity
Indus	China, India, Pakistan	39.4%	12
Tigris/Euphrates	Syria, Turkey	5.3%	6
Murray	Australia	4.4%	8
Krishna	India	2.4%	9

NOTE: Blue WF (water footprint): 'blue water' is the consumption of surface and groundwater sources.
SOURCE: Franke and Mathews (2013)[28]

FIGURE 7.4   The shrinking Aral Sea

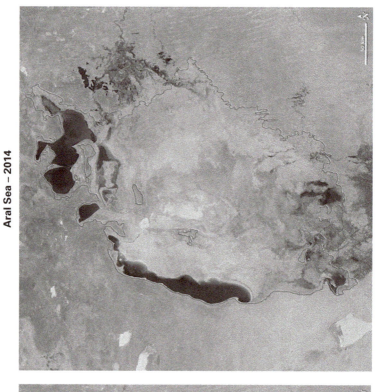

Aral Sea – 2014

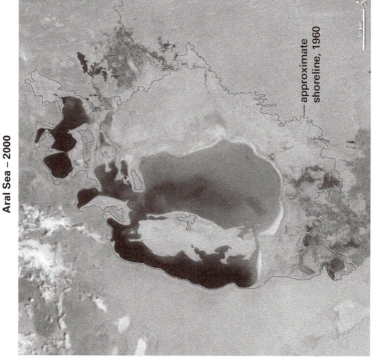

Aral Sea – 2000

— approximate
shoreline, 1960

50 km

50 km

SOURCE: NASA's Earth Observatory

Reports like this are useful for highlighting areas for improvement, such as working with farmers to find ways to reuse water, reduce water consumption through more specific irrigation, look at different planting seasons or seed varieties, and so on. Bodey notes that China 'loses up to US$36 billion each year because of water shortages', losing around 10 per cent of GDP because of pollution-related problems and may 'start to demand higher standards from textile factories'.[29]

Water diverted from the Aral Sea by the Soviet Union in the 1950s, mainly for irrigation of cotton crops, has continued as a means of supporting Uzbekistan's key cotton industries. Hoskins reports that 'exposure of the bottom of the lake has released salts and pesticides into the atmosphere, poisoning both farmland and people alike. Carcinogenic dust is blown into villages causing throat cancers and respiratory diseases.'[30] The local fishing industry (which once employed around 60,000 people) has ceased. NASA announced that the Aral seabed had dried up, publishing time-lapsed video recordings showing the difference between 2000 and 2014, shown in Figure 7.4. The faint black line on each photograph shows the shoreline in 1960.

Ravasio reports that '14.4 per cent of an apparel retailer's total water footprint relates to manufacturing', compared with 54 per cent for the jeans example. Figure 7.5 shows the life-cycle impacts of a pair of jeans, with a total water impact measured at over 3,700 litres. Levi Strauss & Co already has a Water<Less® programme for its jeans, with several innovations helping it to save over 1 billion litres of water by 2015, so the water footprint

FIGURE 7.5   Footprint analysis for jeans

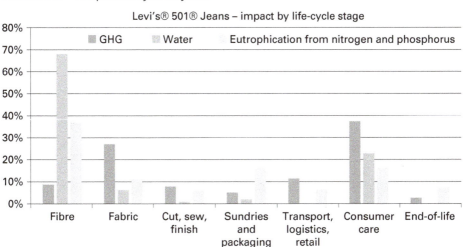

SOURCE: Levi Strauss & Co (2015)[31]

for these jeans is likely to be 'industry-leading', with many products and manufacturers using much higher levels of water.

A typical figure for 1 kilogram of cotton is 20,000 litres. A conventional cotton t-shirt typically uses between 2,700 and 4,300 litres. Leather shoes typically require around 8,000 litres; this can also vary enormously depending on the local climate and whether the animals are reared for meat or milk, rather than primarily for leather.

Resources: land

The amount of **land used** to grow cotton has been in the range of 30–35 million hectares in the last few decades, as improved cotton yields provided the increased production tonnage. However, there is growing pressure on land use from the need to grow more food, and regenerate forestry, plus the issues of agricultural land degradation that we looked at in Chapter 6.

Fertilizer use is also a concern, as we saw in Chapter 6, with industrial fertilizers causing GHG emissions together with harmful effects from nitrogen and phosphorus run-off into water sources.[32]

Balanced scorecard

We can summarize the sustainability issues using the Natural Step criteria we looked at in Chapters 5 and 6. Figure 7.6 shows a simple scorecard, with the kind of assessment that any fashion brand or manufacturer might use as a starting point to track their sustainability improvements over the long term.

There are wide-ranging issues along the supply chain, for both natural and man-made materials, covering use of scarce materials, safety issues from chemicals (for both human health and for living systems), and damage to ecosystems at every stage. Working conditions are often poor, perhaps unsafe, with long hours and poor pay, and use of forced and child labour. Even in use, there may be safety issues from toxins in the fabrics and dyes.

Extended supply chains for most fashion brands means production efficiency improvements are largely the responsibility of individual manufacturers, often small enterprises struggling to fund investments in new machinery and innovative approaches.

FIGURE 7.6   Sector issues – fashion

	Supply chain stage				
Natural Step criteria	Raw materials	Manufacture	Logistics and sales	Use	End-of-life
Scarce materials taken from the earth	⬇	⬂	⬇	⬂	⬆
Man-made toxic and persistent chemicals	⬂	⬇	⬂	⬂	⬂
Destruction and pollution of nature	➚	⬇	⬂	⬂	⬇
Work and/or use conditions	⬂	⬂	➚	⬂	⬇

Key:	Good	Quite good	Quite bad	Bad	Don't know
	Positive impacts, no concerns	Positive or neutral impacts, few concerns	Negative or neutral impacts, many concerns	Negative impacts, widespread /major concerns	Not enough information
	⬆	➚	⬂	⬇	?

SOURCE: Adapted from Streamlined Life Cycle Assessment (based on Natural Step System Conditions), Sustainable Wealth Creation, 2007, with kind permission of Forum for the Future

Circular economy developments

The fashion industry is facing pressure to change its ways, from material choice to lowering 'consumption', and from reducing energy and 'fashion miles' to improving working conditions in fields and factories. We are seeing examples of circular innovations across the sector, including circular business models, together with new and recycled materials. Many of these are from startups, and the 'supertanker' global brands seem to be finding it harder to step off the take-make-waste, revenue-generating model. Being 'first-mover' seems to be a risk – but is there a bigger risk of disruption from a startup or expanding smaller brand?

The industry is looking at ways to create disposable garments using 'waste is food' principles, but this raises questions of how to justify the energy and water used in production and the supply chain.

Consultancy Circle Economy (2019) highlights the importance of switching to circular business models, especially extending the active use of garments – using a 'garment just three months longer can lower its water, carbon and waste footprint by 5 per cent to 10 per cent'. It notes that people buy 60 per cent more items than they did 15 years ago and wear them for half as long. Seventy per cent of clothes usually go unworn and it is estimated that one-third of women wear items as few as five times before disposing of them. Circle Economy encourages brands to see the value-adding scope of reselling and renting, pointing out that 'consumer attitudes towards wearing "used" clothing are rapidly shifting with 64 per cent of women now buying or willing to buy secondhand products'.[33]

Business models

The main challenge for fashion brands is how to move away from that ever-faster model of consumption underpinning most business models. With very few exceptions, they aim to persuade customers to either expand their wardrobes or replace clothing with increasing regularity. How do they transition from this high-volume, low-margin model to a strategy of **slowing the flow** and **intensifying the loop**? This would mean a few styles that customers will invest in, wearing them regularly over a few years (at least), and/or having resale options that are both easy and will recover a healthy proportion of the original cost.

A circular fashion sector must also collaborate to **close the loop** and **regenerate** its own materials. There are significant challenges here, with little effective recycling infrastructure and poor-quality recycling outputs, not helped by the vast array of mixed materials and chemical inputs.

SLOW THE FLOW

Designing for 'emotional durability', using fabrics that will last and making garments easy to repair are some of the strategies that help slow the flow of clothing. Clothes from respected brands, in timeless designs and with standard sizing are also likely to have a resale value, helping to keep them in circulation for longer. (See the WRAP Sustainable Clothing Guide in Further Resources.)

Outdoor brand Patagonia has offered free repairs for many years, and Barbour, Finisterre and others offer a repair service. Repairs were common

FIGURE 7.7   Circular Economy Framework 2.0 – business models

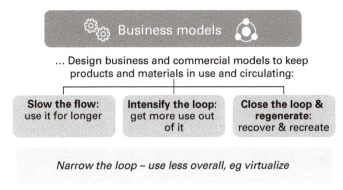

SOURCE: © Catherine Weetman

for shoes, and there are signs that this is set to return. Nudie Jeans offers ethically sourced denim, with an upcycling reuse programme, repair kits and a free repair service.

CLOTHES DOCTOR – WARDROBE MAINTENANCE[34]

Clothes Doctor launched in the UK in 2017 and aims to become the 'UK's largest wardrobe maintenance service, with digital convenience, 5-star quality, and sustainability at its core'. It offers repairs and alterations to a wide range of clothing, via online ordering with repairs undertaken at its workshop in Cornwall, and partners with major high-street fashion retailers to offer in-store services.

INTENSIFY THE LOOP

Clothing designed for durability and recirculation supports the viability of access and sharing models – operated by a circular service provider, or by the brand itself.

Chapter 3 highlighted several fashion-related business models for exchanging, sharing and renting clothes to be used again, used more intensively or for longer. Rent the Runway in the United States and Girl Meets Dress in the UK are successfully renting a range of clothes, enabling consumers to meet their fashion needs without investing cash into a wardrobe of clothes destined for disposal. Clotho started by organizing a clothes swap for friends to recycle unwanted clothes, followed by 'cherry picking some of the coolest vintage and retro pieces as a way to reuse great clothes from the past'.[35]

Rental and subscription models are emerging, with Mud Jeans offering a 'lease' option and Nike Adventure Club providing a subscription service for children's sneakers. Babywear and children's clothing subscriptions and rental work well for customers, providing access to high-quality, well-tailored clothing plus other occasional items like sleeping bags. Examples include Vigga in the Netherlands, Räubersachen in Germany, MiniLoop in Switzerland, and Bundlee in the UK. Belles and Babes offers 'stylish maternity clothing and luxury organic baby clothing to hire across the UK'.

GIRL MEETS DRESS: FASHION RENTAL AND SUBSCRIPTIONS[36]

Girl Meets Dress, based in the UK and launched in 2009, claims to be the world's first online fashion rental service. The company stocks over 4,000 designer dresses from over 200 brands. Customers can order and try on several dresses, returning anything unworn for a refund. They can shop online or at the London showroom, and book either two- or seven-night rental periods. Added services include stylist advice, free dry cleaning, insurance, next-day delivery to the UK and Europe, and prepaid return postage. There is an optional monthly subscription for £99, to rent unlimited dresses.

Larger brands are experimenting, with H&M announcing a rental trial in its Stockholm store in 2019, with customers able to rent three pieces from the Conscious Exclusive collections. In the US, Banana Republic, Bloomingdale's and Urban Outfitters all launched new clothing subscription services in 2019.

CLOSE THE LOOP AND REGENERATE

There is a huge opportunity to set up effective, efficient recovery systems, aiming to collect, sort and reroute end-of-use clothing so it can have further lives. New developments in mechanical and chemical recycling offer potential to reproduce fibres at a high-enough quality to become textiles again, but the main gap seems to be systems to return the original garment to the loop.

In 2019, Fashion United reported that US supermarket Asda would trial 'Re-Loved', a resale pop-up; German online giant Zalando was piloting 'Zircle', a second-hand clothing pop-up in Berlin; and US department store chains Macy's and JC Penney both announced they had entered into partnerships with resale company ThredUp.[37]

FIGURE 7.8   Circular Economy Framework 2.0 – safe, sustainable inputs

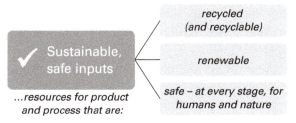

SOURCE: © Catherine Weetman

THREDUP: CLOTHING EXCHANGE PLATFORM[38]

ThredUp started in 2009, and says it is 'not your typical thrift store'. It aims to give people the 'easiest way to clean out their closets'. It ensures 'every single one of the 15K new arrivals we add to the site every day is 100 per cent authentic and in such good shape anyone could mistake them as new. No knockoffs here—just knockoff prices.' Stock, including 35,000 brands and 2 million items of clothing, comes from customers who 'clean out their closets and fill a ThredUp bag' with clothes that are clean and in good enough condition to be resold.

Describing itself as 'the creative community's mobile marketplace', Depop was established in 2011 and now has over 15 million users in 147 countries. With a big focus on fashion, it has staged events and pop-ups in the US and UK, as well as expanding through its mobile app.

ThredUp's 2019 Resale report says resale has grown 21 times faster than the retail apparel market over the past three years, and predicts the overall market will more than double by 2023.[39]

Safe, sustainable inputs

Figure 7.8 reminds us of the 'circular input' aims for safe and sustainable materials: recycled materials; replacing finite materials with renewable inputs; ensuring materials are safe for both humans and living systems; aiming to select materials that will provide secure supplies into the future.

We have seen that there are serious sustainability issues for both natural and man-made fibres. Comparing environmental impacts of a range of natural and synthetic fibres, including acrylic, cellulosic, nylon, polyester, silk and viscose:[40]

- synthetics use lots of energy, but have lower water and land footprints;
- cotton has the highest water and pesticide use;
- wool has the highest land footprint and generates the most wastewater;
- natural bast fibres and regenerative cellulosic provide a good balance across energy, water, land use and emissions – *but* (unless produced using closed-loop methods) they are criticized for heavy chemical use and pollution.

The Cradle to Cradle Products Innovation Institute website lists a range of companies producing Cradle to Cradle™ certified apparel and work-wear,[41] including reworx®, a sustainable, wood-based cellulosic fibre and infinito® fibre, a synthetic, biodegradable polymer.

There is great scope for developing recycled fibres from synthetic textiles or finding ways to recycle biological waste products into fibres to create new forms of renewable inputs. *Green chemistry* is helping to develop fibres from seaweed and algae.

RECYCLED AND RECYCLABLE INPUTS

Recycling fibres from end-of-use fabrics is difficult, with similar challenges to recycling paper and card. The fibres become shorter in each cycle and so unsuitable for reuse in the same kind of fabric. Often textiles are *down-cycled*, perhaps into wadding for lining outdoor coats, or for upholstery, insulating materials, etc. Green chemistry and technology innovations aim to find solutions for this, and to develop other regenerated fibres derived from polymers.

Patagonia has developed a range of recycled fabrics, including cotton, down, nylon, wool and Woolyester (a wool, nylon and polyester blend). Adidas has committed to using much more recycled content by 2024.

Polyethylene terephthalate (PET) is the most common of the polyester fibres. Recycled PET (rPET) is manufactured from end-of-use waste plastic bottles. Japan-based Teijin Fibers developed its 'Eco Circle™' closed-loop chemical recycling processes in 2002, to refine old polyester into recycled raw material equivalent to the new material (made from petroleum).[42] Teijin claims the technology reduces energy consumption and CO_2 emissions compared with making new polyester, and now has 150 participating companies worldwide.

Other organizations are recycling different materials to create yarns and textiles, with plenty of examples from the food industry.

TIDAL VISION: GREEN CHEMISTRY AND WASTE = FOOD[43,44]

Tidal Vision in Alaska is 'reducing waste and encouraging sustainable fishing by upcycling sustainable ocean byproducts'. It has 'invented two patent-pending methods for processing ocean by-products into aquatic leathers and Chitoskin™, with applications in textiles, consumer goods and other industries'. Tidal Vision says that its closed-loop processing system is 'the only one in the world that fully utilizes crab shells, [to] extract chitin from crab shells and turn it into chitosan. Our co-product—which "closes the loop"—is natural nitrogen source fertilizer.'

Tidal Vision suggests that Chitosan can replace chemicals, often at a lower cost, including heavy metal and other toxic antimicrobials, inorganic flocculants and coagulants, pesticides and insecticides.

RENEWABLE INPUTS

Whilst fibres from cotton, wool, linen and other plant or animal sources are renewable, pressure on land use, and the environmental impacts of production, undermine their suitability for a truly sustainable process. Wool can be a by-product from sheep meat production; however, over centuries, specific breeds of sheep, such as merino, were bred to provide wool fibres suited to clothing, thus producing high quantities of wool instead of meat. Natural fibres may also have mineral sources, such as asbestos – which does not meet our 'safe' criteria for a textile fibre!

To minimize the use of land, we should follow a hierarchy of priorities for biomaterials, using agricultural or manufacturing waste flows, followed by post-consumer waste, then looking at crops that can grow on poor land, or perhaps from sustainable forests (harvesting some leaves, cork bark, etc) without displacing food crops.

Plant-based

Natural fibres produced using **organic farming** methods have lower environmental footprints. The Textile Exchange, a non-profit organization, has a website dedicated to organic cotton. It explains that cotton is often grown in water-scarce areas using irrigation, whereas organic cotton is 80 per cent rain-fed, which reduces pressure on local water sources.[45] Organic farming does not use synthetic pesticides, meaning water running off the fields is cleaner and safer. Organic farming uses 80 per cent less energy and thus produces 80 per cent fewer GHG emissions. Organic fibres may be linked to

FIGURE 7.9　Piñatex™ intended life-cycle

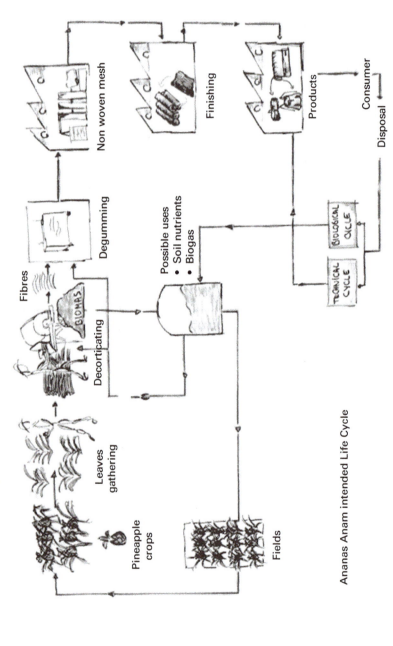

Ananas Anam intended Life Cycle

food crops: cottonseed oil is used in a variety of food products and is also fed to livestock. Every cotton garment made by outdoor brand Patagonia, from 1996 onwards, is organic.

Improvements in natural fibres include hemp and other 'bast' fibres (plant fibres collected from the phloem, or outer skin of certain plants, such as ramie, hemp or nettle). Patagonia says it blends hemp with TENCEL® lyocell and organic cotton for superior strength and durability, creating a soft, lightweight and breathable material.

Camira, a UK textile company, uses nettles and hemp to make textiles for upholstery, health care, transport and domestic sectors. Camira highlights the inherent fire-retardant properties of its wool and bast fibre ranges, also including flax and jute recycled from coffee sacks. These need 'no chemical treatments to meet the main contract and domestic flammability standards'.[46]

Choosing fibres that can be a co-product of food production helps make better use of land and production resources, and may reduce problematic waste at the farm.

ANANAS ANAM PIÑATEX™ FABRIC: RENEWABLE INPUTS[47,48]

Researching the development of natural fibre products in the Philippines, Dr Carmen Hijosa realized she could create a non-woven textile, using pineapple leaf fibres as an alternative to leather and linen. Early uses included bags and shoes.

Piñatex™ raw material is waste from pineapple farming, needing no further inputs of water, fertilizers or pesticides. The fibres are around 60 centimetres long and retain dyes well. Processes are labour-intensive, starting with fibre extraction, washing, then open-air drying and waxing to detangle the fibres, and the yarns are woven into fabric. At end-of-use, the fabric can be recycled into geotextiles.

Figure 7.9 illustrates the flows in the Piñatex™ manufacturing process (included with kind permission from Dr Carmen Hijosa of Ananas Anam).

Man-made – cellulosic

TENCEL® is a lyocell fibre, extracted from wood grown in sustainable forest plantations. The manufacturer, Lenzing, uses an award-winning closed-loop process to recycle almost 100 per cent of the solvents used in the spinning process, describing the fibre production as 'extremely eco-friendly'.

A life-cycle analysis highlighted a number of environmental benefits over cotton, for example using 10–20 times less water. Lenzing claims that TENCEL® textiles (Lyocell and Modal) are 'more absorbent than cotton, softer than silk and cooler than linen'.[49]

Some brands advertise as an 'eco-textile'. Although bamboo is rapidly renewable and requires few agricultural pesticides, there are sustainability concerns. The Made-By fibre classifications,[50] referred to earlier, show the branded Monocell® lyocell-process bamboo fibre in class B,[51] whereas bamboo viscose is ranked lower in class D. The viscose rayon production method involves many chemicals and is highly energy-intensive compared with cotton. An article exposing an 'organic bamboo' fraud highlights the most common solvent in viscose rayon production, carbon disulphide, which is both highly toxic and a dispersant, with high levels of the substance released into the air when used.[52]

Another development is banana fibre, and its spinnability, fineness and tensile strength are said to be better than bamboo. Banana fibres can make textiles with different weights and thicknesses, depending on what part of the banana stem is used. Lotus leaves are a traditional fibre in some countries, with a time-consuming process that produces luxurious fabric similar to silk or raw linen.

Man-made from other sources

Other edible products can be processed into textiles, including fermented foods like kombucha and even soured milk. Using a process similar to making cheese, fabric from waste milk was produced commercially in Italy in the 1930s and is now attracting interest (Qmilk is one example). Coffee beans can add antibacterial properties to fabric, and mycelium (part of fungi) can 'grow' fabric, with MycoTEX and MYX as examples.

Designers are also repurposing fabrics from other applications into fashion products, including from car seats, ocean plastics from fishing nets (examples include Adidas and RubyMoon) and fire hoses.

ELVIS & KRESSE: UPCYCLED INPUTS[53]

Fire brigades across the UK (and Europe) use fire hoses made from a hardwearing material, designed to withstand wear and tear over 25 years then discarded before they are likely to fail. Design duo Elvis & Kresse were struck by the hose itself, a deep red colour, made from tough, flexible and multilayer material. Separation of the layers would be costly, but they realized that the hose itself had 'provenance' and a great story: saving lives.

They decided to transform it into something practical and desirable, 'something you would want even if it were not recycled, even without the ethics'. The aim is to create classic and timeless designs, with high-quality craftsmanship to ensure the new products will last for as long as the reclaimed materials. Products including belts, wallets and bags feature linings from *upcycled* materials such as parachute silk or wedding tablecloths.[54]

Chapter 2 introduced some by-products from orange juice production, and OrangeFiber has successfully turned citrus waste into high-quality fabric similar to silk. The company sees great potential to create textile value from that waste, estimating that orange juice manufacturers create as much as 25 million tonnes of waste, including peel and seeds, each year. There are other sources of fibres made from food by-products, some of which have been in use for centuries.

Design for durability and recovery

What features should we see in clothes and shoes designed for a circular economy? We need durable, timeless, well-made apparel, designed to fit its intended customers. Designs should use fewer, simpler, sustainable materials, and should enable ease of care, repair and recycling at the end of life. Circular design should avoid mixing synthetic and natural fabrics and fibres, to make it easier to regain value when recycling the clothing at end-of-use.

FIGURE 7.10   Circular Economy Framework 2.0 – product design

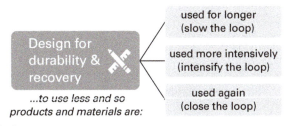

SOURCE: © Catherine Weetman

DESIGN SO THE PRODUCT AND MATERIALS ARE IN USE FOR LONGER

Designing fashion for subsequent lives after the first use is the antithesis of 'fast fashion', but some designers and brands are embracing this. Designing for function helps: Patagonia insists that each product must fulfil its function, so a climbing jacket must allow freedom of movement.

PETIT PLI: INSPIRED BY ORIGAMI[55]

Often, children's clothes are hardly worn before they are outgrown, with children growing through seven sizes in their first two years. Petit Pli designed durable and appealing clothes that grow with the child, with sizes covering 9 months to 4 years old. The design team were inspired by space engineering and the ingenious folding techniques of origami, and designed garments that are windproof, rainproof and folded in a way that allows for tops and bottoms to expand and fit each child for years.

In 2019, luxury department store Harvey Nichols announced it would expand its after-care service for shoes and bags (an initiative in partnership with The Restory) from London to its five regional UK stores. In Canada, Frankie Collective is dedicated to reworking garments that would otherwise end up in landfill into high-demand streetwear styles. Vintage garments and overstock that would otherwise end up in landfill are salvaged and reworked by a local, skilled team.[56]

WRAP developed a Clothing Longevity Protocol in 2014, offering good practice guidelines, with a checklist to use throughout the product development process.[57] It aims to help the industry create longer-lasting clothing, highlighting business benefits including fewer returns, greater customer loyalty and environmental improvements.

DESIGN TO USE PRODUCT AND MATERIALS MORE INTENSIVELY

Patagonia sets stringent design criteria for each of its new product ideas. It aims to make its designs fulfil more than one function, so a ski jacket should double up as a waterproof for hiking and even commuting, meaning the user can get more wear (and value) out of it, and needs fewer clothes overall. Sizing is important, especially if the product is likely to be used by more than one person. Patagonia's customers come in all sorts of shapes and sizes. Those doing adventure sports tend to be younger and slimmer, whereas fishermen are older and so may want a more relaxed fit. Patagonia uses three size blocks: slim fit, regular, and relaxed. Consistent and well-described sizing can also reduce returns from online orders.

Modular designs aim to overcome that conflict, with a durable, high-quality base product that the wearer can customize to change the 'look' or functionality of the item. One example is the 'Ze o Ze' shoe by Israeli industrial designer Daniela Bekerman. The basic shoe is plain and flat and users can buy easily swappable components, including different heel sizes, to change it from a party shoe to a brogue, change the colours and so on.

For clothing, modular designs enable children's clothing to last longer. Nula Kids makes adjustable styles that fit a wide range of body shapes, helping the clothes fit for three to four times longer and reducing the risk of returns from online shopping. Organic cotton and hemp fabric blends are durable and sustainable.[58] The clothes incorporate a range of well-tested design features, such as an adjustable waistband with buttonhole elastic or a dress lengthened with hidden add-on pieces.

DESIGN TO USE PRODUCT AND MATERIALS AGAIN – WASTE = FOOD!

Designing easily disassembled garments and footwear can recover materials at end-of-use, for remanufacturing into new garments or recycling into new materials. Puma launched its InCycle collection in 2013,[59] with apparel, shoes and accessories that are either biodegradable (shirts and a sneaker) or recyclable (a track jacket and a backpack). The recyclable products use materials that are homogeneous, avoiding mixed or composite materials, to enable easier separation at end of life. Puma calculates that the waste created during production and at end of life for its conventional suede sneakers is almost two-thirds lower; biodegradable sneakers can go to industrial composting facilities.[60]

Puma sees benefits from reduced energy, air pollution and land use compared with using virgin raw materials. Puma plans to use its 'Bring Me Back' programme, with recycling company I:CO, to educate and encourage consumers to return items for recycling.[61]

In addition to simplifying the bill of materials for designs – using fewer different materials and avoiding blended fabrics – better labelling would improve fibre recovery. New technology including intelligent tags, or machine-readable codes that link back to the product's materials database, could help to sort and prioritize the most suitable fabrics for recycling into high-quality textiles.

Process design

Circular improvements for process design (shown in Figure 7.11) aim to recover production inputs, including energy, water and chemicals; and ensure that all 'waste is food', so removing toxins from effluents and emissions to the air and recovering other 'technical' or synthetic resources for reuse.

FIGURE 7.11   Circular Economy Framework 2.0 – process design

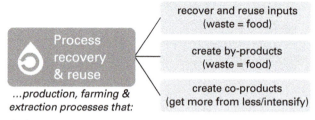

SOURCE: © Catherine Weetman

Traditional methods of leather tanning use lots of water and harmful chemicals, linked to health issues for workers and communities around the tannery. Shoe brand Ecco developed DriTan technology, which uses the natural moisture in the hide to reduce the water footprint and resulting chemical 'sludge'.

> ### BLUESIGN® TECHNOLOGIES: SUSTAINABLE TEXTILE CERTIFICATION[62]
>
> bluesign® technologies, based in Switzerland, began working with Patagonia in 2000. bluesign® helps to evaluate and reduce resource consumption in its materials supply chain, also assisting with managing the chemicals, dyes and finishes used in the process. At each step in the textile supply chain, bluesign® works to approve chemicals, processes, materials and products that are safe for the environment, safe for workers and safe for the end-user.

RECOVER AND REUSE INPUTS

At every stage of the supply chain, we should be narrowing and closing the loop. Procuring production inputs, such as chemicals and dyes, as a service can reduce waste, reduce virgin material use and encourage better outcomes for the textile manufacturer. **Chemical Leasing Toolkit** is an interactive tool providing guidelines, materials, best practice case studies and lessons learned from 10 years of work at UNIDO's Global Chemical Leasing Programme.

Companies are investing in water reduction and recovery, with examples including H&M, Levi Strauss & Co's Water<Less™ programme for its jeans, Patagonia for its denim, Lenzing and the Better Cotton Initiative.

Digital technology is developing, enabling 'printing' of more precise colour on to fabric rather than immersing the entire fabric in dyes, using 95 per cent less water and 75 per cent less energy.[63]

CREATE BY-PRODUCTS AND CO-PRODUCTS

Manufacturing process waste can create new products: **waste = food**. In the cutting process, patterns for the different parts of the garment, in a range of sizes, are arranged on top of several fabric layers on a long cutting table. Gaps in between each pattern piece will vary in size, according to the difficulty of making an efficient jigsaw puzzle from the mix of shapes and sizes. These 'gaps', or offcuts, become process waste, and reusing these recovers lost value.

The clothes manufacturing process may waste up to 15 per cent of fabric. A Global Change Awards finalist is designing a database to track leftover material and make it available for other companies to use.[64] In 2015, Speedo announced a collaboration with Aquafil to develop a new line of products, 'PowerFLEX Eco', made from surplus material from its manufacturing processes.[65] Aquafil's ECONYL® treatment depolymerizes and repolymerizes with no loss of quality.

In Chapter 2, we noted that Elvis & Kresse (a certified B Corp) and luxury brand Burberry had announced a five-year partnership to see at least 120 tonnes of leather offcuts from Burberry made into new products designed and sold by Elvis & Kresse. Profits from the sale of the products go to charitable causes and inspiring craftspeople.

Recovery flows

Reports from McKinsey (2016)[66] and the Ellen MacArthur Foundation (2017)[67] indicate that **only around 1 per cent of the material used to make clothing is eventually recycled into new clothing**, and that **nearly three-fifths of all clothing produced ends up in incinerators or landfills within a year of being made**. Germany outperforms most countries by collecting almost three-quarters of all used clothing, reusing half and recycling the remainder. Elsewhere, collection rates are far lower: 15 per cent in the United States, 12 per cent in Japan, and 10 per cent in China.

> APPARELXCHANGE: MAKING IT EASY TO REUSE SCHOOL
> UNIFORMS[68]
>
> ApparelXchange, a Scottish social enterprise, works with schools across
> Glasgow to gather, process and reuse pre-owned uniforms. There is an online
> shop, a store and pop-up shops in schools, with donations at the shops and at
> collection points in schools. Everything is sorted and quality-checked, and

anything below the quality standard is recycled by a registered textile recycler. Clothes in excellent reusable condition are washed, ironed and then made available for resale.

The benefits go beyond value-for-money. ApparelXchange reminds us that wearing 'pre-loved' items instead of buying new avoids using raw materials, energy, carbon emissions and water and the reuse processes require very little energy and transportation.

FIGURE 7.12   Circular Economy Framework 2.0 – recovery flows

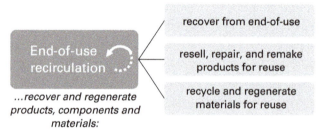

SOURCE: © Catherine Weetman

Figure 7.12 reminds us of the main options for recovery, or circular flows. Online platforms and apps are making it easier to recover value from end-of-use apparel. The ReGain app encourages users to donate unwanted fashion at local drop points, in return for discounts from clothing brands. The donated clothing is reused or recycled, to avoid landfill. New technologies such as dissolvable thread can simplify separation of materials, and improve the efficiency of repairs or refurbishment, such as for workwear.

Companies, designers and technology innovators are realizing that recycling has potential to recover value of inputs 'embodied' in the finished products. Figure 7.13 compares embodied energy in a number of textile materials, which covers a wide range, from flax at the lower end of the scale, to nylon, requiring 25 times more energy.

A Global Change Awards startup developed new technology processes to dissolve old cotton clothing into a cotton-like material, which can then be spun into new fibres.[69] Another has found a way to recycle polyester, now the most common raw material used for clothing and one that is hard to recycle without loss of quality. A new type of microbe can eat the old fabric, breaking down the polymer into a raw material to sell to polyester manufacturers. The process also works on mixed material fabrics, such as cotton and polyester (polycotton), and is cheaper than using new materials.

FIGURE 7.13   Embodied energy in textile fibres

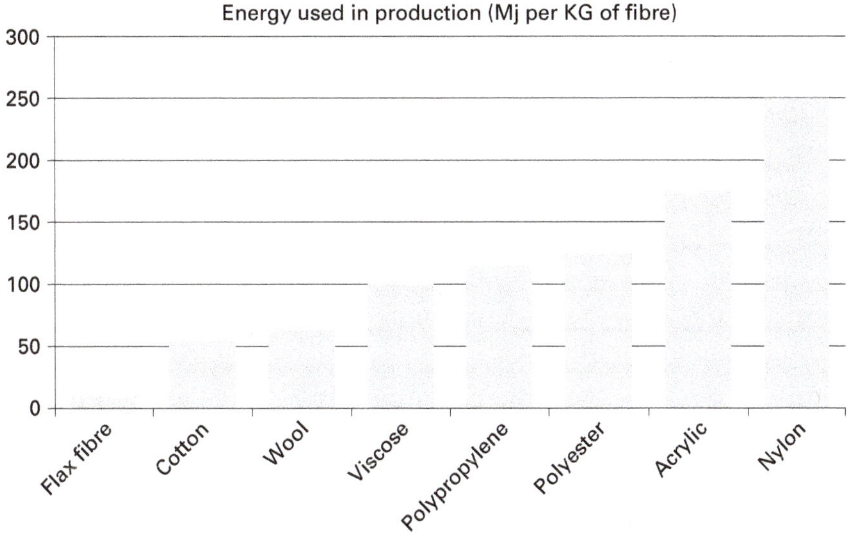

Energy used in production (Mj per KG of fibre)

SOURCE: Summerscales (2006)[70]

There are developments to transform textile waste into new materials, such as Spintex that spins 'silk' from post-consumer waste. Fibersort is a technology that automatically sorts large volumes of mixed post-consumer textiles by fibre type. Once sorted, these materials become reliable, consistent input materials for high-value textile to textile recyclers.

Patagonia helps consumers to find **reuse** routes for its outdoor activity and lifestyle products, collaborating with the exchange platform Trove to swap products, and operating a trade-in programme for used Patagonia clothing, with sales routes through its retail stores and online. Recognizing that 'nothing lasts forever', it offers easy recycling options once products reach the end of their useful lives and can no longer be repaired. Customers are encouraged to take the product to their local Patagonia retail store, or post it direct to Patagonia. The company recycled 82 tonnes of clothing between 2005 and 2015.[71]

LOOPTWORKS: UPCYCLING[72]

Looptworks makes desirable sports and leisure products from recycling materials, such as laptop sleeves from end-of-use neoprene wetsuits. Looptworks's aim was to design a product range, Loopt Classics, with a goal of longevity, prioritizing function over aesthetics, and clean, timeless design.

Excess leather, from manufacture of bespoke motorcycle clothing, is perfect to meet these criteria, and the leather is upcycled into handbags, tote bags and wallets. Looptworks uses other 'pre-consumer flows', including 'cut and sew' offcuts, end of roll, seasonal excesses, damaged textiles and finished clothes.

Enablers

What **enabling** approaches can companies use to support circular strategies? We have seen examples of *green chemistry* and technology developments helping to innovate processes, product design and material choice. *Biomimicry* approaches are also creating new materials. Spider silk is tougher than Kevlar, stronger than steel and more flexible than nylon. Spiber in Japan is making Qmonos, a synthetic spider silk, by incorporating spider silk DNA into microbes that then make a protein. *3D printing* is finding new uses in fashion, with Nike 3D printing running shoes and football boot soles, and an industrial designer mimicking honeycomb to create a 3D woven flexible shoe sole.

FIGURE 7.14   Circular Economy Framework 2.0 – enablers

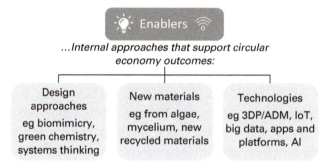

SOURCE: © Catherine Weetman

CIRCULAR.FASHION: CLOSING THE LOOP WITH DIGITAL IDENTITIES[73]

circular.fashion has developed a digital system which provides designers with knowledge and tools on how to design with recyclable intent. The specifications are then saved as a digital identity, a circularity.ID, which customers can scan for information on the best options at end-of-use, encouraging reuse, updating or recycling.

There are opportunities to use 'big data' to improve the product or to find and share resources, and there are good examples of platform technology for knowledge and resource exchanges.

Accelerators

What external forces are likely to drive the change? There seems to be little appetite from governments for product-stewardship legislation, but campaigners and NGO initiatives, like Greenpeace's Detox campaign, are helping galvanize the industry towards 'slow, sustainable fashion'. Collaborations and sector-certification standards are growing, though many of these are criticized for lack of ambition and a resulting slow pace of change. We can see there are opportunities to improve transparency and safety for materials, and we will look at life-cycle assessment and product life-cycle management in Part Three.

FIGURE 7.15   Circular Economy Framework 2.0 – accelerators

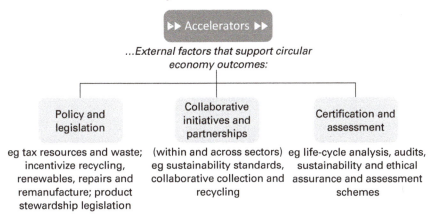

SOURCE: © Catherine Weetman

Sector collaborative initiatives include:

- Fashion Positive supports and promotes the development of Cradle to Cradle Certified™ products and materials, aiming to increase transparency and provide low-interest loans to help innovation and closed-loop developments.

- The Sustainable Apparel Coalition[74] is building the Higg Index, a standardized measurement tool helping industry participants to understand the environmental, social and worker impacts of making and selling their products and services, along the supply chain.

- Textile Exchange[75] shares best practices on farming, materials, processing, traceability and product end-of-life, to reduce the textile industry's impact on water, soil and air, and the human population.

- The Circular Textiles Programme, managed by consultants Circle Economy with brands, collectors, sorters and recyclers, aims to 'produce the critical data, tools, and pilot projects [...] building the new foundation for a circular textiles industry'. It is developing a Circular Fashion Tool and supports a cotton recycling project and the Fibersort initiative.[76]

- The United Nations Alliance for Sustainable Fashion aims to contribute to the Sustainable Development Goals through coordinated action in the fashion sector.[77]

- Ellen MacArthur Foundation's Make Fashion Circular (originally the Circular Fibres Initiative) aims to stimulate the level of collaboration and innovation to create a circular textiles economy. It outlines four steps: phase out substances of concern and microfibre release; transform the way clothes are designed, sold, and used to break free from their increasingly disposable nature; radically improve recycling by transforming clothing design, collection, and reprocessing; and make effective use of resources and move to renewable inputs.[78]

Summary

The Global Fashion Agenda predicts global apparel consumption to reach 102 million tonnes by 2030, an increase of 63 per cent from 2017, and equivalent to 500 billion additional t-shirts.[79] The fashion and textiles sector is under pressure to improve its transparency and ethics, and to clean up materials and processes. However, despite recent attention on the 'take-make-waste' issues across the industry, so far the focus seems to be on doing a 'bit less bad' across supply chains, and improving the volume and effectiveness of recycling.

Ellen MacArthur Foundation's Make Fashion Circular (see Further Resources), pointing out that over US$500 billion in value is lost every year from the fashion system, details four steps for a circular textile economy:

1 Phase out substances of concern and microfibre release.

2 Transform the way clothes are designed, sold, and used to break free from their increasingly disposable nature.

3 Radically improve recycling by transforming clothing design, collection and reprocessing.

4 Make effective use of resources and move to renewable inputs.

We are starting to see innovative materials, processes and product designs. Using renewable energy, recycled water from production processes and renewable process inputs are all highly relevant for apparel manufacturing. Companies are embarking on supply chain initiatives to recover value from waste. Governments, NGOs and companies encourage consumers to repair, reuse and resell, though this needs to go much further than well-meaning messages if it is to close the loop on fashion and textiles.

There are two options for sustainable fashion: to produce durable, high-quality garments to slow the flow or intensify the loop (with higher prices and profit margins) and that can also be recovered for recycling at the end of life, and to find safe, sustainable materials for the fast-fashion low-margin model. Both options must use renewable energy and closed-loop production processes, and provide 'food' for nature or another industrial process at the end of life.

Closing the loop and regenerating inputs is essential, and the industry faces a major challenge to create the networks and develop systems to make this happen at scale – and without substantial value leakage. Business models based on durable, repairable designs, using safe and sustainable materials, seem to be a rare find in the world of fashion.

> At Nike, we are pursuing new business models that move away from the take, make, and waste linear models of the past. Our success depends not only on the work within our own value chain, but on disruptive partnerships across a broader textile production and manufacturing ecosystem.
>
> Cyrus Wadia, VP, Sustainable Business & Innovation, Nike, Inc[80]

Further resources

Allwood, JM, Laursen, SE, Rodriguez, CM and Bocken NMP (2006) [accessed 16 March 2016] Well Dressed? *The present and future sustainability of clothing and textiles in the United Kingdom*, University of Cambridge, Institute for Manufacturing [Online] https://www.ifm.eng.cam.ac.uk/insights/sustainability/well-dressed/ (archived at https://perma.cc/S3ER-Z3GT)

Centre for Sustainable Fashion [accessed 1 June 2016] [Online] sustainable-fashion.com/ (archived at https://perma.cc/7JUT-3H25)

Circular Fashion online platform [accessed 1 November 2019] [Online] circularfashion.com (archived at https://perma.cc/YX9U-C42C)

Circular Textiles Programme (2019) [accessed 2 November 2019] *Circle Economy* [Online] www.circle-economy.com/textiles/ (archived at https://perma.cc/2QQ2-BTQH)

Ellen MacArthur Foundation (2017) [accessed 1 November 2019] *A New Textiles Economy: Redesigning fashion's future* [Online] www.ellenmacarthur foundation.org/publications (archived at https://perma.cc/44DG-FJVV)

Fixing Fashion: Clothing Consumption and Sustainability (2019) [accessed 2 November 2019] House of Commons Environmental Audit Committee (UK), 5 February [Online] publications.parliament.uk/pa/cm201719/cmselect/cmenvaud/2311/2311.pdf (archived at https://perma.cc/7AX2-DTZG)

Greenpeace International (nd) [accessed 2 November 2019] *Detox My Fashion campaign* [Online] www.greenpeace.org/international/act/detox/ (archived at https://perma.cc/6CK5-XXKN)

Greenpeace International (2017) [accessed 2 November 2019] *Fashion at the Crossroads* [Online] www.greenpeace.org/international/publication/6969/fashion-at-the-crossroads/ (archived at https://perma.cc/985U-HUQ9)

WRAP (2017) [accessed 2 November 2019] *Valuing Our Clothes: The cost of UK fashion*, 11 July [Online] www.wrap.org.uk/sustainable-textiles/valuing-our-clothes%20 (archived at https://perma.cc/L4TH-NL6F)

WRAP Sustainable Clothing Guide (2017) – 'a practical guide to help brands and retailers to enhance the durability and quality of the clothing they produce' [accessed 2 November 2019] [Online] www.wrap.org.uk/sustainable-textiles/scap/extending-clothing-life/guides/sustainable-clothing-guide (archived at https://perma.cc/PZ8V-YW3R)

Notes

1   Chouinard, Y (2010) [accessed 28 March 2016] Interview on YouTube [Online] www.youtube.com/watch?v=O3TwULu-Wjw (archived at https://perma.cc/Y6XH-5RPQ)

2   Allwood, JM, Laursen SE, Rodriguez, CM and Bocken NMP (2006) [accessed 16 March 2016] *Well Dressed? The present and future sustainability of clothing and textiles in the United Kingdom*, University of Cambridge, Institute for Manufacturing [Online] https://www.ifm.eng.cam.ac.uk/insights/sustainability/well-dressed/ (archived at https://perma.cc/S3ER-Z3GT)

3   Burgen, S (17 August 2012) [accessed 21 March 2016] Fashion chain Zara helps Inditex lift first quarter profits by 30%, *The Guardian* [Online] www.theguardian.com/business/2012/aug/17/zara-inditex-profits (archived at https://perma.cc/AK4T-89LG)

4 Ellen MacArthur Foundation (2017) [accessed 1 November 2019]
   A New Textiles Economy: Redesigning fashion's future [Online]
   http://www.ellenmacarthurfoundation.org/publications (archived at
   https://perma.cc/44DG-FJVV)

5 Statistica (2016) [accessed 16 March 2016] [Online] www.statista.com/topics/
   965/apparel-market-in-the-us/ (archived at https://perma.cc/MG8F-YRXK)

6 Stotz, L and Kane L (February 2015) [accessed 22 March 2016] *Facts on
   the Global Garment Industry*, Clean Clothes Campaign [Online]
   www.cleanclothes.org/resources/publications/factsheets/general-factsheet-
   garment-industry-february-2015.pdf (archived at https://perma.cc/SCC2-65LN)

7 Ellen MacArthur Foundation (2017) [accessed 1 November 2019]
   A New Textiles Economy: Redesigning fashion's future [Online]
   http://www.ellenmacarthurfoundation.org/publications (archived at
   https://perma.cc/44DG-FJVV)

8 Carmichael, A (2014) [accessed 21 March 2016] *Man-Made Fibers Continue
   to Grow*, Textile World [Online] www.textileworld.com/textile-world/
   fiber-world/2015/02/man-made-fibers-continue-to-grow/ (archived at
   https://perma.cc/6G87-G7PR)

9 Organic Cotton (part of the non-profit Textile Exchange) [accessed
   2 November 2019] [Online] aboutorganiccotton.org/ (archived at https://perma.cc/
   F7Q2-BC5Q)

10 Siegle, L (8 May 2011) [accessed 16 March 2016] Why fast fashion is slow
   death for the planet, *The Observer* [Online] www.theguardian.com/
   lifeandstyle/2011/may/08/fast-fashion-death-for-planet (archived at
   https://perma.cc/PG3F-PRZL)

11 WRAP (2017) [accessed 2 November 2019] *Valuing Our Clothes: The cost of
   UK fashion*, 11 July [Online] www.wrap.org.uk/sustainable-textiles/valuing-
   our-clothes%20 (archived at https://perma.cc/L4TH-NL6F)

12 Council for Textile Recycling (2016) [accessed 21 March 2016] [Online]
   www.weardonaterecycle.org/ (archived at https://perma.cc/CMQ6-6D4K)

13 Butler, S (2018) [accessed 1 November 2019] Is fast fashion giving way to
   the sustainable wardrobe? *The Observer*, 29 December [Online]
   https://www.theguardian.com/business/2018/dec/29/fast-fashion-giving-way-
   sustainable-wardrobe (archived at https://perma.cc/XKE7-TH2V)

14 Made-By (2016) [accessed 24 May 2016] *Environmental Benchmark for
   Fibres* [Online] www.made-by.org/consultancy/tools/environmental/ (archived
   at https://perma.cc/5DDQ-Z4KU)

15 Better Cotton Initiative [accessed 21 March 2016] *Q&A* [Online]
   bettercotton.org/about-bci/qa/ (archived at https://perma.cc/E8CN-CGTQ)

16 EJF (2007) *The Deadly Chemicals in Cotton*, Environmental Justice
   Foundation in collaboration with Pesticide Action Network UK, London

17 Chouinard, Y (2016) *Let My People Go Surfing*, Penguin Books, London,
   p 95

18 Ecotextiles (October 2011) [accessed 24 May 2016] *Polyester and Our Health* [Online] oecotextiles.wordpress.com/2011/10/13/polyester-and-our-health/ (archived at https://perma.cc/65UM-WGJ8)

19 Van Elven, M (2018) [accessed 27 September 2019] *Fashion United*, 15 November [Online] fashionunited.com/news/fashion/how-sustainable-is-recycled-polyester/2018111524577 (archived at https://perma.cc/57XG-SFXX)

20 Ravasio, P (7 March 2012) [accessed 16 March 2016] How can we stop water becoming a fashion victim?, *The Guardian* [Online] www.theguardian.com/sustainable-business/water-scarcity-fashion-industry (archived at https://perma.cc/JB26-HKNU)

21 Greenpeace (2012) [accessed 16 March 2016] *Toxic Threads: The big fashion stitch-up* [Online] www.greenpeace.org/international/big-fashion-stitch-up/ (archived at https://perma.cc/T6LT-WE2Q)

22 ZDHC (2015) [accessed 24 May 2016] *Zero Discharge of Hazardous Chemicals* [Online] www.roadmaptozero.com/ (archived at https://perma.cc/VX7T-DW4U)

23 Zaffalon, V (2008) [accessed 28 March 2016] Climate change, carbon mitigation and textiles, *Textile World* [Online] oecotextiles.wordpress.com/2011/01/19/estimating-the-carbon-footprint-of-a-fabric/ (archived at https://perma.cc/XHN9-2KPX)

24 Remy et al (2016) *Style That's Sustainable: A new fast-fashion formula*, McKinsey and Company

25 Rupp, J (2008) [accessed 28 March 2016] Ecology and economy in textile finishing, *Textile World*, Nov/Dec [Online] oecotextiles.wordpress.com/2011/01/19/estimating-the-carbon-footprint-of-a-fabric/ (archived at https://perma.cc/XHN9-2KPX)

26 Franke, N and Mathews, R (August 2013) [accessed 21 March 2016] *C&A's Water Footprint Strategy: Cotton clothing supply chain*, Water Footprint Network, with C&A Foundation [Online] http://waterfootprint.org/media/downloads/CA_Strategy_Final_Report_Formatted_06.08.2013.pdf (archived at https://perma.cc/SP9Y-C2KT)

27 Levi Strauss (2015) 501® Jeans Impact [Online] http://levistrauss.com/sustainability/planet/lifecycle-assessment/ (archived at https://perma.cc/6AE3-CQKJ)

28 Franke, N and Mathews, R (August 2013) [accessed 21 March 2016] *C&A's Water Footprint Strategy: Cotton clothing supply chain*, Water Footprint Network, with C&A Foundation [Online] http://waterfootprint.org/media/downloads/CA_Strategy_Final_Report_Formatted_06.08.2013.pdf (archived at https://perma.cc/SP9Y-C2KT)

29 Bodey, A (9 August 2012) [accessed 21 March 2016] *Water Sustainability is Becoming Fashionable*, 2degrees & Best Foot Forward [Online] www.2degreesnetwork.com/groups/2degrees-community/resources/water-sustainability-becoming-fashionable/ (archived at https://perma.cc/6SDD-V6CB)

30 Hoskins, T (2014) [accessed 21 March 2016] Cotton production linked to images of the dried up Aral Sea Basin, *The Guardian* [Online] www.theguardian.com/ sustainable-business/sustainable-fashion-blog/2014/oct/01/cotton-production-linked-to-images-of-the-dried-up-aral-sea-basin (archived at https://perma.cc/ V3EP-VHDY)

31 Levi Strauss & Co (2015) *The Lifecycle of a Jean* [Online] http://levistrauss.com/ sustainability/planet/lifecycle-assessment/ (archived at https://perma.cc/6AE3-CQKJ)

32 Organic Cotton (2016) [accessed 22 March 2016] *The Risks of Cotton Farming* [Online] organiccotton.org/oc/Cotton-general/Impact-of-cotton/ Risk-of-cotton-farming.php (archived at https://perma.cc/2FDC-P7V6)

33 Switching Gear (2019) [accessed 2 November 2019] *Circle Economy* [Online] new.circle-economy.com/textiles/switching-gear (archived at https://perma.cc/ 6TGZ-DJZD)

34 Crowdcube (2019) [accessed 15 August 2019] [Online] www.crowdcube.com/ companies/clothes-doctor/pitches/bvQaDZ (archived at https://perma.cc/ EU5R-L9ZG)

35 Clotho [accessed 24 March 2016] [Online] www.clotholondon.co.uk/ (archived at https://perma.cc/9GNB-VQEN)

36 Girl Meets Dress – email 9 October 2019 and website [accessed 9 October 2019] [Online] www.girlmeetsdress.com/

37 Hughes, H (2019) [accessed 4 November 2019] Asda trials resale with second-hand clothing pop-up, 'Re-Loved', 3 September [Online] fashionunited.uk/ news/retail/asda-trials-resale-with-second-hand-clothing-pop-up-re-loved/ 2019090345054 (archived at https://perma.cc/7ELX-T5XR)

38 ThredUp [accessed 3 November 2019] [Online] www.thredup.com (archived at https://perma.cc/V3GN-23EQ)

39 ThredUp Annual Resale Report (2019) [accessed 3 November 2019] [Online] www.thredup.com/resale (archived at https://perma.cc/K928-6AUQ)

40 Turley, DB et al (2009) *The Role and Business Case for Existing and Emerging Fibres in Sustainable Clothing*, Final report to the Department for Environment, Food and Rural Affairs (Defra), London

41 Cradle to Cradle [accessed 23 March 2016] [Online] www.c2ccertified.org/ products/registry/search&category=apparel_shoes_accessories/ (archived at https://perma.cc/E9AD-FJ7N)

42 Teijin Fibers (2016) [accessed 24 May 2016] *Closed-Loop Recycling System: Eco Circle* [Online] http://www.teijin.co.in/solutions/ecocircle/ (archived at https://perma.cc/UKL3-DP4H)

43 Tidal Vision (2019) [accessed 2 November 2019] [Online] tidalvisionusa.com/ story-2/ (archived at https://perma.cc/JBH7-CFDT)

44 Tidal Vision (2019) [accessed 2 November 2019] [Online] tidalvisionusa.com/ chitosan/ (archived at https://perma.cc/68WE-LXLU)

45 Organic cotton platform from Textile Exchange and others [accessed 2 November 2019] [Online] https://organiccotton.org/oc/Organic-cotton/ Organic-cotton.php (archived at https://perma.cc/4Q86-PZW7)

46 Camira (2016) [accessed 24 June 2016] [Online] www.camirafabrics.com/ sustainability/Cut-from-a-different-cloth (archived at https://perma.cc/ A863-EM9J)

47 Ananas Anam (2016) [accessed 22 March 2016] [Online] www.ananas-anam.com/ pinatex/ (archived at https://perma.cc/E7YY-36TK)

48 Hijosa, C (5 November 2015) *Designing a Business Fibre by Fibre*, Disruptive Innovation Festival

49 Lenzing AG (2016) [accessed 24 May 2016] [Online] www.lenzing-fibers.com/ en/tencel/tencelr/ (archived at https://perma.cc/ATD4-2SZW)

50 Made-By (2016) [accessed 24 May 2016] *Environmental Benchmark for Fibres* [Online] www.made-by.org/consultancy/tools/environmental/ (archived at https://perma.cc/5DDQ-Z4KU)

51 Monocel (2016) [accessed 24 May 2016] [Online] monocel.com/this-is-monocel/ (archived at https://perma.cc/PJ8S-RZPF)

52 Vos, M (2014) [accessed 24 May 2016] No such thing as organic bamboo clothing: Chinese company leads apparent global market fraud, *Epoch Times* [Online] www.theepochtimes.com/n3/427295-no-such-thing-as-organic-bamboo-clothing-chinese-company-leads-apparent-global-market-fraud/ (archived at https://perma.cc/CP6X-Y853)

53 Elvis & Kresse (2016) [accessed 22 March 2016] [Online] elvisandkresse.com/ innovation/ (archived at https://perma.cc/G2D6-P96Z)

54 Provenance (2016) The fire-hose accessory collection [Online] www.provenance.org/stories/elvis-kresse-the-fire-hose-accessory-collection (archived at https://perma.cc/9GYA-SUD4)

55 Clothes that Grow (2019) [accessed 3 November 2019] Global Change Award Winner [Online] https://globalchangeaward.com/winners/clothes-that-grow/ (archived at https://perma.cc/UD2Y-NDKH)

56 Frankie Collective (2019) [accessed 3 November 2019] *About Us* [Online] https://frankiecollective.com/pages/about (archived at https://perma.cc/ D28F-GG82)

57 WRAP (2014) [accessed 24 May 2016] *Clothing Longevity Protocol* [Online] www.wrap.org.uk/content/clothing-longevity-protocol-1 (archived at https://perma.cc/L3WH-2KLP)

58 Buczynski, B (7 May 2013) [accessed 23 March 2016] Organic, vintage-inspired kids clothing that fits for 3 years, *Ecosalon* [Online] ecosalon.com/organic-vintage-inspired-kids-clothing-that-fits-for-3-years/ (archived at https://perma.cc/ 84KC-CNQK)

59 King, B (9 October 2012) [accessed 23 March 2016] New Puma line closes the loop on shoes, shirts and bags, *Sustainable Brands* [Online]

www.sustainablebrands.com/news_and_views/articles/new-puma-line-closes-loop-shoes-shirts-and-bags (archived at https://perma.cc/9JV3-3U37)

60 King, B (9 October 2012) [accessed 23 March 2016] New Puma line closes the loop on shoes, shirts and bags, *Sustainable Brands* [Online] www.sustainablebrands.com/news_and_views/articles/new-puma-line-closes-loop-shoes-shirts-and-bags (archived at https://perma.cc/9JV3-3U37)

61 Puma (17 April 2012) [accessed 23 March 2016] *Newsroom* [Online] about.puma.com/en/newsroom/corporate-news/2012/april/puma-launches-product-recycling-program-in-puma-stores-in-germany (archived at https://perma.cc/QLM7-43FM)

62 Inside Patagonia (2019) [accessed 25 October 2019] *Materials and Technologies: bluesign* [Online] https://eu.patagonia.com/gb/en/bluesign.html (archived at https://perma.cc/JWC3-6N46)

63 Breyer, M (4 September 2012) 10 awesome inventions changing the future of fashion, *Treehugger* [Online] www.treehugger.com/sustainable-fashion/10-awesome-innovations-changing-future-fashion.html (archived at https://perma.cc/5Z8C-N33U)

64 Peters, A (2 January 2016) [accessed 23 March 2016] 5 new solutions for the fashion industry's sustainability problem, *Fast Company & Inc* [Online] www.fastcoexist.com/3055925/5-new-solutions-for-the-fashion-industrys-sustainability-problem (archived at https://perma.cc/9KKM-FLYR)

65 Iles, J (August 2015) [accessed 23 March 2016] Speedo develop high performance range from surplus material, *Circulate News* [Online] circulatenews.org/2015/08/speedo-develop-high-performance-range-from-surplus-material/ (archived at https://perma.cc/JCR7-VNXV)

66 Remy et al (2016) *Style That's Sustainable: A new fast-fashion formula*, McKinsey and Company

67 Ellen MacArthur Foundation (2017) [accessed 1 November 2019] *A New Textiles Economy: Redesigning fashion's future* [Online] www.ellenmacarthurfoundation.org/publications (archived at https://perma.cc/44DG-FJVV)

68 ApparelXchange (2019) [accessed 20 September 2019] [Online] www.apparelxchange.co.uk (archived at https://perma.cc/8W66-Y5NT)

69 Peters, A (2 January 2016) [accessed 23 March 2016] 5 new solutions for the fashion industry's sustainability problem, *Fast Company & Inc* [Online] www.fastcoexist.com/3055925/5-new-solutions-for-the-fashion-industrys-sustainability-problem (archived at https://perma.cc/9KKM-FLYR)

70 Summerscales, J (2006) From fabric and your carbon footprint, *O Ecotextiles*, 3 October [Online] oecotextiles.wordpress.com/2013/10/03/fabric-and-your-carbon-footprint/ (archived at https://perma.cc/8YVF-4D2G)

71 Patagonia (2016) [accessed 23 March 2016] *Worn Wear* [Online] www.patagonia.com/us/reuse-recycle (archived at https://perma.cc/Y44F-QD6P)

72 Looptworks (8 October 2015) [accessed 23 March 2016] *Looptworks and Langlitz Partner Up* [Online] www.looptworks.com/blogs/looptworks-blog/69478915-looptworks-and-langlitz-partner-up (archived at https://perma.cc/3N22-HHM7)

73 circular.fashion (2019) [accessed 4 November 2019] [Online] https://circular.fashion/ (archived at https://perma.cc/45RJ-B9ZW)

74 Sustainable Apparel Coalition [accessed 15 August 2016] [Online] http://apparelcoalition.org/the-coalition (archived at https://perma.cc/3HJG-9ANH)

75 Textile Exchange [accessed 1 November 2019] [Online] textileexchange.org/about-us/ (archived at https://perma.cc/99VF-4CZX)

76 Circular Textiles Programme (2019) [accessed 2 November 2019] *Circle Economy* [Online] www.circle-economy.com/textiles/ (archived at https://perma.cc/2QQ2-BTQH)

77 United Nations Alliance for Sustainable Fashion [accessed 1 November 2019] [Online] https://unfashionalliance.org/ (archived at https://perma.cc/H3GN-AJRK)

78 Ellen MacArthur Foundation (nd) [accessed 1 November 2019] *Make Fashion Circular* [Online] www.ellenmacarthurfoundation.org/our-work/activities/make-fashion-circular (archived at https://perma.cc/4XPM-5VLL)

79 Global Fashion Agenda (2017) [accessed 23 August 2020] *Pulse of the Fashion Industry: 2017 executive summary* [Online] https://www.globalfashionagenda.com/wp-content/uploads/2017/05/Pulse-of-the-Fashion-Industry_Executive-summary.pdf (archived at https://perma.cc/NRN3-VG37)

80 Ellen MacArthur Foundation (2017) [accessed 1 November 2019] *A New Textiles Economy: Redesigning fashion's future* [Online] http://www.ellenmacarthurfoundation.org/publications (archived at https://perma.cc/44DG-FJVV)

8

Consumer electricals and electronics

We're not just looking at niche opportunities – we see this as our opportunity to decouple economic growth from the depletion of the earth's natural resources for HP, our customers and other industries.

JOHN ORTIZ, DIRECTOR OF PRODUCT STEWARDSHIP AT HP[1]

This fast-growing sector includes some of the world's largest companies. We begin with the background, and then:

- review the **issues and challenges**, including business models, resources, end-of-use and legislation;
- look at some of the **ethical and health issues;**
- review **circular economy developments**, covering business models, the 'design and supply chain', enablers and accelerators.

Background

Global sales of consumer electrical and electronic equipment (EEE) grew to around US\$1.5 trillion in 2018. New product development accelerates, with digital technologies, tablets, smartphones, 3D TVs and other innovations, and each new technology wave sees more rapid dissemination. Better, cheaper devices help shorten product life-cycles, resulting in ever-faster product obsolescence: driven by technology developments and advances, a drive for revenue growth and 'consumer preferences' (likely to be influenced by marketing).[2]

Demand for 'greener, longer-lasting devices' is increasing,[3] yet the majority of products consist of finite materials, with some classified as 'critical' by

FIGURE 8.1   Supply chain map for electronics

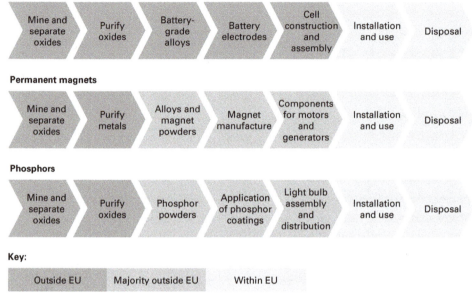

SOURCE: EC (2014)[4]

the EU. Each year, consumer electronics and household appliances with input (purchase) values totalling around US$390 billion reach end of life.[5] Complex designs, using a multitude of different materials, create supply chain challenges and complicate recycling and remanufacture.

Major brands 'offshored' and outsourced manufacturing to low-cost economies after the World Trade Organization (WTO) agreements reduced tariff and import barriers in the mid-1990s. Typical supply chain maps for three common electronic components sold in the EU show mining and the majority of manufacturing processes taking place outside the EU (see Figure 8.1).

Dhekne and Chittal (2011)[6] highlight supply chain challenges for the sector. These include planning and demand forecasting, reverse logistics, legislation, and user demand for safe, sustainable products, together with:

- **Collaboration and outsourcing** as manufacturing is commoditized whilst 'vertically integrating' core competencies such as design and innovation. Lenovo, for example, increased outsourcing of notebook production from less than 10 per cent to over 50 per cent.

- **Risk management:** extended global supply chains are more vulnerable to disruption risks from extreme weather, terrorism and geopolitics.

Product lifetimes undermine brand trust: in the UK, WRAP (2014)[7] found that one-third of washing machines and fridges, and one-quarter of vacuum cleaners do not meet the average customer's expectations for durability. It reported that around two-thirds of consumers would welcome different business models, providing repair, reuse and trade-in, if provided by the right organizations.

Business models and consumption

As consumption grows, so too does waste. Global **e-waste** is set to increase from 41.2 Mt (million tonnes) in 2014, to 52.2 Mt by 2021.[8]

Each new model is marketed as a 'must-have' with improved functionality and performance – though this may be software-enabled, not reliant on new components. Modular designs could be a game-changer, enabling both easy repairs and upgrades. In 2013, the Phonebloks project,[9] aiming to create a modular, customizable, open-sourced mobile phone design, was taken on by Motorola (at the time owned by Google). By spring 2016, the project scope had been reduced and the launch date delayed, earning criticism from original creator Dave Hakkens.[10] In 2018, Samsung and Apple were both fined by the Italian authorities, for millions of euros, for 'planned obsolescence' built into their smartphones.

To keep products in the loop, we need repair facilities and spares, otherwise, even a small malfunction makes a product unusable. However, spare parts present challenges – shortening product life-cycles and technology developments mean component specifications evolve rapidly, sometimes requiring new production technology too. That can make it expensive to make spares for old devices – even those just a few years old. Stocking parts in advance would be expensive too, and difficulty of forecasting demand could result in both stock-outs and waste.

Resources: technical

A range of metals and plastics feature heavily in EEE products, with some newer materials such as carbon fibre and graphene starting to feature. The European Commission assessed a wide range of **critical raw materials**, based on economic importance for a range of industrial sectors, together with the supply risk (including political stability, availability, violence and other factors). The 2017 assessment covered 78 materials, designating 27 with primary sources outside the EU as critical.[11]

New electronic technology often uses scarce and expensive resources, including rare earth elements and precious metals, with 'around 10 per cent of total gold worldwide used for their production'. Rare earth elements are extremely difficult to recycle. The intrinsic value of materials embedded in e-waste is estimated at 48 billion euros globally, dominated by gold, copper and plastics.

Mobile phones contain valuable materials, such as gold, silver and rare earth elements, plus silicon, ceramics and plastics. The Ellen MacArthur Foundation (2018)[12] estimated that almost 1.5 billion smartphones are shipped each year, containing components with potential value of US$1.5 billion. A study in Japan highlighted the gold yield from 1 tonne of discarded mobile phones at 150 grams, compared with just 5 grams produced from 1 tonne of ore from an average gold mine.[13] The same tonne of discarded mobile phones contains around 100 kilograms of copper and 3 kilograms of silver, plus other metals.

EEE also contains a range of oil-based plastics, and many products use several different types of plastic, creating further complexities for end-of-use disassembly and reuse.[14] These may be extremely difficult to separate at end-of-use. Often the recycling process shreds the plastic content, resulting in low-value mixed-material recyclate, suitable only for *downcycling*.

Many elements and compounds in EEE are known to be toxic for humans and living systems, including polyvinyl chloride (PVC) and brominated flame retardants (BFRs), which produce dioxins – highly toxic and carcinogenic – that are released throughout the product's life.

Resources: energy

Increased global sales of EEE, with increasing items per household or business and more frequent product replacement, mean higher-energy demand for both manufacturing and device usage. The trend towards offshoring manufacturing to East Asia, where 'coal power still dominates energy production and is the leading cause of climate change',[15] means that emissions for the industry continue to rise. The **'rebound' effect** is also a concern. As new appliances include additional functions (eg water dispensers on fridge doors), they consume more energy, potentially more than offsetting the increased efficiency of the new appliance.

Resources: water

Water footprints of EEE are high, with a smartphone using over 1,000 litres,[16] and a 2-gram microchip requiring 32 litres.[17] A heavy share of this is in mining, 'probably the second-largest industrial user of water' after energy generation, using 7–9 billion cubic metres of water annually.[18] Environmental and social impacts include overexploitation and toxic effluents from tailings contaminating rivers and lakes. Mining is increasingly competing with local communities and farmers for access to water supplies.

Flooding is a serious risk, with dams constructed to store mining tailings and effluent. In 2016, a dam burst at an iron-ore mine operated by Samarco (a joint venture between BHP Billiton and Vale), 'unleashing a wave of wastewater that flattened a village and polluted a 400-mile stretch of the River Doce'; 17 people died and a multi-billion lawsuit was filed by Brazilian prosecutors.[19]

Resources: biological

Land use, for the mine itself and the 'storage' of wastewater or solid tailings, reduces available land for farming and destroys biodiversity. Releasing effluents further destroys local ecosystems, leaching toxins into soil, water and air. In addition to water use and pollution, mining causes deforestation and land degradation.

End-of-use

Leading industrial ecologist Thomas Graedel, in a report for UNEP (2011),[20] notes that our 'personal stocks' of metals, in bicycles, cars, computers, phones, fridges, TVs and so on, are increasing. Walter Stahel highlights 'hibernating' stocks, such as obsolete undersea cables, with products no longer in use, but not yet recycled. Stocks of EEE are hibernating in households, with mobile phones at the back of drawers and so on.

Research by Rhys Charles and his team (2018)[21] used data from Graedel and others to show the average end-of-life functional recycling rates (EoL-RR) of elements highlighted in recent criticality assessments, shown in Figure 8.2. The recycling rate of the majority (32 out of 37) of these speciality metals is close to zero.

The first 'Global E-waste Monitor' report, from the UN University, was published in 2014. Figures for 2016, illustrated in Figure 8.3, show increasing levels both overall and per person.[22] The world generated 44.7 Mt (million metric tonnes) of e-waste in 2016, equivalent to 6.1 kg per person, and this is expected to grow to 52.2 Mt, or 6.8 kg per person, by 2021. E-waste growth is driven by trends including growing numbers of internet and mobile users; increasing disposable incomes enabling people to spend

FIGURE 8.2   Global recycling rates for metals and minerals

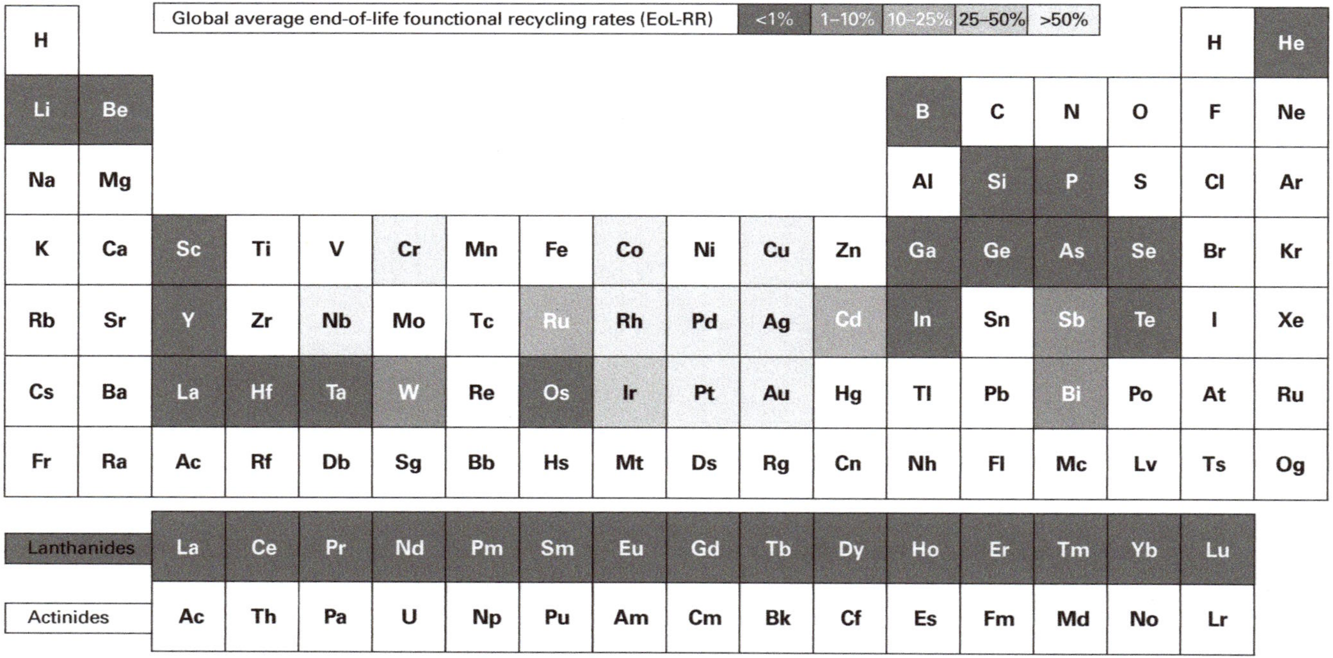

| Global average end-of-life founctional recycling rates (EoL-RR) | <1% | 1–10% | 10–25% | 25–50% | >50% |

H																	He
Li	Be											B	C	N	O	F	Ne
Na	Mg											Al	Si	P	S	Cl	Ar
K	Ca	Sc	Ti	V	Cr	Mn	Fe	Co	Ni	Cu	Zn	Ga	Ge	As	Se	Br	Kr
Rb	Sr	Y	Zr	Nb	Mo	Tc	Ru	Rh	Pd	Ag	Cd	In	Sn	Sb	Te	I	Xe
Cs	Ba	La	Hf	Ta	W	Re	Os	Ir	Pt	Au	Hg	Tl	Pb	Bi	Po	At	Ru
Fr	Ra	Ac	Rf	Db	Sg	Bb	Hs	Mt	Ds	Rg	Cn	Nh	Fl	Mc	Lv	Ts	Og

Lanthanides	La	Ce	Pr	Nd	Pm	Sm	Eu	Gd	Tb	Dy	Ho	Er	Tm	Yb	Lu
Actinides	Ac	Th	Pa	U	Np	Pu	Am	Cm	Bk	Cf	Es	Fm	Md	No	Lr

SOURCE: Image created by Rhys Charles et al (2018) (see chapter-endnote 23) using the following data sources: Global end-of-life functional recycling rates (EoL-RR) of elements highlighted as critical in recent assessments (adapted from Graedel et al, 2011); critical materials identified by EC (2011), EC (2014a) Harfield et al (2014) Deloitte Sustainability et al (2017b); data on recycling rates from Graedel et al (2011) Deloitte Sustainability (2017a)[23]

FIGURE 8.3   Global e-waste quantities

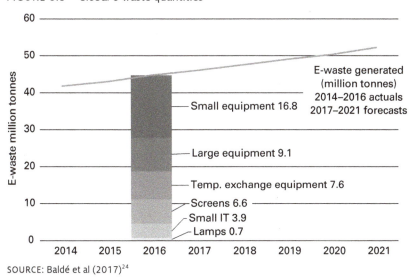

SOURCE: Baldé et al (2017)[24]

more on electronic and electrical equipment (including owning more than one device); together with shortening replacement cycles for mobile phones, computers and other devices.

Only 20 per cent (8.9 Mt) of e-waste is documented as collected and properly recycled. Of the 80 per cent (35.8 Mt) not documented, 4 per cent (1.7 Mt) in higher-income countries goes into general residual waste; the fate of the rest – 76 per cent (34.1 Mt) – is not known, but likely to be 'dumped, traded or recycled under inferior conditions'. Figure 8.4 shows the regional differences: Asia generated the largest amount of e-waste, though the second-lowest per inhabitant, whereas Oceania generated the highest e-waste per person at 17.3 kg and had the second-lowest recycling rate, at only 6 per cent.

The report estimates the value of all raw materials in e-waste at 55 billion euros in 2016 ('more than the Gross Domestic Product of most countries in the world'), with circular economy opportunities likely to far exceed that of the raw materials.

Recycling systems for households and businesses may limit reuse and recovery: throwing a TV into a waste container with other EEE is likely to damage it, and products are vulnerable to further damage during transport. E-waste is mixed into other waste streams, especially for small equipment, meaning recovery opportunities are lost. Trading of e-waste, legally or illegally, is also problematic. The Global E-waste Monitor highlights a case study on Nigeria, showing that in 2015–16, 'EU countries were the origin of

FIGURE 8.4   E-waste by region

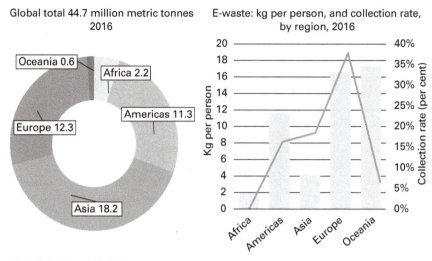

Global total 44.7 million metric tonnes 2016

E-waste: kg per person, and collection rate, by region, 2016

SOURCE: Baldé et al (2017)[25]

around 77 per cent of used EEE imported into Nigeria', and notes that 'used equipment' turns out to be broken on arrival, and should have been considered as e-waste instead. Although some equipment parts may be reusable or repairable, the remainder is likely to become e-waste. Toxic chemicals are often released during recycling, especially informal recycling and incineration.

Legislation

The Global E-waste Monitor notes that only 66 per cent of the global population is covered by national e-waste management laws, though this is a significant increase on the 44 per cent covered in 2014. The report highlights a 'high risk that pollutants are not taken care of properly', or recycled informally, without properly protecting the workers from the toxins present in e-waste. Legislation does not guarantee successful enforcement, and there may be insufficient or inadequate management, or lack of effective, robust systems to deal with e-waste.

EU legislation aims to improve the environmental management of waste EEE (WEEE), contributing to a circular economy and enhancing resource efficiency by improving collection, treatment and recycling. It aims to make producers responsible for products at end-of-use, through additional charges or take-back schemes (note that each country may implement different schemes). WEEE includes most products that have a plug or need a battery.

The regulations outline 10 broad categories of WEEE, including household appliances, IT and telecoms, entertainment (eg TVs), lighting, toys and sports, medical devices, monitoring and control equipment (eg smoke detectors) and automatic dispensers.

Related EU waste legislation covers batteries; restriction of the use of certain hazardous substances in electrical and electronic equipment (RoHS Directive); and packaging. EU regulations cover ecodesign requirements for energy-using products (EuP); the Energy Labelling Directive; and registration, evaluation, authorization and restriction of chemicals (REACH).

A global 'right to repair' movement is emerging, aiming to allow users to be able to repair their devices. Companies cite safety, security and intellectual property risks as reasons for not providing instruction and spare parts. In 2017, 'fair repair' legislation was proposed in the state of Nebraska, but was blocked by industry bodies and companies, including Apple.

Ethical and health issues

Electronics is the primary user of **conflict minerals**, raising major issues for supply chains. These relate to 'informal' mining in the Democratic Republic of Congo (DRC), and elsewhere, where small teams of people clear jungle, dig and extract easily accessible minerals. Revenue can fund civil wars, with horrific social impacts. US legislation (the Dodd-Frank Act) and OECD Due Diligence Guidance defines 'conflict minerals' in the eastern DRC as tin, tantalum, tungsten and gold.[26] Gold, in particular, is subject to smuggling and becomes a focus of land disputes. Even outside conflict regions, there are adverse social impacts, including use of child labour, pollution (eg from mercury), low wages and unsafe working conditions. In these communities, mining is often a critical source of income and employment. Ethical concerns related to **fair pay, working conditions and child labour** put global brands in the media spotlight in the early 2010s.

E-waste is often **hazardous** with potential to cause major environmental and health problems. Toxic pollution is a major concern, with annual figures including 2.2 million tonnes of lead glass, 0.3 million tonnes of batteries and 4 kilo-tonnes of ozone-depleting substances, chlorofluorocarbons (CFCs), plus many others. There are safety issues for both production and recycling, especially from toxins such as mercury, plus lead and cadmium (used in batteries). There are issues for safe disposal in many countries that lack suitable management facilities.[27]

GreenBiz reports that research highlights products and packaging containing chemicals linked to chronic diseases. As we increase circularity, these

FIGURE 8.5   Circular economy value opportunities

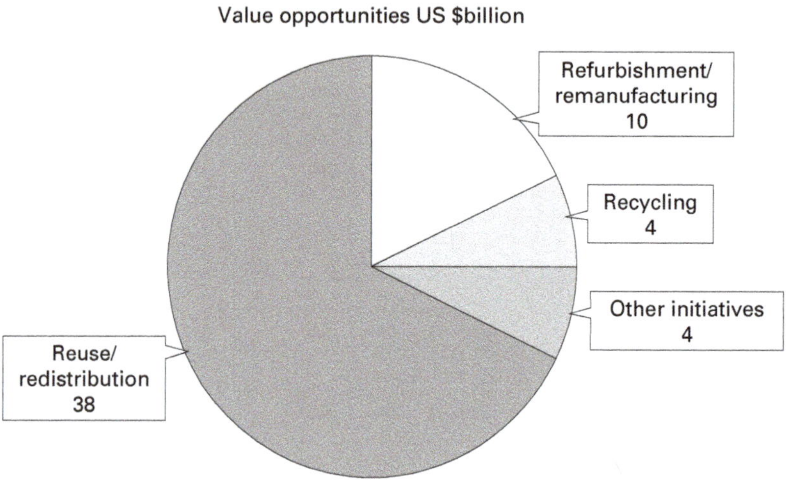

Value opportunities US $billion

Refurbishment/
remanufacturing
10

Recycling
4

Other initiatives
4

Reuse/
redistribution
38

SOURCE: WEF (2015)[28]

hazardous chemicals could be unintentionally recycled into future products. For example, flame retardants used in TV cases do not break down in nature and can accumulate in our bodies, causing infertility, cancer or hormone disruption. When these electronics are recycled at end of life, these hazardous flame retardant chemicals can end up in materials for new products including toys – exposing employees and children to harmful substances.[29]

Circular economy developments

For consumer electricals and household appliances, the World Economic Forum (2015)[30] calculated modest improvement scenarios showing that reuse, remanufacturing and recycling, aided by asset tracking, could recover US$52 billion annually, as shown in Figure 8.5. Reuse and redistribution offer the potential for US$38 billion, equating to nearly 10 per cent of the end-of-life annual total of US$390 billion noted at the start of this chapter.

In a blog for thinkstep (2019),[31] Dr Constantin Herrmann from the C-Servees European initiative says, 'companies fear that going circular will cannibalize their current business.' However, he thinks they risk being 'cut out of the market by competitors that offer affordable and valuable circular alternatives'. He goes on to predict that 'when resources and emissions have a price tag (and they will soon enough), companies will immediately need to rethink their business models. Right now, they are still not responsible for the true cost of their resource use and emissions.'

FIGURE 8.6   Circular Economy Framework 2.0

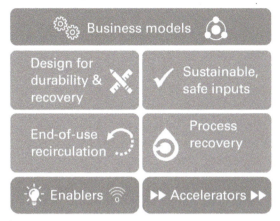

SOURCE: © Catherine Weetman

There are widespread opportunities for circular innovations. Figure 8.6 highlights the areas to explore, including new ways of thinking about resources, product design, recovering valuable materials for reuse and, of course, looking for disruptive opportunities and business models.

Business models

For electronic devices like smartphones, tablets and PCs, cloud computing enables 'on-demand' use and greater storage capacity, and also means users are less attached to their devices – seeing pre-used or rented products as a viable option. Retailers and circular service providers are developing business models that create, conserve and circulate value, and brands are starting to experiment, too.

Apple's sales of iPhones have slowed, and it's now developing software and entertainment services to provide a more engaging offer (and more consistent revenue streams). Apple has committed to a circular economy model (albeit without target dates), declaring 'we want to one day manufacture products without mining any new materials from the earth.' Apple acknowledges 'it's a big challenge. But we know we can make the best products in the world while leaving the planet better than we found it.'[32]

BEST BUY: KEEPING ELECTRONICS IN PLAY[33]

Best Buy's electronics takeback programme began with in-store parking lot events in 2009 and grew into a complex logistics operation spanning all of its retail sites. Its 20,000 Geek Squad tech-support representatives, who repair 5 million items a year, also collect electronics from clients' homes. All in all, the retailer has collected 900 million kg of old PCs, cables, TVs and other electronics.

For Best Buy, circularity means that an electronic purchase moves through consumer usage and into repair, trade-in or recycling, and it aims to nudge and support both suppliers and consumers in that direction. In 2019, Best Buy announced a partnership, enabling consumers to bring Apple products to over 1,000 Best Buy stores for Apple-certified repairs.

HOMIE: PAY-PER-USE HOME APPLIANCES[34]

Homie, in the Netherlands (a spin-off from the circular economy team at TU Delft), offers pay-per-use home appliances. Homie installs and maintains the appliances for free, and for washing machines, users pay with each wash. A digital tracker collects information on the wash programme and temperature, with lower fees for shorter, lower-temperature washes. It found that customers changed their clothes-washing habits, washing at significantly lower temperatures and on average 30 per cent less than before.

GIAB: CLOSING THE LOOP ON INSURANCE CLAIMS[35]

GIAB, in Sweden, started in 2012, working with insurance companies to collect damaged technology products from household claims. After this was implemented, claims were reduced by around one-third. For smartphones, GIAB offers a rapid replacement with an equivalent product or a five-day turnaround for repair of the original product. GIAB is now working with brands and retailers to improve circularity on e-commerce and supply chain damages.

The market for **reselling** used devices is growing fast, with global estimates for used smartphone sales expected to increase from 53 million in 2012 to 257 million by 2018. Apple's iPhone was the most popular phone, commanding higher prices than brands using the Android operating system.[36]

There are many resellers of used PCs, and now Dell and Hewlett-Packard are recognizing the opportunities, selling refurbished products in the UK. Dell also offers new PCs as a service for business customers.[37]

Our circular strategy of last resort should be recycling. Designing for circulation at the outset helps companies make a success of circulating products, components and materials. But, all too often, the difficulty of accessing and identifying materials can make it cost-prohibitive – alloys, laminates and bonded or glued materials can be impossible to separate. For example, Green Alliance (2013)[38] tells us that a reused iPhone retains almost half its original value, but recycling recovers less than a quarter of 1 per cent of the value of a new phone. In other words, reusing the iPhone recovers 200 times more value, as well as increasing Apple's customer base – and those new customers are likely to buy music and other subscription services from Apple.

Industrial ecologist Thomas Graedel sees '*urban mining*' as an important generator of secondary raw materials. For example, the 'largest municipal recycling park in China is capable of recovering 1 million tons of copper per year', over twice the capacity of the largest copper mine in China. Deposits of metal in landfill can be recycled through urban mining. In 2011, global stockpiles of copper were estimated at 225 million tonnes.[39]

Design for durability and recovery

Although electronics and electricals have great potential for redesign – for durability, ease of repair and effective end-of-use disassembly for remanufacture and recycling – only a few companies have embraced this so far. Durability often doesn't meet consumer needs. Research by WRAP (2012)[40] found that over 80 per cent of consumers said they 'would be prepared to pay more for a washing machine with a longer guarantee'. This opens up space for 'disruptors' to create products with consumer appeal that can break the 'take, make, waste' cycle, with designs that 'slow the flow'.

IAMECO: 'SUSTAINABLE, ECOLOGICAL, HIGH-PERFORMANCE COMPUTERS'[41]

iameco (I-am-eco) designs modular, upgradable products designed to last up to 10 years – about three times longer than the average computer. Compared with typical computers, they are designed to use a third less energy and harmful materials (eg brominated flame retardants, PVCs and heavy metals such as lead, cadmium and mercury) are excluded. Recycled wood is used for cases and reusable components are sourced through European partners, including the Berlin ReUse Network and Rehab (Ireland). For every computer sold, iameco also offers a repair, upgrading, and replacement and take-back service.

Designing to use fewer, simpler materials, and less of each can make a big difference to the recyclability and repairability of technology products, and Fairphone is a good example of this.

FAIRPHONE 2: MODULAR, DURABLE AND REPAIRABLE[42,43]

Fairphone aims to minimize both the social and environmental impact of production, limit composite materials, favour homogeneous materials, maximize the use of recycled materials and minimize the use of coatings. Fairphone 2, launched in 2015, is rugged, durable and easy to repair.

The average smartphone contains 62 different materials; Fairphone 2 still uses 46 different elements, but its modular design makes it easier and more productive to separate valuable elements like magnesium, tungsten and tantalum. The design also means it is easy for owners to open and repair their own phones, with a diagnostic on the website helping users find the problem module and order a replacement. Replaceable modules include the external case, battery pack, 'core unit', display unit, speakers, cameras and so on.

Users can repair their own phone or use Fairphone's repair service. Fairphone sells spare parts in its online shop, partnering with iFixit to create specific open-source repair guides. iFixit scored the phone as 10/10 for 'repairability', 'the highest score given to a mobile phone'. In 2019, Fairphone began offering refurbished smartphones across the EU.

The Ellen MacArthur Foundation (2018)[44] reports that 'cascading' of components is starting to happen, with some parts of end-of-use electronic products used in other applications. **Software upgrades** can improve functionality on products to extend their lifetimes. **Standardization** of basic components, such as screens, batteries, sensors, hard drives and chips, could reduce the proliferation of parts, simplify materials specifications and support cascading.

Safe, sustainable inputs

As we have seen, there are widespread issues with many of the materials used in EEE, with hazardous and toxic chemicals present in mining, production, use and end-of-use.

Major companies are **rethinking material inputs,** to exclude toxic, harmful and non-recyclable materials. They see the benefits of **securing key resources,** avoiding hazardous materials, improving brand perception, and reducing supply chain risk. A focus on 'safe' inputs is critical – eliminating pollution and toxins along the supply chain, improving conditions for processors, communities, users, recyclers and, of course, living systems.

APPLE: SAFE, RECYCLED, RENEWABLE MATERIALS[45]

Companies are starting to adopt material health strategies, and Apple's Chemical Management Program will help suppliers develop a comprehensive approach to managing chemicals safely. The programme includes 113 facilities across several upstream tiers of suppliers, enabling Apple to develop a Regulated Substances Specification list of all of the chemicals used in its production, to identify and eliminate harmful substances in its products. By 2019, Apple had eliminated mercury, brominated flame retardants, PVC, phthalates and beryllium from its products including computers and phones. Apple's risk assessment tools, including GreenScreen, evaluate substances against 18 hazards, including carcinogens, mutagens and endocrine disruptors.

In 2017, Apple announced its goal to make all new iPhones, Macs and other products from **100 per cent recycled or renewable** materials. By 2019, its progress included working on a menu of 13 materials, including aluminium, cobalt, zinc and plastic. There are major challenges. Some of these recycled material flows are robust, for example for recycled tin, but not for rare earth elements. Apple uses recycled tin solder in logic boards in 11 products, but to use fully recycled aluminium in the casing of Mac devices, it had to create its own alloy.[46]

Interest in both recycled and renewable materials is growing, as we've already seen with the recycled wood used in the computer cases from iameco.

DELL: RECYCLED AND RENEWABLE INPUTS, CLOSED-LOOP PROCESSES[47,48]

Dell has developed circular initiatives for both products and packaging. A *closed-loop* supply chain for recycled plastics began in 2014. By late 2015, it had recycled nearly 2 million kilograms of plastics into enclosures for new products, including flat-panel monitors and some Dell OptiPlex desktops. Working with a specialist partner, Dell also recovers carbon fibre source materials. Excess carbon fibre and production process scraps create material suitable for inclusion in new Dell products. This diverts carbon fibre from landfill, reducing the carbon footprint of the product by 11 per cent compared with using virgin material.

Intel published results of a survey finding that 70 per cent of millennials would avoid buying from companies that have negative impacts on society. Only 35 per cent of respondents had heard of conflict minerals, but Intel found that once consumers knew about the issue, the majority would favour those companies seeking to eliminate dubious supplies.[49]

FAIRPHONE: FAIRTRADE-CERTIFIED SUPPLY CHAIN FOR GOLD[50,51]

In 2016, Fairphone announced the first pilot supply chain for Fairtrade-certified gold in the electronics sector, supporting responsible mining of gold in Peru to provide materials for its Fairphone 2 smartphone.

Fairphone has mapped its supply chain, tracing the sources of materials it plans to use and looking for opportunities to improve social and environmental outcomes. Social initiatives range from employee welfare to e-waste and recycling.

For the Fairphone 2, the conflict-free mineral-sourcing scope includes tin, tantalum and tungsten, looking for opportunities to select and build relationships with like-minded suppliers.

Process design

Standardization of parts can improve supply chain flexibility and reduce inventory and obsolescence. Recovery of resources from production waste, combined with closing the loop on water and chemicals, plus the use of renewable energy, can all improve circularity and reduce costs.

Packaging of EEE products often happens at the final assembly plant, a long way from the retail market. This can significantly increase the storage and transport 'cube' for each product, adding to long-distance logistics costs. Packaging, and potentially assembly, closer to the final market allows postponement, customization and savings from improved load density of bulk shipments.

Recovery flows

Recycling technologies are developing for metals, with pyrometallurgy, hydrometallurgy and other electrochemical processes, and also for plastics (see Chapter 10 on packaging).[52]

Repair and maintenance services are normal for cars and industrial machinery, but technology has made servicing more complicated, and often it is impossible to access a service manual for 'DIY' repairs. In developed economies, clever marketing persuades us to accept shorter product life-times and limited, expensive repair options for many products.

But there is a quiet rebellion happening. Around the world, Repair Cafés are growing in popularity and online 'wiki' site iFixit.com is providing tools, parts and user-friendly instructions to help us repair a wide range of products, with almost 150,000 solutions for over 14,000 products as at June 2019. (See case studies later in this chapter.) As we noted earlier, there is a 'right to repair' movement, supported by iFixit, which says:

> Manufacturers say that repair information is proprietary and [they] work to shut down independent repair shops. Fortunately, not all companies are that way. Support companies that are repair friendly, like Dell and Patagonia, help us create documentation for companies that aren't.[53]

In a survey in the EU, 50 per cent of respondents said that in the past 12 months they had 'decided against repairing a faulty product because repair costs were too high'.

Although demand for reusable and repairable products is growing, manu-facturers are generally not designing products or their components to make this easy for consumers, or repairers. In an EU survey, 50 per cent of respondents said that they had decided not to repair a faulty product in the last year because the repair costs were too high, and 92 per cent thought that producers should indicate the lifespan of products.[54] Often the neces-sary repair is for a simple component, and the same kinds of components fail across different brands for the same product, such as pumps and drum bearings in washing machines, or screens and batteries in phones, laptops and tablet devices.

CIRCULAR COMPUTING™: THE 'WORLD'S FIRST COMPUTER REMANUFACTURER'[55]

In 2019, UK-based Circular Computing™ announced it was setting up a network of partners across Europe to sell its range of 'carbon neutral enterprise-grade laptops'. It reports that 160,000 laptops are disposed of every day in the EU alone and that over 70 per cent of discarded laptops could be reused. Circular Computing™ takes thousands of ex-lease computers from large corporations each month, and puts them through a rigorous five-hour remanufacturing process, during which they are dismantled, cleaned, repaired, upgraded and refinished, ready for sale.

TECH TAKEBACK: POP-UP EVENTS GETTING END-OF-USE CONSUMER TECHNOLOGY BACK INTO THE LOOP[56]

In the UK, Tech Takeback provides a government-compliant data-wiping service, sorts the equipment and arranges for secure refurbishment, reuse or recycling.

At Tech Takeback's first three pop-ups, more than 1,000 people brought along over 3,500 end-of-life electronic and electrical items, including laptops, mobile phones, hard drives, monitors, and lots of cables. Tech Takeback calculated that reusing the technology and materials saved over 19 tonnes of CO_2 equivalent.

Companies are developing effective ways to recover their own products. Those offered through service or rental contracts offer easy opportunities, as the product is returned when the contract ends. Ricoh, with its Comet Circle™ and GreenLine product renewal process, is a good example of 'closing the loop'.[57] Exchange platforms, including well-known examples like eBay, Freecycle, Gumtree and others, make it easy to sell pre-owned devices, but authenticity and condition are difficult to determine. This opens up space for trusted brands and specialist resellers, who can check for fakes and provide refurbishment and repair if necessary.

TELEFONICA UK – O2 RECYCLE: REWARDING RECOVERY FLOWS[58]

Telefonica UK Ltd launched O2 Recycle in 2009, and by 2019 had prevented more than 3 million handsets from reaching landfill, saving 450 tonnes of waste from landfill and paying over £225 million back to customers. All devices are data-wiped and either reused or recycled. As many as 95 per cent are in suitable condition to be resold, with the remainder disposed of responsibly and the valuable materials returned to the supply chain. The operation, supported by Redeem, deals with functioning, faulty and broken devices; questions on the website assess the value accordingly.

APPLE: TRADE IN[59]

Apple offers a Trade In programme, with credit towards a future purchase for eligible products. Non-eligible devices are recycled for free. In 2019, an iPhone XS could earn up to US$500 credit. Customers answer a few questions about device condition, and are given a trade-in estimate. Users are shown how to safely back up and wipe their data, and can opt for a prepaid shipping label, or take it to an Apple Store.

ENVIRONCOM: CIRCULAR SERVICE PROVIDER

Environcom, founded in 2003, is the UK's largest independent reuse and recycling specialist of waste electrical and electronic equipment (WEEE). Its strategy evolved from 'mining' specialist components to focus on reuse. It processes more than 100,000 tonnes and 5 million items each year, across four sites.[60] Products include household appliances, TVs and IT equipment.

Figure 8.7 illustrates the typical process. Waste from a variety of sources arrives at the sites and products are inspected, to decide if they are suitable for refurbishment and/or repair. Otherwise, they are recycled to recover chemicals, spare parts and materials, removing chemicals and gases required by EU WEEE regulations.

The four purpose-built processing plants separate metals, plastics and foam for recovery, and safely collect non-recyclable materials for disposal.

FIGURE 8.7   Environcom – outline process

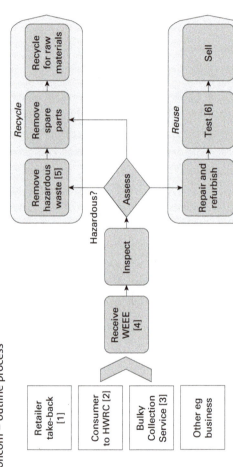

Key
1. For example, from free collection of end-of-life product, either during home delivery, or take-back at store
2. Household waste recycling centres (HWRC), operated in England and Wales by local councils
3. Bulky collection service – may be operated by local councils, or charities. Large electrical items and furniture **may** be collected free of charge
4. Mixed product streams are received and sorted
5. For example, from fridges, automatically extracted in controlled environments at dedicated fridge plants
6. Final cleaning, comprehensive tests including PAT

Enablers

Researchers are developing **new materials,** with examples of bio-based plastics, carbon fibre alternatives using lignin (from wood) and other bio-origin materials.

A number of existing companies are developing new **recycling processes,** aiming to extract a wider range of materials and create more value. In 2011 Umicore, with French company Solvay, began recycling rechargeable metal hydride batteries.[61] These contain valuable materials, with around one gram of rare earth elements in an AAA battery. Walter Stahel (2016)[62] reminds us that the 'ultimate goal is to recycle atoms'. His examples also include Umicore, extracting gold and copper from e-waste, plus Batrec (a Swiss firm) removing zinc and manganese from batteries. Stahel warns of energy-intensive processes, only partly recovering the metals, requiring 'new technologies to de-polymerize, de-alloy, de-laminate, de-vulcanize and de-coat materials'.

Production technologies like *3D printing (3DP)* can replace complex sub-assemblies with a single 3D printed component. 3DP developments include batteries, transistors and LEDs,[63] as well as 3DP circuit boards. This can simplify both manufacturing and recovery, eliminating mixed materials in difficult-to-disassemble components. 3DP can also support 'mass customization'.

The World Economic Forum Asset Tracking project, announced in 2015, aims to accelerate the adoption of **asset tracking** in a couple of pilot value chains, including consumer electronics and medical equipment.[64] The Internet of Things and sensors can monitor performance and flag the need for servicing, and provide data on component durability.

APPLE: MATERIAL RECOVERY ROBOTS[65]

Automation can reduce disassembly costs, improving the business case for repair, remanufacture and recycling. Apple's **material recovery robots** (known as Daisy) have evolved to disassemble 15 different iPhone models at the rate of 200 per hour, meaning each robot could disassemble more than a million devices per year. Apple refurbished more than 7.8 million devices in 2018, diverting more than 48,000 metric tons of e-waste from landfills. Although the recovered materials represent a tiny proportion of the 60 or so elements found in an iPhone, Apple prioritized the highest-value raw materials based on their environmental, social and supply impacts. In 2019, it opened a Material Recovery Lab and will partner with academic institutions to drive innovation in recycling and device disassembly.

Mobile apps and *platforms* can connect like-minded consumers together, sharing design ideas or helping to understand and repair products.

IFIXIT: KNOWLEDGE-SHARING PLATFORM[66]

In 2003, iFixit began helping users to repair a wide range of equipment, including mobile phones, computers and ICT (information and computer technology), and domestic appliances. iFixit is:

> a wiki-based site that teaches people how to fix almost anything. It now has over 15 years' experience in training and supporting thousands of repair businesses worldwide, with around 5 million users each month. Anyone can create a consumer-oriented repair manual for a device, and edit the existing set of manuals to improve them.[67]

iFixit supplies toolkits and spare parts, and supports independent repair shops, providing technical information, plus business and supply-chain expertise.

iFixit also publishes scorecards for popular products such as mobile phones and computers, highlighting their ease of repair. Through information from users, iFixit analyses product durability, including common failure causes (whether through normal wear and tear, malfunction or accidental damage). For smartphones, it finds that 10 per cent break in the first year, and 24 per cent break in less than two years. Often it may be the screen, speaker, buttons, vibrator, etc, that fail. The main causes of breakages include being dropped (76 per cent) and liquid damage (20 per cent).

Governments can encourage reuse and repairs too, for example in the UK through the 'RecycleNow' website.[68] Information for consumers includes guidance on removing personal data from devices before passing on or recycling, with a range of suggestions including charities and reuse organizations, online platforms, friends, family, reuse shops, etc. For broken items, it suggests checking online repair information sources, including www.ifixit.com.

Accelerators

Government **policy** can encourage repairs: for example, Sweden is trialling **tax incentives** for repairs of household products. In the European Union, the **Ecodesign** standards are likely to be expanded to include operational hours, performance and durability of key components, such as with the Ecodesign guidelines for vacuum cleaners.

HP, Teleplan, IKEA, Philips and iFixit recently embarked on a year-long **collaborative project** (Co.Project) exploring new applications of 3D printing technology for spare parts. Instead of warehouses full of parts (that might never be needed), the parts can be printed on-demand, needing only digital files, or even a 3D scan of the existing part. For companies like IKEA, with around 12,000 types of products (and many more components), the potential benefits are substantial.[69]

The C-SERVEES project aims to boost a resource-efficient circular economy in the electrical and electronic sector through the development, testing, validation and transfer of new circular economic business models based on systemic, eco-innovative services.[70] There are four target products: washing machines, toner cartridges, TV sets/displays and access link monitoring (telecom) equipment. Funded by H2020, members include large enterprises, SMEs, research centres and others.

Community projects enable people to share skills and tools. The Restart Project is a social enterprise aiming to reduce electronic waste, for example with 'repair parties' in London.[71] It helps people 'learn to repair their own electronics in community events and in workplaces', and gives talks on repair and resilience.

REPAIR CAFÉ: KNOWLEDGE-SHARING POP-UPS[72]

Repair Café, a non-profit organization, has grown from an idea in 2007, to have over 1,600 groups, holding nearly 20,000 meetings and repairing 350,000 products in 2018. The concept recognizes that in developed economies we often throw away items with almost nothing wrong with them: because we have forgotten or not learned simple repair skills. Repair Cafés aim to involve those people with these skills to pass on their knowledge, so products last longer instead of being thrown away. The cafés are also meeting places, fulfilling social as well as practical and learning functions. The tools and materials are available, and clothes, furniture, electrical appliances, toys, bicycles and more can be repaired, with help from expert volunteers.

Certification and assessments can also share knowledge and build trust in the brands using them. TCO Certified is a sustainability label for IT products, covering a broad range of social and environmental factors across the product life-cycle. In 2019, it is available for eight product categories, with more than 3,500 products certified.

In 2019, Apple promised to source gold for its electronic products from miners registered under the Salmon Gold partnership, a scheme combining mining sites with projects to restore ecosystems and improve nearby watercourses for salmon. Apple plans to trace all the gold sourced this way from the mine to the refiner, using blockchain technology.[73]

Summary

Linear business models depend on increasing market penetration to offset reducing product prices (and profit per item). Levels of waste are increasing, exacerbated by shortening product life-cycles, ineffective recovery systems and lack of incentives for circular flows. Extended, complex supply chains are more vulnerable to disruption risks, and shortening product life-cycles adds challenges to planning, forecasting and inventory management.

Externalities occur all along the supply chain, from environmental and social issues with mining; to using (and polluting) with hazardous chemicals and heavy metals in production; to unethical and unsafe reverse flows and recycling processes. Transparency and reputation risks are encouraging brands to 'professionalize' their supply chains to ensure that all actors are operating to agreed ethical, safe and legal standards. Costs of raw materials are likely to continue increasing (we have used up all the easy-to-access sources), encouraging recovery of increasingly valuable resources for reuse.

Consumers, seeking performance and access rather than ownership of (soon-to-be-outdated) products, will prefer service, performance and rental contracts. These are suitable for more durable, modular products, easily upgraded and repaired for further use cycles.

Systems thinking approaches are vital – there are lots of connected factors: material specifications impact safety and future recycling viability; standardization and refurbishment technology can increase value of recovered products and enable parts to be harvested for repairs or 'cascading'; modular designs, new technology and software, if 'designed in' at the start, can make upgrades and reuse attractive, extending the useful life of products. Brands like Apple are already focusing more on services (apps and entertainment) and less on selling new products, and have declared their circular economy ambitions.

We want to make but not take. … Our ambition to end mining is as big as anything we've undertaken at Apple, and it's inspired some of our most innovative solutions.

> Sarah Chandler, Senior Director of Operations and Environmental Initiatives, Apple Inc. (2019)[74]

Further resources

Circular Consumer Electronics: An initial exploration (2018) Ellen MacArthur Foundation www.ellenmacarthurfoundation.org/publications/circular-consumer-electronics-an-initial-exploration (archived at https://perma.cc/2MET-NLT6)

EC Critical Raw Materials [Online] ec.europa.eu/growth/sectors/raw-materials/specific-interest/critical/index_en.htm (archived at https://perma.cc/C8PM-DGUP)

Global E-waste Monitor: http://ewastemonitor.info/ (archived at https://perma.cc/U9EY-ZC8H)

WRAP (2019) [accessed 2 December 2019] *Electrical and Electronic Equipment Sustainability Action Plan 2025 (esap 2025)* [Online] www.wrap.org.uk/sustainable-electricals/esap (archived at https://perma.cc/2HLW-A2HT)

Notes

1 Hower, M (2015) [accessed 30 June 2019] HP, Tetra Pak win big with the circular economy, *GreenBiz*, 24 November [Online] www.greenbiz.com/article/hp-tetra-pak-win-big-circular-economy (archived at https://perma.cc/89DJ-F34F)

2 EMF (2015) [accessed 24 April 2016] *Growth Within: A circular economy vision for a competitive Europe*, Ellen MacArthur Foundation with SUN and McKinsey [Online] www.ellenmacarthurfoundation.org/publications/growth-within-a-circular-economy-vision-for-a-competitive-europe (archived at https://perma.cc/J7PG-GAE9)

3 Cobbing, M and Dowdall, T (2014) [accessed 24 April 2016] *Green Gadgets: Designing the future*, Executive Summary, Greenpeace International [Online] www.greenpeace.org/international/en/campaigns/detox/electronics/Guide-to-Greener-Electronics/Green-Gadgets/ (archived at https://perma.cc/T5XN-DT8Z)

4 EC (2014) *Report on Critical Raw Materials for the EU: Critical raw materials profiles*

5 WEF (2015) [accessed 30 May 2016] Project MainStream – Status Update, Prepared with Ellen MacArthur Foundation and McKinsey [Online]

www3.weforum.org/docs/WEF_Project_Mainstream_Status_2015.pdf
(archived at https://perma.cc/MU8D-54LR)

6   Dhekne, R and Chittal, SS (May 2011) [accessed 24 April 2016] *Supply
    Chain Strategy for the Consumer Electronics Industry*, WIPRO [Online]
    www.wipro.com/documents/insights/the-future-of-supply-chain-strategy-for-
    consumer-electronics.pdf (archived at https://perma.cc/Z3PG-MFVJ)

7   WRAP (2014) [accessed 2 February 2016] *esap – Generating Value for
    Business through Sustainability* [Online] www.wrap.org.uk/sites/files/wrap/
    esap-summary-2014.pdf (archived at https://perma.cc/V5V9-D268)

8   Baldé, CP et al (2017) [accessed 4 December 2019] *The Global E-waste
    Monitor – 2017*, United Nations University (UNU), International
    Telecommunication Union (ITU) & International Solid Waste Association
    (ISWA) [Online] http://ewastemonitor.info/ (archived at https://perma.cc/U9EY-
    ZC8H)

9   Phonebloks (2013) [accessed 30 May 2016] [Online] phonebloks.com/journey
    (archived at https://perma.cc/AV8L-2K7K)

10 Hakkens, D (2016) [accessed 30 May 2016] [Online] davehakkens.nl/news/
    re-think-project-ara/ (archived at https://perma.cc/4DML-TQMP)

11 EC (2017) [accessed 2 December 2019] *Critical Raw Materials* [Online]
    https://ec.europa.eu/growth/sectors/raw-materials/specific-interest/critical_en
    (archived at https://perma.cc/8CPE-AL86)

12 Ellen MacArthur Foundation (2018) [accessed 1 December 2019]
    Circular Consumer Electronics: An initial exploration [Online]
    www.ellenmacarthurfoundation.org/publications/circular-consumer-
    electronics-an-initial-exploration (archived at https://perma.cc/2MET-NLT6)

13 Yoshikawa, M (2008) [accessed 24 April 2016] Urban miners look for
    precious metals in cell phones, *Reuters* [Online] www.reuters.com/article/
    us-japan-metals-recycling-idUST13528020080427 (archived at https://perma.cc/
    U7G9-B6PS)

14 Goosey, M (2013) [accessed 2 February 2016] ieMRC, *The Materials Content
    of WEEE – Plastics* [Online] www.lboro.ac.uk/microsites/research/iemrc/
    Events%20write%20up/Events%20write%20up/MTGIeMRCBrussels170413.pdf
    (archived at https://perma.cc/55MB-WNRR)

15 Cobbing, M and Dowdall, T (2014) [accessed 24 April 2016] *Green Gadgets:
    Designing the future*, Executive Summary, Greenpeace International [Online]
    www.greenpeace.org/international/en/campaigns/detox/electronics/Guide-to-
    Greener-Electronics/Green-Gadgets/ (archived at https://perma.cc/T5XN-
    DT8Z)

16 McCarthy, E (15 October 2014) [accessed 24 April 2016] *The Surprising
    Water Footprints of 15 Common Things* [Online] mentalfloss.com/
    article/59480/surprising-water-footprints-15-common-things (archived at
    https://perma.cc/LE26-7USU)

17 Zygmunt, J (2007) *Hidden Waters: A waterwise briefing* [Online] http://waterfootprint.org/media/downloads/Zygmunt_2007_1.pdf (archived at https://perma.cc/UKH2-Y3RW) [accessed 24 April 2016]

18 Gasson, C (2011) [accessed 24 April 2016] Don't waste a drop: water use in mining, *Mining Magazine*, October [Online] www.globalwaterintel.com/dont-waste-drop-water-mining/ (archived at https://perma.cc/3BYE-4VSY)

19 Yeomans, J (11 March 2016) [accessed 24 April 2016] BHP Billiton's disaster-hit mine Samarco to reopen by end of year, *The Telegraph* [Online] www.telegraph.co.uk/business/2016/03/11/bhp-billitons-disaster-hit-mine-samarco-to-reopen-by-end-of-year/ (archived at https://perma.cc/223S-ZG5Y)

20 Graedel, TE et al (2011) [accessed 23 April 2016] *Assessing Mineral Resources in Society: Metal stocks and recycling rates*, UNEP International Resource Panel [Online] www.unep.org/resourcepanel/publications/recyclingratesofmetals/tabid/56073/default.aspx (archived at https://perma.cc/R5JT-WU7H)

21 Charles, RG et al (2018) [accessed 5 October 2019] Platinized counter-electrodes for dye-sensitised solar cells from waste thermocouples: A case study for resource efficiency, industrial symbiosis and circular economy, *Journal of Cleaner Production*, 202, 20 November, pp 1167–1178 [Online] https://doi.org/10.1016/j.jclepro.2018.08.125 (archived at https://perma.cc/J6WX-HFJZ)

22 Baldé, CP et al (2017) [accessed 4 December 2019] *The Global E-waste Monitor – 2017*, United Nations University (UNU), International Telecommunication Union (ITU) & International Solid Waste Association (ISWA) [Online] http://ewastemonitor.info/ (archived at https://perma.cc/U9EY-ZC8H)

23 Charles, RG et al (2018) [accessed 5 October 2019] Platinized counter-electrodes for dye-sensitised solar cells from waste thermocouples: A case study for resource efficiency, industrial symbiosis and circular economy, *Journal of Cleaner Production*, 202, 20 November, pp 1167–1178 [Online] https://doi.org/10.1016/j.jclepro.2018.08.125 (archived at https://perma.cc/J6WX-HFJZ)

24 Baldé, CP et al (2017) [accessed 4 December 2019] *The Global E-waste Monitor – 2017*, United Nations University (UNU), International Telecommunication Union (ITU) & International Solid Waste Association (ISWA) [Online] http://ewastemonitor.info/ (archived at https://perma.cc/U9EY-ZC8H)

25 Baldé, CP et al (2017) [accessed 4 December 2019] *The Global E-waste Monitor – 2017*, United Nations University (UNU), International Telecommunication Union (ITU) & International Solid Waste Association (ISWA) [Online] http://ewastemonitor.info/ (archived at https://perma.cc/U9EY-ZC8H)

26 Foreign and Commonwealth Office (2013) [accessed 24 April 2016] *Guidance: Conflict minerals* [Online] https://www.gov.uk/guidance/conflict-minerals (archived at https://perma.cc/9FHW-2G6D)

27 UNEP (2016) [accessed 24 April 2016] *Lead and Cadmium* [Online] www.unep.org/chemicalsandwaste/LeadandCadmium/PbandCdBatteries/tabid/6175/Default.aspx (archived at https://perma.cc/3RB5-5PCW)

28 WEF (2015) [accessed 15 August 2016] Project MainStream – Status Update; prepared with Ellen MacArthur Foundation and McKinsey [Online] http://www3.weforum.org/docs/WEF_Project_Mainstream_Status_2015.pdf (archived at https://perma.cc/MU8D-54LR)

29 Greiner, T (2019) [accessed 2 December 2019] How Apple and Ahold Delhaize are ensuring the new materials economy is safe, *GreenBiz*, 8 November [Online] www.greenbiz.com/article/how-apple-and-ahold-delhaize-are-ensuring-new-materials-economy-safe (archived at https://perma.cc/8T6U-Z64R)

30 WEF (2015) [accessed 15 August 2016] Project MainStream – Status Update; prepared with Ellen MacArthur Foundation and McKinsey [Online] http://www3.weforum.org/docs/WEF_Project_Mainstream_Status_2015.pdf (archived at https://perma.cc/MU8D-54LR)

31 Herrmann, C (2019) [accessed 2 December 2019] Being 'smart' ain't enough – circular economy in the electronics sector, *thinkstep blog*, 17 June [Online] www.thinkstep.com/blog/circular-economy-and-the-electronics-sector (archived at https://perma.cc/2R2B-947V)

32 Apple (2019) [accessed 7 December 2019] *Environment* [online] https://www.apple.com/environment/our-approach/ (archived at https://perma.cc/AM4K-Q3J2)

33 Wenzel E (2019) [accessed 2 December 2019] Apple and Best Buy reveal their circular visions (and a new partnership), *Greenbiz*, 20 June [Online] www.greenbiz.com/article/apple-and-best-buy-reveal-their-circular-visions-and-new-partnership (archived at https://perma.cc/5U2P-GVP7)

34 Interview with Nancy Bocken, co-founder, Homie (14 November 2019) and Homie www.homiepayperuse.com/ (archived at https://perma.cc/47Y3-CGFU) [accessed 5 December 2019]; and Bocken, N, Mugge, R, Bom, C and Lemstra, H (2018) Pay-per-use Business Models as a Driver for Sustainable Consumption: Evidence from the case of HOMIE, *Journal of Cleaner Production*, **198**, 498–510

35 Circular Economy Podcast, Episode 15 (17 November 2019) www.rethinkglobal.info/episode-15-matilda-jarbin-giab/ (archived at https://perma.cc/85YM-R8PM) and www.godsinlosen.se (archived at https://perma.cc/HXJ2-K7M2)

36 Guglielmo, C (7 August 2013) [accessed 14 May 2016] Used smartphone market 'poised to explode', *Forbes* [Online] www.forbes.com/sites/connieguglielmo/2013/08/07/used-smartphone-market-poised-to-explode-apple-iphone-holding-up-better-than-samsung-galaxy/#1948ccb4ccd9 (archived at https://perma.cc/YX62-84U8)

37 Dell (2019) [accessed 5 December 2019] [Online] www.dell.com/en-us/work/ shop/pc-as-a-service-for-business/cp/pcaas (archived at https://perma.cc/ XG9T-LCYB)

38 Benton, D and Hazell, J (2013) [accessed 2 December 2019] *Resource Resilient UK*, Green Alliance, 16 July [Online] https://www.green-alliance.org.uk/ page_816.php (archived at https://perma.cc/F3JJ-BJTQ)

39 Graedel, TE et al (2011) [accessed 23 April 2016] *Assessing Mineral Resources in Society: Metal stocks and recycling rates*, UNEP International Resource Panel [Online] www.unep.org/resourcepanel/publications/recyclingrates ofmetals/tabid/56073/default.aspx (archived at https://perma.cc/R5JT-WU7H)

40 WRAP (2012) [accessed 3 February 2016] *Switched on to Value* [Online] www.wrap.org.uk/sites/files/wrap/Switched%20on%20to%20Value%20 12%202014.pdf (archived at https://perma.cc/L8EM-M6CV)

41 iameco (2019) [accessed 5 December 2019] [Online] http://www.iameco.com/ our-vision/product-service-strategy/ (archived at https://perma.cc/4N5F-2P6B)

42 Fairphone (2016) [accessed 19 April 2016] [Online] www.fairphone.com/ phone/ (archived at https://perma.cc/GYV6-WDET)

43 Fairphone Fact Sheet [accessed 19 April 2016] [Online] www.fairphone.com/ wp-content/uploads/2016/01/Fairphone-factsheet-EN.pdf (archived at https://perma.cc/5UY9-388U)

44 Ellen MacArthur Foundation (2018) [accessed 1 December 2019] *Circular Consumer Electronics: An initial exploration* [Online] www.ellenmacarthurfoundation.org/publications/circular-consumer- electronics-an-initial-exploration (archived at https://perma.cc/2MET-NLT6)

45 Greiner, T (2019) How Apple and Ahold Delhaize are ensuring the new materials economy is safe, *GreenBiz*, 8 November [Online] www.greenbiz.com/ article/how-apple (archived at https://perma.cc/UZC2-D55H)

46 Wenzel E (2019) [accessed 2 December 2019] Apple and Best Buy reveal their circular visions (and a new partnership), *Greenbiz*, 20 June [Online] www.greenbiz.com/article/apple-and-best-buy-reveal-their-circular-visions-and- new-partnership (archived at https://perma.cc/5U2P-GVP7)

47 Wark, C (5 Oct 2015) [accessed 6 February 2016] Dell is at it again, with use of industry-first recycled carbon fiber, *2degrees Network* [Online] www.2degreesnetwork.com/groups/2degrees-community/resources/dell-at-it- again-with-use-industry-first-recycled-carbon-fiber/ (archived at https://perma.cc/ 8BTG-474T)

48 Mattison, D (26 June 2015) [accessed 6 February 2016] The Circular Economy, Interview with Oliver Campbell of Dell [Online]. Website no longer available, but see https://sustainablepackaging.org/people/olivier-campbell/ (archived at https://perma.cc/NJ36-JVLA)

49 Innovation Forum [accessed 2 February 2016] *Will Intel's Conflict-Free Computers Engage the Millennial Consumer?* [Online] innovation-forum.co. uk/analysis.php?s=will-intels-conflict-free-computers-engage-the-millennial- consumer (archived at https://perma.cc/MN8R-JTBL)

50 Sustainable Brands (29 January 2016) [accessed 7 February 2016] *Fairphone Achieves First-Ever Fairtrade-Certified Gold Supply Chain for Consumer Electronics* [Online] disq.us/96gxe3 (archived at https://perma.cc/5HUA-Z4M5)

51 YouTube [accessed 7 February 2016] *Fairphone: 2011 DRC Trip* [Online] www.youtube.com/watch?v=WWVFXesVScA&feature=youtu.be (archived at https://perma.cc/J7NV-KNNH)

52 Ellen MacArthur Foundation (2018) [accessed 1 December 2019] *Circular Consumer Electronics: An initial exploration* [Online] www.ellenmacarthurfoundation.org/publications/circular-consumer-electronics-an-initial-exploration (archived at https://perma.cc/2MET-NLT6)

53 iFixit (2019) [accessed 2 December 2019] *Right to Repair* [Online] www.ifixit.com/Right-to-Repair/Intro (archived at https://perma.cc/S2TN-EN5K)

54 Make Resources Count [accessed 12 May 2016] The European Environmental Bureau [Online] makeresourcescount.eu/policy-in-action/repairable-products-that-last/

55 World's first carbon neutral laptops arrive in Denmark (2 April 2019) [accessed 4 December 2019] *Circular Computing* [Online] https://www.circularcomputing.com/news/worlds-first-carbon-neutral-laptops-arrive-in-denmark (archived at https://perma.cc/N3A7-U2D8)

56 Circular Economy Podcast, Episode 14 (3 November 2019) [Online] www.rethinkglobal.info/episode-14-david-greenfield-of-tech-takeback/ (archived at https://perma.cc/DCB5-ZM5G) and techtakeback.com/ (archived at https://perma.cc/Q669-7CBT)

57 Ellen MacArthur Foundation (2012) [accessed 23 April 2016] *Towards the Circular Economy: Economic and business rationale for an accelerated transition*, p 29 [Online] www.ellenmacarthurfoundation.org/publications/towards-a-circular-economy-business-rationale-for-an-accelerated-transition (archived at https://perma.cc/657J-4UBW)

58 McCaskill, S (2019) [accessed 4 December 2019] O2 Recycle saves 3m devices from landfill, *TechRadar*, 29 October [Online] https://www.techradar.com/uk/news/o2-recycle-saves-3m-devices-from-landfill (archived at https://perma.cc/4WNG-ME5A)

59 Trade In, Apple (2019) [accessed 6 December 2019] [Online] https://www.apple.com/shop/trade-in (archived at https://perma.cc/J7ZK-XER4)

60 Environcom (2014) [accessed 4 January 2015] Business & Education Minister Nick Boles MP Launches Enterprise Scheme with Grantham Recycler [Online] www.environcom.co.uk/page.php?article=846&name=NIck+Boles+Visit+to+Environcom (archived at https://perma.cc/YTE6-Y8E2)

61 Jones, N (2013) [accessed 23 April 2016] A scarcity of rare metals is hindering green technologies, *Environment 360* [Online] e360.yale.edu/feature/a_scarcity_of_rare_metals_is_hindering_green_technologies/2711 (archived at https://perma.cc/A6C6-SYJ8)

62 Stahel, WR (2016) Circular Economy, *Nature*, **531**, 24 March, p 435

63 Cohen D, Sergeant M and Somers K (2014) *McKinsey Quarterly*, January, p 1

64 World Economic Forum (2015) Project MainStream – Status Update, prepared with Ellen MacArthur Foundation and McKinsey, p17 [Online] www3.weforum.org/docs/WEF_Project_Mainstream_Status_2015.pdf (archived at https://perma.cc/MU8D-54LR)

65 Phipps, L (2019) [accessed 2 December 2019] Apple dials up its circular materials aspirations, *Greenbiz*, 18 April [Online] www.greenbiz.com/article/apple-dials-its-circular-materials-aspirations (archived at https://perma.cc/YS93-LCVW)

66 WRAP (2014) WRAP Resources Limited Conference [Online] www.wrap.org.uk/content/wraps-resources-limited-conference (archived at https://perma.cc/EUW2-EDNM) iFixit Kyle Wies Video [Online] youtu.be/Q-fFx3QtlCU?list=UUcKVP2iloKVUHE3MgLaAoog (archived at https://perma.cc/LH37-X7GF) [accessed 2 February 2016]

67 iFixit (2016) [accessed 4 February 2016]*About Us* [Online] www.ifixit.com/Info (archived at https://perma.cc/DG8D-VTS6)

68 WRAP (2016) [accessed 24 April 2016] *RecycleNow* [Online] http://www.recyclenow.com/what-to-do-with/electrical-items (archived at https://perma.cc/3GV2-J87L)

69 Iles, J (2018) [accessed 2 December 2019] Brands team up to see how 3D printing can revolutionise repair, *Circulate News*, 8 November [Online] medium.com/circulatenews/brands-team-up-to-see-how-3d-printing-can-revolutionise-repair-86d882d2a95d (archived at https://perma.cc/3UDG-6GTE)

70 Herrmann, C (2019) [accessed 2 December 2019] Being 'smart' ain't enough – circular economy in the electronics sector, *thinkstep blog*, 17 June [Online] www.thinkstep.com/blog/circular-economy-and-the-electronics-sector (archived at https://perma.cc/2R2B-947V)

71 Du Cann, C (2015) [accessed 18 September 2016] Food waste cafes and urban orchards: five ways people are building a new economy, *The Guardian* [Online] www.theguardian.com/sustainable-business/2015/sep/17/economy-grassroots-projects-local-social-austerity?CMP=new_1194&CMP= (archived at https://perma.cc/89T5-4T3V)

72 Repair Café [accessed 2 December 2019] [Online] repaircafe.org/ (archived at https://perma.cc/X6AC-R7CS)

73 Cuff, M (2019) [accessed 2 December 2019] 'Salmon gold': Apple promises to embrace fish-friendly gold mining, *Business Green*, 19 August [Online] https://www.greenbiz.com/article/salmon-gold-apple-promises-embrace-fish-friendly-gold-mining (archived at https://perma.cc/UAP6-3HBG)

74 Wenzel E (2019) [accessed 2 December 2019] Apple and Best Buy reveal their circular visions (and a new partnership), *Greenbiz*, 20 June [Online] https://www.greenbiz.com/article/apple-and-best-buy-reveal-their-circular-visions-and-new-partnership (archived at https://perma.cc/5U2P-GVP7)

9

Industrial manufacturing

You can completely ignore all the concepts of the circular economy, but if one of your competitors picks it up and it's successful, then you have solved your problem, because your company will disappear.

PROFESSOR WALTER STAHEL[1]

We have looked at what is happening across the food, fashion and consumer electronics sectors, and we will look at packaging in Chapter 10. The circular economy is progressing in a wide range of other sectors too: automotive, chemicals, construction, medical equipment, pharmaceuticals and more. Here we touch on a few examples to show some of the ways the circular economy is gaining traction in businesses of all shapes and sizes, across the world.

We will cover the issues, including key materials, and then look at examples for each of the circular economy components.

Issues

We covered the global trends in Chapter 5 and explored more sector-specific challenges in the other chapters in Part Two. On top of these challenges, society, governments and business leaders face complex, serious risks, such as those reported by the World Economic Forum in Chapter 3, illustrated in Figure 9.1.

Population growth, increasing consumption and urban living needs more infrastructure: housing, roads, hospitals, schools and so on. Growth in consumer demand means growth in support products for manufacturing: machinery, packaging and materials. Increasing affluence means more

FIGURE 9.1   Global risks

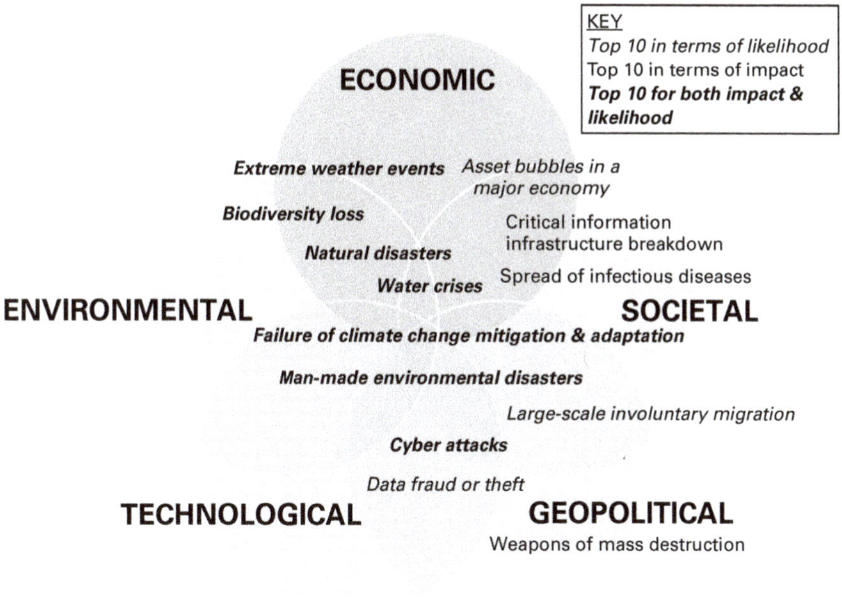

KEY
Top 10 in terms of likelihood
Top 10 in terms of impact
Top 10 for both impact & likelihood

ECONOMIC

Extreme weather events   *Asset bubbles in a major economy*

Biodiversity loss   Critical information infrastructure breakdown

Natural disasters

Water crises   Spread of infectious diseases

ENVIRONMENTAL   **SOCIETAL**

Failure of climate change mitigation & adaptation

Man-made environmental disasters

Large-scale involuntary migration

Cyber attacks

Data fraud or theft

TECHNOLOGICAL   **GEOPOLITICAL**

Weapons of mass destruction

SOURCE: Adapted from World Economic Forum Global Risks Report 2019

people want to own cars, or to 'dial a ride' instead of walking, cycling or using public transport. Throughout the book, we can see evidence that these needs depend on finite resources – technical materials, and biological materials that require available land, water, energy, and often, chemicals.

Reliance on critical materials is a major concern. Chapter 5 mentioned Circle Economy's Circularity Gap Report (2018),[2] which calculates that global resource flows are only 9.1 per cent circular, with just 8.4 billion tonnes of materials recycled each year as part of the 92.8 billion tonnes entering the global economy. Resource extraction, already increased by a factor of 12 between 1900 and 2015, is forecast to further double by 2050. Two-thirds of global greenhouse gas emissions relate to material management, meaning that circular strategies are essential tools in combating global heating.

A later report, in 2020,[3] says the 'gap is widening', with the global economy now only 8.6 per cent circular. It explains that there are three related underlying trends: high rates of extraction, ongoing stock build-up, plus low levels of end-of-use processing and recycling. Figure 9.2 shows the types of resources and their major uses, and the 2018 report maps this to seven 'key societal needs': housing and infrastructure, nutrition, mobility,

FIGURE 9.2   Resources entering the global economy

Resources (extracted and recycled) – billion tonnes per year

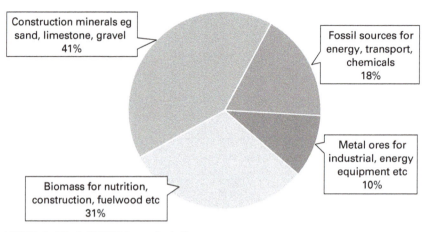

Construction minerals eg sand, limestone, gravel 41%

Fossil sources for energy, transport, chemicals 18%

Metal ores for industrial, energy equipment etc 10%

Biomass for nutrition, construction, fuelwood etc 31%

SOURCE: De Wit et al (2018) (see endnote 2)

consumables, services, healthcare and communication. **Housing and infra-structure** account for nearly half of total resource use, with 42.4 billion tonnes per year.

The report highlights 'stocks', as well as flows: all those materials used for buildings, equipment, infrastructure – and even cars, phones and clothing – that are kept in use over the long term. Every year we put 36 billion tonnes of materials into these stocks. At the same time, we demolish, repair and replace these items, removing 14.5 billion tonnes per year and meaning we increase our global stocks by 21.5 billion tonnes every year – more roads, bridges, buildings, cars and so on, that are in use.

We mentioned the European Union Critical Raw Materials list earlier in the book, and these are materials important to the EU economy (for industry or for citizens' well-being), but assessed as having risks for security of supply, whether from lack of known reserves, geopolitical risks, increasing demand and so on. As an example, Table 9.1 shows the key materials for UK industrial sectors.[4]

Low-carbon strategies change the outlook for metals and minerals, especially for aluminium (and its key component, bauxite), cobalt, copper, iron ore, lead, lithium, manganese, the platinum group, rare earth metals, silver, steel, titanium and zinc.[5]

Automotive companies face significant challenges, from disruptive competitors like Tesla and from disruptive technologies. Internal combustion engines are both inefficient and complex, with hundreds of different parts

TABLE 9.1 Examples of sector-specific key resources

Material	Palm Oil	Timber	Aggregates	Antimony	Cement	Chromic oxide	Chromium	Cobalt	Copper	Fluorspar	Gallium	Glass	Indium	Iron	Lead	Lithium	Magnesium	Mineral sands	Molybdenum	Nickel	Niobium	Phosphates	Phosphorus	Platinum group metals	Rare Earths	Rhenium	Silicon carbide	Steel	Tantalum	Tin	Tungsten	Yellow phosphorus
Recycling rate% [1, 2]				▪			▪	▪	▪	▪	▪		▪	▪	▪	▪	▪		▪	▪	▪	▪		▪	▪	▪			▪	▪	▪	
S Automotive							▪	▪					▪		▪		▪							▪	▪						▪	
E Chemicals				▪						▪						▪					▪	▪	▪	▪								▪
C Construction		▪	▪		▪									▪	▪												▪	▪				
T Cosmetics	▪																															
O Electronics and IT Hardware								▪	▪		▪		▪												▪				▪	▪	▪	
R Mechanical, elec., and process engineering							▪		▪					▪			▪		▪							▪				▪	▪	

Key: **Bold** = Listed as **Critical Material** by the EU (2013 update)

Note: Silicon is listed as a critical material by the EU

Recycling rates: ▪ < 20%   ▪ < 40%, >= 20%   ▪ < 60%, >= 40%   ▪ < 80%, >= 60%   ▪ >= 80%

[1] BIS Defra (2012) Resource Security Action Plan: Making the most of valuable materials, pp 21, 30 – sector resources; recycling rates

[2] The 'End-of-life recycling input rate' measures the proportion of metal and metal products that are produced from end-of-life scrap and other metal-bearing low grade residues in end-of-life scrap worldwide. (Source: 2014, Report on critical raw materials for the EU. Available from http://ec.europa.eu/growth/sectors/raw-materials/specific-interest/critical_en)

– electric motors have around 20 and need little maintenance. This has ramifications for suppliers and dealers, reliant on servicing and sales of spare parts. Congestion, lack of parking, and cost of ownership are all making 'ride-hailing' and pay-per-use models attractive, and major brands including BMW and Toyota are investing to provide 'mobility services' instead of selling cars. This has impacts on the design of roads, buildings, parking lots, and public transport – as well as for vehicles.

Resources

We have covered the challenges for key materials in specific sectors in earlier chapters. Here we will touch on some of the other materials we rely on.

Plastics made from petrochemicals, with their light, cheap and flexible properties, are increasingly prevalent but causing serious concerns. The word plastic comes from the Greek word 'plastikos' meaning 'fit for moulding', and plastic now replaces many traditional materials, such as wood, stone, horn and bone, leather, metal, glass and ceramics. Plastic has transformed many familiar products, often by reducing cost and weight and improving performance, comfort and safety.

Plastics Europe explains the plastics 'families':[6]

- **Thermoplastics** can be melted when heated and hardened when cooled. These characteristics are reversible, meaning they can be reheated, reshaped and frozen repeatedly. They include polyethylene (PE), polypropylene (PP), polyvinyl-chloride (PVC), polyethylene terephthalate (PET), polystyrene (PS), ABS, polycarbonate (PC) and many more.
- **Thermosets** undergo a chemical change when heated, creating a three-dimensional network. After heating and forming, these plastics cannot be re-melted and reformed. Thermosets include polyurethane (PRU), unsaturated polyesters, acrylic epoxy and phenolic resins, melamine resin, silicone and more.

Geyer, Jambeck and Law, authors of *Production, Use and Fate of all Plastics Ever Made* (2017),[7] report that since the 1950s, the world has produced over 8.3 billion tonnes of plastic, resulting in 6.3 billion tonnes of plastic waste – of which only 9 per cent has been recycled. Figure 9.3 shows the inflows and outflows from 1950 to 2015.

Plastic micro-particles are a major concern. They are being discovered everywhere, in rivers, oceans, beaches, mountains, even the Antarctic, finding their way into living systems, into our drinking water and food. In Chapter 7, we highlighted the issue of **micro-fibres** escaping from polyester

FIGURE 9.3   Global plastic flows

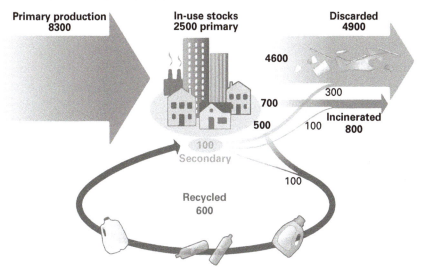

Global production, use, and fate of polymer resins, synthetic fibres, and additives (1950 to 2015; in million metric tons).
SOURCE: Geyer et al (2017)[8]

clothing when we wash it, ending up in sewage sludge, which is then used as fertilizer.

There are health concerns too, with plastic found in the food chain and affecting soil health.[9] In 2018, plastic particles were found in over 90 per cent of samples of bottled water from 11 leading worldwide brands. The average was 325 particles per litre of water.[10]

Glass uses liquefied sand, sodium carbonate, limestone, and various additives. Compared with plastic, glass is heavy, bulkier and fragile. Glass bottles are 100 per cent recyclable and an estimated 80 per cent is recycled into new glass bottles, needing less energy.

World **steel** production has almost doubled since 2000, rising from 850 million tonnes to 1,665 million tonnes in 2014.[11] Global consumption of **chromium** and **nickel,** used for stainless steel production, have increased too.[12] **Aluminium** consumption increased by a factor of three between 1970 and 2005, much more than other non-ferrous metals, and copper and zinc consumption increased roughly twofold. **Nitrogen** extraction has increased rapidly too. China supplies over two-thirds of *rare earth elements* used globally, many of which are essential for renewable energy, technology and healthcare products.

Metals have great potential for recycling, creating circular inputs and improving resource security. Like glass, **aluminium** is completely recyclable and products like cans are commonly recycled worldwide as part of municipal recycling programmes. Aluminium cans can be recycled repeatedly with no limit.

The World Steel Association describes steel as a 'permanent material, which can be recycled over and over again without losing its properties'.[13] We are likely to think of all metals as permanent materials; and there are widespread opportunities to transform our approach to product design, recovery and use of high-quality, secure circular flows. Recycling already shows significant benefits: 1 tonne of steel saves 1,400 kilograms of iron ore, 120 grams of limestone and 70 per cent of energy, and it creates local jobs. Professor Julian Allwood calculates that globally, 'all future growth in demand for steel can be met by recycling', with steel available for recycling set to 'treble in the next 30 to 40 years'.[14] However, steel mixed with other materials is difficult to recycle. In packaging, tin is used to coat steel cans; copper and steel are mixed in motors and wiring. This leads to steel being *downcycled*, eg recycled car steel becomes low-value reinforcing bar.

Global resource extraction, including metal ores, non-metallic minerals, fossil fuels and biomass, is predicted to more than double between 2015 and 2050.[15]

Circular economy developments

Businesses in automotive, construction and infrastructure, healthcare and other manufacturing sectors are seeing the opportunities of a circular economy, and deciding how to evolve their strategies to include circular approaches along the value chain. Figure 9.4 reminds us of the framework and components, or intervention points.

Well-publicized examples of circular approaches in industrial sectors include the Rolls-Royce 'power by the hour' performance model for aerospace engines (dating from 1962),[16] and remanufacturing activities, including high-profile brands such as Caterpillar, GKN, and Siemens Healthcare. Companies like Interface Global have gone further, with their 'Mission Zero', initiated in 1994 by founder Ray Anderson.[17] Mission Zero aims to 'eliminate any negative impact our company may have on the environment by 2020'. Previous chapters have mentioned the internet-based Chemical Leasing Toolkit, which provides guidelines, materials, best practice case studies and lessons learned from UNIDO's Global Chemical Leasing Programme.

FIGURE 9.4   Circular Economy Framework 2.0

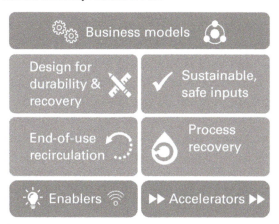

SOURCE: © Catherine Weetman

SCHNEIDER: CIRCULARS 2019 MULTINATIONAL AWARD-WINNER[18,19]

Schneider says:

> The circular economy is part of everything we do at Schneider: it lowers total cost of ownership for our customers; it preserves precious natural resources for the future; and it creates new revenue and jobs for our own company. It's a win-win-win for the triple bottom line.

Schneider's approach includes:

- ecodesign of products with minimum use of virgin raw materials;
- circular value propositions (connected objects, services, leasing, repair, take-back, etc);
- a circular supply chain including reverse logistics, repair and reconditioning centres;
- four 'circular economy' indicators in the quarterly Schneider Sustainability Impact metrics, linked to management reward schemes.

Schneider already has 12 per cent revenue from circular approaches and plans to avoid 100,000 tonnes of primary resource consumption from 2018–2020.

Business models

In the *Institute for Manufacturing Review*, Neely (2014)[20] highlights business procurement trends shifting from buying products to solutions and replacing transactions with relationships. Business-to-business (B2B) markets are well suited to business models based on outcomes and performance, rather than purchase and ownership. Business models for performance could apply extensively across industrial manufacturing and construction, and some chemical companies already sell the use of solvents, not ownership. As Walter Stahel explains, the contract tender for the Millau Viaduct in France assigned maintenance costs to the constructor.[21] This led the successful bidder to design a rapidly built structure with minimal liability and maintenance costs over the 75-year lifespan. Closer relationships with the end-user can improve the design and the outcomes for all parties.

PHILIPS: CIRCULAR SOLUTIONS MAKE GOOD BUSINESS SENSE[22]

Philips aims to deliver 15 per cent of total revenues from circular solutions by 2020. CEO Frans van Houten says 'Innovative service models, smart upgrade paths, and product take-back and remanufacturing programs are not only good for the planet and improving people's lives, they also make good business sense.'

Philips' circular economy developments include its Diamond Select Advance system, offering pre-owned, refurbished healthcare products such as MRI scanners. A well-publicized example is its 'pay per lux' LED lighting solution, whereby Philips offers light as a service and retains responsibility for the performance of the lighting.

Other global businesses are starting the transition to circular approaches, and we are seeing startups and small businesses disrupting existing models. Some of these are 'gap exploiters' (see Whalen et al in Chapter 3), seeing the opportunity to recover and capture value from end-of-use equipment and products.

Axioma Solucions, in Spain, offers reusable surgical polyester material as a service. The fabric is from recycled sources and completely recyclable after its 75 uses.[23]

CASE STUDY: RYPE OFFICE: OPEN-LOOP REMANUFACTURING

Rype Office supplies high-quality remanufactured office furniture, including a bespoke office design service to deliver an attractive, sustainable, budget-friendly workspace. Remanufacturing enables Rype Office to deliver sustainability and cost benefits without compromising on product quality and durability.

Recognizing the untapped potential of remanufacturing, Lavery/Pennell, a consulting and venturing firm, set the business up in 2014. Rype Office builds on the founders' work, developing circular economy systems for clients and their in-depth study on the potential for remanufacturing: The Next Manufacturing Revolution (2013).[24]

Researching purchasing decisions for higher-specification office furniture showed that customers prioritize attractive, high-quality furniture that meets the defined budget. Staff productivity from better ergonomic design and sustainability (through reduced raw materials, energy and emissions in manufacturing) are seen as additional benefits.

The Rype Office marketing strategy aims to demystify the remanufacturing concept, using straightforward terms such as 'refreshed' and 'remade', and focusing on the 'like-new' performance with substantial cost benefits.

FIGURE 9.5   Sustainable office furniture comparisons

	Cost saving [1]	Quality [2]	Choice	Ease of purchase [3]	Sustain-ability [4]
New					
Reused					
Refreshed					
Remade					

Key:
[1] Cost compared to purchase of new items
[2] Quality assurance, warranty, product durability
[3] Difficulty and time for purchaser to fulfil the project
[4] Use of virgin materials, energy and water footprint etc

Notes:
Recycled is furniture made from components reclaimed from used furniture, then separated, shredded, melted down, remade into parts and then assembled into furniture
Reused is second-hand or used furniture, with no upgrading or refurbishment
Refreshed includes a 'facelift' eg reupholstering to replace fabric
Remade (remanufactured), replacing 'soft' parts such as fabric and reusing appropriate long-life components

SOURCE: After Rype Office team (2015)[25]

Figure 9.5 compares methods of purchasing office furniture against criteria based on typical purchaser priorities.

Rype Office emphasizes seven layers of quality in its operations:

- choosing used furniture to remanufacture from proven brands with timeless aesthetics, long-life components and great ergonomics;

- sourcing good-condition pieces and materials from top suppliers;

- using the latest precision equipment for flawless finishes;

- developing new techniques to restore surfaces;

- applying rigorous processes, including testing and inspection;

- grading to strict A+, A and B standards to meet customer needs and budgets;

- warranting parts and workmanship.

Rype Office provides design assistance to meet the client's needs for branding, quality and aesthetics, and to incorporate the latest ergonomic, productivity and sustainability features in the layout. After procuring suitable pieces of furniture, components and materials from a range of trusted suppliers, Rype Office manages the inbound logistics and remanufactures to the customer's required standard, before delivery and installation to meet the client's project requirements. Figure 9.6 illustrates the supply chain.

Rype Office is a fully circular business, offering leasing or buy-back options to reacquire the furniture at the end of each life, to remanufacture it for further lives. **Benefits**, for the client and wider society, include:

- reduced cost, with over 50 per cent saving compared with the list price of new furniture;

- reduced lead time, usually faster than the sector 'standard' of 6–8 weeks;

- bespoke designs for clients, including resizing desks, or matching the preferred colours, fabrics, patterns, shapes and sizes;

- integration with current interior designs or with existing furniture that is no longer in production;

- less than one-third of the environmental impact compared with new furniture;[26]

- increasing local, semi-skilled employment by remanufacturing locally to minimize two-way furniture transport.

FIGURE 9.6   Rype Office supply chain

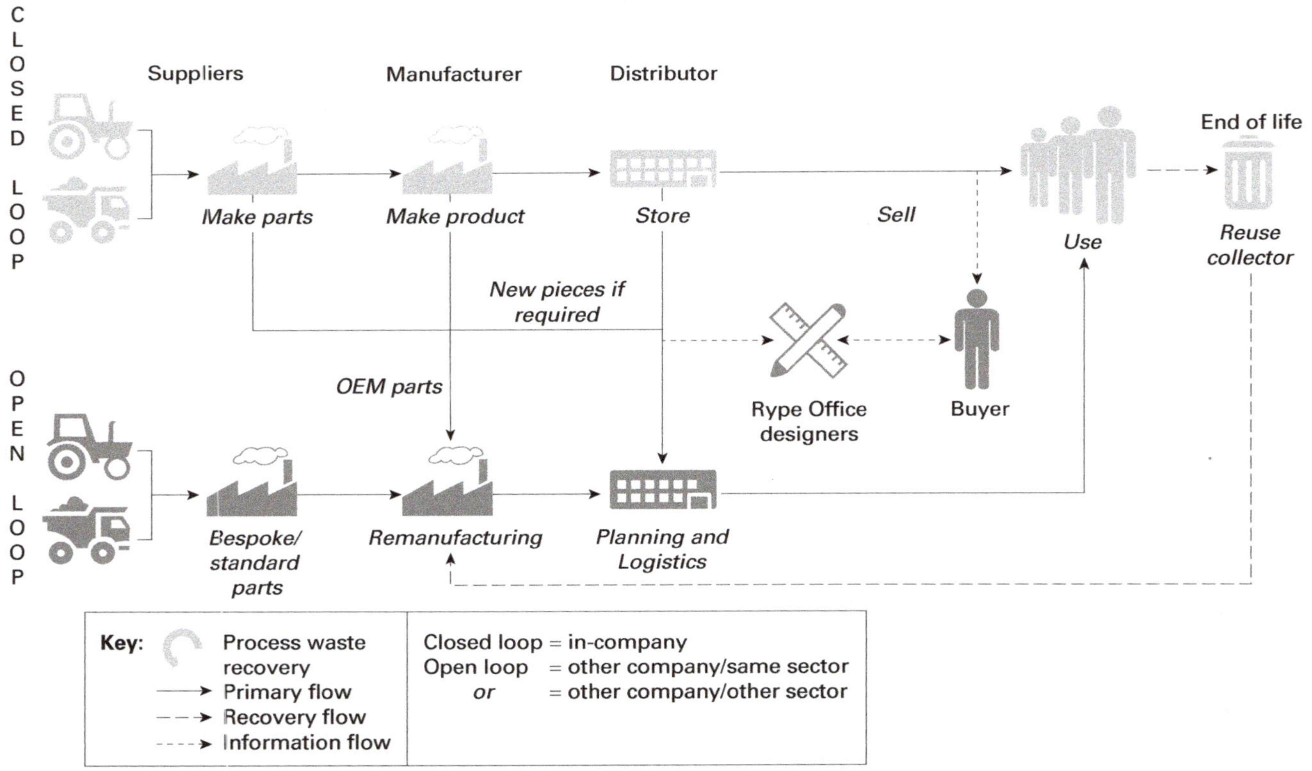

SOURCE: © Catherine Weetman (2015)

Design for durability and recovery

Design for disassembly and reuse provides value opportunities for **major construction projects**. A new bridge in Ohio used salvaged beams from the previous structure; an entire 3,270-tonne steel structure was moved from a UK wartime airship hangar and reassembled to become a Building Research Establishment (BRE) test facility.[27] Organizations like BRE (a UK charity focusing on research and education in the built environment) provide codes (such as BREEAM) and methodologies to help create sustainable buildings, homes and communities. The US Green Building Council (USGBC) developed Leadership in Energy and Environmental Design (LEED), with projects worldwide able to earn one of four LEED rating levels to show they are resource-efficient, use less water and energy and emit fewer *GHG* emissions.

Buildings As Material Banks (BAMB) is a European Union-funded Horizon 2020 programme of 15 partners. After demolition or refurbishment, reuse of construction materials is rare. Instead, they are wasted, becoming a cost instead of an asset (financially, socially and environmentally). BAMB aims to utilize the true value of these materials and enable a circular building industry, starting with the project foundations – Materials Passports and Reversible Building Design. BAMB reimagines a building as a dynamic data-tracked repository of tradable value.[28]

Research by Swansea University's SPECIFIC Innovation & Knowledge Centre (2019)[29] says energy consumption could be reduced by more than 60 per cent if homes were designed to generate, store and release their own solar energy. The concept is operating successfully in the UK's first energy-positive classroom, combining an integrated solar roof and battery storage with solar heat collection on south-facing walls – over six months it has generated more energy than it has consumed.

For all products, designing with reparability and recovery in mind is essential. Steelcase's Think® office chair, launched in 2004, became the world's first Cradle to Cradle Certified™ product.[30] Disassembly for recycling takes about five minutes using common hand tools (eg hammer, screwdriver).

HERMAN MILLER: DESIGN FOR RECYCLABILITY[31,32]

Herman Miller has several Cradle to Cradle Certified™ (C2C) certifications across its office furniture products. By 2009, more than half the company's sales came from C2C products. Its 'Design for Environment Programme', launched in the 1990s, uses the MBDC C2C design protocol, evaluating new product designs for recyclability and safety, including: design for disassembly, recyclability and materials chemistry evaluation, including human and ecological health criteria.

Using fewer, simpler materials helps simplify the reuse opportunities and make it easier to keep track of materials used. Wood can be a high-tech construction material and is good at absorbing seismic shocks. Tall buildings are already using wood as a structure, and the Plyscraper in Tokyo, planned for 2041, will be 350 metres high.

RENAULT: REMANUFACTURING, REUSE AND 'CASCADING'[33]

Since 1949, Renault has remanufactured components at its site in Choisy-le-Roi, France, now including injectors, injection pumps and turbo compressors. In 2014, Renault's remanufactured gearboxes contained around 75 per cent pre-used parts, and engines around 38 per cent.

At its Indra site, also in France, Renault has a joint venture with recycling specialist Suez. Workers extract parts from End of Life Vehicles (ELV) for use in vehicle repairs. In 2017, it handled 350,000 ELV. In addition, Renault *cascades* the used batteries from its electric vehicles, for example to power buildings, giving the batteries a second life.

Safe, sustainable inputs

Companies are becoming more conscious of chemicals in our living and working environments, as we understand more about the effects of 'off-gassing' from fabrics, paint, furniture, flame retardants and so on.

ROHNER: CLIMATEX LIFECYCLE FABRIC[34]

Climatex Lifecycle biodegradable fabric, produced by Swiss firm Rohner, is used extensively in office furniture manufacturing. It reduces agricultural inputs (fertilizers, pesticides, water), eliminates petroleum-based fibres and uses fewer, more benign chemical inputs. The project started in 1991, aiming for a more benign and compostable product, a 'safely disposable fabric'. Just 16 safe chemicals were chosen, from around 8,000 chemicals commonly used in fabric processing. The materials included wool from free-range sheep, and pesticide-free ramie (a 'bast' fibre in the nettle family, in use for around 6,000 years). In 2001, DesignTex, Rohner and MBDC agreed to allow the entire textile industry to use the Climatex manufacturing process, to create safe, completely biodegradable fabrics.

BIOMASON: MICRO-ORGANISMS TO GROW CONSTRUCTION MATERIALS[35]

bioMASON, in the US, reminds us that over 4 billion tonnes of cement are produced each year, accounting for around 8 per cent of global CO_2 emissions. Its proprietary manufacturing processes and materials use micro-organisms to grow biocement™ based construction materials. It says the strength of biocement™ materials is comparable to traditional masonry, and the products are produced in ambient temperatures using locally available materials, saving energy and 'enabling zero carbon emissions'.

Process design

Throughout the book, we have seen examples of by-products, co-products and resource recovery. There are opportunities to find high-value uses for scrap materials, either recovered for reuse internally or sold as a *by-product*, with examples for steel shown in Figure 9.7. Car maker Jaguar LandRover and aluminium producer Novelis set up the REALCAR project, aiming to close the loop on one of its key materials, aluminium. They set a target for 75 per cent recycled content for every automotive aluminium sheet, 50 per cent of which will be sourced from scrap generated by JLR's own manufacturing and supply chain, and 25 per cent from post-consumer waste streams.[36]

In Chapter 12, we look at the Kalundborg symbiosis project: exchanging by-products and waste for energy between industrial companies, and in Chapter 2, we mentioned the UK's National Industrial Symbiosis Project, aiming to 'match-make' waste flows from one organization to feed resources into another. There are other symbiosis projects, including WISP (Western Cape Industrial Symbiosis Project), in Africa.

Distributed manufacturing, in smaller, local facilities rather than central-ized 'mass production' sites, is growing, assisted by 3D printing, cloud computing and team networking tools.

Opendesk describes itself as 'a global platform for local making'.[37] Opendesk is an online marketplace that hosts independently designed furniture and connects its customers to local makers around the world. It is

FIGURE 9.7   Steel by-products

Main steelmaking by-products and their uses

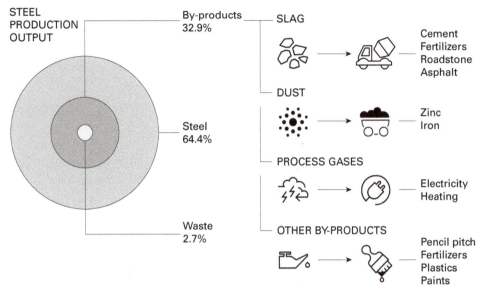

SOURCE: worldsteel.org (2016)

creating a distributed and ethical supply chain through a global maker net-work, instead of mass manufacturing and shipping worldwide.

More accurate planning can reduce resource inputs, work in progress stock and finished stock, and big data and AI can improve demand forecast-ing accuracy – all helping reduce overstocks, obsolescence and lost sales.

Recovery flows

Plastics Europe explains the different options for **plastics:**[38]

- **Mechanical recycling**, which avoids directly changing the chemical structure of the material, accounts for 99 per cent of plastics recycling in Europe. In principle, all types of thermoplastics can be mechanically recycled with little or no quality impairment.

- **Feedstock recycling** means any thermal process that converts polymers into shorter molecules, ready for new chemical reactions. These could be for reuse (chemical recycling) or for energy production.

- **Chemical recycling** means the plastic and/or polymer are modified by a chemical agent or process, so they can be used again. For energy production, processes including gasification and pyrolysis break down plastic waste to produce synthesis gas (syngas) as well as other liquid and semi-liquid products.

Julian Allwood sees new approaches for recovery and circular flows of metals, especially **steel**, including robotic cutting and handling and new sorting technologies.[39] Veolia is developing new ways of extracting materials for high-value reuse, with case studies covering *permaculture*, frugal innovation and renewable energy on its '#Living Circular' webpage.[40]

EXCESS MATERIALS EXCHANGE: A 'DATING SITE' FOR MATERIALS[41]

Excess Materials Exchange is a digital facilitated marketplace that uses four bespoke tools:

1   resources passport: to identify materials;

2   tracking and tracing: identifiers to link materials to the resources passports and follow them through their life-cycles;

3   valuation: calculating the financial, environmental and societal impact of the matches;

4   matchmaking platform: to find the highest-value reuse of materials and products.

Recovery systems are emerging for paints, chemicals and other difficult-to-recycle products. Paintback, a collaborative initiative in Australia, has drop-off points in major cities for trade and household customers to return unused paint. Community RePaint is a UK-wide paint reuse network, sponsored by Dulux, that aims to collect leftover paint and redistribute it to benefit individuals, families, communities and charities in need at an affordable cost.

Startups are finding ways to create value from waste biological and mixed materials. RamBrick™ is 'Africa's first 5-star eco-standard rated brick manufactured from local resources and inert waste'. The RamBrick™ system converts waste soils and rubble from landfill into building products for all types of housing, with at least a third less carbon footprint than conventional materials.[42]

Enablers

In Chapter 4, we looked at different approaches to design and problem-solving. We saw how *biomimicry* is helping companies to create new materials, new ways of recycling, and design products, and throughout the book, we've seen examples of *green chemistry* and *biorefining*, reducing use of finite materials, and conserving and circulating value from 'waste'.

Katie Beverley, author of the **Ecodesign** section in Chapter 4, describes Riversimple as one of her favourite circular economy examples. Riversimple's RASA car design will 'deliver a step-change in fuel efficiency and environmental performance. It is powered by hydrogen; built with lightweight but strong composite materials; weighs less than half as much as a conventional car and is highly aerodynamic and stable.'[43] Riversimple will offer mobility as a service. 'For a fixed monthly fee, our customers will receive a car – their car – and all the maintenance, insurance and fuel to run it.'

Systems thinking led a UK council to create a '**pop-up village**', providing cost-effective social housing for families living in temporary accommodation and allowing the council to use 'brownfield' land whilst longer-term projects are being finalized.[44] The architect-designed flats evolved from the YMCA 'Y-cube', have a design lifespan of 60 years and can be moved several times. They are factory built and well insulated, arriving in two pieces: a living area with built-in services, and the bedrooms.

The pressure on finite resources is stimulating research into **new materials**, especially those that use abundant, natural materials. Chip[s] Board®, in the US, has developed bioplastics from coffee grounds, pine flour, potato waste and oak shavings.[45] Continental Tire is growing dandelions close to its factory in Germany, to replace latex from rubber trees, grown around the equator (and on the EU Critical Raw Materials list).[46]

Algae is abundant, and can be problematic, for instance when fertilizer run-off causes 'algal bloom', with serious issues for other living systems. In Chapter 4, we read about the research team in Germany that developed a process that created carbon fibres from algae oil.[47] As well as using less energy than production of steel or concrete alternatives, algae absorbs CO_2 during its life, so the CO_2 gets 'locked in' to the raw material for the carbon fibre, allowing storage of atmospheric carbon whilst the material is intact.

BRICKS FROM HUMAN URINE[48]

University of Cape Town researcher Suzanne Lambert has created a zero-waste building material made with human urine, which hardens at room temperature. It is an alternative to traditional bricks, kiln-fired at temperatures of more than 1,000 degrees Celsius and producing huge carbon emissions.

> The process combines urine, loose sand and a bacteria that produces the enzyme urease – this triggers a chemical reaction to produce calcium carbonate (ie limestone, the main component of cement), solidifying the bricks.

Innovations in recycling are also creating value. Every year, over 1 billion tyres are being landfilled or burned worldwide, releasing toxic chemicals. Black Bear upcycles end-of-life tyres into high-quality carbon black and other raw materials (steel, rubber, etc), reducing both pollution and CO_2 emissions.[49]

For **technology**, the *IoT*, sensors and *big data* can track product use and condition, supporting service models, and we see examples of 3DP innovations in Chapter 4.

In Chapter 8, we saw that HP, Teleplan, IKEA, Philips and iFixit are collaborating on a project (Co.Project) exploring new applications of 3D printing technology for spare parts. Instead of warehouses full of parts (that might never be needed), the parts can be printed on-demand, needing only digital files, or even a 3D scan of the existing part. For companies like IKEA, with around 12,000 types of products (and many more components), the potential benefits are substantial.[50]

GENERAL ELECTRIC (GE): 3D PRINTING[51]

In 2016, GE Aviation began 3D printing fuel nozzles for the LEAP engine on the Airbus A320neo, claiming a world-first for the passenger airline industry. The original design had 20 separate parts; by using 3D printing, they were able to design the nozzle as a single piece. Each nozzle is five times more durable; the number of brazes and welds reduced from 25 to 5, and the finished component weights 25 per cent less than an ordinary nozzle.

In 2016, GE spent more than US$1 billion to buy controlling stakes in two leading manufacturers of industrial 3D printers. GE intends its new Additive division to become a leading supplier of additive machines, materials, and software for sectors including aerospace, power generation, automotive, medical, and electronics.

Accelerators

Product stewardship legislation, carbon pricing, incentives for repairs and other **policy initiatives** will help switch the focus from linear models (with externalized costs for health risk, waste and pollution, etc) to circular ones, aiming to create, conserve and recirculate value. We are seeing collaborative initiatives and partnerships, aiming to 'get more from less'.

Collaborative exchange platforms are emerging. For the **construction** sector, the biggest contributor to landfill in the UK, orders tend to include extra materials to provide a safety margin for order quantity or damage. Enviromate is an online marketplace for builders to 'find and trade leftover materials' and reduce storage or landfill costs.[52] It sees the cost of waste, typically 2–3 per cent of the project cost, as a value opportunity. United States Materials Marketplace, a project supported by the World Business Council for Sustainable Development and others, aims to scale up B2B materials reuse across the United States.[53] The Furniture Reuse Network works with over 300 charities and has 'Approved Re-use Centres' covering the whole of the UK.[54] Cohealo, in the US, shares healthcare equipment. There are many other sector-specific and public sector reuse networks such as Warp It.

WARP IT: REUSE PLATFORM[55]

Warp It, based in the UK, aims to provide a network 'where buying new is the last resort and nothing is wasted', enabling redistribution of reusable items, including furniture, electrical equipment, office consumables, laboratory and medical equipment.

The network includes over 1,000 charities, 1,000 schools, over half the UK universities, plus councils, the NHS and private sector companies.

Car maker Nissan, and Ovo, a UK energy supplier, are to offer a vehicle-to-grid programme. Ovo will manage the battery's energy, buying power during off-peak periods and selling in peak.[56] Peer-to-peer car-hiring apps, such as Turo and Getaround, are popping up, allowing car owners to earn revenue from idle assets.

Volkswagen's MOIA ride-sharing service has plans to offer pooling services in 50 cities across Europe and the US. The Hamburg operation will work with 'switchh', a shared user service operated by Hamburg's underground transport operator and which already uses BMW DriveNow and Daimler car2go vehicles.

In Chapter 8, we mentioned Apple's **material risk assessment** tools, which included GreenScreen.

Retailers and manufacturers are using the Chemical Footprint Project tool to track, measure and report progress on safer chemical alternatives.[57] This requires significant input from suppliers at every stage of the supply chain, helping to understand which materials can be safely recovered and used in future products.

Summary

We have scanned a tiny sub-set of industrial and other manufacturing developments, outlining the vast potential for companies to transform their supply and value chains. Consumers are beginning to prefer access to ownership, and for businesses, the procurement and performance benefits are already clear. For producers, there are additional benefits from closer customer relationships and improved understanding of product performance, plus the opportunity to develop service and maintenance capabilities (and revenue). There are some challenges, such as financing the switch from sales-based cash flow to contracts, with potential risk around customer insolvency, etc.

The recovery flows, with potential for high-quality recycling, remanufacture and maintenance services, pose challenges too: not least providing effective, efficient and secure reverse supply chains. We return to this in Part Three.

Braungart and McDonough, in their seminal work, *Cradle to Cradle: Remaking the way we make things*, ask whether manufacturers should feel guilty about their role in this so-far 'destructive agenda', concluding that it does not really matter. They remind us that:

> insanity has been defined as doing the same thing over and over and expecting a different outcome. Negligence is described as doing the same thing over and over even though you know it is stupid, dangerous and wrong. Now that we know, it's time for a change. Negligence starts tomorrow.[58]

Further resources

BIS Defra (2012) *Resource Security Action Plan: Making the most of valuable materials* [Online] www.gov.uk/government/uploads/system/uploads/attachment_data/file/69511/pb13719-resource-security-action-plan.pdf (archived at https://perma.cc/6H3F-4UCW)

Braungart, M and McDonough, W (2009) *Cradle to Cradle: Remaking the way we make things*, Vintage Books, London

Buildings as Material Banks (2019) www.bamb2020.eu/ (archived at https://perma.cc/ ED7E-TVG6)

De Wit, M et al (2018) *The Circularity Gap Report: an analysis of the circular state of the global economy*, Circle Economy, January [Online] www.circle-economy.com/the-circularity-gap-report-our-world-is-only-9-circular/ (archived at https://perma.cc/Z36M-K4QG)

Geyer R, Jambeck, JR and Law KR (2017) Production, use, and fate of all plastics ever made, *Science Advances*, 3 (7), doi: 10.1126/sciadv.1700782

Hawken, P, Lovins, AB and Lovins, LH (2010) *Natural Capitalism: The next industrial revolution*, Earthscan, London

Institute for Manufacturing, University of Cambridge [Online] http://www.ifm.eng.cam.ac.uk/ (archived at https://perma.cc/S2FD-KQ2Z)

Lavery, G, Pennell, N, Brown, S and Evans S (2013) *The Next Manufacturing Revolution: Non-labour resource productivity and its potential for remanufacturing* [Online] https://www.ifm.eng.cam.ac.uk/ (archived at https://perma.cc/9RC3-6TJL)

Rogich, DG and Matos, GR (2008) *The global flows of metals and minerals: U.S. Geological Survey Open-File Report 2008-1355* [Online] http://pubs.usgs.gov/ of/2008/1355/ (archived at https://perma.cc/7XTF-FB8T)

Notes

1 Stahel, WJ (2013) [accessed 15 August 2016] The Circular Economy: Interview with Walter Stahel by Daan Elffers, *Making It Magazine*, 28 June [Online] www.makingitmagazine.net (archived at https://perma.cc/T4QA-37MH)

2 De Wit, M et al (2018) [accessed 22 November 2019] *The Circularity Gap Report: An analysis of the circular state of the global economy*, Circle Economy, January [Online] www.circle-economy.com/the-circularity-gap-report-our-world-is-only-9-circular/ (archived at https://perma.cc/Z36M-K4QG)

3 Circle Economy (2020) [accessed 24 August 2020] *The Circularity Gap Report* [Online] https://www.circularity-gap.world/2020 (archived at https://perma.cc/ R2R5-PZUQ)

4 BIS Defra (2012) [accessed 15 August 2016] *Resource Security Action Plan: Making the most of valuable materials*, pp 21, 30 [Online] www.gov.uk/ government/uploads/system/uploads/attachment_data/file/69511/pb13719-resource-security-action-plan.pdf

5 World Bank Group (2017) [accessed 8 December 2019] *The Growing Role of Minerals and Metals for a Low Carbon Future* [Online] http://documents.worldbank.org/curated/en/207371500386458722/pdf/117581-WP-P159838-PUBLIC-ClimateSmartMiningJuly.pdf (archived at https://perma.cc/2AXF-KQH5)

6 *Thermoplastics/Thermosets from Plastics – the facts 2019*, Plastics Europe Association of Plastics Manufacturers (2019) [accessed 12 November 19] [Online] www.plasticseurope.org/en/resources/publications/1804-plastics-facts-2019 (archived at https://perma.cc/BY2P-78AB)

7 Geyer, R, Jambeck, JR and Law, KR (2017) Production, use, and fate of all plastics ever made, *Science Advances*, **3** (7), doi: 10.1126/sciadv.1700782

8 Geyer, R, Jambeck, JR and Law, KR (2017) Production, use, and fate of all plastics ever made, *Science Advances*, **3** (7), doi: 10.1126/sciadv.1700782

9 Plastic planet: How tiny plastic particles are polluting our soil, *UN Environment*, 3 April 2018 [accessed 7 December 2019] [Online] https://www.unenvironment.org/news-and-stories/story/plastic-planet-how-tiny-plastic-particles-are-polluting-our-soil (archived at https://perma.cc/8E5R-EAG6)

10 Redfearn, G (2018) [accessed 7 December 2019] WHO launches health review after microplastics found in 90% of bottled water, *The Guardian*, 15 March [Online] https://www.theguardian.com/environment/2018/mar/15/microplastics-found-in-more-than-90-of-bottled-water-study-says (archived at https://perma.cc/2M7L-TV6R)

11 World Steel Association (2015) [accessed 19 May 2016] *World Steel in Figures 2015* [Online] www.worldsteel.org/dms/internetDocumentList/bookshop/2015/World-Steel-in-Figures-2015/document/World%20Steel%20in%20Figures%202015.pdf (archived at https://perma.cc/X3EG-JAWG)

12 Rogich, DG and Matos, GR (2008) [accessed 7 December 2019] *The global flows of metals and minerals: U.S. Geological Survey Open-File Report 2008-1355* [Online] http://pubs.usgs.gov/of/2008/1355/ (archived at https://perma.cc/7XTF-FB8T)

13 World Steel Association (2016) [accessed 15 August 2016] *Steel – The permanent material in the circular economy*, p 3 [Online] http://circulareconomy-worldsteel.org/ (archived at https://perma.cc/2NYN-GU9H)

14 Allwood, J (2016) [accessed 15 August 2016] *A Bright Future for Steel*, University of Cambridge [Online] www.cam.ac.uk/system/files/a_bright_future_for_uk_steel_2.pdf (archived at https://perma.cc/H7AR-RA99)

15 De Wit, M et al (2018) [accessed 22 November 2019] *The Circularity Gap Report: An analysis of the circular state of the global economy, Circle Economy*, January [Online] www.circle-economy.com/the-circularity-gap-report-our-world-is-only-9-circular/ (archived at https://perma.cc/Z36M-K4QG)

16 Rolls-Royce PLC (2012) [accessed 1 June 2016] [Online] http://www.rolls-royce.com/media/press-releases/yr-2012/121030-the-hour.aspx (archived at https://perma.cc/P9GF-RLXV)

17 Interface Global (2016) [accessed 1 June 2016] [Online] www.interfaceglobal.com/careers/mission_zero.html (archived at https://perma.cc/E94C-9KEG)

18 *Schneider Sustainability Report 2018–2019: Circular economy overview* [accessed 8 December 2019] [Online] https://sdreport.se.com/en/circular-economy-overview (archived at https://perma.cc/C6BX-VM2H)

19 The Circulars (2019) [accessed 8 December 2019] [Online] https://thecirculars. org/our-finalists/filter/eyJyZXN1bHRfcGFnZSI6Im91ci1maW5hW5hbGlzdHNc L2ZpbHRlciIsImNhdGVnb3J5IjoiMzkiLCJzZWFyY2g6Y3g6Y3NfeWVhciI6IjIw MTkifQ (archived at https://perma.cc/77TY-DZM2)

20 Neely, A (2014) Making the shift to services, *University of Cambridge Institute for Manufacturing Review*, **2**, October, pp 10–11

21 Stahel, WJ (2016) Circular Economy, *Nature*, **531**, 24 March, p 438

22 Koninklijke Philips N.V., Press Release (2018) [accessed 19 September 2019] [Online] www.philips.com/a-w/about/news/archive/standard/news/ articles/2018/20180124-philips-spearheads-the-circular-economy-with-firm-2020-pledge.html (archived at https://perma.cc/A96H-UKR8)

23 Axioma Solucions (2019) [accessed 6 December 2019] [Online] http://www.axiomasolucions.com/ (archived at https://perma.cc/7DLL-AKAW)

24 Lavery, G, Pennell, N, Brown, S and Evans S (2013) [accessed 15 August 2016] *The Next Manufacturing Revolution: Non-labour resource productivity and its potential for remanufacturing* [Online] https://www.ifm.eng.cam.ac.uk/ (archived at https://perma.cc/9RC3-6TJL)

25 Rype Office team (2015) *What is Most Sustainable Office Furniture?* [Online] http://www.rypeoffice.com/what-is-the-most-sustainable-office-furniture/ (archived at https://perma.cc/NE8A-J4PY)

26 Rype Office (2015) [accessed 23 December 2015] [Online] www.rypeoffice. com/office-furniture-sustainability/ (archived at https://perma.cc/X6XX-U7XN)

27 Sustainable in Steel (2016) [accessed 27 April 2016] *Examples of Reuse* [Online] www.sustainableinsteel.eu/p/539/examples_of_reuse.html (archived at https://perma.cc/J3XE-VTH7)

28 Buildings as Material Banks (2019) [accessed 6 December 2019] [Online] www.bamb2020.eu/ (archived at https://perma.cc/ED7E-TVG6)

29 Turning homes into power stations could cut household fuel bills by £600 or more – report (2019) [accessed 9 December 2019] *News*, Swansea University [Online] www.swansea.ac.uk (archived at https://perma.cc/PF57-3E4L)

30 Steelcase [accessed 8 December 2019] [Online] www.c2ccertified.org/ innovation-stories/steelcase (archived at https://perma.cc/Y54L-P7BY)

31 GreenBiz Group (2009) [accessed 24 February 2016] [Online] www.greenbiz. com/news/2009/05/12/herman-miller-earns-design-recycling-award (archived at https://perma.cc/LG3S-ECBN)

32 Rossi, M, Charon, S, Wing, G and Ewell, J (2005) [accessed 24 February 2016] *Herman Miller's Design for Environment Program* [Online] chemicalspolicy. org/downloads/HermanMillerDardenCaseStudy8Nov05.pdf (archived at https://perma.cc/E2NK-5HHR)

33 McEvoy, P (5 June 2014) [accessed 13 February 2016] *Groupe Renault, News, Corporate Blog* [Online] group.renault.com/en/news/blog-renault/circular-economy-recycle-renault/ (archived at https://perma.cc/R6J8-SEDN)

34 Investor Environmental Health Network (2016) [accessed 23 March 2016] *Case Studies, Rohner Textiles: Cradle-to-Cradle Innovation and Sustainability* [Online] www.iehn.org/publications.case.rohner.php (archived at https://perma.cc/M7VV-6NLK)

35 bioMASON (2019) [accessed 8 December 2019] [Online] biomason.com/ (archived at https://perma.cc/9RB9-8KJ6)

36 University of Cambridge Institute for Sustainability Leadership (CISL) (2016) [accessed 8 December 2019] *Collaboration for a Closed-Loop Value Chain: Transferable learning points* [Online] www.cisl.cam.ac.uk/publications/low-carbon-transformation-publications/collaboration-for-a-closed-loop-value-chain (archived at https://perma.cc/UH6B-R949)

37 Opendesk (2019) [accessed 9 December 2019] [Online] https://www.opendesk.cc/ (archived at https://perma.cc/EW22-HGGM)

38 Plastics Europe Association of Plastics Manufacturers (2019) [accessed 12 November 19] *Recycling and Energy Recovery* [Online] www.plasticseurope.org/en/focus-areas/circular-economy/zero-plastics-landfill/recycling-and-energy-recovery (archived at https://perma.cc/HF8H-4V77)

39 Allwood, J (2016) [accessed 15 August 2016] *A Bright Future for Steel*, University of Cambridge [Online] www.cam.ac.uk/system/files/a_bright_future_for_uk_steel_2.pdf (archived at https://perma.cc/H7AR-RA99)

40 Veolia (2016) [accessed 29 April 2016] [Online] livingcircular.veolia.com/en (archived at https://perma.cc/9X6R-J34U)

41 Excess Materials Exchange (2019) [accessed 24 September 2019] [Online] excessmaterialsexchange.com/ (archived at https://perma.cc/A5GJ-J7BG)

42 Rambrick (2019) [accessed 8 December 2019] [Online] www.rambrick.co.za/ (archived at https://perma.cc/63WT-ZP88)

43 Riversimple (2019) [accessed 8 December 2019] [Online] https://www.riversimple.com/whole-system-design/ (archived at https://perma.cc/R4NQ-J9MM)

44 Osborne, H and Norris, S (2016) Moving day: London council tackles housing crisis with portable village, *The Guardian*, 19 March, p 41

45 Chip[s] Board (2019) [accessed 9 December 2019] [Online] www.chipsboard.com/materials (archived at https://perma.cc/96HY-K425)

46 Weetman, C (2019) [accessed 2 December 2019] *Circular Economy Bicycle Design* [Online] www.rethinkglobal.info/circular-economy-bicycle-design/ (archived at https://perma.cc/RV6V-R56P)

47 Kennedy, S (2019) [accessed 22 October 2019] Researchers turn algae into a material as hard as steel, *Yale Climate Connections*, 15 October [Online] www.yaleclimateconnections.org/2019/10/researchers-turn-algae-into-a-material-as-hard-as-steel/ (archived at https://perma.cc/Y65V-QAZN)

48 Aouf, RS (2018) [accessed 10 December 2019] Bio-bricks made from human urine could be environmentally friendly future of architecture, *Dezeen*, 6 November [Online] www.dezeen.com/2018/11/06/bio-bricks-human-urine-environmentally-friendly-university-cape-town/ (archived at https://perma.cc/59HL-LSWF)

49 Climate-KIC (2019) [accessed 9 December 2019] *Black Bear: Upcycling end-of-life tyres into high quality carbon black* [Online] www.climate-kic.org/success-stories/bbc-2-0-upcycling-end-life-tyres-high-quality-carbon-black/ (archived at https://perma.cc/BVQ8-ELWE)

50 Iles, J (2018) [accessed 2 December 2019] Brands team up to see how 3D printing can revolutionise repair, *Circulate News*, 8 November [Online] medium.com/circulatenews/brands-team-up-to-see-how-3d-printing-can-revolutionise-repair-86d882d2a95d (archived at https://perma.cc/U7FP-K9ZZ)

51 Kellner, T (2017) [accessed 26 October 2019] *An Epiphany of Disruption: GE Additive Chief explains how 3D printing will upend manufacturing*, GE, 13 November [Online] www.ge.com/reports/epiphany-disruption-ge-additive-chief-explains-3d-printing-will-upend-manufacturing/ (archived at https://perma.cc/CWN6-WJHT)

52 Enviromate Reuse Ltd (2015) [accessed 27 April 2016] [Online] enviromate.co.uk/#s=1 (archived at https://perma.cc/GKK2-39TQ)

53 United States Materials Marketplace (2016) [accessed 29 April 2016] [Online] www.materialsmarketplace.org/#about (archived at https://perma.cc/NM3W-D3Z3)

54 Furniture Reuse Network [accessed 15 August 2015] [Online] www.frn.org.uk/ (archived at https://perma.cc/46EG-LX3P)

55 WarpIt reuse network [accessed 16 December 2015] [Online] www.warp-it.co.uk/ (archived at https://perma.cc/3PYH-KMZS)

56 Nissan and OVO announce a new collaboration to accelerate the adoption of home battery storage in the UK (October 2017) [accessed 7 December 2019] Ovo Energy Press Releases [Online] www.ovoenergy.com/ovo-newsroom/press-releases/2017/october/nissan-and-ovo-announce-a-new-collaboration-to-accelerate-the-adoption-of-home-battery-storage-in-the-uk.html (archived at https://perma.cc/VY2A-BCVW)

57 Chemical Footprint Project (2019) [accessed 8 December 2019] [Online] www.chemicalfootprint.org/ (archived at https://perma.cc/M3P8-DL3W)

58 Braungart, M and McDonough, W (2009) *Cradle to Cradle: Remaking the way we make things*, Vintage Books, London, p 117

10

Packaging and plastics

Recycling, packaging, businesses are changing all of those things because that's what consumers want.

JERRY GREENFIELD, CO-FOUNDER, BEN & JERRY'S ICE CREAM[1]

We buy with our eyes, and companies know this. In the 21st century, packaging is no longer a means of getting the product delivered safely. Instead, it's a critical element in the marketing mix, persuading us to buy things we probably don't need. New developments, especially with plastics, allow packaging designers to be more creative – and create more waste. Multiple different materials, non-recyclable elements, lack of recycling infrastructure and few regulations mean that packaging pollution and waste is a major headache for society and our living planet.

Plastic packaging is under the spotlight. Writing for the World Economic Forum (2018),[2] Ellen MacArthur and Paul Polman (former CEO, Unilever) sum up the change: 'In just half a century, plastic has moved from being a symbol of modern domestic bliss to a magnet for derogatory adjectives.' They point out that globally, most plastic goes into packaging, and yet almost none is recycled. 'Over the past 50 years, we have moved from reusable solutions to disposable, single-use items. But the recycling system hasn't kept pace. Today, just 2 per cent of the plastic on the market is turned into new packaging.'

In this chapter, we cover:

- a quick look at the evolution of modern packaging;
- purpose and design aims;
- the issues emerging, for society and our living planet;
- circular economy solutions, including business models, product design, sustainable materials, circular process and recovery flows;

- circular economy enablers and accelerators;
- summary and recommendations.

Evolution and global trends

Packaging has evolved in leaps and bounds over the last century or so. Innovations like moulded glass, metal cans and early plastics have improved product protection, extended shelf life and improved transportability, underpinning sales growth and product development.

Packaging has been around for thousands of years: primitive humans made containers with shells, leaves, plant fibres, wood and animal skins to protect, store and move food, medicines and other items. Later, metals and pottery helped develop more sophisticated packaging, and by the 1950s, packaging had become an integral part of the 'marketing mix', along with product, price, promotion and the other '7 Ps'. Often, it's what the customer first sees, and can make the difference between a product being chosen, or ignored.

Purpose and design aims

Packaging to protect and prolong the life of the product, often based on plastic, has revolutionized retail, e-commerce and logistics. Projects to 'lightweight' packaging, aimed at reducing logistics costs, often meant swapping from glass to plastic bottles. But public perception is changing, and we are all realizing how much damage discarded plastic is causing – to our water, to living creatures including fish, birds and animals, to our food chain, and to communities.

Figure 10.1 shows the typical design aims for the different forms of packaging:

- **primary packaging** (eg a tube for toothpaste, a plastic or paper wrapper for breakfast cereals);
- optional **secondary packaging** (eg the box containing the toothpaste tube or cereal wrapper);
- for some products, **tertiary packs** and **shelf packs**;
- **transit packaging**, to protect the product between manufacture and delivery.

FIGURE 10.1   Packaging – design aims

	Theme	Description
Physical protection	Storage	maintain the condition of the contents until ready for use/end of product life
	Distribution	protect against potential hazards during transport and handling at each stage
	Safety/security	safe to handle, and protect the environment from the product; deter/prevent tampering, pilferage, counterfeit, unauthorized sales
Information	Product info	provide information to those who may handle, store, buy or use the product
	Track and trace	production/packing location, status, serial/batch numbers
Relevance	Ease of use	user-friendly at all stages, eg optimal pack size (primary, secondary, transit), handling and display
	Aggregation/ portion control	relevant quantity or portion size; portion control (eg drugs)
📈	Marketing	support product marketing and establish, maintain or enhance the brand
£	Economy	optimize cost of packaging and effectiveness
↻	End of life	reusability, recoverable materials, ease of recycling

SOURCE: © Catherine Weetman

Each stakeholder may have different aims for packaging design, and Figure 10.2 illustrates some of the differing priorities. Influence from stakeholders can change design aims – such as to be eye-catching or low-cost.

Issues

In the 21st century, however, packaging has become a problem. Like fashion and many other consumer goods, it flows through the economy in a linear system. Plastic packaging could be the poster child for our 'waste economy' – take, make, use and throw it away.

Perhaps plastic seems so essential, and relatively cheap, that we don't value it. When we discard it, we destroy the value of the packaging, the materials, and all the other resources, energy and labour invested in it along the process. Whenever we choose to throw plastic away, we have to replace it, which means finding new petrochemical sources, often in ever-more difficult and expensive locations. Worse still, many of the materials (the pack, print,

FIGURE 10.2   Stakeholder perspectives for packaging

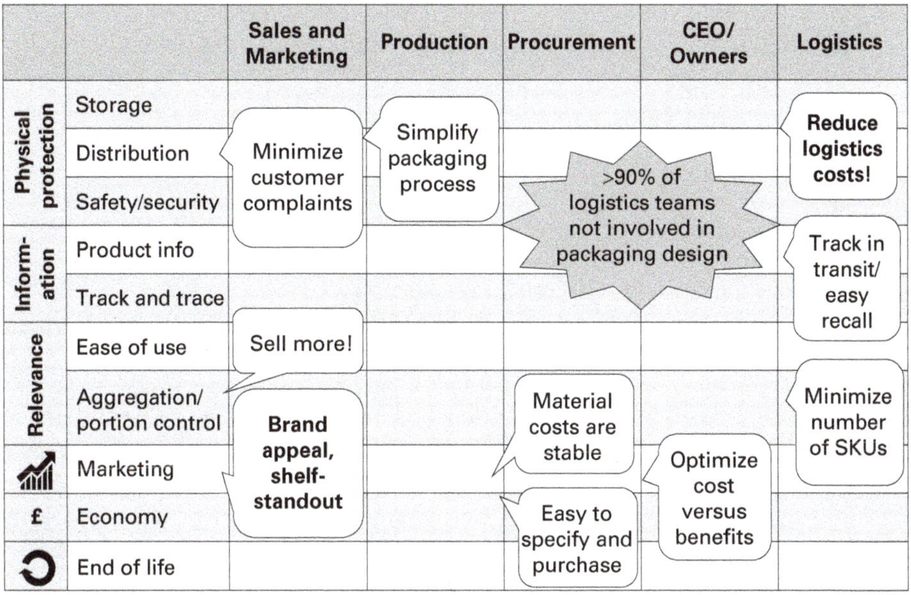

		Sales and Marketing	Production	Procurement	CEO/ Owners	Logistics
Physical protection	Storage		Simplify packaging process			Reduce logistics costs!
	Distribution	Minimize customer complaints		>90% of logistics teams not involved in packaging design		
	Safety/security					
Information	Product info					Track in transit/ easy recall
	Track and trace					
Relevance	Ease of use	Sell more!				
	Aggregation/ portion control	Brand appeal, shelf-standout		Material costs are stable		Minimize number of SKUs
📈	Marketing				Optimize cost versus benefits	
£	Economy			Easy to specify and purchase		
↻	End of life					

SOURCE: © Catherine Weetman

coatings and other additives) are creating pollution and waste, leaching toxins into living systems and our food chain.

Recycling can save energy, reduce pollution and carbon emissions *and* cost less – as long as the plastic is suitable for recycling. A better option is reuse, and companies are starting to explore ways to do this, as we'll see later.

In Europe, the average recycling rate for plastic packaging in 2018 was 42 per cent. Czechoslovakia, Spain and Switzerland achieved over 50 per cent, whereas Greece, Hungary, France and Finland managed less than 30 per cent.[3] China, which dealt with around half the world's waste plastic for three decades, began restricting imports in early 2017. In 2018, China's 'National Sword' policy meant it stopped importing most residential recyclable waste, creating major headaches for government and business worldwide. Now other countries in Asia are increasing their plastic waste imports, raising environmental concerns about their ability to handle such large volumes of recyclables.

In its Circular Economy paper (2019),[4] Plastics Europe tells us that the plastic waste collected and sent to recycling is never 100 per cent plastic, and often contains food residues, metal parts, paper labels and more contaminants.

Plastic may be labelled as degradable, biodegradable, or compostable – but be careful! 'Degradable' doesn't mean it creates food for nature – only that it breaks down and doesn't disrupt the composting process of other natural materials.

BIODEGRADABLE, COMPOSTABLE, BIOPLASTICS – WHAT DO THEY MEAN?

These terms can be confusing, especially for householders. The European Commission highlights the differences:[5,6]

- **Biodegradable:** A material is biodegradable if it can, with the help of micro-organisms, break down into natural elements (eg water, carbon dioxide and biomass). (However, see **Bioplastics** below.)

- **Compostable:** A material is compostable if it undergoes biodegradation by biological processes in home- or industrial-composting conditions and timeframes, leaving no toxic residues. (In other words, composting is enhanced biodegradation under managed conditions. For industrial composting, there are internationally agreed standards like EN13432 and ISO 18606.)

- **Oxo-degradable:** Oxo-degradable (or oxo-biodegradable) packaging is plastic packaging with additives that cause it to break down into microscopic particles. It can contribute to the bioplastics and can be biobased (made from a renewable resource), biodegradable (able to break down naturally) or both. Biodegradable bioplastics can be just as durable as other types of plastic, as they only break down in specific conditions. Oxo-degradable plastic packaging is not the same as biodegradable.

Bioplastics are plastics that are either created from a renewable, bio-based source; or are biodegradable; or both bio-based and biodegradable. The European Bioplastics Association reminds us that bioplastics, therefore, can be made from fossil-fuel sources.[7]

Bio-based plastics are made from a wide range of biological materials, including agricultural crops such as corn and sugar cane, ligno-cellulosic feedstocks like wood and other non-edible plants, and organic waste feedstocks.[8]

Reputational risks are coming to the fore, too. Crisp and snack packets often consist of several layers, making them unrecyclable. After a widespread UK social media campaign in 2018, and when angry customers began posting crisp packets back using a Freepost customer service address, Pepsico brand Walkers Crisps decided to set up recycling services with TerraCycle.

Business models and consumption

Plastic food packaging has helped grow the markets for imported food, ready meals and 'food to go', and enabled people to shop less frequently. One oft-cited study says an unpackaged cucumber will be past its best after three days, yet when wrapped in plastic film, it will stay fresh for 14 and so reduce food waste, and other studies show how plastic wrapping extends the shelf life of cheese, meat and other perishables.

Most packaging is designed for single use, meaning that billions of pieces of packaging are discarded every year. For example, globally, 480 billion plastic bottles were sold in 2016, an increase of 60 per cent in a decade.

Product design

The design of the packaging influences its environmental impact. Using multiple materials in the packaging makes recycling (and labelling for recycling) more complex.

Packaging with several different layers laminated together can be very difficult to recycle – though, as we see later, TerraCycle manages to convert some of these into other plastic products. Examples include beverage cartons with card, plastic and foil; crisp and snack packets with multiple layers of foil and plastic.

Toothpaste tubes and other tube-based containers are almost impossible to recycle, due to their small size, blended materials and contamination from leftover contents.

A survey of UK food and beverage manufacturers found that in 90 per cent of cases, logistics teams were not involved in the design of product packaging, resulting in sub-optimal volume efficiency (the amount of product on a pallet, or in a delivery vehicle). In consumer-packaged goods and food products, including logistics factors in design reduced logistics costs by over 10 per cent. According to McKinsey,[9] for two products of identical volume, more rectangular packaging can **increase packing density by up to 40 per cent**.

Consider transit packaging too – could you get a better 'fill' on the pallet base and available height: improving utilization of warehouse space, delivery vehicle and so on. Designing for supply-chain efficiency helps reduce costs for the company and its retail customers, but few companies tap into the knowledge of their logistics teams. Sometimes it seems there is a 'Russian doll' approach with multiple boxes. We need to move the product, not fresh air!

Resources: materials

In industrialized countries, packaging materials like glass, aluminium, steel, paper and board have effective recycling systems. The Packaging Resources Action Group reports that:[10]

- Glass packaging can be recycled indefinitely without losing performance, and most glass contains some recycled material, known as 'cullet'. However, the glass collected for recycling needs to have the same colour as the final glass – for food and beverages, this is usually green, amber or clear.

- Metal packaging such as aluminium and steel may contain over 50 per cent of recycled content, and products like cans can be infinitely recycled without loss of quality. Steel cans from recycled material may require only 25 per cent of the energy needed to make a can from virgin material, and for aluminium, only 5 per cent is needed.

- Paper, card and board are easily recycled, and carton board and corrugated board usually contain a high proportion of recycled material. However, during recycling, paper fibres become shorter and weaker each time they are recycled. This means that some virgin fibre has to be included to achieve the strength and quality of the end-product – the higher the performance demand, the more virgin fibre is likely to be needed.

Recycling systems are expanding for plastics such as PET (polyethylene terephthalate) and HDPE (high-density polyethylene), both common in food and drinks.

Generally, conventional plastics cannot be recycled indefinitely without loss of quality, and in the EU, plastic for food applications must comply with legislation to protect against contamination. In practice, this means recycled plastic must flow through *closed-loop* systems. For transit packaging, expanded polystyrene (EPS) as a filler is difficult to recycle.

There may be issues with the process chemicals, inks and coatings, too. Some of the **additives and colourants** in plastic are toxic, with potential to harm humans and living systems even whilst in use: causing cancer and disrupting hormones. There is little research into what happens when plastics begin to degrade and release those chemicals, but more research is emerging about the risks from chemicals leaching out of food and drink plastic packaging. *The Guardian* (2018)[11] reported on a UK study showing that BPA (bisphenol A), used to create polycarbonate, was found in 80 per cent of teenagers. BPA is an endocrine disruptor and research raises concerns about its effect on liver and kidney functions. France has banned the use of BPA in any packaging that comes into contact with food.

We are learning about microplastics problems: researchers from Canada, studying 'pyramid'-shaped plastic teabags, found that near-boiling water caused billions of microplastics and nanoplastics from just one teabag to escape into the cup.

Resources: energy

The energy footprint of packaging is complex and depends on a range of factors, including the materials, the production process, the supply chain and the recovery process (if available).

Lucy Siegle, answering the question 'Are plastic jars worse for the environment?' (2013),[12] reports that compared with a glass jar, a PET (a thermoplastic polymer resin) jar 'uses twice as much abiotic material (minerals and fossil fuel) to produce and 17 times more water (predominantly from cooling power plants) and produces five times the greenhouse gas emissions.' However, she reminds us that we need to factor in the logistics energy consumption, so 'the lightest wins. A PET jar shipped 1,000km in lieu of a glass jar saves 19g of CO_2e (carbon dioxide equivalent).' If we consider the end-of-use scenarios, glass is much more likely to be recycled, and can be recycled infinitely with no loss of quality.

Resources: water

The Water Footprint Network (2017)[13] reminds us that modern packaging puts pressure on water resources in those countries producing the raw materials and manufacturing the packaging, 'equivalent to between 650 and 800 billion cubic metres of water annually.' In addition to the water used in packaging production, it creates a large grey water footprint (the amount of water needed to assimilate pollutants to avoid compromising water quality standards), with plastics and paper being the worst. For example, the grey water footprint for producing plastic packaging is 'up to 330 billion cubic metres per year, which could supply China with domestic water for six months'.

Metals also have grey water footprints. For example, in producing aluminium drinks cans, the raw material (bauxite mineral) mining pollutes the water. The Water Footprint Network points out that 'many of the regions where mining and production of packaging materials occur are already severely impacted by water pollution and water scarcity, such as China, Brazil and the USA.'

Plastics are polluting our oceans, rivers and beaches too. Ocean Conservancy's 2018 beach clean-up top 10 list of items retrieved includes nine food- and drink-related items, with food packaging at number two, and plastic cutlery now in the list too.[14]

Resources: land

Recent research is discovering the many downsides of landfilling waste, with methane emissions and microplastics escaping into the soil, as well as water. Chemical changes in plastics allow toxic chemicals to leach out too, damaging ecosystems and making their way into the food chain.

While paper, card and bio-based plastics may seem better than difficult-to-recycle petrochemical-based plastic, there are concerns about their impact on land use. Replacing native trees with fast-growing varieties can reduce biodiversity, and growing crops purely for packaging diverts much-needed land from food production – as well as risking deforestation. Industrial agriculture means more synthetic fertilizers and pesticides too, with all their adverse impacts, and may put pressure on local water supplies.

Mining for metals, especially bauxite for aluminium, harms the environment and biodiversity as well as affecting water use and quality.

End-of-use

Governments all around the world are starting to regulate packaging and plastics. Plastic bottles and bottle caps rank as the third and fourth most collected plastic trash items in the Ocean Conservancy's 2019 beach clean-ups in more than 100 countries,[15] and activists are campaigning to ban plastic bottles, together with plastic shopping bags. Small towns in the US and Australia have banned bottles, as have numerous public spaces and buildings in Europe and the United States. There are serious implications for the developing world – where over 2 billion people still do not have access to clean drinking water, according to the United Nations, and bottled water is often the only safe option. Kenya announced a ban on single-use plastics at beaches and in other conservation areas from June 2020, and Delhi banned disposable water bottles in all city offices.

THE EU PACKAGING WASTE DIRECTIVE[16]

The European Council Directive 94/62/EC on Packaging and Packaging Waste was first introduced in 1994, with defined targets for the recycling and recovery of packaging waste across the European Union (EU). Each member state was free to define mechanisms for delivering the directive's targets.

A revision in 2015 relates to the consumption of lightweight plastic carrier bags, and revisions in 2018 contain updated measures to contribute to the transition towards a circular economy.

The directive covers all packaging placed on the European market and all packaging waste, whether it is used or released at industrial, commercial, office, shop, service, household or any other level, regardless of the material used.

EU countries must take measures to meet certain recycling targets. By 31 December 2030, at least 70 per cent by weight of all packaging must be recycled, including 55 per cent of plastic, 30 per cent of wood, 80 per cent of ferrous metals, 60 per cent of aluminium, 75 per cent of glass and 85 per cent of paper and cardboard.

In the UK, this EU Packaging Waste legislation requires each large company putting packaging into the market to pay for Packaging Recovery Notes (PRN), based on the quantity and type of packaging. However, these PRN fees recover only about 10 per cent of the cost of collection and recycling – so most costs are 'externalized' by business, meaning UK citizens pick up the rest of the costs and suffer the health and environmental consequences of non-recycled waste. The UK government introduced a small charge for single-use plastic carrier bags in 2015, resulting in an 85 per cent reduction in bags used.

Whilst internationally agreed recycling symbols exist, there is no international law forcing manufacturers to use them, and companies can design their own symbols. These may be genuinely helpful, or meaningless – but are likely to cause confusion and frustration for the user. There are also issues with contamination in use – for example, food remnants on packaging can contaminate an entire recycling stream. Colours and coatings in the packaging can also prevent or add cost to recycling, with an obvious example being black plastic trays, used to extend the shelf life of meat.

Since China's ban on recycling imports, the lack of regulations for recycling and waste management in developing countries has become a key issue. Many developing countries don't have regulations or systems for managing solid waste and collecting garbage, and receiving exported waste from other countries (often illegally) exacerbates the issues. Burning and informal dumping risks health and damage to ecosystems.

Campaigners and NGOs have been highlighting the problem and calling for action. In 2019, almost all of the countries in the world agreed to restrict shipments of hard-to-recycle plastic waste to poorer countries, by extending the terms of the Basel Convention.[17] Whereas previously, exporting countries could send lower-quality waste to private organizations without approval from the importing country's government, they will now have to obtain consent. The agreement covers contaminated, mixed or unrecyclable plastic waste.

Circular economy developments

Companies are beginning to rethink packaging altogether, and develop a wide range of different approaches to narrow, slow, intensify, close and re-generate packaging. New business models, materials and recycling processes are emerging, and technology innovations are adding value and improving recovery options.

Could you use less packaging? Are you optimizing product fill in the final transit packaging? In 2015, preparing for a presentation to Zero Waste Scotland, I measured six similar packs of oatcakes from different brands. The most-efficiently packed one had a volume density of more than double the least efficient one – and was the second cheapest per 100 grams.

Packaging Insights notes that sustainability dominated the trends in 2018, 'largely driven by anti-plastic sentiment'.[18] It highlights the world's first plastic-free supermarket aisles in the UK and the Netherlands, wide-spread bans on single-use plastic and the Ellen MacArthur Foundation-supported New Plastics Economy Global Commitment. Research shows that consumers are more likely to buy organic, premium brands if the pack-aging is 'natural-looking'. Examples include cardboard replacing polysty-rene discs for Aldi's pizzas, and Morrisons using 'vacuum skinboard' (VSB) to replace its black (hard to recycle) plastic meat trays.

Business models

Let's look at how companies are developing ways to make the product packaging more circular, and even create new business models for packag-ing itself. Strategies for circular business models are shown in Figure 10.3.

NARROW THE LOOP

Is all the packaging necessary? How could you rethink the product and the packaging to improve the volume density, minimizing materials and foot-prints? Cosmetic brand Lush sells soaps in 'naked' packaging, and plastic-free supermarket aisles (and even whole supermarkets) are popping up (see above). Companies are developing toothpaste and mouthwash in tablet form, delivered through subscription services, and Cozie in France sells organic beauty products through dispensers that allow customers to refill their empty bottles.

FIGURE 10.3   Circular Economy Framework 2.0 – business models

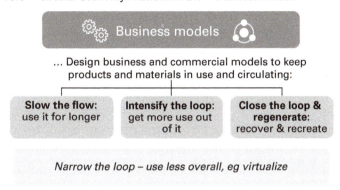

SOURCE: © Catherine Weetman

Aim for fewer and simpler materials, to improve resource efficiency and aid recycling. Could you lightweight the design, using thinner-walled bottles or cans to reduce materials, costs, energy and *GHG* emissions? Could you print onto the pack instead of applying a label, reducing printing costs as well as improving recyclability?

ALGRAMO – SHARING THE SAVINGS OF BULK DISTRIBUTION

Algramo started in Chile back in 2013, selling food and hygiene products through vending machines. Customers purchase reusable containers, and can then dispense goods such as lentils, rice and cleaning supplies in over 2,000 stores. Convenience stores are expensive, but distributing in bulk means the products are 30 to 40 per cent cheaper, and Algramo shares the profits with the stores. In 2019, Algramo announced a partnership with Unilever to trial deliveries using electric tricycles.

SLOW THE FLOW

How could you design to prolong the usable life of the packaging? That can be a difficult challenge for something for which the purpose is to protect the contents inside.

In the UK, Costa Coffee launched a new reusable 'Clever Cup' that enables contactless payments and comes in packaging made from coffee cups containing recycled fibre from one 'medio' sized cup from Costa's own waste stream.

Some companies are aiming to use longer-lasting or refillable packaging as part of product-as-service models.[19] The Evian (re)new app and bottle from Danone is an 'in-home water system' with a collapsible 5-litre recyclable 'bubble', made from 100 per cent recycled PET (rPET). Danone says it uses two-thirds less plastic than its normal 1.5-litre bottle. A button on the appliance is connected to the (re)new app, which can track the water consumed, notifying the user when a refill is needed. Pepsico, meanwhile, acquired Sodastream and launched its 'Beyond the Bottle' strategy. A new hydration platform includes a water dispenser, with a variety of flavour options; a companion smartphone app; and a personalized QR code sticker for reusable bottles allowing the dispenser to recognize consumers. The app can track users' water intake against personalized hydration goals and customize flavour and carbonation preferences.

In the UK, sales of reusable cups and water bottles have increased, with some coffee chains introducing discounts for the growing numbers of customers bringing their own cup. For water, UK retailers can sign up to the Refill app, which encourages consumers to ask for a free refill (a legal right in much of the UK).

INTENSIFY THE LOOP

Reusable packaging can transform people's habits, by swapping single-use items for more durable items that can be recycled at the end of life. We could learn from the Dabbawala system in India – a workers' collective delivering 200,000 lunch boxes, every day, from people's homes to their offices, routed through consolidation and deconsolidation stations. It's highly efficient, same-day delivery, with a superb accuracy rate, using simple coding and no computers.

Food-to-go reuse systems and shared-use schemes are emerging, such as CupClub in London, RECUP in Germany and Green Caffeen in Australia.

ARK REUSABLES – REUSABLE AND RECYCLABLE FOOD-TO-GO CONTAINERS[20]

Ozarka offers returnable, responsible, sustainable, zero-waste takeaway boxes for prepared food businesses, through food outlets in Amsterdam and Utrecht in the Netherlands, and plans to expand across the US and Europe. Its ARK Reusables food-to-go containers are made from reusable recyclable silicone and pack flat so they are easy to carry.

Subscription services offer several business benefits, by creating a direct relationship with the consumer. This helps build trust and brand loyalty, and helps to understand how customers use the product, with scope for personalization. In contrast, the traditional distribution method puts the brand under constant price pressure from low-cost supermarkets and online retailers. Offering refills can cut distribution costs and enables users to choose quantities.

LOOP – MAKING REUSE EASY AND ATTRACTIVE[21]

Loop, a 'global circular shopping platform' started by recycling specialist TerraCycle, aims to transform products and packaging from single-use to 'durable, multi-use, feature-packed designs'. Loop offers food, household personal care products from well-known brands, including Procter & Gamble, Mars, Nestlé, PepsiCo and Unilever and more, in upgraded, durable and reusable packaging.

The pack designs aim to look attractive in your bathroom and kitchen, and some have other value-adding features, for example, containers that keep ice cream cooler for longer.

When the pack is empty, customers place used product containers in the Loop tote and schedule a free pickup from their home. Loop then cleans and refills the products, and delivers the replenished packs to the customer. TerraCycle says the containers recover the environmental cost of production after three to four uses, and they are designed to be reused 100 times or more, or easily recycled. Deposits encourage consumers to return the packaging.

Loop's 2019 pilot in the United States starts as a standalone system, with logistics company UPS delivering and collecting from consumers. It will soon become part of retailer e-commerce offers, and in spring 2020, Loop plans to work with UK retailer Tesco to put Loop products on its store shelves.

For household cleaning, Ecover provides **refillable** bottles, with farm shops and wholefood outlets stocking the bulk product and providing 'refill stations'. In Europe, RePack offers **reusable packaging** for home delivery, with a reward system to encourage the successful return. Other transit packaging schemes include Chep pay-per-use pallets, and Pallite's reusable cardboard pallets (see Chapter 12).

CLOSE THE LOOP AND REGENERATE

Returnable packaging works well for closed supply chains, such as deliveries of bottles in returnable crates. AB Inbev has returnable bottle fleets in

FIGURE 10.4   Circular Economy Framework 2.0 – product design

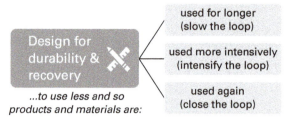

SOURCE: © Catherine Weetman

most of its sales geographies, and says it gets 40 cycles out of each glass bottle, noting that the costs of transport and cleaning the bottles are massively outweighed by the benefits of not making new bottles each time.

TERRACYCLE – RECYCLING HARD-TO-RECYCLE WASTE[22]

TerraCycle, founded in 2001, provides solutions for collecting and repurposing hard-to-recycle waste. By 2019, it was operating in over 20 countries, recycling 'billions of pieces of waste' through various collection schemes. It offers services to industrial and municipal clients, and for communities. TerraCycle offers free recycling programmes funded by brands, manufacturers and retailers. Examples in the UK include baby food sachets, bread bags, household cleaning and personal care product containers. Other services include fluorescent lamps, batteries, e-waste, organic waste and medical waste, and it sells upcycled products from its website. By 2019, TerraCycle had received waste from 202 million people worldwide, raising over US$44 million for charities around the world.

Design for durability and recovery

Our chosen design approaches can ensure the packaging is fit for its intended lifetime, that it is easy to recover and is designed to have multiple lives – see Figure 10.4.

DESIGN TO USE LESS

How can we reduce the amount of packaging and materials? Suggestions from the UK-based Packaging Resources Action Group Packaging and Recyclability[23] guide include:

- ask if each element of packaging (primary, secondary, tertiary, etc) is necessary, or could be redesigned and reduced;
- lightweighting and designing out unnecessary layers or elements of packaging;
- design the most efficient shape – a shorter, squat bottle would normally use less material than a tall, thin bottle – avoid awkward shapes, 'head space' or voids;
- don't overspecify, and consider alternative materials – eg double-walled rather than triple-walled corrugated board may meet the use specification;
- make the packaging work harder – for example, could you print information on the primary pack, or on the inside of outer packaging, rather than including a separate leaflet;
- consider a 'buy in bulk' option to reduce the ratio of product to packaging.

Companies are changing product configurations, for example with concentrates for liquid products, or reducing the materials and the footprint for the product, the packaging and in the supply chain. Many B2B suppliers now offer better-value concentrated cleaning products and in the US, Dazz concentrated refill tablets are available in Walmart and on Amazon. Replenish refillable systems are available worldwide, and in the UK, Splosh is well established.

SPLOSH – CONCENTRATED REFILLS FOR HOUSEHOLD CLEANING PRODUCTS[24]

UK brand Splosh launched in 2012, creating concentrated formulations for household cleaning and personal care products. Splosh points out that for the majority of home cleaning and laundry products, the first-named (highest volume) ingredient is 'aqua' – water, typically accounting for 70–85 per cent of the whole contents.

Single-use, disposable bottles made sense for both supermarkets and big brands, as they are easy to distribute, there's no mess and the big bottles imply value for money (and justify a high margin). Splosh also highlights the difficulties of recycling bottles used for home and personal care products, due to 'taint' – the residue left from the perfumes and other chemicals. This means laundry and cleaning products would contaminate plastic recyclate for food use, and so instead, they are downcycled. The result is that even if these bottles are recyclable and fed into the local recycling network, they won't become a replacement for a new household cleaning product bottle.

> Splosh users buy full bottles to start with, then order concentrated refills that fit through a letterbox. A mobile app saves time, the refill boxes are small and easy to store, and Splosh guarantees the bottles and caps for life.

DESIGN SO THE PRODUCT AND MATERIALS ARE IN USE FOR LONGER

Packaging durability is relevant if it will extend the usable life of the product, or create reuse opportunities. Perhaps you can rethink the system of delivering the product – as with Nespresso capsules and coffee machines and the Evian and Sodastream examples earlier. Nespresso encourages return for recycling for its aluminium capsules in many countries, though it is unclear how successful and effective this is. Designing for durability would consider how the packaging will be stored, transported and handled in use. If designing for refills, you might think about aesthetics too – would the user prioritize your product if it looks more attractive on the bathroom shelf? Some of the products in the Loop range aim to achieve this.

DESIGN TO USE PRODUCT AND MATERIALS MORE INTENSIVELY

Reusing packaging reduces raw material use and postpones end-of-life waste, but it may need more energy and materials to make the packaging suitable for several use cycles. Reuse options include:

- by the user – for example a refillable biscuit tin or coffee tin;
- at the retailer – refill options for dry food products (pasta, legumes, grains), household cleaning bottle, trigger spray, etc. We mentioned Ecover and similar refill stations earlier;
- in return systems – this is common for transit packaging such as roll-cages, pallets and totes (eg Bakers Basco in the UK bakery sector), and is still used for bottles in some countries.

DESIGN TO USE PRODUCT AND MATERIALS AGAIN – WASTE = FOOD!

If we aim to recover the packaging, we should consider how easily the user can find suitable recycling facilities. How and where will the product be used, and where will the packaging be removed? People may consume a soft drink at work, at an event, in the street, or at home. Try to design for the majority of scenarios, not the example that's the easiest option for the manufacturer!

If it's likely to go into 'mainstream' recycling services, ensure the design simplifies recycling:

- Use materials that are recyclable *and* recycled.

- Use fewer materials and mono-materials where possible, and avoid laminates and dark colours which are difficult to sort, separate and recycle.

- Avoid additional items that might contaminate recycling streams, such as a non-recyclable bottle top or label.

- Clear labelling to help the user understand what the packaging is, and where it can be recycled, will encourage recycling and reduce the risk that unsuitable materials will contaminate otherwise valuable recyclate.

Globally, the Coca-Cola Company's World Without Waste initiative includes a goal to recover and recycle a bottle for every one it sells by 2030. In Great Britain, the packaging it uses is 100 per cent recyclable and its bottles contain up to 25 per cent recycled plastic or plant-based material, and it has committed to using 50 per cent recycled plastic in all its plastic bottles by 2020.[25]

Coca-Cola Simply brand juices are in PET bottles, but the larger bottle had an integrated handle made from PETG, causing significant issues in processing the PET for recycling. This bottle also had a label and adhesive that was hard to wash off during recycling. Both issues meant the bottle wasn't recyclable and could contaminate recycling streams, so Coca-Cola redesigned the bottle in recyclable PET with a recycling-compatible label.[26]

GARÇON WINES —·FLAT WINE BOTTLES SAVING RESOURCES, VOLUME, WEIGHT AND ENERGY[27]

Garçon Wines, in the UK, has developed award-winning flat bottles made from 100 per cent recycled, food-grade and recyclable PET. They are 87 per cent lighter than traditional glass wine bottles, and 40 per cent smaller. The flat shape means they can be 'packed like books', reducing storage space. The single-bottle pack is designed for e-commerce, complies with Amazon's ISTA 6-Amazon.com Tier 1 certification, and can be delivered through most UK letterboxes. A case of 10 bottles is the same size as one that would carry four, rounded, glass bottles of the same volume.

Laminates and composite packaging that uses multiple materials presents major challenges for a packaging closed loop. However, single ('mono') material alternatives may be heavier, bulkier, and potentially offer lower durability and performance.

FRUGALPAC – RECYCLABLE MULTI-LAYER BEVERAGE CARTON[28]

Beverage cartons often consist of a laminate of several layers of plastic tightly bonded to cardboard, meaning they need specialist recycling facilities. And poor recycling rates might mean only a small percentage of the cartons reach the recycling facility. Sustainable packaging company Frugalpac developed the Frugal Carton so it can be processed at any paper recycling facility in the UK. Instead of bonded layers, the Frugal Carton outer shell is 100 per cent paperboard and a foil bag sits inside as a waterproof layer. By tearing off the carton top at the end of use, the user can separate the carton and foil, recycling it through easily accessible systems.

In addition to choosing structural materials (plastic, metal, board, etc) for easy recovery and reuse, we must consider the labels, print, sleeves, adhesives and barrier materials. These must also be safe, sustainable and compatible with our intended recovery methods. For example, using a PVC sleeve on a PET bottle may contaminate the PVC recycling stream, causing black spots in the recycled PET (rPET).

HOW2RECYCLE – TAKING THE GUESSWORK OUT OF RECYCLING[29]

How2Recycle began in 2008 as a Sustainable Packaging Coalition project, supported by a coalition of brands including Amazon, Aldi, Bayer, Campbells, Dow, Mattel and Unilever. By 2019, it was operating in the US and Canada.

The labels make it clear which packaging component the label refers to and include a website link for more information, showing:

- how to prepare it for recycling, and whether any additional steps are required, such as rinsing off food debris;
- whether the item falls into one of four categories – Widely Recycled, Check Locally, Not Yet Recycled, Store Drop-Off;
- what type of material the packaging is made from.

Safe, sustainable inputs

Is it single-use? Is it likely to be reused or disposed of? Material choices should consider the end-of-use options. Can you make it easier to recycle, perhaps by using alternatives to plastics, including glass, metals, cardboard

FIGURE 10.5   Circular Economy Framework 2.0 – safe, sustainable inputs

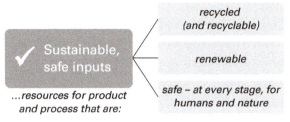

SOURCE: © Catherine Weetman

and paper? Otherwise, aim to use renewable, bio-based materials, so at the end of life, waste becomes food for nature: compost. Figure 10.5 reminds us of the aims.

In 2018,[30] bioplastics were estimated to account for 6 per cent of all plastic packaging. Bioplastic and compostable packaging are expected to grow, especially for pre-packaged 'food to go' and snacks.

Safety and sustainability apply to all the materials used in the packaging and the manufacturing process, including colourants, coatings, inks and glues. We should not forget these, or leave them to the printer or service provider to apply later in the packing process.

RECYCLED AND RECYCLABLE INPUTS

Glass and metal are still common, especially for food and beverage packaging, and many countries have effective recycling systems for these. Cardboard and paper are easy and cost-effective to recycle, but results in shorter fibres and thus reduced quality compared with virgin materials. This means that at least a small proportion of the fibres have to be from virgin materials. Most plastic recycling also results in lower-quality materials, limiting the number of cycles to around five. As such, using recycled plastic might require an extra layer of protection or an increase in material thickness and bulk.

There are developments in creating **perpetually recyclable polymers**. In 2018, scientists in Colorado announced they had discovered plastic-like material (a new polymer) that can be recycled infinitely, through de-polymerization.[31] The new material avoids the need to use petrochemicals too.

RENEWABLE INPUTS

TU Delft summarized the range of renewable materials.[32] These include non-plastics, like fibres, wood-based, animal-based (wool, leather, silk), cork, bamboo and clay. In 2019, British company Lush announced its 'carbon positive' packaging for solid shampoos and other 'naked' products, made out of biodegradable cork.

Renewable bio-based plastics can be biodegradable, with PHAs, Bio PBS and PHB (all from bacterial fermentation), cellophane (from wood, cotton or hemp) and PLA (from sugar cane or corn starch). There are non-biodegradable bio-based plastics, too, including Bio-PET, Bio-PE and PEF, from sugar cane, sugar beet, wheat grain and algae.

Nestlé announced a recyclable paper wrapper for its YES!® healthy snack bars, and Carlsberg is working on the Green Fiber Bottle – a 'paper' beer bottle made from sustainably sourced wood fibre: 100 per cent bio-based and fully recyclable. By 2019 it had two prototypes, using a thin plastic film for the inner barrier – with one containing recycled PET and the other a 100 per cent bio-based PEF.[33]

For transit packaging, polystyrene can be replaced with corn or potato starch 'chips', or shredded paper and cardboard. Valueform, in the UK, developed processes to convert cereal waste into replacements for polystyrene and paper pulp.

New bioplastic developments are using abundant resources like algae, fungus and seaweed, or from agricultural waste. UK Start-up Notpla has developed Ooho flexible packaging and sachets for food. It is edible, biodegradable and made from renewable brown seaweed. Ecovative uses mycelium to convert straw and other agricultural waste into strong, lightweight protective packaging. In the UK, Woolly Shepherd uses sheep's wool to provide food-grade insulation for home delivery.

However, using the same principle that we should avoid using agricultural land for textiles and biofuels, it is critical that we do not grow crops purely for packaging. Paper and other wood or cellulosic materials should come from certified, renewable sources. Certification labels include Forestry Stewardship Council (FSC) and the Programme for the Endorsement of Forest Certification (PEFC).

As research discovers more about how plastics degrade, both in use and at end-of-use, it is critical to ensure packaging materials are safe – at every stage of the supply chain, for humans and nature. Materials used today may be discovered to be unsafe in the future – can you demonstrate that you have used the best available science to decide on all the materials you have used?

Process design

Figure 10.6 highlights the aims for process design. We have highlighted the importance of **safe and sustainable** materials, including labels and print. In

FIGURE 10.6   Circular Economy Framework 2.0 – process design

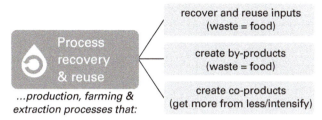

SOURCE: © Catherine Weetman

2017, EPEA, with support from the DOEN Foundation, launched a healthy printing initiative (www.HealthyPrinting.eu (archived at https://perma.cc/U8B3-F57S)) to scale up availability of healthier substances in printing for packaging and publishing, and to improve recycling. It has a knowledge platform, case studies and other resources.

As with any other production process, it is important to **recover** the energy, water and process chemicals for reuse, and **reuse** any process waste.

In India, Dell is working with a supplier that removes soot from diesel generator exhausts and refines it to make carbon black, for ink. Dell uses the ink to print on over 1.5 million packages it sends out across India every year, cleaning the equivalent of the air breathed in by over 100,000 people.[34]

How else could you make the process more circular – could you create *by-products* or produce a food product and use the waste to make a packaging *co-product*?

Recovery flows

Figure 10.7 reminds us of the objectives for recovery and regeneration. As we have seen, it is critical to ensure the packaging is either easily recyclable or returnable/reusable. Recycling packaging is complicated – in the UK, government-funded Recycle Now lists 27 different recycling symbols used on packaging: including the seven resin code numbers. Biodegradable and bioplastic materials may not have widely available recycling options, but instead be collected as general waste (and so go to landfill or incineration), or even mistakenly added to plastic recycling streams, causing contamination.

Governments are setting and strengthening product stewardship regulations, including bans on plastic carrier bags and other single-use items. The European Commission packaging recycling targets stipulate that EU countries must reach a recycling rate of 75 per cent of packaging waste by 2030.

FIGURE 10.7   Circular Economy Framework 2.0 – recovery flows

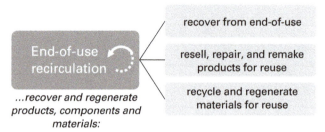

SOURCE: © Catherine Weetman

RECOVER FROM END-OF-USE

Could you set up systems to recover primary, secondary and transit packaging for your own reuse, or as part of a sector collaboration? There are systems for beer kegs and returnable bottles, and now there is a solution for e-commerce delivery packaging, with RePack. As we noted earlier, companies can encourage recycling and recovery, by providing clear information about the packaging materials, and the options for end-of-use recovery or recycling.

Reverse vending machines can improve the practicalities and economics of recovering packaging for recycling. Similar to other vending machines, they are automated machines using advanced technology to identify, sort, collect and process used beverage containers, and are in use for bottle collection, as well as other forms of waste collection such as batteries and light bulbs. Users may be rewarded, perhaps with discounts for future purchases.

RESELL, REPAIR AND REMAKE PRODUCTS FOR REUSE

I have struggled to find examples of repairable product packaging, though transit packaging has well-established examples, such as wooden pallets. The TerraCycle example earlier mentioned selling plastic products upcycled from the waste streams it processes. These include picnic benches, chairs, litter bins, tote bags and more.

RECYCLE AND REGENERATE MATERIALS FOR REUSE

As we mentioned, recycling of metals, glass and paper/card is already common. For plastics, mechanical recycling, with plastics ground and chopped into smaller fragments, is almost the sole type of recycling in Europe. Research into chemical recycling (depolymerization) aims to increase the quality of the recycled output and enable efficient and effective closed loops.

P&G PURECYCLE – RESTORING USED PLASTIC TO 'VIRGIN-LIKE' QUALITY[35]

In 2017, Procter & Gamble (P&G) announced a patented technology that restores used polypropylene plastic (PP) to 'virgin-like' quality. The technology, licensed to PureCycle in the US, is capable of removing virtually all contaminants and colours from used plastic. This has potential to replace virgin materials in a broad range of applications, such as car interiors, packaging, electronics, construction materials, home furnishings and more.

New developments are improving recycling options. **Plastic-eating enzymes** can convert waste into new, high-quality plastic. In 2018, scientists accidentally created a mutant enzyme that breaks down plastic drinks bottles. Their research was triggered after discovering the first bacterium that had naturally evolved to eat plastic, at a waste dump in Japan in 2016.[36]

Enablers

Different ways of thinking and designing, such as *systems thinking, biomimicry* and *green chemistry* can help revolutionize packaging, innovating the product, the packaging and the business model (see Figure 10.8). Examples include Notpla's Ooho edible packaging and plenty of compact products.

We have also seen examples of **new materials**, for example from algae, mycelium, seaweed, food waste and more. Other material innovations are focusing on proper plastic recycling so it is reused as packaging. In 2019, BP announced Infinia – 'enabling circularity for unrecyclable PET plastic

FIGURE 10.8   Circular Economy Framework 2.0 – enablers

SOURCE: © Catherine Weetman

waste'.[37] BP expects its pilot plant in the US to be operational by 2020, and it envisages scaling up with multiple plants around the world, with 'potential to prevent billions of PET bottles and trays from ending up in landfill and incineration each year'.

New **technologies** are helping, with *3D printing* offering potential to upcycle plastic packaging waste into new products, apps helping provide information and customer-use insights, and *AI* revolutionizing collection and sorting systems. New **mechanical sorting** developments include robotic waste pickers and sophisticated sorting machines.

The Plastic Bank has set up '**social plastic' exchanges** in some of the world's poorest places, by incentivizing people to bring marine and other plastic waste to recycling collection areas for export. They are rewarded with digital tokens paid into a smartphone-accessible bank account, which they can then exchange for food, water, phone minutes and more.[38]

Accelerators

FIGURE 10.9   Circular Economy Framework 2.0 – accelerators

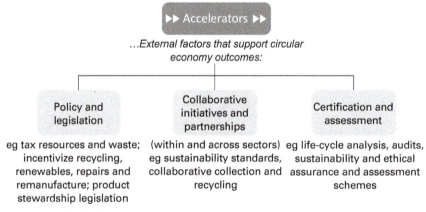

SOURCE: © Catherine Weetman

With six main types of plastic in common use, **product stewardship legislation** could ensure every piece of plastic put into the market should be properly recyclable, and regions could work together to collect and recycle every type. Research by Plastics Europe compares mixed-waste collection schemes with separated waste at home or commercial collections, noting that plastic waste recycling rates are 10 times higher when collected separately.[39]

Policies like the EU Packaging Waste Regulations could be used to recover the full costs of collection and processing from producers and retailers and help fund research and innovation. Policies should penalize those companies using additives, coatings or colourants that reduce the quality of the recycled material or make it much more difficult to recycle.

There are a number of large-scale, sector-wide **collaborative initiatives** to improve sustainability and close the loop.

The New Plastics Economy Global Commitment, launched in 2018, unites businesses, governments and other organizations behind a common vision and targets to address plastic waste and pollution at source. It is led by the Ellen MacArthur Foundation in collaboration with UN Environment, and by 2019 it united more than 400 organizations on its common vision of a circular economy for plastics, to keep plastics in the economy and out of the ocean.[40]

The Sustainable Packaging Coalition, which set up How2Recycle, is a membership-based collaborative that believes in the power of industry to make packaging more sustainable.

Brands and manufacturers are establishing partnerships with specialist recyclers, such as Veolia and TerraCycle. In 2018, TetraPak teamed up with Veolia to ensure each of its carton components would have an end-of-use recycling value.[41] Partnerships and direct engagement with specialists can make a difference too. In 2018, Coca-Cola announced a loan agreement with Ioniqa Technologies, to process the harder-to-recycle PET for reuse in its bottles.

Specialist investment funds like Closed Loop Partners and initiatives like the Recycling Partnership are also bringing companies and municipalities together to transform waste into valuable resources.

How2Recycle says its survey analysis in 2017[42] found 54 per cent of consumers change their behaviour as a direct result of the How2Recycle label, sending more valuable packaging to the recycling stream, and reducing the risk of contamination with non-recyclable packaging.

CERTIFICATION AND ASSESSMENT

Life-cycle assessment may help to provide a more holistic analysis, but it is important to consider how likely it is that the best end-of-use options will actually happen. Where will the product be used (and the packaging discarded) and how easy is it to access an effective recycling stream?

Summary

Is your packaging future-fit? Is it making a positive contribution to society and nature, and meeting your customer's needs: in delivery, in use and after use? There are multiple issues to overcome. The absence of product steward-ship policies, combined with a massive increase in packaged goods (for pro-cessed food, drinks, food-to-go, personal care and much more) and multiple packaging innovations, have created a perfect storm. Packaging made from non-renewable materials, designed for single use and with very few effective recycling options, means ever-increasing levels of production, and of course, waste and pollution. Just 2 per cent of all plastic on the market is turned into new packaging.

Encouragingly, sustainability is becoming a priority for consumers and is driving new approaches from businesses and governments. We are seeing new materials, new designs for products and packaging, and new business models, to narrow, slow and intensify the flows.

Recycling is evolving too, with more effective and efficient recovery sys-tems and technological developments to close the loop, creating packaging from end-of-use packaging materials.

Circular economy and 'zero waste' approaches improve sustainability, the user experience *and* save money. Reputation may be at stake here, too. If your product is recyclable, but it ends up discarded on beaches, that's not going to be a great advert for your brand.

Plastic is the biggest challenge. We're starting to hear about exciting developments, with new polymers that can be recycled infinitely, and bacte-ria that can transform plastic back into its base materials. But it could take years to replace all the single-use plastic with better materials. We should treat plastic as a fantastic resource, now, and keep it circulating in our economy.

Further resources

British Plastics Federation [accessed 11 November 2019] [Online] *Standards for Compostability* www.bpf.co.uk/Topics/Standards_for_compostability.aspx (archived at https://perma.cc/E3WM-3RDK)

European Commission (2019) [accessed 11 November 2019] *A Circular Economy for Plastics: Insights from research and innovation to inform policy and funding decisions* [Online] op.europa.eu/en/publication-detail/-/publication/33251cf9-3b0b-11e9-8d04-01aa75ed71a1/language-en/format-PDF/source-87705298 (archived at https://perma.cc/7LZL-VAE7)

European Commission: Circular Economy Plastics Factsheets and Documents [accessed 9 November 2019] [Online] ec.europa.eu/commission/publications/factsheets-european-strategy-plastics-circular-economy_en (archived at https://perma.cc/T7JZ-958Y)

TU Delft online course on sustainable packaging design for a circular economy [accessed 11 November 2019] [Online] online-learning.tudelft.nl/courses/ sustainable-packaging-in-a-circular-economy/ (archived at https://perma.cc/ ZBG8-MDZ6)

UN Environment [accessed 11 November 2019] *Interactive Guide to Beat Plastic Pollution* [Online] www.unenvironment.org/interactive/beat-plastic-pollution/ (archived at https://perma.cc/4M5D-TX6H)

Notes

1 Njus, E (2011) [accessed 24 March 2020] Ben & Jerry's co-founder Jerry Greenfield talks business ethics, non-profit partners and Occupy Wall Street, *The Oregonian* [Online] https://www.oregonlive.com/business/2011/11/ben_ jerrys_co-founder_jerry_gr.html

2 MacArthur, E and Polman, P (2018) [accessed 12 November 2019] *4 Things Companies Can Do to Fix the Plastics Problem*, World Economic Forum, 2 February [Online] www.weforum.org/agenda/2018/02/how-companies-can- fix-plastics-ellen-macarthur-paul-polman (archived at https://perma.cc/ JXJ8-UPLC)

3 Plastics Europe Association of Plastics Manufacturers (2019) [accessed 12 November 2019] *Plastics – the facts 2019* [Online] www.plasticseurope. org/en/resources/publications/1804-plastics-facts-2019 (archived at https://perma.cc/QZ68-DZFP)

4 Plastics Europe Association of Plastics Manufacturers (2019) [accessed 12 November 2019] *The Circular Economy for Plastics – A European overview* [Online] www.plasticseurope.org/en/resources/publications/1899- circular-economy-plastics-european-overview (archived at https://perma.cc/ U2C5-XWFW)

5 Directive (EU) 2018/852 of the European Parliament and of the Council of 30 May 2018 amending Directive 94/62/EC on packaging and packaging waste, PE/12/2018/REV/2 ELI: data.europa.eu/eli/dir/2018/852/oj (archived at https://perma.cc/4SCT-7YYV) [accessed 11 November 2019]

6 Packaging and Packaging Waste (2018) *Summaries of EU Legislation*, EU-Lex, 6 November [Online] https://eur-lex.europa.eu/legal-content/EN/TXT/ ?uri=legissum:l21207 (archived at https://perma.cc/W45P-4G2R)

7 European Bioplastics Association (2019) [accessed 12 November 2019] *What are Bioplastics?* Fact Sheet [Online] https://www.european-bioplastics.org/ bioplastics/

8 European Bioplastics Association (2019) [accessed 12 November 2019] *What are Bioplastics Made of?* FAQ [Online] https://www.european-bioplastics.org/ news/faq/

9   McKinsey & Company, *By Rethinking Packaging, a Company Reduces Production Costs While Enhancing Brand* [Online] www.mckinsey.com/ business-functions/operations/how-we-help-clients/reduce-packaging-costs

10   PRAG: Packaging Resources Action Group (2009) [accessed 11 November 2019] *An Introduction to Packaging and Recyclability*, November [Online] www.wrap.org.uk/sites/files/wrap/Packaging%20and%20Recyclability%20 Nov%2009%20PRAG.pdf (archived at https://perma.cc/593E-AQXA)

11   Cox, D (2018) [accessed 12 November 2019] Are we poisoning our children with plastic? *The Guardian*, 19 February [Online] www.theguardian.com/ lifeandstyle/2018/feb/19/are-we-poisoning-our-children-with-plastic (archived at https://perma.cc/TK4E-N5VG)

12   Siegle, L (2013) [accessed 13 November 2019] Are plastic jars worse for the environment? *The Guardian*, 12 May [Online] www.theguardian.com/ environment/2013/may/12/are-plastic-jars-better-than-glass (archived at https://perma.cc/B5XU-2NJZ)

13   Water Footprint Network (2017) [accessed 13 November 2019] *Reducing Wastewater by Recycling Packaging*, Blog, March [Online] https://waterfootprint.org/en/about-us/news/news/reducing-wastewater-recycling-packaging/ (archived at https://perma.cc/BP8M-C2LL)

14   Parker, L (2018) [accessed 13 November 2019] Plastic food packaging was most common beach trash in 2018, *National Geographic*, 3 September [Online] https://www.nationalgeographic.com/environment/2019/09/plastic-food-packaging-top-trash-global-beach-cleanup-2018/

15   Parker, L (2019) [accessed 11 November 2019]How the plastic bottle went from miracle container to hated garbage, *National Geographic*, 23 August [Online] https://www.nationalgeographic.com/environment/2019/08/plastic-bottles/

16   Packaging and Packaging Waste (2018) *Summaries of EU Legislation*, EU-Lex, 6 November [Online] eur-lex.europa.eu/legal-content/EN/TXT/ ?uri=legissum:l21207 (archived at https://perma.cc/W45P-4G2R)

17   Holden, E (2019) Nearly all countries agree to stem flow of plastic waste into poor nations, *The Guardian*, 10 May [Online] https://www.theguardian.com/ environment/2019/may/10/nearly-all-the-worlds-countries-sign-plastic-waste-deal-except-us (archived at https://perma.cc/4H5H-UZ4F)

18   Poole, J (2019) [accessed 15 November 2019] Packaging trends 2019: Part 1 – The search for sustainability, *Packaging Insights*, 8 January [Online] www.packaginginsights.com/news/packaging-trends-2019-part-1-the-search-for-sustainability.html

19   Trending: Billerudkorsnäs, Evian, PepsiCo aim to redesign how we hydrate, *Sustainable Brands*, 22 April [accessed 11 November 2019] [Online] sustainablebrands.com/read/chemistry-materials-packaging/trending-billerudkorsnaes-evian-pepsico-aim-to-redesign-how-we-hydrate (archived at https://perma.cc/ACB5-TKKQ)

20 Massa, B (2019) [accessed 30 October 2019] Episode 13, Circular Economy Podcast [Online] www.rethinkglobal.info/episode-13-beth-massa-ark-reusables/ (archived at https://perma.cc/CX4Z-ZYEY)

21 Loop (2019) [accessed 11 November 2019] [Online] loopstore.com/ (archived at https://perma.cc/LL2F-ESZ4)

22 About TerraCycle (2019) [accessed 13 November 2019] [Online] www.terracycle.com/en-GB/about-terracycle (archived at https://perma.cc/8WAL-F3EB)

23 PRAG: Packaging Resources Action Group (November 2009) [accessed 11 November 2019] *An Introduction to Packaging and Recyclability* [Online] www.wrap.org.uk/sites/files/wrap/Packaging%20and%20Recyclability%20Nov%2009%20PRAG.pdf (archived at https://perma.cc/593E-AQXA)

24 Splosh (2019) [accessed 11 November 2019] *About Us, Home, Zero Waste* [Online] www.splosh.com/ (archived at https://perma.cc/GLE2-Q25N)

25 Coca Cola Great Britain (2019) [accessed 12 November 2019] *Is This Our Chance to Stop Plastic Becoming Waste?*, 21 May [Online] www.coca-cola.co.uk/stories/stop-plastic-becoming-waste (archived at https://perma.cc/D9K5-6HXG)

26 Baldwin, C (2019) [accessed 16 November 2019] Evolving plastic packaging strategies – beyond the straw, *Sustainable Brands*, 15 May [Online] sustainablebrands.com/read/chemistry-materials-packaging/evolving-plastic-packaging-strategies-beyond-the-straw (archived at https://perma.cc/8J4K-6W59)

27 Garçon Wines (2019) [accessed 9 November 2019] [Online] https://www.garconwines.com/

28 Frugal Cartons and wooden wind turbines: the best green innovations of the week, *EDIE Newsroom*, 27 October 2017 [accessed 9 November 2019] [Online] https://www.edie.net/news/8/Frugal-Cartons-and-wooden-wind-turbines--the-best-green-innovations-of-the-week/

29 How2Recycle (2019) [accessed 15 November 2019] [Online] how2recycle.info/ (archived at https://perma.cc/M6B6-V5EN)

30 Poole, J (2019) [accessed 15 November 2019] Packaging trends 2019: Part 1 – The search for sustainability, *Packaging Insights*, 8 January [Online] www.packaginginsights.com/news/packaging-trends-2019-part-1-the-search-for-sustainability.html

31 Colorado State University (2018) [accessed 15 November 2019] 'Infinitely' recyclable polymer shows practical properties of plastics, *Phys.org/Science*, X, 26 April [Online] phys.org/news/2018-04-infinitely-recyclable-polymer-properties-plastics.html (archived at https://perma.cc/4Q9C-D8DD)

32 TU Delft online course on sustainable packaging design for a circular economy [accessed 11 November 2019] [Online] online-learning.tudelft.nl/courses/sustainable-packaging-in-a-circular-economy/ (archived at https://perma.cc/ZBG8-MDZ6)

33 Carlsberg Green Fiber Bottle (2019) [accessed 15 November 2019] [Online] www.carlsberg.com/en/green-fibre-bottle/ (archived at https://perma.cc/X4GC-V5BP)

34 Dell (2019) [accessed 9 November 2019] [Online] corporate.delltechnologies.com/en-gb/social-impact/advancing-sustainability/sustainable-products-and-services/materials-use/waste-as-a-resource.htm (archived at https://perma.cc/CT5G-CAUW)

35 Revolutionary P&G technology restores used plastic to virgin-like quality, *Sustainable Brands*, 21 July 2017 [accessed 9 November 2019] [Online] sustainablebrands.com/read/cleantech/revolutionary-p-g-technology-restores-used-plastic-to-virgin-like-quality (archived at https://perma.cc/W2C3-3CNK)

36 Carrington, D (2018) [accessed 15 November 2019] Scientists accidentally create mutant enzyme that eats plastic bottles, *The Guardian*, 16 April [Online] www.theguardian.com/environment/2018/apr/16/scientists-accidentally-create-mutant-enzyme-that-eats-plastic-bottles (archived at https://perma.cc/2GWU-QZLM)

37 BP plc (2019) [accessed 15 November 2019] *Sustainability* [Online] www.bp.com/en/global/bp-petrochemicals/sustainability.html (archived at https://perma.cc/QT3W-SNK5)

38 How blockchain is helping the Plastic Bank create a global economy of 'social plastic', *Sustainable Brands*, 11 April 2018 [accessed 19 November 2019] [Online] sustainablebrands.com/read/finance-investment/how-blockchain-is-helping-the-plastic-bank-create-a-global-economy-of-social-plastic (archived at https://perma.cc/3EUZ-A7SM)

39 Plastics Europe Association of Plastics Manufacturers (2019) [accessed 12 November 2019] *The Circular Economy for Plastics – A European Overview* [Online] www.plasticseurope.org/en/resources/publications/1899-circular-economy-plastics-european-overview (archived at https://perma.cc/U2C5-XWFW)

40 New Plastics Economy (2019) [accessed 12 February 2019] *Global Commitment 2019 Progress Report* [Online] https://www.newplasticseconomy.org/about/publications/global-commitment-2019-progress-report

41 Poole, J (2019) [accessed 15 November 2019] Packaging trends 2019: Part 1 – The search for sustainability, *Packaging Insights*, 8 January [Online] www.packaginginsights.com/news/packaging-trends-2019-part-1-the-search-for-sustainability.html

42 Cramer, K (2017) [accessed 15 November 2019] For How2Recycle, 2017 was a year of acceleration, *How2Recycle*, 13 March [Online] how2recycle.info/news/2018/for-how2recycle-2017-was-a-year-of-acceleration (archived at https://perma.cc/SA3W-PQ67)

PART THREE

What does this mean for supply chains?

11

Supply chain strategy and planning

If repair, remanufacturing and recycling become commonplace, would we still ship our raw materials across great distances to be recycled?

DR DAI MORGAN, INSTITUTE FOR MANUFACTURING,
UNIVERSITY OF CAMBRIDGE (2014)[1]

This chapter focuses on how our 'traditional' supply chains will evolve to support the transition to circular approaches: for products, services, processes or entire business models. After a quick reminder of the global **drivers and megatrends** and the **features of traditional supply chains**, we examine **supply chains for the circular economy**, asking:

- How will supply chain **strategies** evolve, with expanded **scope** and a more **complex** range of choices and trade-offs, and aiming for resilience and agility?

- What kind of **network designs** will best support circular models, with **distributed manufacturing** and locally recovered materials? What are the key **principles** for these sustainable models?

- Switching from ownership to **access** models and delivering **performance** instead of products will create radically different flows of materials and components and feature new partnerships and support systems. How do we design supply chains to support these new flows of materials and value? Which **enabling technologies** will change inbound flows, manufacture and repair, and provide rich sources of information?

- How can the **supply chain** develop its own **circular initiatives**, particularly for packaging, consumables and 'assets', including warehouses and vehicles?

- How will we define and measure **criteria** for supply chain **success**?
- What kind of changes will we need to incorporate in **planning** supply chain activities? A section by Jo Conlon looks at how **product life-cycle management** supports circular approaches.

Global drivers and megatrends

In Chapter 5, we looked at the complex factors affecting economics and geopolitics, consumer behaviour, business success and supply chain resilience. The continuing population growth, global power shifts and supply and demand imbalances all create risks for businesses. Consumer behaviour is changing, with millennials seeing access to products and services as more important than ownership. The maker and trader movements are enabling anyone to become a 'prosumer', turning their hobby into an income stream and maybe into a business. Demand for more individual or personalized products is driving **mass-customization** approaches, postponing the last stage of manufacture until confirmation of the order and final specification.

Technology is transforming both capture of and access to knowledge and data: what is that product made from? How can I repair my phone? Where is the nearest rental car? Can I 'sell' the spare seat on my daily commute? The World Economic Forum lists its 'Top 10 emerging technologies of 2015', including *additive manufacturing* and *distributed manufacturing* (referred to as 'redistributed manufacturing by other organizations, including a European research programme, RECODE).[2] Both of these will present challenges for the global, long-distance supply chains we see now for many sectors. We look at distributed manufacturing in more detail in Chapter 12.

Risk management and resilience is now a critical success factor for supply chains, and in Chapter 5, we reviewed the World Economic Forum Risks Report. Supply chain risks include climate-related weather disruptions (droughts, floods, hurricanes, etc), other natural disasters, supply or demand shocks (potentially exacerbated by 'hedging' and stockpiling), geopolitical issues, brand reputation, terrorism, security and corruption.[3] We return to sourcing and supply risks in Chapter 12.

Traditional supply chains

As companies 'offshored' in the early 21st century to find cheaper costs of labour and new sources of materials, supply chains became more complex, with multiple tiers of suppliers and transport links. The World Business Council for Sustainable Development (WBCSD) describes a 'supply web', with a disaggregated network of suppliers who 'cooperate and compete to extract or grow the primary resource, to process and manufacture it and many other ingredients or components. These are then transported and stored at intermediate points, before final distribution and sale to the end-user.'[4] These supply webs include 'enabling functions' such as finance, security and insurance. They rely on technology, with enterprise resource planning systems, vendor-managed inventory, consignment tracking and other systems to reduce cost, improve service levels and optimize inventory. For example, in automotive supply chains, electric vehicle batteries require four stages:

1 **material extraction:** with 10 different metals and minerals;
2 **processing:** involving six different smelting, binding and other manufacturing processes for the various materials;
3 **component manufacture:** producing eight different types of compound materials and components;
4 **final manufacture** of the battery cell.

Traditional supply chains **optimize forward flows**, aiming to balance the cost and service trade-off, with reverse flows seen as inconvenient. Reverse logistics may exist only to return incorrect, unwanted or malfunctioning products, in small, irregular quantities or (worse) as part of a major product recall. The increase in 'omnichannel' logistics, with consumers ordering online or in-store, and collecting from the store or choosing a delivery method, has also increased 'consumer power'. Consumers expect choice, including efficient and user-friendly ways to return products should they wish to. This forces retailers, in particular, to adjust ways of working and adapt operations to support reverse flows. Modern supply chains tend to be:

- **long,** in both fulfilment timescales and distance;
- **complex,** in numbers and tiers of suppliers and countries involved;
- involving greater quantities of **stock** and higher levels of **obsolescence,** worsening as product life-cycles shorten to stimulate demand for the latest version;
- **lacking transparency,** with the final product manufacturer, brand or retailer unable to be certain about the actors involved in their supply chain. Identities of suppliers, in which countries, the exact nature of the

FIGURE 11.1   Supply chains for a circular economy

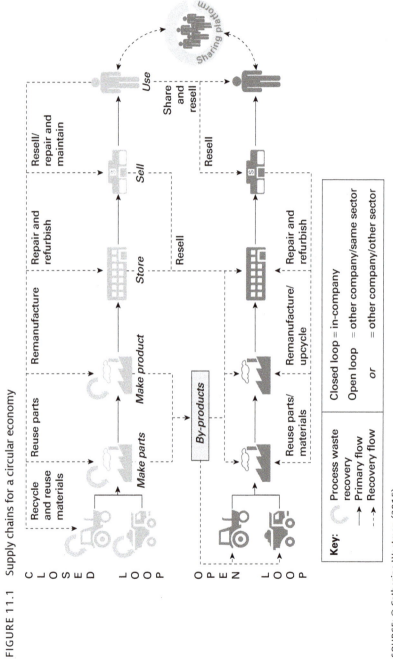

SOURCE: © Catherine Weetman (2015)

materials and their sources, and the ethical and legal standards may be unclear.

Reputational risk is high on the agenda, with supply chain teams aiming to avoid appearing in the headlines (such as the negative news stories from the Rana Plaza and UK 'horsemeat' scandals).

In its report *Beyond Supply Chains – Empowering responsible value chains* (2014),[5] the World Economic Forum looks at how the supply chains of leading companies evolve to underpin 'improvements in profitability while benefiting society and the environment', gaining a 'triple advantage'. Scope extends with a 'landscape of supply chain practices', including product design, end-of-life activities and 'cross-functional practices'. The cross-functional practices include technologies to trace materials and improve supply chain visibility through data and analytics, and 'labour standards', for example, fair wages, and 'high environment, health, safety standards'.

Supply chains for a circular economy

The circular economy will transform these 'traditional' supply chains, extending beyond the point of sale, and creating complexity and new challenges for supply chain teams:

- engaging with the end-user to help maintain the product, perhaps refilling or repairing on site;
- finding ways to recover the product successfully for refurbishment, remanufacture or recycling;
- engaging with new partners and customers to exchange by-products and recycled/recyclable materials.

A more holistic view of the supply chain can optimize value from reverse and by-products or symbiotic resource flows, in addition to delivering the 'mainstream' product and subsidiary flows. Figure 11.1 illustrates the typical flows in a circular economy, with recycled materials, by-products and recovery of products and materials.

Network design

Network designs will evolve, as each business finds and implements additional circular flows and transitions to new commercial models, based on service and performance. Early-stage partnerships with local specialists can simplify and de-risk changes, with the opportunity to bring key processes in-house to improve assurance and control or take advantage of critical mass. Modular product designs and increased material recovery may need different logistics networks and operations. New by-products may be perishable or hazardous (eg biofuels), with fluctuating volumes. Reverse logistics must retain product value and manage fluctuating volumes and multiple return loops.

McKinsey sees companies 'splintering monolithic supply chains into smaller, nimbler ones', improving service whilst reducing complexity and cost.[6] As companies consolidated manufacturing and expanded into new sales territories, products (and *stock-keeping units*) proliferated, making it difficult to forecast sales and maintain high service levels. Companies are rethinking networks, perhaps using Pareto analysis to segment the product range:

- manufacturing high-volume stable products centrally, in low-cost locations;
- making volatile, high-volume demand locally;
- while low-volume and low-demand-volatility products may be 'near-shored' to reduce production costs.

Faster market access, minimizing lost sales at the same time as maintaining low inventories, optimizes the cost-to-service trade-off. Producing close to the point of demand allows much shorter lead times, enabling demand-driven, rather than forecast-driven, supply chains.

Figure 11.2 compares features of distributed and centralized supply chains. The asset-light, lower-cost benefits of centralized networks contrast with more resilient, agile, decentralized networks. Disruption to flows can cause serious issues in centralized networks, whereas the extra nodes and links in decentralized systems include more sources and options for working around blockages and supply issues. McKinsey found that 'agile companies' achieved deliveries of 94 per cent on time and in full (OTIF) with 20 per cent less inventory, compared with 87 per cent OTIF in other companies.[7]

The linear supply chains for some high-volume mass production sectors, such as automotive, feature 'supplier parks', with key suppliers co-located next to assembly plants. Circular supply chains will develop **industrial ecosystem** approaches, with by-products and other symbiotic flows allowing eco-park occupants to share technology, get more from materials and inputs, co-create energy and recover value from outputs. These industrial eco-park models are emerging in several countries, supporting symbiotic flows

FIGURE 11.2   Supply chain network design

Centralized network	Centralized		Distributed	Distributed network
• Low operating and asset costs	✦	Reliability	★	• Agile, resilient, responsive
• Make to stock	★	Assets	*Local partners*	• Make on demand
• Long lead times and higher inventories, more obsolescence	★	Cost	✦	• Choice of materials and sources
	☆	Agility	★	• Multiple stock locations to reduce risk from regional issues
• Postponement and kitting to customize for local market	☆	Resilience	★	
	✦	Responsiveness	★	
	Many	Suppliers and tiers	*Few*	
• Transport efficiency – larger, fewer loads	*Many*	Stock and SKUs	*Few*	• Transport mode to match urgency
	Global	Scale	*Local*	
	Disposal	End of life	*Recovery*	

Key: ★ high need   ☆ low need

SOURCE: © Catherine Weetman

between businesses, with shared facilities to process effluent (and recover nutrients) and generate clean energy on site. The United Nations is helping to transform industrial zones in Vietnam into eco-industrial parks.[8] The aim is to create environmentally sound, sustainable networks using cleaner production and new technologies to minimize hazardous waste, *GHG* emissions and water pollution, and properly manage chemicals.

Key principles

From the perspective of sustainability, or SixSigma, we could view logistics as a series of wastes. Every transport link, storage and handling operation involves energy and equipment, with inputs of fossil fuels and consequential harmful emissions to air and atmosphere (and for shipping, polluting water). In 2010, developing tools to help businesses understand the challenges and opportunities of sustainable business models, I created a set of design principles for supply chains. This became the '8 Sustainability (8S) Principles', shown in Figure 11.3.

1 **Simplify** the design and *bill of materials*. Aim to reduce complexity and waste, using simpler and more natural materials. Simpler resources require less energy and cost to separate for reuse or biodegrading. Mixed materials are more likely to be *downcycled*. How can you apply 'resource

FIGURE 11.3   '8S' principles for supply chains

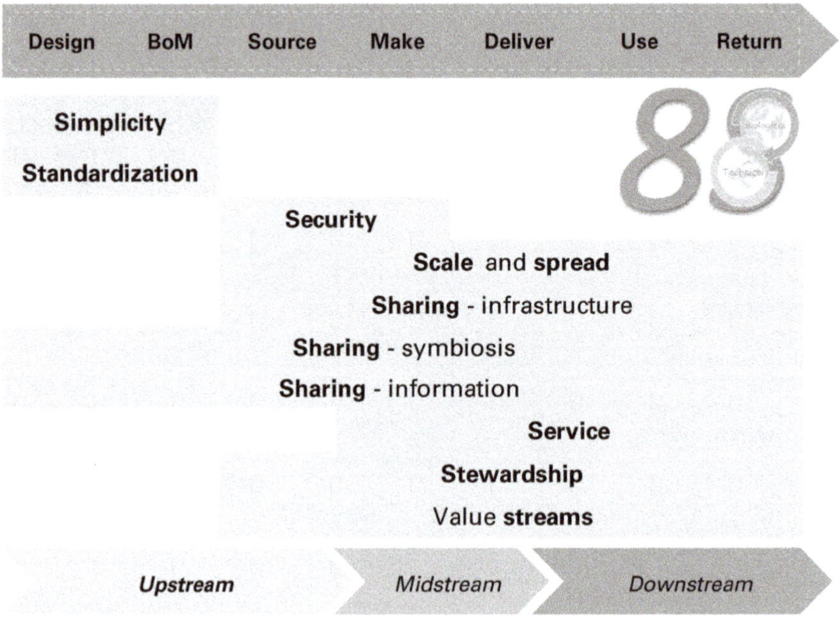

SOURCE: © Catherine Weetman (2015)

efficiency' to the materials themselves, by reducing 'embedded' resources (especially from overseas), reducing energy and eliminating waste? *Life-cycle assessment* (LCA) may help this, and we cover this in Chapter 12.

2 **Standardize** design, across brands, with the ability to repair or upgrade later. Modular designs can help with remanufacturing, parts swap-out and on-site repairs, and future product upgrades. Modular approaches and clear design principles can enhance the efficiency of future product development. Are there opportunities to collaborate with your sector peers, to create industry standards for non-core parts (similar to the industry-standard charger for mobile phones)?

3 Improve **security** of supply, for both materials and suppliers. Priorities for future supplier and production locations will focus on where resources will be available, rather than the lowest labour or supply costs. Can you improve the security of supply by finding recycled inputs to replace virgin materials? Recycled materials will not be risk-free, but you may be able to reduce price volatility, avoid geopolitical supply risks and so on. Do your suppliers, in all the upstream tiers, meet environmental standards? Are there risks of climate-related or geopolitical disruption? You might consider sourcing similar or substitute materials from more than one geographic region, to minimize the impact of disruptions to supply. The

supply chain team should recommend what to buy, from where in the world and from which sustainable suppliers. Are the materials themselves safe, or might they contain undesirable chemicals? How can you assure this into the future? How robust is the data from suppliers? Can you trust it enough to publish it? Are there certifying bodies, or do you need to audit the suppliers?

4 Supply chain networks for circular models will aim to reduce both **scale** and geographic **spread**. Resilient manufacturing, geared to customize products for local markets, is adopting decentralized, **distributed** models. As energy costs increase, and pressure to decarbonize supply chains grows, shorter supply chains make more sense. Fewer supplier tiers improve transparency and closer connections help with understanding potential supply issues. Supply networks that include a range of suppliers in different regions, and have options for alternative or substitute materials or components, will improve resilience and reduce risks for security of supply. Increasing the number of stock-holding locations tends to increase safety stock (an accepted formula is the square root of the increase in locations; so increasing from two locations to four would double safety stock, whilst decreasing the number of locations from four to two would halve the safety stock). However, shorter lead times for replenishing inventory, and potentially smaller batch sizes (as manufacturing is now local) would decrease stock. Holding more stock of raw materials from distant locations may be cheaper and less risky than holding stock of finished products made in those locations.

5 **Shared approaches** can create multiple benefits along the supply chain:

o **Shared-user infrastructure**, such as platforms and exchanges, can reduce costs or improve response times, especially if your own network lacks sufficient critical mass. There are also examples of collaborative logistics networks with apparent competitors working together, such as milk cooperatives in the UK, and the Openfield farmer-owned storage facilities. We look at outbound distribution networks in Chapter 12.

o Are there opportunities to **share facilities or equipment** with supply chain partners, or with local businesses? Can you work with neighbours to build a critical mass for more specialist and cost-effective waste processing or energy production?

o Can you share value, setting up **symbiotic flows**, transforming waste materials to *by-products*, or recovering energy or water as a resource for a local partner?

o You could **share information** with **customers** and end-users about the supply chain impacts of products and materials, about sources, materials, supplier certifications and so on. It may include sharing 'footprint' details for the product or materials, including energy, water use, chemicals, emissions, etc. It aims to provide 'product honesty': is it safe, ethical, energy- and water-efficient, and does it use renewable resources?

o How might you **share information** with your **supply chain partners** to help their efficiency and effectiveness? Providing your sales data or forecasts could help them forecast future demand for their products, or you might work more closely with a range of suppliers and other supply chain partners to look at market trends and forecasts.

6 **Service** and performance models have more complex supply chain needs:

o For your customers, you may need to set up a **service** and maintenance network, with a supporting supply chain to provide engineers with parts, tools and consumables. What repair and refurbishment are required – will it be maintenance on site, or supply to field engineers? How will products return at end-of-use, and how will you protect their value and functionality during the reverse flows?

o Are there opportunities to procure services instead of products or access straightforward rent/lease models for assets or consumables in your supply chain? Could you buy 'tyres by the mile' for vehicles or 'pay per lux' for lighting in your warehouse?

7 Product **stewardship** approaches will become more common, aiming to take responsibility for the entire life-cycle of the product and materials. How will you design and organize the supply chain to support this? Are you recovering products to process in-house, or routing them to specialist partners, for dismantling and recycling?

8 New **streams** of by-products, co-products, symbiotic and circular flows will develop, into and out of your supply chain. These may have different logistics requirements, such as bulk transportation, temperature control or hazardous elements. Their volumes may be difficult to predict or control, making planning more complex and challenging. There may be new reverse flows for repair/reuse/upgrade/remanufacture, or take-back initiatives for product, packaging and waste. How can you design and manage supply loops to retain the value of all material, component and products – the *nutrients* – as they flow through the network? British

Sugar produces 12 different by-products from its raw material input, sugar beet.[9] Some of these, such as soil and aggregate, use bulk transport. Others, such as bio-ethanol, are hazardous. Customers span several different market sectors, such as agriculture, animal feed producers and even cosmetics.

Delivering access and performance

Moving to a service or performance business model will require fundamental changes to the supporting supply chains:

- finding effective ways to monitor the condition of products and equipment at customer sites;

- deciding how best to provide maintenance services (in the field or return to a repair site, in-house or subcontracted to a repairer);

- setting up flows of maintenance parts and consumables ('service parts logistics').

Optimum solutions for all of these will evolve, as we switch to access from ownership and as the patterns of durability, breakages and maintenance cycles settle down. A survey of supply chain practitioners in 2016 – 'The Growth of the Circular Economy' – ranked the most effective 'circular' incentives for customers and industry.[10] The top incentives thought to encourage consumer returns were rebates; making it easy to return a product to a 'brick-and-mortar' location; and pre-paid shipping options. The top three incentives for industry were physical reclaim of the product by the producer or distributor; offering a turnkey packaging and pickup service; the manufacturer refurbishing the product and returning it for continued use.

The design and supply chain

The focus of the supply chain will switch from forward flows, concentrating on delivering the primary products or services, to providing a 'nutrients network', receiving and distributing a wide range of materials and products into and out of other organizations in the same industry sector or across into other sectors. These flows will prioritize renewable or recycled materials, aiming to achieve 'zero extraction'.

FIGURE 11.4 Nutrient flows – recycled or renewable

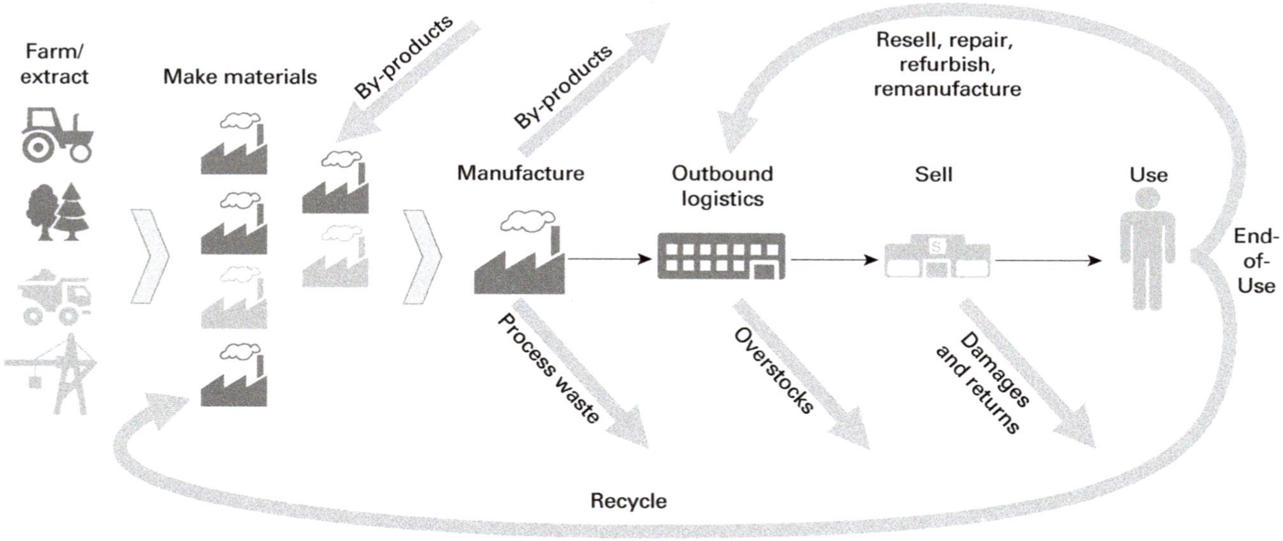
Farm/ extract
Make materials
By-products
By-products
Resell, repair, refurbish, remanufacture
Manufacture
Outbound logistics
Sell
Use
End-of-Use
Process waste
Overstocks
Damages and returns
Recycle

SOURCE: © Catherine Weetman (2016)

Many of the new 'nutrient flows' illustrated in Figure 11.4 will bring supply chain challenges. In addition to 'mainstream' flows, such as boxed, long-life product being delivered to fulfil orders, there may be bulk flows of (at least initially) unpredictable volumes of by-products, perhaps perishable. Forward orders for these new by-products may be difficult to secure, with supply chain teams finding buyers for whatever quantity and grade of by-product or recyclate the production process generates, on a day-to-day basis.

As these flows increase, you might look for opportunities to supply higher-value markets. *Green chemistry* and *biorefining* might create new, valuable products in addition to energy recovery from waste, or you might find a niche market, needing different packaging. Getting involved in product and process design means you can help generate ideas for new flows and markets, and flag benefits or issues for the different options.

Partnership approaches and knowledge-sharing will replace traditional, more adversarial relationships between suppliers and buyers. **Procurement** teams can help speed up the circular economy journey, pushing to continuously improve on materials, and secure future resources. Can you find new sources of recycled materials? Alternatively, could you collaborate with a specialist or university to develop specific recycling processes? Are your sources sustainable (including their land use), or competing with food production? Can you encourage your suppliers to explore circular economy opportunities for their businesses? Recovery loops for remanufacturing and repair may need new partnerships and relationships, with innovative contracts and ways to measure and share value and knowledge. Again, you may choose to outsource at the start, and then develop in-house capabilities to either create more value or protect intellectual property.

In the next chapter, we look more deeply at how circular inputs, product and process design, and circular flows all affect supply chain scope, complexity and organizations.

Enabling technologies

In Chapter 4, we saw a wide range of digital technologies supporting the transition to a circular economy. Some of these will have disruptive effects on supply chains. The *Internet of Things* and *big data* can provide richer sources of information about products, their location, their condition and performance, as well as feeding information from suppliers and logistics providers to illuminate the supply chain itself. Data will be more accurate and up to date and can be interrogated as required, or used as a dashboard to direct attention where needed. The internet can link together multiple supply chain partners, improving transparency and trust and helping optimize cost, service, agility and resilience.

Additive manufacturing and *3D printing* will extend across more industries to enable local, on-demand and bespoke manufacturing as well as transforming spare parts supply chains and product longevity. We look at the practical use of these in Chapter 12.

Accelerators

In reviewing the 8S principles, we looked at product stewardship approaches and collaboration options, sharing facilities and information with companies in your sector or supply chain. Major companies are setting up **knowledge-sharing** networks, encouraging their suppliers to share ideas and best practice on a range of topics, including environmental sustainability. At least two of the 'big four' UK supermarkets created supplier collaboration programmes, with one promising not to use improvements as a cost-reduction lever. Specialist 'curated' platforms can help the exchange of knowledge, reaching across geographic boundaries. 2degrees Network provides 'fully linked collaboration' to help 'major organizations cut costs, reduce risks and grow'. It provides both public and private online services, enabling clients to collaborate with an unlimited number of stakeholders, sharing best practice and information to solve practical problems. Members can ask for help in finding information or solving a problem, post articles or attend conferences and workshops. A report in 2015 lists improvements in energy-efficiency, waste recirculation, procurement and logistics, plus strategic benefits including innovation, risk reduction, transparency and brand reputation.[11]

Circular initiatives in the supply chain

Even if your organization is not yet adopting circular strategies, you can integrate circular approaches into the supply chain, especially for facilities, assets and consumables. Earlier in this chapter, we looked at shared-user platforms, exchanges and facilities. For equipment and consumables, can you work with your suppliers to help them become 'circular'? The sharing economy could include collaborating with local businesses to share equipment for peaks, or perhaps a sector initiative for returnable transit packaging. You may be able to buy good-as-new remanufactured or used items and sell your unused or end-of-life assets – platforms like Warp It connect businesses to exchange equipment. For packaging, can you influence pack design to be more logistics-efficient? Is the outer and transit packaging reusable and recyclable?

Success criteria

How should we change our approach to measuring success and progress? Instead of return on capital employed (ROCE), business measures will focus on **return on resources employed** (RORE), aiming to extract value from every molecule of materials, energy and water that comes into the business. Having purchased the raw materials and other inputs to make the product, consigning some of them to waste (and perhaps having to pay to dispose of that waste) does not make good business sense.

Success criteria for supply chains will broaden beyond cost and service, to include agility, risk management and progress towards circular goals. How transparent is the supply chain? Which suppliers, materials and processes do you have confidence in, and which are more obscure? Targets for 'zero waste to landfill' and GHG reduction will switch to measuring increasing flows of nutrients and value, both into and out of the business.

The Future-Fit Business Benchmark, an open-source initiative based on *Natural Step* principles, issued its second public draft in 2015.[12] The Future-Fit Business Benchmark (FFBB) recognizes that a fundamental change is required, to move global companies away from a belief that 'reducing their impacts year-on-year is sufficient. But science tells us that we're already living far beyond the carrying capacity of the planet.' The FFBB aims to 'give business leaders the tools to see where the destination is, and to assess how far away they are'. The benchmark includes 'a set of performance criteria that describe a company that is fit for the future: one that will flourish while adding to the well-being of society as a whole'. The goals cover physical resources, operational waste, physical presence, product use and waste, as well as employees, communities, customers, suppliers and company owners. How will you measure new forms of value created, perhaps in recovering higher quality and greater volumes of products and materials at end-of-use?

Supply chain planning

Supply chain planning will also be more complex, reflecting the difficulties of predicting return flows of products and materials, with different rates of recovery at each stage. Measuring flows from different sectors and market channels, together with ratios of product for resale, refurbishment, remanufacture or recycling, will merge with predictions for improvements designed to improve product longevity, rates of return or reduced damages in the reverse supply chain.

FIGURE 11.5   ERP II modules

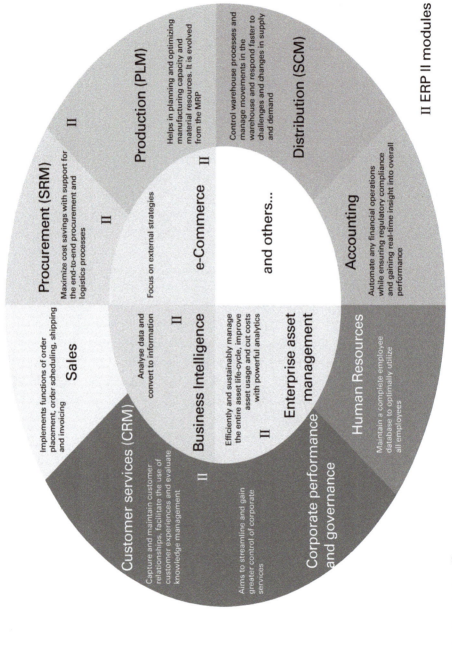

II ERP II modules

Procurement (SRM)
Maximize cost savings with support for the end-to-end procurement and logistics processes

Production (PLM)
Helps in planning and optimizing manufacturing capacity and material resources. It is evolved from the MRP

Distribution (SCM)
Control warehouse processes and manage movements in the warehouse and respond faster to challenges and changes in supply and demand

Sales
Implements functions of order placement, order scheduling, shipping and invoicing

e-Commerce
Focus on external strategies

and others...

Accounting
Automate any financial operations while ensuring regulatory compliance and gaining real-time insight into overall performance

Customer services (CRM)
Capture and maintain customer relationships, facilitate the use of customer experiences and evaluate knowledge management

Business Intelligence
Analyse data and convert to information

Enterprise asset management
Efficiently and sustainably manage the entire asset life-cycle, improve asset usage and cut costs with powerful analytics

Human Resources
Maintain a complete employee database to optimally utilize all employees

Corporate performance and governance
Aims to streamline and gain greater control of corporate services

SOURCE: Shing Hin Yeung[13]

Many companies use enterprise resource planning (ERP) to integrate procurement, production, distribution, inventory management and sales (see example in Figure 11.5). ERP evolved from early material requirements planning (MRP) and manufacturing resource planning (MRP II). ERP systems track a range of business resources: including raw materials, manufacturing capacity, inventory and cash, plus commitments such as sales and purchase orders. Databases in ERP track and share this data across business functions, and potentially to outside stakeholders.

Designing products that use fewer, simpler materials and components, require fewer (or less harmful) process inputs, and are more durable and repairable, presents challenges to product designers, operations management, and for obtaining and incorporating feedback from users and those involved in disassembly, recovery and recycling. Product life-cycle management (PLM) systems provide a means of sharing this information and engaging stakeholders all along the supply chain, with the aim of improving the design of products to be used again, and for longer.

Product life-cycle management

Contribution by Jo Conlon

Across manufacturing industries, companies are innovating to meet the challenges of global competition, such as short product development and delivery times, growing customer needs, tighter regulations and legislation.[14] A product's life-cycle is characterized by a sequence of stages that reflect the competitive environment: introduction, growth, maturity and decline. Product life-cycle management (PLM) systems enable the '3Ps' (people, processes and product data) to be integrated across the extended enterprise, helping to manage the complexities of product that is created, sourced and retailed globally,[15] enabling reduced product cost, time to market and improved quality (see Figure 11.6).

PLM developed from computer-aided design (CAD), product data management (PDM) and collaborative production management (CPM) and continues to evolve to support the integration of SMAC (social, mobile, analytics and cloud) technologies and the strategic ambitions of the future digital enterprise. The PLM market has grown in traditional engineering industries like automotive and transportation, as well as expanded into non-traditional PLM markets like fast-moving consumer goods, energy, architectural and construction. Stark (2011)[16] explains that this is driven by a

FIGURE 11.6   PLM supporting and driving the value chain

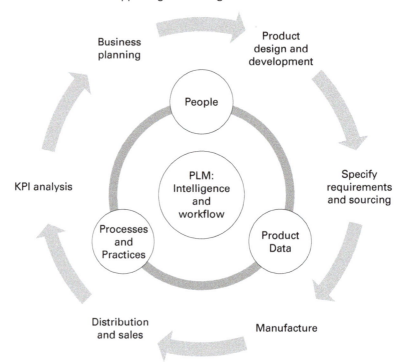

need for organizations to improve and formalize their capability to manage products across their life-cycle.

How businesses use PLM

Today's complex global supply chains have evolved to benefit from the substantial cost advantages available from offshore sourcing and manufacturing. The main features of PLM are categorized by Corallo et al (2013)[17] as managerial, technological and collaborative, defining PLM as 'a strategic business approach that supports all the phases of product life-cycle, from concept to disposal, providing a unique and timed product data source. Integrating people, processes and technologies and assuring information consistency, traceability and long-term archiving, PLM enables organizations to collaborate within and across the extended enterprise'.

Connected PLM systems enable collaborative design of both product and process, with ideas, information and feedback from designers, engineering, suppliers, service teams, logistics, customers and users. Typical stages in product design and development include:

- concept design and specifications;
- specify a bill of materials;
- implementation: procure, manufacture, assemble, sell and deliver/install;
- in-use: operate/use, maintain, support;
- end-of-use: recover or dispose, refurbish, remanufacture, resell, recycle.

Figure 11.7 shows the types of information provided at each stage of the supply chain, supporting efficient and effective product development processes and providing critical data to people in each function of the business.

There are significant benefits along the supply chain, for the company, its suppliers and partners. Integration of data into a central hub provides universal, real-time access to all users, improving efficiency and effectiveness. This, combined with rapid data updates, improves the quality and speed of decision-making and reduces time to market. Other benefits include:

- increased efficiency with easy retrieval of the latest version means less time 'searching and checking';
- reduced material costs;
- increased accuracy in shared documentation, eg QA manuals/customs requirements, etc;
- transparency and legislation compliance;
- intellectual property can be reused and shared at enterprise level;
- easier dissemination of best practice;
- enterprise resource planning and customer relationship management data can be integrated with PLM for better decision-making;
- potential to integrate tracking data (eg from the Internet of Things).

The scope and functionality of PLM systems are extending and evolving to improve management of environmental risk, life-cycle cost and customer and end-user service demands.

PLM for a circular economy

Consumers are asking for more visible information about clothing and the environmental aspects of textile and apparel production.[18] Organizations are increasingly collaborating, tackling global challenges by sharing product information and sustainability performance across industry sectors. An example is the Sustainable Apparel Coalition (SAC), which originated in 2009. The coalition's main focus is to build on the Higg Index, a standardized supply

FIGURE 11.7 Information and data flow

	Design and BoM	Source and procure	Manufacture	Logistics and sales	Use and recovery
Product	Material library, CAD, parts lists, technical and performance specs, trend analysis, substitutions	Materials: define, cost, elements, origin, footprint, certificates	Time (cost), construction specification, quality standards	Parts lists, substitutes, technical specifications	Product, part and material durability feedback
Process	Plan, concept definition and development, prototyping and material test results	Compliance and CSR audits, contract terms, supplier evaluation	Set-up/ clean-down, safety and quality results, compliance to legislation	End-of-use guidelines; sales and seasonality patterns, purchase order management	In-use test results
People	Designers, engineers, suppliers, service inputs	Suppliers: standards, audit results, quotations	Outsource partner standards and audits	Sales and logistics feedback eg packaging, installation	Service technician and user feedback

chain management tool for all industry participants to understand the environmental and social and labour impacts of making and selling their products and services.

Generating and using product data at the design and manufacturing stages is straightforward. Generating product data during use and end-of-use phases is more complex, and there is often an information gap after the point of sale. Figure 11.8 illustrates how PLM can help close this information gap, feeding information about in-use and end-of-use to inform product development, material selection and support circular business models.

Largely driven by the circular economy, companies see the value of maintaining information on a product throughout its life-cycle; and PLM is extending to manage this rich level of data to support decision-making. Technologies such as IoT, GPS and RFID supported by next-generation PLM solutions offer a new approach establishing an information cycle through the whole product life-cycle (ie BOL, MOL, EOL). This information then provides feedback to inform improvements regarding design, performance and durability. There are further opportunities in extending PLM to connect with other companies through industrial symbiosis (IS) to promote sharing of information regarding materials, water, energy and infrastructure.[19] This information flow or digital thread could continue seamlessly through reuse to the end-of-use, with further feedback to the designer and producer, supporting sustainable development. PLM systems are a key enabler for new business models featuring closed-loop supply structures, supply chain transparency and collaboration.

FIGURE 11.8   Closing the information loop

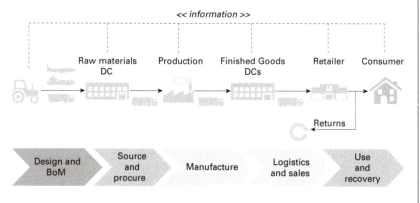

Summary

The World Economic Forum concludes that 'circular business models will gain an ever-greater competitive advantage in the years to come because they create more value from each unit of resource'.[20] Circular approaches mean rethinking and redesigning complex systems, with collaboration and knowledge-sharing amongst *all* the stakeholders. The scope and scale of supply chains will change profoundly, with increased engagement both upstream and downstream (perhaps using PLM to share feedback and designs).

Markets for more durable products and 'product as a service' offers mean different designs and sustainable materials: purer, non-toxic, renewable, recycled and recyclable. Each input will need a traceable 'backstory': origin and purity of ingredients; quality and consistency; supplier ethics. Effective, efficient, agile and resilient supply chains will create a foundation for circular strategies, with redesign of products, safe and secure material sources, sharing and collaboration. Rethinking commercial approaches, including service or performance models, may require new supply chains for maintenance or recovery, flows of new and evolving by-products and symbiotic flows may involve different logistics challenges, and recovery of products and resources adds complexity to reverse supply chains.

There are circular opportunities inside the supply chain, even if the business has not yet embraced the concept. Opportunities include procuring assets and consumables as a service, shared infrastructure and equipment, or finding ways to create value from waste.

Measuring success will focus on return on resources employed (RORE). How can you use the supply chain to create new value? Where might value be lost or destroyed, for the company, suppliers, customers, employees, local communities and other living systems? How can you keep raising the bar higher, to move from 'less bad' to 'more good', recovering and regenerating resources and revitalizing living systems?

Further resources

Future-Fit Business Benchmark [Online] http://futurefitbusiness.org (archived at https://perma.cc/MB76-6CE2)

WBCSD, ERM (2015) [accessed 8 April 2016] *Building Resilience in Global Supply Chains* [Online] wbcsdpublications.org/project/building-resilience-in-global-supply-chains/ (archived at https://perma.cc/ZKS7-KMKQ)

Notes

1 Morgan, D (2014) Predicting the unpredictable: the future of manufacturing, *Institute for Manufacturing Review*, **1**, University of Cambridge

2 Meyerson, B (4 March 2015) [accessed 8 April 2016] *Top 10 Emerging Technologies of 2015*, World Economic Forum [Online] www.weforum.org/agenda/2015/03/top-10-emerging-technologies-of-2015-2/#distributed-manufacturing (archived at https://perma.cc/E73F-ZHCG)

3 Manners-Bell, J (2014) *Supply Chain Risk: Understanding emerging threats to global supply chains*, Kogan Page, London

4 WBCSD, ERM (2015) [accessed 8 April 2016] *Building Resilience in Global Supply Chains* [Online] wbcsdpublications.org/project/building-resilience-in-global-supply-chains/ (archived at https://perma.cc/ZKS7-KMKQ)

5 World Economic Forum (2015) *Beyond Supply Chains* [Online] www.weforum.org/reports/beyond-supply-chains-empowering-responsible-value-chains (archived at https://perma.cc/Q9L2-TQ9V) [accessed 19 February 2016]

6 Malik, Y, Niemeyer, A and Ruwadi, B (2011) Building the supply chain of the future, *McKinsey Quarterly* (January)

7 Dubeauclard, R, Kubik, K and Nagall, V (2015) How agile is your supply chain? *McKinsey Quarterly* (April)

8 United Nations (2014) [accessed 8 April 2016] *UNIDO Launches Landmark Eco-Industrial Park Project in Viet Nam* [Online]. Web page no longer available, but see https://www.unido.org/news/new-unido-project-viet-nam-focuses-eco-friendly-industrial-zones (archived at https://perma.cc/2CYD-43XC)

9 British Sugar (2016) [accessed 16 April 2016] How Our Factory Operates [Online]Website no longer available, but see https://www.britishsugar.co.uk/about-sugar/our-factories (archived at https://perma.cc/GRM5-8H7G)

10 UPS/GreenBiz (2016) [accessed 6 April 2016] *The Growth of the Circular Economy* [Online] sustainability.ups.com/media/UPS_GreenBiz_Whitepaper.pdf (archived at https://perma.cc/GLV4-EMQX)

11 2degrees Network (October 2015) [accessed 15 August 2016] *Joining Forces: The Case for Collaboration* [Online] https://www.2degreesnetwork.com/groups/2degrees-community/resources/joining-forces-case-collaboration-brought-you-by-2degrees/attachments/3849/ (archived at https://perma.cc/6LDF-UJN3)

12 The Future-Fit Business Benchmark [accessed 8 April 2016] [Online] futurefitbusiness.org/about/introduction/ (archived at https://perma.cc/XR9Y-CSXM)

13 Shing Hin Yeung – own work, CC BY-SA 3.0 [Online] https://commons.wikimedia.org/w/index.php?curid=27867977 (archived at https://perma.cc/2M5R-G6AN)

14 Saaksvuori, A and Immonen, A (2008) *Product Lifecycle Management*, 3rd edn, Springer, Berlin, Chapter 1, pp 1–6

15 Ameri, F and Dutta, D (2005) Product lifecycle management: closing the knowledge loops, *Computer-Aided Design and Applications*, **2** (5), pp 577–90

16 Stark, J (2011) *Product Lifecycle Management: 21st century paradigm for product realization*, 2nd edn, Springer, London, Chapter 1, pp 1–16

17 Corallo, A et al (2013) *Defining Product Lifecycle Management: A journey across features, definitions, and concepts*, ISRN Industrial Engineering

18 Vehmas, K, Raudaskoski, A, Heikkilä, P, Harlin, A and Mensonen, A (2018) Consumer attitudes and communication in circular fashion, *Journal of Fashion Marketing and Management: An International Journal*, **22** (3), pp 286–300

19 de Oliveira, SF and Soares, AL (2017) *A PLM Vision for Circular Economy*, *Working Conference on Virtual Enterprises*, Springer, Berlin, pp 591–602

20 World Economic Forum (2014) *Towards the Circular Economy: Accelerating the scale-up across global supply chains*, produced in collaboration with the Ellen MacArthur Foundation and McKinsey

12

Supply chain operations

*Sourcing and procurement, manufacturing,
distribution and reverse logistics*

The future is already here, it's just not evenly distributed.

WILLIAM GIBSON[1]

In this chapter, we explore how supply chain operations – including sourcing and procurement, manufacturing, distribution and reverse logistics – need to evolve for a circular economy. This does not depend on the business adopting circular strategies for products and services – there are many ways the supply chain itself can use and benefit from circular approaches. We will start with the background and issues for 'traditional' supply chains: often long-distance, extended networks with several 'tiers' of (numerous) suppliers and sub-contractors. Moving onto supply chains for the circular economy, we look at:

- upstream: sourcing and buying circular inputs and the need for transparency and trust;
- midstream production of materials, components and products: local versus global, including trends towards distributed manufacturing; industrial symbiosis, by-products and co-products; remanufacturing; and transit packaging;
- downstream: the complexities and broadening the scope of distribution and reverse supply chains, including rethinking to support service and performance models;
- reverse supply chains, a section by Dr Regina Frei;

- enablers: life-cycle assessments; and other technology enablers including blockchain, 3D printing, big data, communications and IoT;
- accelerators: relationships, partnerships and collaboration;
- finally, we explore value opportunities: creating new value and setting criteria for success.

Background and issues

Upstream procurement has evolved into a specialist business function over the last few decades, as the drive for lower-cost materials and products led to replacing local, 'domestic' suppliers with international sources. As each new source country developed and wages rose, another country would develop its industrial capabilities, allowing buyers to move onto this next 'low-cost economy'. As functional teams handed over their purchasing responsibilities, materials and components for products came into scope, followed by consumables, services, equipment and maintenance categories. Professional procurement teams aggregate contract volumes and negotiate to achieve the lowest cost supplies against the defined specification, looking for 'best value'. This approach tends to prioritize the cost price over aspects such as supplier ethics, the sustainability of sources (eg deforestation), *externalities* from the production process, employee working conditions and so on. These other aspects may not even be visible to the procurement team, obscured by the **multiple 'tiers' of suppliers** in modern supply chains.

Often, there are many 'tiers' of suppliers: tier 1, supplying directly to the brand or main supplier, may be supported by several further tiers, starting with farming and extraction (eg mining), then raw material processing, compounds and sub-assemblies, components, and finally the end product. As an example, a supply chain for electric vehicle batteries involved four different stages before the final manufacture of the car, including 10 materials, six processing activities and eight different manufacturing activities. Chapter 7 outlined the typical supply chain for garment manufacture, often with multiple processes between the raw material and the finished garment (see Figure 12.1).

Suppliers may sub-contract all or part of their contract to supply, with or without the knowledge and permission from the end customer. These issues of supply chain **transparency and trust** were highlighted by a delay of several days before some major UK brands could confirm whether or not they were involved in the Bangladesh Rana Plaza factory collapse or the UK horsemeat scandal (both in 2013).

FIGURE 12.1   Fashion supply chain

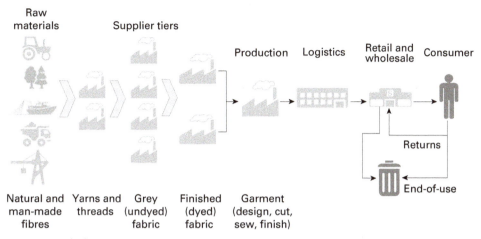

SOURCE: © Catherine Weetman

Long-distance, extended supply chains, evolving as companies switched to the next lowest-cost manufacturing base, have intrinsic **risks**. Events on the other side of the world can invoke chaos in local supply chains, as happened in the automotive industry after the Japan tsunami in 2011. Other weather-related events can impact raw material production, manufacturing or shipping. Geopolitics, volatile costs and corruption can all disrupt supply.

The rapidly changing global landscape, plus increased awareness of large-scale risks, makes it less attractive to invest in mega-facilities. Instead, companies may prioritize local, distributed solutions to avoid 'all the eggs in one basket'.

In Chapter 11, we highlighted the challenges for traditional supply chains, with shortening product life-cycles and an ever-increasing range of stock-keeping units (SKUs) to manage. Long-distance extended supply chains, based on low-cost source locations, result in longer-term (and so less accurate) sales forecasts and higher levels of inventory. **Multichannel retailing** increases complexity, with a range of distribution methods and pack sizes (maybe even extra SKUs), additional packaging and an increasing likelihood of returns. **Reverse logistics** is generally unplanned and often sub-optimal (not unlike a 'distress purchase'). Most companies handle waste from products and packaging at retail outlets and customer locations. There are cost pressures too, with increasing fuel costs, road congestion, retailer demands for 'little and often' deliveries, and the rising popularity of e-commerce and home delivery.

Supply chains for the circular economy – upstream

Leading companies are investing time and effort to better understand their supply chain risks, looking at ethical, social and environmental conditions as well as risks affecting supply itself. They seek to improve resilience and robustness across ethical, environmental and economic criteria. They may set their own **supply chain standards,** or engage in collaborative initiatives like the Better Cotton Standard System or the Roundtable on Sustainable Palm Oil.

Procurement teams see **collaboration and relationships** as key themes. High-performing and trusted suppliers need to be nurtured (or lost to the competition), with deeper exchanges of information between buyer and supplier. Externally, this includes building partnerships with service providers, for logistics, contract manufacturing and data analysis. Internally, it means working closely with design and manufacturing teams to deepen understanding of their needs and offer ideas and options.

Cost-to-buy decisions will evolve to **full-life cost perspectives.** This means creating and measuring value for a wider range of stakeholders. Full-life costs need information from all stages of the product life, from farming and extraction, through production, use and end-of-use. A whole-system approach would include the business owners, together with other groups at every stage through to disposal: communities, employees, suppliers, customers and the planet (living systems, water basins, healthy soils, *GHG* and air pollution within safe boundaries). If a material can be improved or changed to provide better durability, how does this affect the full-life costs and stakeholder value?

Transparency of the extended supply chain is becoming critical: which suppliers and materials, from where in the world, and whether ethically produced. Customers want evidence for ethical and sustainable products, expecting this to be backed up by proof of the sustainability of raw materials, inputs and all other aspects of the extended process – from 'farm to fork' and so on. Companies embarking on this are finding it to be a major challenge – even knowing who produces what at each stage of the business may be more complex and obscure than anticipated. For companies with complex supply chains and a history of ethical or fraudulent issues, there may be concerns about the reliability of data provided by suppliers, leading to a reluctance to publish the data. For example, the Indonesian palm oil industry has over 2 million smallholders operating over 40 per cent of plantations.[2] Trying to understand which farms are involved in your supply chain could be virtually impossible. The Fairphone example in Chapter 8, with a

Fairtrade-certified supply chain for gold, shows how even a small company can improve the ethics and transparency of its sourcing for materials at risk from corruption.

Social media means that any suspicion of wrongdoing, harmful materials or perceived conflicts between a company's actions and its stated 'values' or *corporate social responsibility* policies can be publicized around the world within hours. Campaigns by *NGOs* are highlighting the reputational risks of lack of transparency – or worse: continuing to procure from unethical or unsustainable sources (eg palm oil linked to destruction of rainforests). Social media can publicize the issue and persuade consumers to engage directly, by posting messages on the brand's social media feeds. Campaigns extend to political issues, for example, *The Guardian*'s #Keepitintheground campaign, aiming to stop fossil fuel mining and extraction. A partnership between Ceres Investor Network on Climate Risk and Aiming for A calls on oil companies to stress-test their business strategies against the Paris Agreement goal.[3]

As we have seen, contracts based on access and performance can be a win-win for both the provider and the user, and so can be a central strategy for procurement, supported by extending and deepening long-term business **relationships with suppliers and customers.** These models can help both buyer and supplier develop shared aims and rewards, for reliability, performance or outcomes of the product, rather than the price and volume for a single transaction. The cash-flow implications may need support from a specialist finance provider, to overcome the initial 'hole' in cash flow for the supplier. Finance providers such as DLL (a division of Rabobank), are seeing the potential for services to support these circular models.[4]

Decisions should evaluate **full-life costs,** rather than just the purchase cost. This may be more complex for products designed for second or subsequent 'lives', or use cycles. What value will you assign to the product at the end of its first life, and what assumptions for recovery and reuse of the product, components and materials? These assumptions could be conservative at the outset, then improved with detailed evidence over time. 'Shared value' models may help build trust, and avoid conflict when negotiating supplier contracts.

A presentation on 'Procurement and the Circular Economy', by WRAP, highlights elements of contract costs that are often hidden.[5] These include operating and maintenance, exposure to supply chain price volatility, costs of reputational or operational risk, environmental costs, uncertainty around margins and disposal. WRAP examines the role of specifications, comparing

FIGURE 12.2   Circular Economy Framework 2.0 – circular inputs

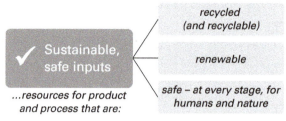

SOURCE: © Catherine Weetman

those based on technical requirements with those aimed at performance. Whilst technical specifications tell the market exactly what you want, you need a technical expert in your team, providing detailed requirements. The proposals from suppliers will be easy to evaluate, but with limited opportunity for innovation, and a risk that your specification does not produce the best outcome. Specifying performance parameters or desired outcomes encourages innovation, but is more difficult to evaluate and so the criteria for bid evaluation needs careful consideration.

Safe, sustainable inputs

As you move towards 'circular inputs' (see Figure 12.2), such as swapping virgin technical resources (eg metals or plastics) for recycled sources, you may need to find new suppliers. To increase resilience, you might source from several small suppliers, developing and scaling-up methods for recovering and recycling materials, rather than one major international company capable of fulfilling all your needs and seasonal variations. Alternatively, could you work with a company at the other end of the value chain, such as a waste processor that sees a future in resource recovery for resale? As your circular business model develops and matures, continuous improvement approaches can 'raise the bar', finding better materials and resilient, trusted and secure sources. You may be able to work with researchers or commercial organizations to develop new materials, using *biomimicry* or *green chemistry* to innovate renewable (especially *by-products* from existing flows) or recycled materials.

Security of supply and safety of materials is critical. Looking both medium and long term, can you highlight those materials at most risk, and with the biggest impact on the company? Impact may be measured by the volume used, the level of spend, their role in a critical component (or high-value product) and so on.

There is a wealth of opportunities to build **agility** and **resilience**, through multiple source options, specifying substitute materials or components, and recovering resources for reuse. Procurement toolkits can help with this – see Further Resources in this chapter.

Supply chains for the circular economy – midstream

For the 'midstream' of the supply chain, we focus on the manufacturing and assembly processes, consolidating and preparing stock for sale to customers. We look at the trend towards **relocalization** and *distributed manufacturing*, **industrial symbiosis, by-products** and **co-products; remanufacturing;** and **packaging.**

Other trends include **mass customization**, with business customers and consumers wanting to select 'bespoke' products to meet specific needs. This could mean choosing options at the last stage of assembly, as for cars, or it may be genuinely unique products as with 'made to measure' medical implants for human joint replacements. Manufacturers may meet these needs using on-demand manufacturing techniques such as *3D printing*, or postponement and local assembly. Technology themes include innovations in social media, mobile internet and cloud computing, all with implications for product design, relationships and interactions with supply chain partners.

Local versus global

A report by the World Economic Forum (2015)[6] examines emerging technologies, including **distributed manufacturing**. Whereas traditional, centralized manufacturing makes large batches of identical products, distributed manufacturing reorganizes the raw materials and manufacture methods to make the final product much closer to the customer. Digital designs allow local manufacturing hubs, using computerized tools or robots, to make parts then assemble them into finished products at local fabrication or assembly shops. Products are made to order rather than for stock, reducing inventory and risk of overstocks or obsolescence. Raw materials are from local sources, speeding re-orders and reducing the energy required for logistics and storage. In Chapter 11, we reviewed the features of distributed and centralized supply chains.

MyMuesli, in Germany, allows customers to customize the final product.

MYMUESLI: BESPOKE BREAKFASTS[7]

Founded in 2007, MyMuesli offers 'mix your own' muesli, sourcing organic ingredients regionally and worldwide. It sells online in France, Germany, Sweden, Switzerland, the Netherlands and the UK. Customers can pick their own recipe combinations on the website, with highly automated mixing machinery capable of mixing '566 quadrillion' combinations of ingredients. Customers can suggest new ingredients and preferences. This becomes 'smart data' to optimize the supply chain, with the customer's individual product specification stored on a product memory tag, then attached to a 575-gram tube. The mixing machine reads the tag and preselects the mix for that customer.

Figure 12.3 reminds us of the aims for process design, which we covered in detail in Chapter 2. In addition to ensuring our process inputs (such as chemicals, coatings, dyes, adhesives, etc) use safe, sustainable inputs (recycled and recyclable, or renewable) and improving resource-efficiency (narrowing the loop), we aim to:

- recover and reuse inputs (waste = food);
- create by-products (waste = food);
- create co-products (get more from less/intensify).

FIGURE 12.3   Circular Economy Framework 2.0 – process design

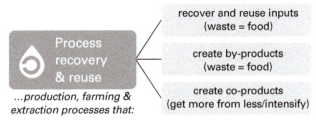

SOURCE: © Catherine Weetman

Industrial symbiosis

In Chapter 2, we learned about the UK's National Industrial Symbiosis Programme (NISP), and in Chapter 11, we saw how the UN is supporting development of eco-industrial parks, looking to use waste from one operation to provide a resource for another.

KALUNDBORG: INDUSTRIAL SYMBIOSIS[8,9,10]

The world's first industrial symbiosis project began at the Kalundborg industrial park in Denmark in 1961. It started with a water management project, with Statoil working with the city of Kalundborg to develop a pipeline to extract surface water from nearby Lake Tissø, to avoid depleting groundwater resources for Statoil's new gas refinery. The next project came in 1972, with Statoil agreeing to supply its excess gas for Gyproc's plasterboard drying ovens. In 1973, the Asnæs power station (now Dong Energy) was connected to the Statoil water pipeline, expanding the project to three partners.

The companies started to discuss new collaboration ideas, aiming to reduce resource costs and circulate waste from one company as inputs to another. The Asnæs plant, a 1,500-milliwatt coal-fired power station, is now the hub of the exchange network, with energy and material links with the local community, as well as other companies. Dong Energy sells steam from the plant to both Novo Nordisk (pharmaceuticals) and Statoil, and sells a by-product, sulphur dioxide, to Gyproc, providing almost all its gypsum inputs. Clinker and fly-ash from the power plant become by-products for the road-building and cement industries. Surplus heat from the Asnæs plant heats 3,500 local homes, plus a nearby fish farm. Sludge from the fish farm becomes a fertilizer by-product.

Both public and private companies buy and sell a variety of wastes between each other in a closed system, with over 30 exchanges between Kalundborg Municipality and eight other companies. Waste flows include steam, ash, gas, heat, sludge and other products. Environmental benefits include the reuse of heat-reducing thermal pollution, previously discharged into the nearby fjord. The gypsum feed to Gyproc reduces open-cast mining and associated pollution and degradation, and the project had saved over 3 million cubic metres of water by 2015.

The project has become a model for private (rather than government-planned) eco-industrial parks. The exchange of resources and the close proximity has helped develop a collaborative culture, with the companies fostering communication, transparency and cooperation, and sharing staff, equipment and information. This drives collective problem-solving, such as a recent project to develop renewable energy for the area.

THE PLANT: AQUAPONICS AND INDUSTRIAL SYMBIOSIS[11,12]

In Chicago, The Plant, housed in a former meat-packing plant, is a community of food businesses with a mission to 'cultivate local circular economies'. Plant Chicago is a non-profit organization established in 2011 by John Edel, with a 'vision for a future where the shift in production, consumption and waste is driven at the local level, generating equity and economic opportunity for all residents'.

On-site indoor and outdoor farmers' markets sell to the public; and tenant businesses supply other farmers' markets, restaurants and local businesses. By 2015, the businesses and demonstration projects included:

- an *aquaponics* farm, supplying vegetables (grown without soil) and raising fish using homemade fish food from a range of sources, including spent grains from the brewery. Another example is black soldier flies, fed on kitchen scraps to produce larvae harvested for use in the fish food;
- an algae bioreactor using waste from the on-site shrimp farm to produce spirulina, a fast-growing nutritious algae for fish food;
- a miniature anaerobic biodigester, converting food waste into biofuel;
- a kombucha tea brewery: using oxygen produced by plants in the aquaponics system and producing carbon dioxide for the plants;
- an indoor mushroom farm: using recycled compost with waste coffee grounds;
- an outdoor farm supplying vegetables to subscribers;
- 'Bike a Bee', supplying honey to farmers' markets from 32 beehives all over the city;
- other businesses, including a brewery, coffee roaster, pie shop and bakery.

Figure 12.4 illustrates the symbiotic flows – by 2019, the community supported 85 full-time-equivalent jobs.

By-products and co-products

As we've seen, finding ways to recover value from every input, including materials, water and energy, can create a whole new range of by-products and co-products. These may evolve over time, as advancements in biorefining help extract valuable elements from bulk materials, with value for specific sectors. You may find different outlets with more value-add potential,

FIGURE 12.4   Industrial symbiosis – The Plant

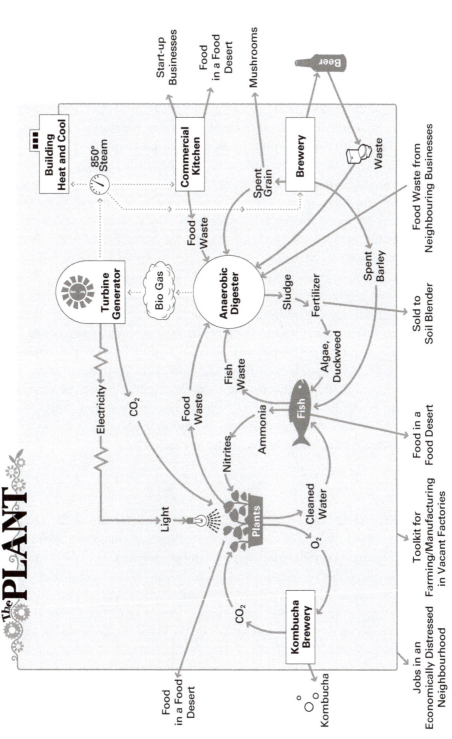

SOURCE: Created by Matt Bergstrom, Bubbly Dynamics, LLC, reproduced with kind permission of John Edel, The Plant

supporting investment in on-site processing to capitalize on these by-products. In previous chapters, we saw how British Sugar developed many by-products from its raw material input, sugar beet. Cleaning the soil from beet, then separating the small stones in the soil produced two separate by-products. Removing the stones improves the soil before returning to the farms, and the stones are available for resale for construction, road-building, etc. Further value could be created by grading the stones and bagging those suitable for sale to consumers through garden centres.

In Chapter 6, we saw the wide range of by-products generated by coffee, whilst in the *FMCG* sector, Procter & Gamble set up a Global Asset Recovery Purchases team to identify new cascades and by-products. One factory, in the United States, sells waste from baby-wipe production for use as an upholstery filling; waste from a toilet paper plant in Mexico is sold for use in low-cost roof tiles; mascara by-products go to the automotive sector; beauty care product waste becomes a leather care product.[13]

New by-products may require different methods of handling and transport. You may want to transport and sell in bulk, or need to provide smaller containers to improve logistics and increase sales potential. Some products, especially chemicals and fuels, may be hazardous or be subject to specific regulations. How easy is it to forecast the production quantities each day or week? Can you find buyers that are more flexible to suit your production patterns, especially in the early stages of developing these new flows? Will you need to store them, even if only to aggregate ahead of a full-vehicle order quantity? Are the products stable, or perishable?

Remanufacturing

Remanufacturing is an important tool in the circular economy toolbox, able to extend the useful life of components, products and equipment with substantial savings in cost, labour, energy and other resources. The UN Resource Panel estimates that remanufactured products save up to 98 per cent of CO_2 emissions compared with the equivalent new products.[14]

In 2015, the European Remanufacturing Network (ERN), a consortium of eight research partners,[15] was funded by the European Commission for a two-year project. Now renamed as the Conseil Européen de Remanufactur, it aims to create greater awareness with the public and policymakers, increase demand, address barriers, improve operations and competitiveness and encourage new businesses to adopt remanufacturing. The ERN Remanufacturing Market Study (2015)[16] refers to the British Standard (BS8887-Part 2), defining remanufacturing as 'returning a product to at least its original performance with a warranty that is equivalent to or better than that of the newly manufactured product'.

US researcher RT Lund, in his Database of Remanufacturers report (2008),[17] defines remanufacturing as 'the process of restoring a non-functional, discarded or traded-in product to **like-new** condition', emphasizing that it 'must meet at least the specifications of the product when new. It may also incorporate upgrades to reflect improvements ... since the product was originally made.'

Remanufacturing is established in the automotive, aerospace and heavy-duty off-road sectors, and for products like toner cartridges, office furniture and equipment, machine tools, electrical equipment and compressors. It is now gaining attention for medical devices and equipment.

Remanufacturing can be a key strategy for different types of business:

- in-house, by the original equipment manufacturer *(OEM)*;
- as a specialist sub-contracted service, potentially for a range of manufacturers;
- by a company in a support sector acting as a key supplier to the OEM (as with Cat Reman for major companies in other industrial sectors);
- by a company existing purely to remanufacture and sell products from other OEMs (as with the Rype Office case study in Chapter 9).

The Database of Remanufacturers lists over 7,000 firms in the United States and Canada active in remanufacture of over 125 different product types.[18] Caterpillar is a well-known example, remanufacturing over US$3.5 billion of parts and components and employing over 5,000 workers through Cat Reman, a 'high technology, low-cost, global brand focused on salvage capabilities'. It offers parts for Caterpillar machines and engines plus remanufacturing for high-profile customers in industrial, automotive and component sectors.[19] Nextant Aerospace in Ohio remanufactures and upgrades Beechcraft aircraft, with 200 employees generating sales of US$100 million each year.

Remanufacturing: the process of restoring a non-functional, discarded or traded-in product to like-new condition.

The Database of Remanufacturers report lists some terms 'equivalent to remanufacturing', used in specific industries. These include 'overhaul' for aircraft engines, 'rebuild' for automotive parts, 'recharge' for laser toner cartridges, 'retread' or 'recap' for tyres, plus others.

FIGURE 12.5   Remanufacturing in Europe

Sectors	Turnover (€bn)	Firms	Employm't ('000)	Core ('000)[1]	Intensity[2]
Aerospace	12.4	1,000	71	5,160	11.5%
Automotive	7.4	2,363	43	27,286	1.1%
EEE[3]	3.1	2,502	28	87,925	1.1%
HDOR[4]	4.1	581	31	7,390	2.9%
Machinery	1	513	6	1,010	0.7%
Medical	1	60	7	1,005	2.8%
Others[5]	0.7	184	7	2,630	0.3 – 1.1%
Total	29.8	7,204	192	132,405	1.90%

[1] Core: a used part intended to become a remanufactured product
[2] Intensity: ratio of remanufacturing to new manufacturing
[3] Electronic and electrical equipment
[4] Heavy duty and off-road equipment
[5] Includes furniture, marine and rail, each below €1 billion turnover

SOURCE: ERN (2015)[20]

Gathering data from nine sectors across the EU, the ERN found that Germany, the UK, France and Italy generated 70 per cent of remanufacturing value. Figure 12.5 summarizes the dimensions for the major industry sectors.

Remanufacturing is already worth 30 billion euros in Europe; however, 'intensity' (the value of remanufacturing as a proportion of total sales) is low, even in those sectors where it is seen as 'mainstream'. The opportunities to increase remanufacturing apply to many established sectors. UNEP reported that remanufacturing accounts for only ~2 per cent of US production, and ~1.9 per cent across the European Union. The ERN Remanufacturing Market Study found that remanufacturing in the EU aerospace sector has the highest intensity, at 11.5 per cent. Heavy-duty and off-road (HDOR) equipment ranks second at 2.9 per cent, and medical equipment is third at 2.8 per cent.

The survey considered motives and barriers for remanufacturing, with top motives including higher profit margins, strategic advantage and increased market share, together with securing spare parts supply, reduced resource security risks, reduced lead times, asset and brand protection. The top barrier was 'customer recognition': for customers to be aware of remanufactured products and their environmental benefits and to understand the workmanship in a high-quality remanufactured product and therefore to pay an appropriate price. Other barriers included access to the required volume of 'core' (parts or products), high labour costs, legal ambiguities, and poor design for remanufacturing. The ERN envisages that with supportive policies and investment from industry, remanufacturing could overcome these barriers to generate an annual value of 70–100 billion euros across the EU by 2030, employing around half a million people.

Packaging

In Chapter 10, we covered packaging, noting that circular design is critical for each element:

- primary packaging (eg a tube for toothpaste, a plastic or paper wrapper for breakfast cereals);
- secondary packaging (eg the box containing the toothpaste tube or cereal wrapper);
- for some products, tertiary packs and shelf packs;
- transit packaging, to protect the product between manufacture and delivery.

We saw that each functional team in the business might have different priorities for packaging design (retail shelf 'impact', logistics costs, packaging materials cost, etc). In many cases, logistics teams are not involved in product packaging design and material choices. Often this meant that packaging compromised the quantity of product on a pallet, or in a delivery vehicle, perhaps with a 'Russian doll' approach of several packs, each enclosing yet more empty space.

Supply chain teams should aim to design (or redesign) packaging to improve the volume density, minimizing materials and footprints. Transit packaging is an important consideration, with potential to improve the 'fill' on the pallet base (not leaving empty space at the edge of the pallet) and available height: improving utilization of warehouse space, delivery vehicle and so on. Designing for supply chain efficiency helps reduce costs for the company and its retail customers, but few companies tap into the knowledge of their logistics teams. According to McKinsey,[21] for two products of identical volume, more rectangular packaging can increase packing density by up to 40 per cent. Move the product, not fresh air!

Involving supply chain teams in the design of both the packaging and the product for **distribution and recovery** is also important. In addition to the logistics gains, there is potential to recover higher value from the returning product or components, and create multiuse packages to reduce costs and inputs. Designing packaging for product recovery presents different challenges, as we saw in Chapter 10. Even if the original packaging can pack flat for easier storage, the user may not retain it. Packaging for a replacement, upgraded or new product could encourage the customer to reuse packaging from the new product to pack and return the old product. If you provide packaging specifically for the return, then flat-pack designs enable easier (and lower cost) delivery. Perhaps you can use pre-cut card in kit form, with simple instructions for the user to construct protective support modules for the product, inside the outer carton. Otherwise, could the collection service take the protective packaging to the product location? The trade-off between the cost of collection and value recovery from the returning product and materials needs careful analysis.

Textile manufacturer Sympatex's 'functional jacket 4.0', showcased in 2017, included a range of circular features. Each jacket is equipped with an integrated return label featuring the Sympatex company address, where consumers can send their product to be recycled.[22]

For bulk orders, recyclable transit packaging materials include metal (beer and wine kegs) and cardboard. The Pallite paper-based pallet is a reusable, recyclable pallet.[23] In standard and bespoke sizes, it is cleaner and drier than new wooden pallets, so highly suited to food, pharmaceutical and exported products (as it is also ISPM 15 exempt), with the benefit of a material that – once the loaded products are used – can be recycled (whereas wooden pallets regularly incur chargeable collection or disposal).

In Chapter 10, we mentioned using (compostable) sheep's wool to keep fresh food cool for home delivery. In Europe, RePack offers reusable packaging for home delivery, with a reward system to encourage the successful return.

Supply chains for the circular economy – downstream

Our 'downstream' supply chain stores and distributes the products and manages their successful recovery. Circular approaches mean rethinking to support service and performance models, and we need to design supply chains for successful circular flows.

In Chapter 5, we noted the trend towards access instead of ownership, and personalization, or 'mass customization', instead of mass-produced, identical products. The personalization trend includes service experiences as well as products, for example being able to save your typical weekly online grocery order. Some predictions include 'smart households', with sensors in your refrigerator to reorder items consumed.

Products designed to be more durable, and used more intensely, will need return loops, coming back for refurbishment, remanufacture or recycling of materials. Reverse logistics will be planned and desirable and can help improve the competitive strength of the organization.

Circular flows are essential to recover resources and reduce waste. In addition to ensuring the products and materials arrive back in good condition, the challenges include managing fluctuating volumes and multiple return loops. These flows must retain value – through secure transport, trusted reverse logistics partners, and protection of products to avoid damage and loss – and be cost-efficient. Options might include:

- an 'Uber-type' freight model, tapping into unused capacity on existing networks;

- collaborating with industry peers to provide critical mass for an economic network;

- finding ways to collect whilst making your outbound deliveries.

The resulting economies of scale enable higher-value recovery from waste, justifying sortation and compaction equipment. Tracking systems can direct and control flows of returning products and materials. End users can classify product condition, reducing inspection and handling costs; in which case, legislation and specific waste licences may apply. For some products, appropriate transit media (or packaging) may resolve the issue, but for others (eg lithium batteries) specific legislative restrictions apply. In Chapter 8, we read about Fairphone's modular design, allowing users to easily identify, order and swap defective parts for new ones, or to upgrade a component.

UPS highlights the logistics cost of reclaiming used goods as a major barrier to 'an effective, global circular economy'.[24] The survey considered factors to encourage product returns in a circular economy, finding that industrial and consumer users include monetary and convenience factors (see Figure 12.6).

FIGURE 12.6   Incentives for product return

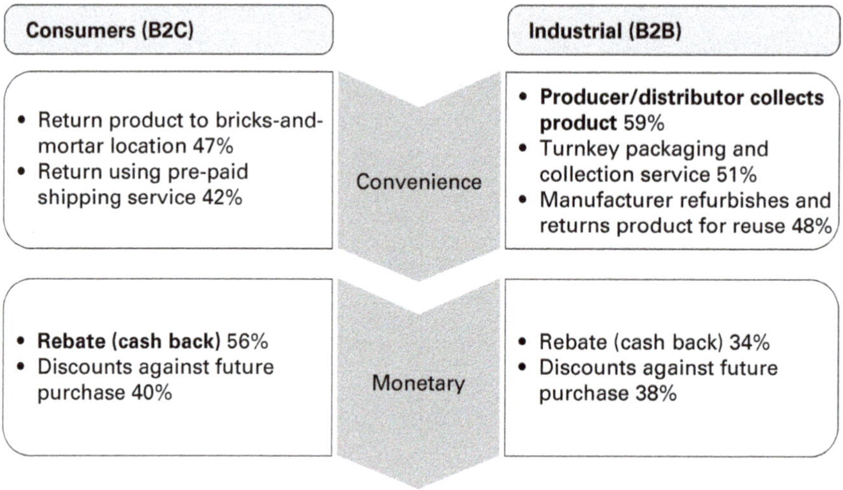

Consumers (B2C)		Industrial (B2B)
• Return product to bricks-and-mortar location 47% • Return using pre-paid shipping service 42%	Convenience	• **Producer/distributor collects product** 59% • Turnkey packaging and collection service 51% • Manufacturer refurbishes and returns product for reuse 48%
• **Rebate (cash back) 56%** • Discounts against future purchase 40%	Monetary	• Rebate (cash back) 34% • Discounts against future purchase 38%

SOURCE: UPS/GreenBiz (2016)[25]

Reverse supply chains
Contribution by Dr Regina Frei

Supply chains become loops in a circular economy, needing robust reverse supply chains (RSCs) to recover products, components and materials. Figure 12.7 shows possible scenarios: product recalls; returns of products delivered wrongly, damaged or obsolete; used products going for resale with or without remanufacturing; and products at the end of their useful life being recycled or disposed of properly.

Besides the reverse logistics (RL) necessary for the transportation and distribution of products and materials in RSCs, many factors are essential for successful operation. We look at examples of products and parts fed back into the market, examine a unifying model for different RSC options and discuss their shared characteristics.

Whilst the idea of returning used and unwanted parts, products and packaging for reuse or recycling is growing in popularity, the implementation is often challenging and companies other than those focusing on recycling are often reluctant to engage beyond their legal obligations due to financial, technical and organizational challenges. However, considering the possible benefits, companies are increasingly starting to explore their RSCs. The following examples illustrate the situation across industries and countries.

Ship dismantling: reverse supply chain and recovery of materials

Iliopoulos (2015) investigated the process of ship dismantling, mostly undertaken in Asia under precarious conditions for workforce and environment.[26] Few ships are dismantled in Europe, where legislation is much more stringent regarding safety and toxin release.

With the various ship types, sub-types and modifications they undergo in operation, there is a lack of information-sharing between the manufacturer, operator and decommissioning crew. This proves challenging for dismantling, done for financial gain: globally acting third parties buy ships and take them apart. The retrieved metals (and sometimes other materials) are sold for recycling. As with most products, dismantling by original manufacturers would be easier and they would be interested in building ships that can be dismantled easily.[27] Maersk (2014) is pioneering this approach with the Cradle-to-Cradle passport, informing about the materials used and changes made during lifetime.[28]

Electronics companies: reverse supply chains

An estimated 42 million metric tons of *e-waste* was produced globally in 2014 and the amount increases every year.[29] Controlling and tracking e-waste flows is difficult because the classifications and codes (UNU-KEYS) may be ambiguous and change when items are processed, or when they age.

Most electronic devices contain a variety of materials including plastics, semi-conductors, metals and ceramics, some of which are scarce and/or valuable. Components are usually difficult to separate, and hence reuse is challenging. Products received at recycling centres vary widely: different types of products, from different generations, in different conditions. This makes disassembly an even more difficult endeavour. Almost impossible to automate, developed countries usually avoid taking products apart, burning them instead. Exceptions to this rule are companies like TRACOuk, where the manual work is covered by a fee charged to customers, as well as selling recovered products. Besides broken and old electronics, e-waste typically contains a considerable proportion of new, used but functional or repairable devices. These could contribute to funding the sorting, testing, refurbishing and recycling, hence creating jobs. Nevertheless, most of the e-waste goes directly to incineration or landfill.

Although EU legislation prevents cross-border transport of waste, electronics from around the world are shipped to developing countries in Asia and Africa and there dealt with under hazardous conditions and often in semi-legal or illegal ways, creating considerable pollution and health problems.

Current business models, aiming for early planned redundancy and devices breaking shortly after the warranty expires – enticing customers to upgrade to new models – exacerbate the e-waste problem. It is problematic that remanufacturing is often considered as a threat to manufacturing due to 'cannibalization' – the sales of the remanufactured product affecting the sales of the new product[30] – whereas these options ought to be integrated, typically addressing different customer segments.[31] Modular designs allowing customers to upgrade devices are more favourable for the environment, but the major electronics companies have been ignoring this possibility. Examples of modular consumer electronics products made for upgrades and repair are the Fairphone and LG's G5, but it remains a niche market. Legislation may be necessary to force the major manufacturers to change strategies. It is essential for them to assume responsibility for the full life-cycle of their products, favouring designs that allow easy upgrade, disassembly and separation of materials.

GameStop (2012) adopts a buy–sell–trade business model refurbishing game consoles and similar electronic devices, without any instructions for disassembly and repair from original manufacturers.[32] It returns 85 per cent of the accepted consoles to the market, and the remainder is used for spare parts or recycled.

There are other examples:

- Global Robots Ltd refurbishes discarded industrial robots. As with cars, robots and their spare parts are resold for a reduced price. Customers are typically unable to purchase new robots at full price. Robots are highly engineered, generally very robust and usually remain operational and reliable for many years.

- Airbus is working on a Cradle-to-Cradle strategy with Tarmac Aerosave, estimating that 90 per cent of an aircraft can be safely dismantled and recycled.[33] Airbus recognizes the learning opportunity when analysing the wear and tear found in old aircraft, and improves their new designs accordingly.

- Japanese manufacturers of photocopiers and single-use cameras were pioneers in *remanufacturing*.[34] Their engagement takes a long-term perspective: fully automated solutions require high investments that will need a decade to break even. With printer ink cartridges and car parts, Japanese OEMs have been slow to engage, and independent companies have moved in. Car parts remanufacturing, however, is fairly common with OEMs in Europe.[35]

FIGURE 12.7   Types of reverse supply chain

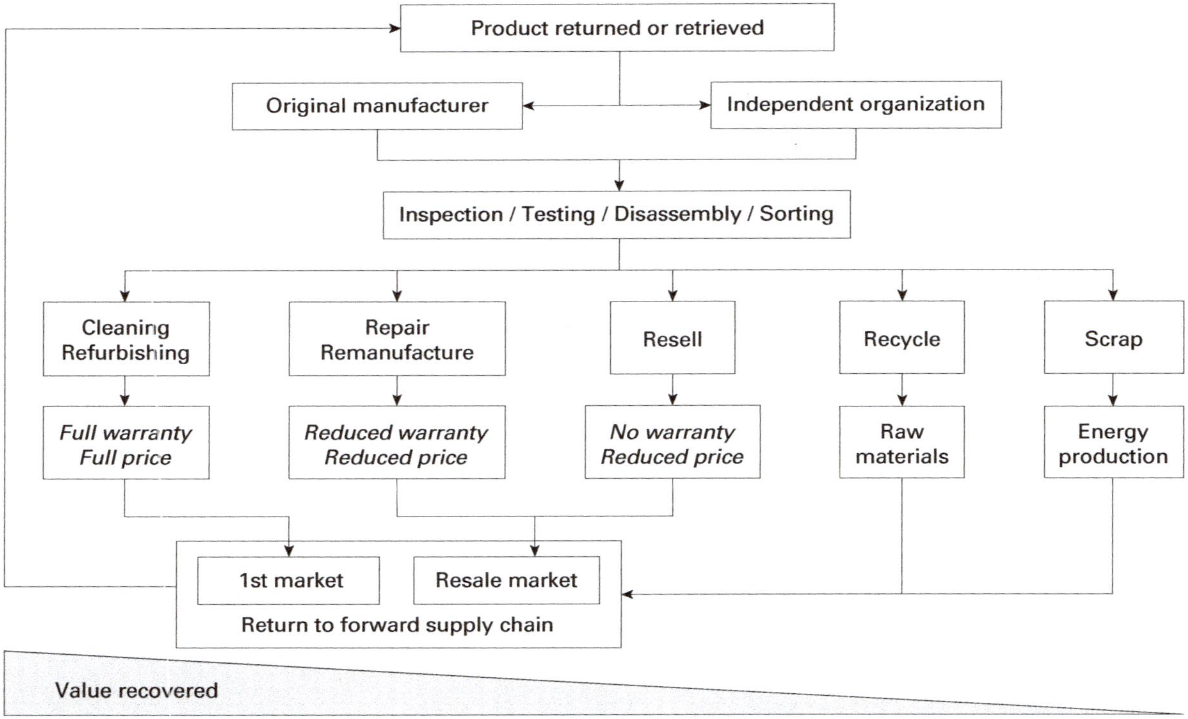

SOURCE: Dr Regina Frei

- Brands including Dyson, Shark, KitchenAid, TomTom and others actively sell **'manufacturer refurbished'** products on their websites, often with reduced warranty. Amazon offer open-box, used, warehouse-damaged and remanufactured products labelled as 'warehouse deals' and without warranty. It remains rather exceptional to find remanufactured products in physical shops, possibly because predicting customer demand is more difficult.

Reverse supply chain model and analysis

Figure 12.7 illustrates different types of RSCs, depending on the value that can be retrieved from the product and the access to resale markets.[36]

Shared characteristics

RSC scenarios are diverse, with a variety of stakeholders, aims and structures, but they share certain characteristics. When advising companies and governments on how best to engage in RSC and what policies to formulate to guide them, it is important to have a clear view of stakeholder interests and to understand how different RSCs work.

When retrieving products or components for reuse or remanufacturing, it is essential that they incur minimal damage, wear and tear. Figure 12.8 illustrates factors to consider in deciding whether to reuse or recycle.

FIGURE 12.8   Product destiny factors

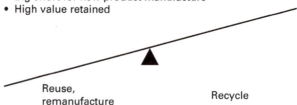

- Small effort for logistics and transformative process
- Good performance of old vs. new product
- Big effort for new product manufacture
- High value retained

Reuse, remanufacture

Recycle

SOURCE: Dr Regina Frei

Typically, *OEMs* manage and operate the RSC for usable parts (possibly outsourcing logistics). However, when the focus is on retrieving materials for recycling, third-party companies may have control, operating in similar ways to a forward supply chain, except that materials are sourced from more diverse locations. The prime objective is to recover value from components or materials without expending uneconomic levels of resources. Options that retain more value and involve less transformative processes usually require less energy, happen earlier after the original sale and have a higher probability of OEM involvement, as Figure 12.9 illustrates.

FIGURE 12.9   Correlated reverse supply chain aspects

SOURCE: Dr Regina Frei

Dismantling products to reuse components or separate materials is usually done manually with considerable effort. The resulting costs encourage shipping of products to lower-wage countries, increasing their environmental impact with transportation and possibly less socially and environmentally favourable conditions.

As seen in various examples above, unless the OEM is involved, disassembly can be complex. For product-service systems (see Chapter 3 for more detail), the manufacturer benefits by designing the product for frequent upgrade, easy repairs, simple disassembly and reuse of components or materials recycling. Modular designs are favoured.

Avoiding fraud and black markets

Controlling the returns is essential for restricting products from black markets with additional detrimental effects on business, such as counterfeiting, or sub-standard products being 'passed off' as new by unlicensed resellers. Consequences for the brand can be reputation impairment, or even major product recalls, as with the car airbag recalls in 2014.

RSC design will depend on the aims and participants: systems designed to keep spare parts off the black market will operate differently from networks of community-organized recycling points, or the returns systems of major retailers.

Fraud in the RSC can seriously affect companies. For instance, many online retailers face return rates of 20–40 per cent or more, providing multiple opportunities for malicious fraud (or unintentional mistakes) by customers, third-party logistics handlers and company employees. Companies need to take preventative measures to avoid losing money, quality and credibility.

Reverse supply chains – measuring success

We discussed a variety of RSC cases and analysed their characteristics and factors influencing how RSCs are organized and operated. Further research is necessary to deepen the understanding of RSCs and their characteristics. Ultimately, a widely applicable method for assessing their economic viability, environmental and social impact needs to be developed. This requires the definition of standard performance metrics taking into account the different RSC types, products involved and their destiny, as well as stakeholders and their interests.

Enablers

In Chapter 4, we explored enablers, which help us to 'think differently', use new materials to replace finite sources with renewable or recycled alternatives (and avoid toxic chemicals), and adopt new technology, to improve system effectiveness and conserve more value.

Maintenance, refilling and repairs will feature in many circular supply chains, and technology will transform approaches and efficiency. The *Internet of Things (IoT)* in vending machines senses the need for refills or malfunctions, and requests the parts or products and automatically assigns the task to the nearest engineer. Refurbishment and repair can be provided by specialist logistics contractors, using 'swap out' parts and 'apps' with diagnosis and repair scripts and collecting parts and consumables from remote, secure lockers en route. Services include product inspection and grading, refurbishment, waste recovery and consolidation. Can you reduce parts inventories, using *3D printing* to print parts on demand and close to the repair location? Could you design modular products with one standard *(OEM)* component shared by many products?

Technology 'enablers' – information-sharing

Procurement teams are increasingly using B2B commerce networks to manage risk, contracts and invoices, transact with suppliers, and analyse supplier performance.[37] Procurement can also take advantage of platforms for exchange and information-sharing. As an example, Sedex is a not-for-profit membership organization, aiming to 'drive improvements in ethical and responsible business practices in global supply chains'.[38] By 2016, it had 36,000 members across 28 industry sectors. Sedex provides a collaborative platform, allowing members to store, exchange and report information about labour standards, environment, ethics and health and safety. Suppliers can enter information and choose to share it with multiple customers via the platform, and buyers have an easier way to view and manage ethical and responsibility data. Suppliers benefit by providing the information once, rather than facing multiple audits, questionnaires or certification assessments. Buyers can validate data through third-party audits of suppliers.

Product life-cycle management platforms (see the section by Jo Conlon in Chapter 11) can help connect the actors in each value chain, enabling everyone to share their learnings from previous circular developments, and potentially to build in feedback from in-use performance data. Blockchain may offer solutions for material passports and transparency reporting, though we should note the heavy energy demands of blockchain's multiple information exchanges.

3D printing

3D printing (3DP) has the potential to transform supply chains. The use of 3D structures to enable strength or flexibility, the nature of the process itself, and the range of materials all have great potential to improve circular models. In manufacture, 3DP changes the nature of inbound material flows. Instead of pre-cut materials (metal sheets or bars, textile fibres or rolls of fabric) and component parts or sub-assemblies, 3DP uses powder, liquid or resin as a raw material. Inbound transport could be bulk containers, as full truckloads, or intermediate containers such as international bulk containers (IBCs) or bulk bags. Unloading bulk liquids or powders means different handling facilities, and storage of bulk materials could use tanks or hoppers. You may need to consider risks such as explosions. Even simple materials like wheat flour (not yet available for 3DP!) have a high risk of explosion, and have specific regulations, such as ATEX in the EU; and DSEAR (Dangerous Substances and Explosive Atmospheres Regulations 2002) in the UK (see Further Resources at the end of this chapter).

Customizable or bespoke designs can be made to order, reducing stock and risk of obsolescence. Instead of large warehouses storing finished goods made in batches, you may be supplying to predetermined delivery schedules with less scope for production and delivery schedule flexibility.

3DP could also transform servicing, whether for your own maintenance, repair and operations (MRO) or to maintain your products out in the field. Making spare parts, on-demand and locally, keeps products in use for longer and provides scope for local, skilled repair services, both for consumer products and industrial technologies. Printing parts on-demand, closer to the service location, will be more productive than holding stocks of parts, 'just in case', whilst risking obsolescence, overstocks and stock-outs – in 2014 shipping company Maersk announced an experiment to install a 3D printer on a tanker, for the crew to print spare parts as needed.[39]

For logistics, Amazon, already disrupting several sectors (purchasing a robot company and trialling drones to deliver food and household goods in the UK), filed a patent for 'on-demand printing aboard Amazon trucks' in 2015.[40] UPS, Staples and Royal Mail are experimenting with offering 3D printing to customers. A website in the United States, Instructables.com, offers instructions to repair items, including a pram with 3D printed parts, sourcing the materials from 3D printing specialist shapeways.com. Instructables.com, operated by Autodesk Inc, was formed at the MIT Media Lab in the mid-2000s.[41]

Products or components made with a single, recyclable material can be more easily recycled, making it more attractive to recover your own end-of-use products. For more on 3DP, see Chapter 4.

Internet of Things, big data and machine learning

Use of sensors, machine-to-machine (M2M) communications and the *Internet of Things*, coupled with predictive analytics and *big data*, is already transforming production lines and improving resource efficiency. Feedback from in-use products, helping to benchmark performance and support preventative maintenance, can streamline the inventory of spare parts. It also helps improve understanding of which components and materials support longer, more intensive product use, and which are constraining longer life-cycles or reuse opportunities.

For reverse logistics, machine learning is already being used to recognize and sort products for recycling, both in large automated sorting facilities and in reverse vending machines, accepting end-of-use batteries, light bulbs and recyclable packaging. Highly accurate object recognition allows rewards to be automatically issued for the correct returns.

Platforms and mobile 'apps'

As we have seen, platforms and apps are supporting sharing and product-as-a-service models, and allow customers to engage more closely with the company. Logistics providers are using apps to communicate with customers, to ensure deliveries can be made first time, securely and conveniently. Apps and scripts can help with returns, assessing condition and deciding whether an unwanted product has value. Circular service providers can operate platforms on behalf of brands, providing all the back-office logistics and other services to help recover and recirculate a wide range of products. Stuffstr works with 'retail customers to recirculate their used clothing effort-lessly – no listings, no shipping, no waiting for payment. Everything happens at the touch of a button'. Noticing the increasing levels of clothes left unworn in the back of wardrobes, they spotted an opportunity, and say, 'Only by making it as easy to recirculate your used clothing as it is to let things pile up and throw them away can we truly begin to change consumer behaviour.'[42]

PATAGONIA AND IFIXIT – 'DO IT YOURSELF' REPAIRS

In 2013, iFixit and Patagonia created a repair partnership.[43] Patagonia provides a lifetime warranty for its outdoor clothing and other products. Customers can return products for free-of-charge repair, either through the original retail shop or via the Patagonia website. Demand for repairs peaks during autumn and winter, making it difficult to provide a rapid response all year round. iFixit worked with Patagonia to understand the most common repair processes, creating scripts to publish online. The process is simple: the consumer enters the style number from the Patagonia product label into iFixit.com to find the corresponding repair guide, and Patagonia's repair department delivers the relevant fabric and replacement materials.

iFixit's market research indicates that supporting user repairs improves the consumer perception of a brand. This increases the probability of purchasing future products from the brand, with a survey of members finding:

- A successful (do-it-yourself) repair increased the likelihood of buying another product from the same manufacturer (95 per cent).
- Repair options/information available on the brand website at the point of purchase makes it more likely that the consumer will buy the product.
- iFixit enabled users to make repairs they would not otherwise have managed (91 per cent).
- The average user had repaired seven products.

Brands are already facing challenges with 'copycat' and fake products being sold online. Some are organizing their own systems for resale, so they can check for authenticity and provide a more trusted service for customers. RFID and other 'active' or 'passive' tags could help ensure the product, components and materials are genuine.

Accelerators

Accelerators include collaborations, independent assessments and certification, financial support, and legislation. Government policy, whether local, national or international, can encourage a shift to circular approaches too.

Collaboration

Chapter 11 highlighted the opportunities for **collaboration** with peer companies in your sector, and with companies providing specialized outsourcing services. Remanufacturing, refurbishing and repair services can all be contracted out, either to companies offering, say, remanufacture for certain products, or by finding manufacturers who can provide the specialist skills and equipment required. Smaller companies, with more flexible processes, may be good potential partners. It may make sense to sub-contract discrete aspects of remanufacture or refurbishment to different companies. If we took the example of a domestic heating boiler, the burner, the electronics and the water storage tanks could all go to specialists and then return for reassembly and testing.

If your own network does not have sufficient critical mass, **shared user platforms** and **exchanges** can help reduce costs or improve response times. Consider using pallet and parcel networks, contract ('third party') logistics 'shared user' fleets and warehouses, freight exchanges and 'fourth-party logistics' (4PL), or 'lead logistics provider' (LLP) solutions. These LLP services, offered by large-scale logistics service providers, manage freight for several clients with a 'control tower'. Consignments are offered to appropriately screened hauliers, able to meet constraints such as collection and delivery times. The hauliers tender for the work, aiming to 'bundle' with nearby consignments to reduce distance and cost.

Can you **share facilities or equipment** with supply chain partners, or with local businesses? A 'cluster' of businesses, all using, for example, forklift trucks, may have activity peaks at different times of the year, enabling exchanges of spare equipment in order to reduce the overall pool size and cost.

Life-cycle assessment

Life-cycle assessments (LCAs) help to understand the footprint of products along the entire value chain, and evaluate the impact of changing the source country, material types, or even the impact of farming methods, such as organic or biodynamic versus industrialized agriculture.

There are international LCA standards for both the principles and framework (ISO 14040:2006) and the requirements and guidelines (ISO 14044:2006). These standards include 20 'impact categories' such as carbon, water depletion, toxicity and eutrophication, and can be applied to products, buildings, supply chains or services.[44]

LCA aims to compare the effects of products or services, by quantifying all the inputs (resources) and outputs (eg emissions and other wastes) for each material flow. The results can then inform decisions on process and policy improvements. Figure 12.10 shows the four stages of LCA outlined by the International Organization for Standardization (ISO), with interconnections at each stage as information emerges and raises questions or issues at other stages:

- **Goal and scope definition** sets the context for the study, including the 'functional unit', the system boundaries, assumptions and limitations, and the chosen impact categories. If several products or functions share the same process, define a methodology for apportioning impact.

- **Inventory analysis** includes all resources (farmed or extracted) used along the entire life-cycle for the product or service. Transport and logistics between each stage is included in the scope, and both use and disposal at end-of-use should be considered. However, there is often little or no control of what happens after the sale of the product or service; information may be obscure and there might be a wide variance in the approaches taken by users.

- **Impact assessment** includes choosing the impact categories, classification of each inventory parameter to an impact category, and measurement to evaluate the potential overall impact.

- The **interpretation** stage draws conclusions and makes recommendations. Results are analysed in detail, looking to identify the key impacts (where, what and which impact categories). Priorities may differ by company or product. Perhaps your priority is to reduce the water footprint or to avoid causing deforestation. Maybe you want to exclude toxic chemicals from the process? Recommendations for improvement may lead to changes in product designs or procurement specifications.

There are other standards, applicable to different sectors too, such as LEED (Leadership in Energy and Environmental Design) for buildings or the Higg Index for apparel. Assessments could be specific to one product for a single company or generic across a sector, such as life-cycle carbon mapping for the apparel industry.[45] LCAs can be extremely detailed; or 'streamlined' by

FIGURE 12.10   Life-cycle assessment overview

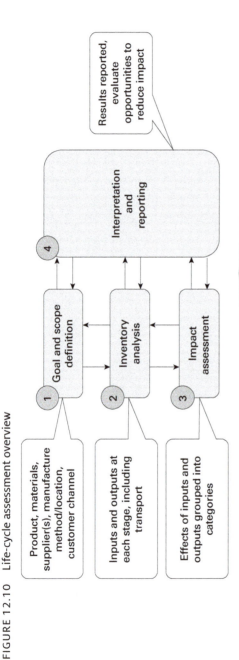

Product, materials, supplier(s), manufacture method/location, customer channel

Inputs and outputs at each stage, including transport

Effects of inputs and outputs grouped into categories

1   Goal and scope definition

2   Inventory analysis

3   Impact assessment

4   Interpretation and reporting

Results reported, evaluate opportunities to reduce impact

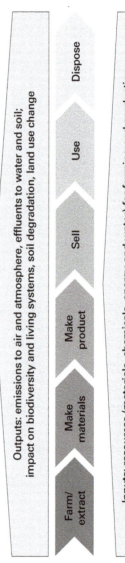

Farm/extract   Make materials   Make product   Sell   Use   Dispose

Outputs: emissions to air and atmosphere, effluents to water and soil; impact on biodiversity and living systems, soil degradation, land use change

Inputs: resources (materials, chemicals, energy and water) for farming and production, transport and logistics along the entire supply chain, facilities and inputs for sales, use and disposal.

omitting smaller, less important processes. Generic LCAs should include representative samples of producers, source countries, etc, to account for differences in methods or regional needs such as water. The footprint analysis for Levi Strauss jeans in Chapter 7 showed the impacts along the supply chain, whilst the LCA for Scotch whisky in Chapter 4 measured climate change, water and land use.

Figure 12.11 shows an example life-cycle assessment for a pair of jeans, undertaken for the French Environment Agency. It measures eight different impacts across nine elements of the supply chain, from cotton cultivation through to use and end of life.

Policies, legislation and product stewardship

Legislation, often created to protect consumer safety, guard against fraud, illegal trading and so on, may be a barrier to circular strategies. Legislation often prevents cross-border movement of 'waste', for example, a returning product being sent for remanufacturing or recycling. Internationally agreed definitions of refurbishment and remanufacturing, perhaps aligned with reputable bodies such as the International Standards Organization, could simplify legal definitions, encouraging more organizations to engage in circular approaches. Trade agreements could also help here.

Product stewardship approaches already make sense for specialist manufacturers, particularly those with strategies for recovery and recirculation – why leave value on the table for a competitor? For some products, including fashion and packaging, sector-wide collaborations may be more appropriate, making it easier to set up locally convenient systems to deal with generic product types.

Value opportunities

Upstream, **procurement** teams can use circular economy approaches to create new value. They can use whole-system approaches to costs and impacts: sourcing circular inputs; reducing environmental, reputational or supply risks; or even switching **from ownership to access models** for support categories such as maintenance, repairs and operations (MRO). Working with suppliers to develop solutions based on **performance**, instead of specifications, can unlock value from more durable or higher-performing products and materials. **Collaborative** approaches could include working with NGOs or academic institutions to make use of their specific expertise, such as the C&A and Water Footprint Network example in Chapter 7.

FIGURE 12.11   Life-cycle assessment for jeans

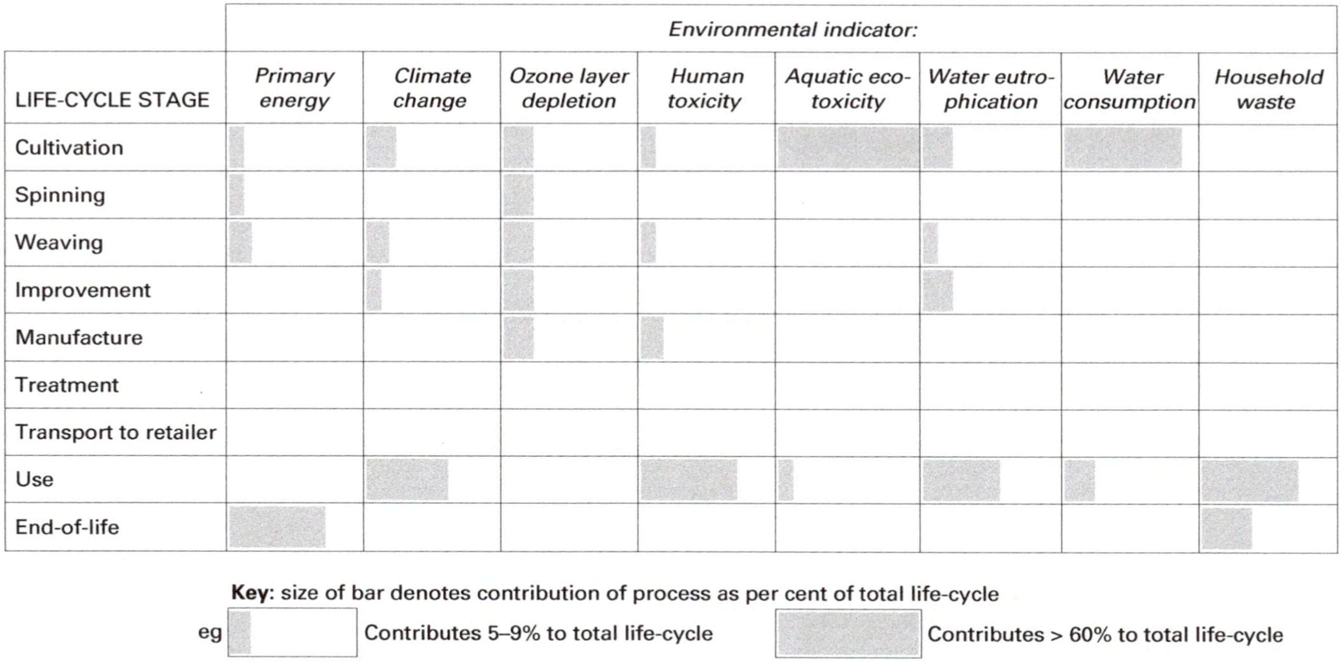

Environmental indicator:

LIFE-CYCLE STAGE	Primary energy	Climate change	Ozone layer depletion	Human toxicity	Aquatic eco-toxicity	Water eutro-phication	Water consumption	Household waste
Cultivation	▪	▪	▪	▪	▪	▪	▪▪	
Spinning	▪		▪					
Weaving	▪	▪	▪	▪				
Improvement		▪	▪			▪		
Manufacture				▪				
Treatment								
Transport to retailer								
Use		▪		▪	▪	▪	▪	▪▪
End-of-life	▪							▪

Key: size of bar denotes contribution of process as per cent of total life-cycle

eg [ ] Contributes 5–9% to total life-cycle   [ ] Contributes > 60% to total life-cycle

SOURCE: Adapted from The Environmental Product Declaration of Jeans, conducted by the Bio Intelligence Service in 2006 for the Department for Eco-Design and Sustainable Development of the French Environment Agency ADEME

In the supply chain **midstream**, development of *by-products* and *co-products*, together with symbiotic flows and eco-industrial parks with shared facilities, adds a new level of complexity to supply chain management. However, it opens up ways of creating new value, converting waste from materials and processes into products and internal resources, with new markets and revenue streams.

Downstream, retaining value by finding effective, efficient ways to recover products and materials can reduce the 'rework' for the product's next use cycle. Implementing circular economy principles adds value: for transit packaging, for warehouse and transport operations, and for reverse supply chains. Prioritizing risk areas, or where most value could be recovered, can create a road map of continuous improvement initiatives.

Could you use your logistics network to recover and consolidate waste from retail stores, restaurants and hotels, or from customers? Higher volumes of waste material, with the potential to separate into 'purer', more specific recyclable streams, may create a business case for sorting and compaction equipment, dedicated space, communication strategies to help improve initial recovery and so on. Perhaps you could collaborate with industrial neighbours to set up joint approaches for separating and recycling packaging or other common streams?

How do we set **criteria for success**, and measure our progress? Approaches to sourcing and procurement will evolve and improve as the business embeds 'circularity' into products and processes. Objectives and performance measurement will evolve too, focusing on more than 'per cent of spend managed' or financial savings. Using the *Natural Step* 'system conditions' scorecard, either the simple version we saw in Chapter 7 or the more detailed, open-source Future-Fit Business Benchmark (FFBB) we covered in Chapter 10, will assess broader environmental, social and ethical themes in addition to the choice of materials and elimination of waste.[46] Alternatively, developing company-specific circular economy objectives into a balanced scorecard can help identify priorities and benchmark a 'base case' and improvements. Include water, energy, value lost (waste) as well as resource inputs, and perhaps focus on 'quick wins' as well as longer-term objectives.

Measuring success might include setting targets for zero waste, and measuring the value earned, both for the sale of by-products and the reduced need for inputs (eg through water-saving, waste to energy, etc). Tracking that value earned, and looking for ways to increase this through improved logistics, different product formats or market channels with more value potential, can turn the supply chain function from a cost centre to a profit generator.

Summary

Involving the whole, extended supply chain is central to the success of circular strategies. Sourcing and procurement teams can play pivotal roles in the transition: for both the product and services provided by the company and in changing how internal services, facilities and consumables are procured. Circular policies can apply to everything – facilities management, back-office, consumables, uniforms and much more – regardless of whether the company is embarking on circular economy strategies.

Business, manufacturing and supply chains have changed profoundly over the last few decades. The 'Third Industrial Revolution', involving digital technologies, continues at pace, with developments in big data, the Internet of Things, robotics and 3D printing. New pressures are emerging, with cost volatility and security of supply for key material resources high on boardroom agendas. Circular models will transform how we think about manufacturing, broadening the scope to include remanufacturing, refurbishing and repair. Reverse manufacturing, or 'un-making', will flourish – developing effective, productive ways to disassemble products and components and recycle materials (maybe at atom level) to provide the next batch of resources.

Distributed manufacturing and local assembly and repair provide opportunities to improve service and resilience. All of these need efficient, agile supply chains to flow used materials, components or products into the 're-' processes, ensuring that transit packaging and handling processes provide effective protection to optimize the value recoverable.

In the last decade or so, supply chain teams have focused on 'last-mile' logistics, aiming to provide efficient, reliable services, with customers choosing from a variety of delivery modes. UPS describes a similar challenge for the circular economy, focusing on 'first-mile' solutions.[47] Ascertaining the condition and thus ideal destination for returning goods helps avoid unnecessary costs and increased risk of loss or damage. Developing systems for these returns, which may lack transit packaging and even require disassembly at the user location, will be challenging. Can you integrate returns with outbound distribution, or is it better to find a suitable collection partner? How can you use technology to monitor the location and condition of products in a 'performance' model, ensuring maintenance or return at the optimum point?

There are many opportunities to embed circular economy approaches into the supply chain, and create new value. Services could replace assets or provide consumables; collaborative solutions could transform asset utilization, utilize specialist skills or create symbiotic flows; reverse supply chains create new value and become the engine in the circular economy; collaborative initiatives can leverage knowledge and create critical mass, to create, conserve and circulate value.

Further resources

BITC Circular Office Guide [Online] https://www.bitc.org.uk/resources-training/resources/research/circular-office-guide (archived at https://perma.cc/VN69-8ZBC)

CIPS WRAP Sustainable Procurement Resources [Online] https://www.cips.org/en-GB/knowledge/procurement-topics-and-skills/sustainability/wrap1/ (archived at https://perma.cc/ZPF8-46HP)

Circular Procurement Guide, MVO Netherlands [Online] https://www.circular-europe-network.eu/library/thematic-guidance-material/roadmap-circular-public-procurement/ (archived at https://perma.cc/66ZW-V3GK)

EU Public procurement for a Circular Economy [Online] https://ec.europa.eu/environment/gpp/pdf/Public_procurement_circular_economy_brochure.pdf (archived at https://perma.cc/2QUU-DHST)

ICLEI Circular Procurement Best Practice Report [Online] http://www.iclei-europe.org/fileadmin/templates/iclei-europe/lib/resources/tools/push_resource_file.php?uid=BDJtTcim (archived at https://perma.cc/9BQX-ZDSL)

Institute for Manufacturing, University of Cambridge [Online] http://www.ifm.eng.cam.ac.uk/ (archived at https://perma.cc/KC8T-YQHR)

Lavery, G, Pennell, N, Brown, S and Evans S [accessed 15 August 2016] *The Next Manufacturing Revolution: Non-labour resource productivity and its potential for remanufacturing* [Online] https://www.ifm.eng.cam.ac.uk/ (archived at https://perma.cc/9RC3-6TJL)

SHAPA (Solids Handling and Processing Association) [Online] http://www.shapa.co.uk/index.php (archived at https://perma.cc/KHU6-EHEY)

Sustainable Procurement Resource Centre (focused on public procurement) [Online] www.sustainable-procurement.org/home/ (archived at https://perma.cc/2FFA-PCEE)

The Future-Fit Business Benchmark [Online] futurefitbusiness.org/about/introduction/ (archived at https://perma.cc/7969-TZP6)

United Nations Global Compact (2010) [accessed 1 June 2016] *Supply Chain Sustainability: A practical guide for continuous improvement* [Online] www.unglobalcompact.org/docs/issues_doc/supply_chain/SupplyChainRep_spread.pdf (archived at https://perma.cc/PZ7Q-7QYC)

UPS/GreenBiz (2016) [accessed 14 April 2016] *The Growth of the Circular Economy: A 2016 UPS/GreenBiz Research Study*, 22 March [Online] sustainability.ups.com/media/UPS_GreenBiz_Whitepaper.pdf (archived at https://perma.cc/GLV4-EMQX)

WEF and UNEP (2018) *Building Circularity into Economies through Sustainable Procurement* [Online] http://www3.weforum.org/docs/WEF_Building_circularity_through_sustainable_procurement_WCEF_2018.pdf (archived at https://perma.cc/7QJP-X88A)

Notes

1 Quoted in *The Economist* on 4 December 2003. Widely quoted online; original date and place of quote is not known, but it's believed to pre-date 1999.

2 Prakarsa, D (30 March 2016) [accessed 10 April 2016] *Supply Chain Traceability Key to Fulfilling Sustainability Promises*, Sustainable Brands [Online] www.sustainablebrands.com/news_and_views/supply_chain/daniel_prakarsa/supply_chain_traceability_key_fulfilling_sustainability (archived at https://perma.cc/2PU4-FWVP)

3 Ceres (2016) [accessed 1 June 2016] Press Release: Ceres Statement on Exxon and Chevron Shareholder Votes [Online] www.ceres.org/press/press-releases/ceres-statement-on-exxon-and-chevron-shareholder-votes (archived at https://perma.cc/CUF2-E6VU)

4 DLL (2015) [accessed 10 April 2016] [Online] www.dllgroup.com/en/press/latest/dll-wins-young-global-leaders-circular-economy-investor-award (archived at https://perma.cc/VJ8W-RKYB)

5 Luckett, T (2014) [accessed 10 April 2016] *Procurement and the Circular Economy*, WRAP [Online] www.sustainable-procurement.org/fileadmin/files/procura-meeting-240914-circular-economy-wrap.pdf (archived at https://perma.cc/DFS4-PZLV)

6 Meyerson, B (4 March 2015) [accessed 8 April 2016] *Top 10 Emerging Technologies of 2015*, World Economic Forum [Online] www.weforum.org/agenda/2015/03/top-10-emerging-technologies-of-2015-2/#distributed-manufacturing (archived at https://perma.cc/ALS5-QZPS)

7 MyMuesli (2019) [accessed 30 November 2019] [Online] uk.mymuesli.com/about-us (archived at https://perma.cc/8HZ2-EFG3)

8 Kalundborg Symbiosis [accessed 15 June 2015] [Online] www.symbiosis.dk/en (archived at https://perma.cc/69T7-DFT9)

9 The Encyclopaedia of the Earth [accessed 21 February 2016] [Online] www.eoearth.org/view/article/153991/ (archived at https://perma.cc/FBB9-3BPS)

10 Ellen MacArthur Foundation (2015) [accessed 21 February 2016] *Case Studies: Kalundborg Symbiosis* [Online] https://www.ellenmacarthurfoundation.org/case-studies/effective-industrial-symbiosis (archived at https://perma.cc/57LY-YQNB)

11 Plant Chicago (2019) [accessed 13 November 2019] [Online] plantchicago.org/
who-we-are/ (archived at https://perma.cc/BK6U-HN7Q)

12 Bubbly Dynamics (2019) [accessed 13 November 2019] [Online]
www.bubblydynamics.com/the-plant/ (archived at https://perma.cc/MU39-TGCG)

13 Himmelfarb, N and O'Dea, K (2015) [accessed 17 April 2016] *From Pepsi to
Unilever, 5 Circular Economy Strategies for Consumer Goods*, GreenBiz
[Online] www.greenbiz.com/article/pepsi-unilever-5-circular-economy-
strategies-consumer-goods (archived at https://perma.cc/A2TA-62EE)

14 Nasr, N et al (2018) [accessed 1 December 2019] *Re-defining Value: The
manufacturing revolution: Remanufacturing, refurbishment, repair and direct
reuse in the circular economy*, A Report of the International Resource Panel,
United Nations Environment Programme, Nairobi, Kenya [Online] UN
Resource Panel re-defining_value_-_the_manfacturing_revolution_full_report_
for_web.pdf

15 ERN (2015) [accessed 13 April 2016] [Online] www.remanufacturing.eu/
about/ (archived at https://perma.cc/VD6C-T65A)

16 Parker, D et al (2015) [accessed 22 November 2019] *Remanufacturing Market
Study*, Report by the European Remanufacturing Network [Online]
www.remanufacturing.eu/assets/pdfs/remanufacturing-market-study.pdf
(archived at https://perma.cc/8XJF-LXV5)

17 Lund, RT (2012) [accessed 13 April 2016] *The Database of Remanufacturers*,
Remanufacturing Studies at Boston University [Online] www.bu.edu/reman/
The%20Remanufacturing%20Database.pdf (archived at https://perma.cc/
W34U-7VYT)

18 Lund, RT (2012) [accessed 13 April 2016] *The Database of Remanufacturers*,
Remanufacturing Studies at Boston University [Online] www.bu.edu/reman/
The%20Remanufacturing%20Database.pdf (archived at https://perma.cc/
W34U-7VYT)

19 Caterpillar (2015) [accessed 8 April 2016] [Online] www.caterpillar.com/en/
company/brands/cat-reman.html (archived at https://perma.cc/3B5L-BNZT)

20 ERN (2015) *Remanufacturing Market Study* [Online]
http://www.remanufacturing.eu/remanufacturing/european-landscape/
(archived at https://perma.cc/5SPS-C6TY)

21 McKinsey & Company (nd) *By Rethinking Packaging, a Company Reduces
Production Costs While Enhancing Brand* [Online] www.mckinsey.com/
business-functions/operations/how-we-help-clients/reduce-packaging-costs
(archived at https://perma.cc/FJ5P-DNMN)

22 Sustainable Brands (30 May 2017) [accessed 1 December 2019] *Trending: Two
new textile innovations aim to take circular fashion towards the mainstream*
[Online] sustainablebrands.com/read/chemistry-materials-packaging/trending-
two-new-textile-innovations-aim-to-take-circular-fashion-towards-the-
mainstream (archived at https://perma.cc/5MMU-KF4S)

23 Pallite UK [accessed 3 June 2016] [Online] http://pallite.co.uk/ (archived at
https://perma.cc/SH6Q-Q6TU)

24 UPS/GreenBiz (2016) [accessed 14 April 2016] *The Growth of the Circular Economy: A 2016 UPS/GreenBiz Research Study*, 22 March [Online] sustainability.ups.com/media/UPS_GreenBiz_Whitepaper.pdf (archived at https://perma.cc/GLV4-EMQX)

25 UPS/GreenBiz (2016) [accessed 14 April 2016] *The Growth of the Circular Economy: A 2016 UPS/GreenBiz Research Study*, 22 March [Online] sustainability.ups.com/media/UPS_GreenBiz_Whitepaper.pdf (archived at https://perma.cc/GLV4-EMQX)

26 Iliopoulos, C (2015) [accessed 17 April 2016] *Reverse Supply Chain of Ships*, MSc thesis, University of Portsmouth, UK [Online] reginafrei.ch/projects.html (archived at https://perma.cc/4KLC-36SP)

27 Jain, KP, Pruyn, JFJ and Hopman, JJ (2014) Influence of ship design on ship recycling, in *Maritime Technology and Engineering*, ed C Guedes Soares and TA Santos, CRC Press London

28 Maersk [accessed 18 April 2016] *Cradle-to-Cradle* [Online]. Web page no longer available, but see http://www.c2c-centre.com/library-item/maersk-cradle-cradle%C2%AE-passport (archived at https://perma.cc/BP7D-T9FQ) and www.maersk.com (archived at https://perma.cc/XQ92-8TL6)

29 Balde, CP et al (2015) *E-Waste Statistics: Guidelines on classifications, reporting and indicators*, United Nations University, IAS-SCYCLE, Bonn, Germany

30 Atasu, A, Guide, VDR and Van Wassenhove, L (2010) So what if remanufacturing cannibalizes my new product sales? *California Management Review*, 52 (2), pp 56–76

31 Abbey, JD, Meloy, MG, Blackburn, J and Guide, VDR (2015) Consumer markets for remanufactured and refurbished products, *California Management Review*, 57 (4), pp 26–42

32 GameStop (2012) [accessed 18 April 2016] *Inside GameStop's Refurbishment Center* [Online] www.gamespot.com/articles/inside-gamestops-refurbishment-center/1100-6389498/ (archived at https://perma.cc/4QRP-CE9H)

33 Airbus (2016) [accessed 18 April 2016] *Eco-services* [Online] www.airbus.com/company/eco-efficiency/eco-services/ (archived at https://perma.cc/ZMH4-9JM8)

34 Matsumoto, M and Umeda, Y (2011) Analysis of remanufacturing practices in Japan, *Journal of Remanufacturing*, 1 (2), pp 1–11

35 Sundin, E and Dunbäck, O (2013) Reverse logistics challenges in remanufacturing of automotive mechatronics devices, *Journal of Remanufacturing*, 3 (2), pp 1–8

36 Frei, R, Lothian, I, Bines, A, Butar Butar, M and Da Gama, L (2015) *Performance in Reverse Supply Chains*, Logistics Research Network Annual Conference (LRN), Derby, UK

37 Cerasis (2015) [accessed 9 April 2016] [Online] cerasis.com/2015/09/17/future-of-procurement/ (archived at https://perma.cc/632X-6VEQ)

38 Sedex (2016) [accessed 10 April 2016] *About Us* [Online] www.sedexglobal.com/about-sedex/ (archived at https://perma.cc/6T2X-9HN6); and *What We Do* [Online] www.sedexglobal.com/about-sedex/what-we-do/ (archived at https://perma.cc/6YD7-D947)

39 Maersk (7 July 2014) [accessed 13 March 2016] *About Us (Spare parts: just press print)* [Online]. Web page no longer available but see shippingwatch.com/suppliers/article10119041.ece (archived at https://perma.cc/4QYR-VEWN) and www.maersk.com (archived at https://perma.cc/XQ92-8TL6)

40 McCormick, R (27 February 2015) [accessed 18 April 2016] Amazon wants to fit trucks with 3D printers to speed up deliveries, *The Verge* [Online] www.theverge.com/2015/2/27/8119443/amazon-3d-printing-trucks-patent (archived at https://perma.cc/WJY5-LH8F)

41 Instructables.com (2016) [accessed 26 May 2016] [Online] http://www.instructables.com/id/How-to-repair-a-Bugaboo-Pram-with-3D-Printing/ (archived at https://perma.cc/R2G2-E4DD)

42 Stuffstr (2019) [accessed 1 December 2019] [Online] www.stuffstr.com/about (archived at https://perma.cc/6UKX-29ZV)

43 Ifixit [accessed 4 February 2016] [Online] ifixit.org/blog/5620/patagonia-ifixits-perfect-partner/ (archived at https://perma.cc/D76Q-63RH)

44 ISO (2006) [accessed 10 April 2016] [Online] www.iso.org/iso/home/news_index/news_archive/news.htm?refid=Ref1019 (archived at https://perma.cc/NUR4-WW7W)

45 Business for Social Responsibility (2009) [accessed 10 April 2016] *Apparel Industry Life Cycle Carbon Mapping* [Online] www.bsr.org/reports/BSR_Apparel_Supply_Chain_Carbon_Report.pdf (archived at https://perma.cc/V3KA-YP2V)

46 The Future-Fit Business Benchmark [accessed 8 April 2016] [Online] http://futurefitbusiness.org/resources/downloads/ (archived at https://perma.cc/EA3U-YLCY)

47 UPS/GreenBiz (2016) [accessed 14 April 2016] *The Growth of the Circular Economy: A 2016 UPS/GreenBiz Research Study*, 22 March [Online] sustainability.ups.com/media/UPS_GreenBiz_Whitepaper.pdf (archived at https://perma.cc/GLV4-EMQX)

PART FOUR

Implementation

13

Making the business case and starting the journey

Closed loop thinking – also known as the circular economy ... engages people and inspires change ... If done well, closed loop innovation can cushion our business from price volatility, provide us with competitive advantage, help us to enter new markets and enable us to build better relationships with customers and suppliers.

SIR IAN CHESHIRE, KINGFISHER PLC[1]

In this chapter, we look at how to implement the circular economy – whether for an entire business, for a product, or perhaps starting with elements of product or process design. We start with a reminder of the **major trends** affecting governments, businesses and citizens, and move on to cover:

- a broader perspective on **the business case** for change, grouped into seven types of rewards;
- **setting strategic direction**, deciding the scope and scale of ambition, involving a wider group of stakeholders and looking for value opportunities and early ideas;
- **risks and opportunities** – factors to consider, including stakeholder needs and competitor pressures;
- common **barriers** and objections, and how to overcome them;
- **beginning the journey**: generating early ideas and plans and moving from ideas to action;
- some **toolkits and resources**, including a section by Barry Waddilove, explaining his card game for whole systems design;
- how to **measure success**.

Trends and drivers

Throughout the book, we have seen the importance of global trends, covering **demand** aspects such as population, demographics and urbanization. The **rules of the game** are changing too, with different business models and commercial relationships, consumer behaviour and technology developments. There are major concerns for **supply**, with resource scarcity and price volatility, and demand for land and water use affecting both affluent and poor regions.

There are critical **system** aspects to consider too, with scientists finding that human impact on our planet is now so significant that we have entered a new geological era, the Anthropocene. Chapter 5 explored the global drivers in more detail, and we covered the challenges for key industry sectors in Chapters 6 to 10. We learned about the massive 'Circularity Gap', with analysis from Circle Economy and others (2018)[2] finding that:

- our global economy is only 9.1 per cent circular;
- resource extraction increased by a factor of 12 between 1900 and 2015, and is forecast to double again by 2050;
- 67 per cent of global *greenhouse gas* emissions (GHG) relate to materials management, meaning circular strategies and solutions are essential tools to address climate change and the Paris Commitments.

We have reached a tipping point, with our increasing demand putting immense pressure on our supply systems (illustrated in Figure 13.1). Our linear approaches to producing food, clothing, housing, consumer goods and transport are not sustainable. We need, urgently, to redesign systems that reduce the load we place on (degenerating) land and living systems and (diminishing) finite resources.

The business case

Many consultancies, governments and other organizations see the circular economy as a win-win for business, people and our planet.

The European Commission's (EC) Circular Economy Action Plan aims to 'close the loop' of product life-cycles.[3] It has 10 billion euros of funding and the EC sees major benefits:

FIGURE 13.1   Tipping point

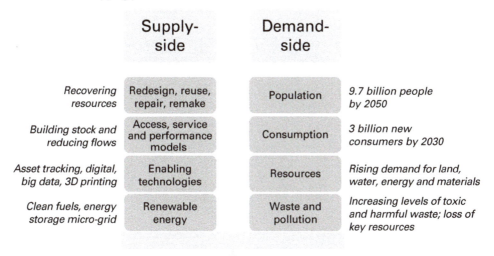

SOURCE: © Catherine Weetman

- 450 million fewer tonnes of EU carbon emissions by 2030;
- savings of 600 billion euros for EU businesses (8 per cent of their annual turnover);
- 580,000 new jobs.

The World Economic Forum believes a 'shift to circular economic activity could help address the global job gap of 600 million', along with many other benefits across a range of market sectors.[4] Accenture estimates that 'shifting to the circular economy could release US$4.5 trillion in new economic potential by 2030'.[5]

However, these macro-economic or industry sector benefits don't easily translate into a business case for smaller-scale circular approaches. You might want to create a compelling business case for your board, or to secure funding – or perhaps you need to convince those around you who are worried about change and uncertainties.

> Businesses that work on the basis of circular principles are amongst the fastest growing in the economy.
>
> Dr Martin Stuchtey, McKinsey[6]

FIGURE 13.2   Seven rewards for circular businesses

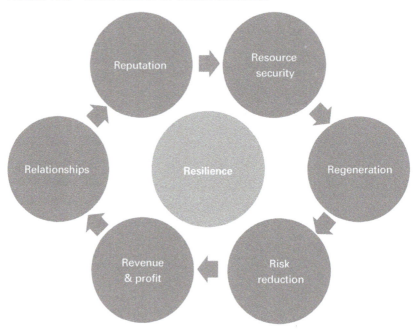

SOURCE: © Catherine Weetman

The hundreds of examples in my circular economy database represent every sector around the world. Many of the examples in this book, and in my talks and workshops, are startups and small businesses, using profitable, resilient, sustainable strategies to disrupt the big corporate 'supertankers'. Circular economy strategies can support a viable business, and you don't need a super-sized research and development budget.

Throughout the book, we have seen how the circular economy creates opportunities for businesses – *and* their customers, suppliers, employees and local communities. I've grouped these into seven circular economy benefits for business: resource security; regeneration; risk reduction; revenue and profit; relationships; reputation and resilience (see Figure 13.2).

Resource security

Pinpointing which materials are critical for your business, and which are most at risk, can be a great starting point for circular approaches. Is future demand likely to exceed supply? Are there geopolitical tensions, likely to affect price or access?

Swapping from finite, potentially risky or under-pressure resources to safe, sustainable materials provides resource security and price stability. For example, Continental Tyres wants to secure its long-term supplies of natural rubber and is developing a more sustainable source of latex, by growing a species of dandelions near its factories in Germany.[7] (The rubber plant is on the EU Critical Materials list.) Similarly, outdoor gear brand Patagonia is securing its resources and reducing its environmental footprint by swapping from high-impact and water-dependent cotton to bast fibres like hemp.

Collecting and recovering your own end-of-life products, components and materials can close the loop in your supply chain and your resource security. Designing for easy disassembly makes this more cost-effective. Tom Harper of Unusual Rigging developed an asset management system, creating opportunities for reuse of equipment and components.[8] Deposit schemes, product-as-a-service, rental and buy-back commercial models can all encourage recovery for your next batch of products – Desso Carpets, Ricoh Greenline copiers and Mud Jeans are benefiting from this.

Regeneration

Applying the circular economy mantra of 'waste = food' – for resources used in both the product and the production process – might involve regenerating your own resources, or partnering with a specialist recycler.

In Chapter 6, we read about a range of new uses for waste coffee grounds. In the Netherlands, Mud Jeans now uses up to 40 per cent recycled denim from jeans returned by its customers.

You could protect both your resources and suppliers by supporting your upstream supply chain to regenerate land, improve biodiversity, water quality and even support communities. Nestlé, realizing its dependency on smallholder farmers, provides training and technology to help those farms be fulfilling and financially viable businesses.

Risk reduction

Resource security and regeneration also reduce business risk; diversifying both the locations and materials in your supply chain can help: a global washing machine brand has production lines based on either magnesium or aluminium, so it can swap between the two to optimize input costs.

Local and distributed manufacturing and assembly can reduce the risk of disruption from geopolitical issues, global trade tensions, or climate change. We're already seeing the impact of climate disruption, especially for agricultural products such as food, textiles, cocoa and rubber.

Might your customers have concerns about risks linked to the product? New science highlighting toxicity, safety or other problems can quickly gain attention. Plastic straws, glyphosate weedkillers and PFCs in outdoor gear are just a few examples where new evidence threatens the entire business model for the companies involved.

What other threats should you consider? Maybe your competitors (existing or soon-to-be) are planning circular economy projects that could undermine your business. Are you at risk from their customer-centric offer, new commercial models, or building their brand purpose to do more good (not just a bit less harm)?

Is your sector gaining attention from governments, concerned about pollution and health? Might they impose product stewardship legislation, taxes or even ban the product itself? Think of those manufacturers of single-use plastics in countries that now have taxes or complete bans. Circular approaches can mitigate those risks, too.

Revenue and profit

New by-products from your recovered waste can open up new markets and sales. Expanding your offer to include repairs, remanufacturing, reselling and sharing can generate new revenue streams. Repair options might need supplies of spares, consumables and even special tools.

Remanufacturing and reselling can open up new markets, by selling to different geographies or demographic groups who might aspire to buy the high-quality, high-functionality product, but can't justify the cost of a brand-new version. For companies like Caterpillar, Cummins and Cisco, remanufacturing is a highly profitable mainstay of their business.

There are new market opportunities from offering services, instead of selling products: BMW started its Drive Now car rental service to make it easy for existing BMW owners to rent their trusted brand of car when away from home. Unexpectedly, plenty of non-BMW owners wanted to rent a BMW too – opening up a new group of potential customers for the company, as well as capturing a bigger share of the rental market.

Another advantage of using instead of owning is that it smooths cash flow, and that can help both buyers and sellers of high-value products, equipment and infrastructure.

Cost savings can come through circular procurement policies, encouraging product stewardship and buying services rather than owning equipment, assets, products and consumables. Negotiating contracts for performance can deliver win-win outcomes for you and your supplier. Avoiding waste disposal costs, import tariffs and long-distance, high-inventory supply chains can save money, too.

Is your business model reliant on product obsolescence? This could incur hidden costs for unnecessary marketing spend, cost of research and development, and writing-off stocks of the old model (and its parts) in your supply chain.

Relationships

Stronger, deeper customer relationships can pay dividends, avoiding expensive marketing to get noticed in an overcrowded and difficult-to-measure media marketplace. Research says that acquiring a new customer is anywhere from five to 25 times more expensive than keeping an existing one.

In Chapter 4, Katie Beverley explained how user-centred design can engage your customer, and designer Adam Fairweather (mentioned in the Greencup case study in Chapter 6) uses *permaculture* principles to design emotionally, socially and industrially durable products.[9]

Circular, regenerative and win-win strategies can strengthen relationships with suppliers, employees, local communities and shareholders, too, helping everyone feel involved in projects that regenerate and support the community and our living planet.

Reputation

Circular economy approaches build stronger brand reputations, by doing things better and doing better things. People are getting more vocal, criticizing companies involved in (or staying quiet on) deforestation, pollution or using unsustainable materials. Brands selling poor-quality products, using non-recyclable packaging or allowing ecosystem destruction are being 'called out' on social media.

Adopting circular economy strategies can attract and retain talent, by ensuring the brand purpose fits your employee values. The oil and plastics industries are worrying about how they will engage forward-thinking employees and investors.

Resilience

Those six benefits of closing the loop all strengthen the core of your business, and help it become more resilient. A systems thinking perspective, understanding more about the ecosystem around your business, can highlight risks, issues and opportunities.

It's also important to think about how to develop interaction and feed-back loops with customers, employees, suppliers and other stakeholders, so you get to know more about each other's needs and aims and create win-win partnerships.

These seven circular economy benefits can build a **compelling business case** for change, by highlighting the opportunities to strengthen your business, so you can get started on a pathway to a resilient, profitable and sustainable business.

Setting the strategic direction

When thinking about the **scope and scale** of the changes and the **speed of transition**, it is useful to involve a wide range of stakeholders, aiming to understand their views on upcoming risks and potential rewards. Starting with a 'quick scan' of priorities and an appetite for change can help define the initial brief for the first project.

What **risks** are already causing concern for the business? These might include **security of supply** or price volatility for key resources, energy or water costs, the cost of waste disposal or packaging, logistics costs, etc. Is this an opportunity to decouple economic growth from the depletion of the earth's natural resources for your company?

Are there risks to **reputation** from suppliers or materials sourced from certain regions, or because you are putting unrecyclable, single-use products into the market? Maybe some of the **materials** you specify are unsafe, making them difficult to recycle? The global risk map we highlighted earlier might be a good starting point (see Figure 13.3 for the top-ranked risks in 2019). The Global Risks reports, published annually by the World Economic Forum, include a comprehensive list of what is worrying global business and government leaders. You can then think about the specific risks facing your business, your industry sector, your key supplier and partners, and your customers. Reviewing risks with different time horizons can also be useful, particularly when deciding which short-term 'quick wins' to pursue and what longer-term, more complex initiatives to commence. We'll return to risks in the next section.

For **stakeholders**, what is their level of interest and buy-in? Are investors, employees and suppliers familiar with circular economy concepts, and do they see the potential? Is it better to start with resource-efficiency and waste reduction, and begin to look at ways to make high-risk inputs more

FIGURE 13.3   Global risks

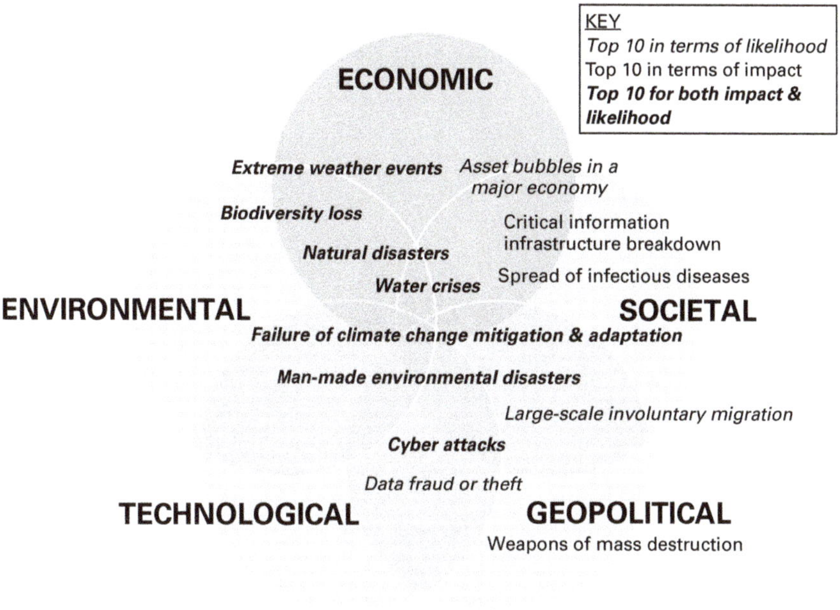

KEY
Top 10 in terms of likelihood
Top 10 in terms of impact
**Top 10 for both impact &
likelihood**

ECONOMIC

Extreme weather events   *Asset bubbles in a
major economy*

Biodiversity loss   Critical information
                             infrastructure breakdown

Natural disasters

Water crises   Spread of infectious diseases

ENVIRONMENTAL   **SOCIETAL**

Failure of climate change mitigation & adaptation

Man-made environmental disasters

                        Large-scale involuntary migration

Cyber attacks

Data fraud or theft

TECHNOLOGICAL   **GEOPOLITICAL**

Weapons of mass destruction

SOURCE: Adapted from World Economic Forum, Global Risks Report 2019

circular? Can you involve stakeholders in an exploratory workshop to generate ideas and discussion?

The Cambridge Value Mapping Tool is an easy-to-use workshop process, helping 'reconcile how a company can create and deliver value for its multiple stakeholders while capturing value for itself'.[10,11] The tool was developed over several years by researchers at the Institute for Manufacturing, based at the University of Cambridge, and has been widely used by industry. It aims to use a holistic approach to redesigning business models, using a **'shared value'** perspective.

In Chapter 3, we noted researchers – Bocken and team, Geissdoerfer and team, Mulrow and Santos – highlighting the need for a clear purpose for circular business models, to ensure we have real 'system value' for all the stakeholders: business, society and the living world we all depend on. In Chapter 5, we talked about 'shareholders versus stakeholders', and mentioned the work of the Future-Fit Foundation.

Companies operate in a range of external systems, with a complex network of stakeholders. Using the unique perspective of each group of stakeholders to understand how value is captured, destroyed or missed can highlight new opportunities. Stakeholders could include consumers,

FIGURE 13.4   Thinking about value

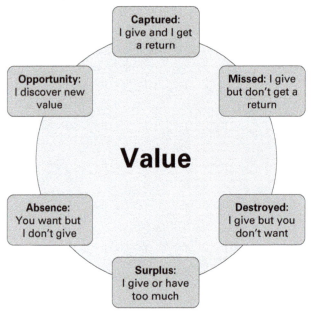

SOURCE: Vladimirova (2015)[12]

customers and specifiers, communities, suppliers and partners, employees, owners, investors or shareholders, and, crucially, the environment and living systems.

The Cambridge Value Mapping Tool helps identify 'failed value exchanges', and uses different viewpoints to 'think about value'. In training sessions on how to use the tool, I have seen the process generate ideas in a range of business contexts, from industrial windows to food packaging. Figure 13.4 summarizes the different value exchanges from the perspective of each of the stakeholders. The tool, developed and refined over a number of years, has been widely used in industry workshops. It is easy to understand and use, and participants take on different stakeholder roles: trying to look at the business, product or service through their eyes. The experience of looking at the problem – from the perspective of customers, suppliers, or communities near the factories in your supply chain – can open up new opportunities for shared value.

Figure 13.5 shows a possible outcome for a food service company, with the issues categorized using the Natural Step system conditions. Many of the issues show value uncaptured for several different stakeholders, and this is a good starting point for discussions and ideas focused on creating value opportunities from those issues. I've adapted the Value Mapping Tool and

FIGURE 13.5 Value uncaptured – foodservice examples

Value uncaptured	Stakeholder →	Planet		People				Profit	
		Living systems	Earth resources	Employees	Customers and end users	Society	Government, NGOs	Owners/ shareholders	Suppliers
Missed	We've created it... / ...but we don't capture value from it				Food waste				
							Employee skills underused		
							Surplus stock		
					Selling non-seasonal food from distant sources				
					Change in land use for outlets and logistics infrastructure				
					Water run-off from buildings				
Destroyed	What we create... / ...has a negative impact			Fossil fuel extraction (and mining waste)					
				Pollution: air, water, soil (and clean up costs/taxes)					
						Demotivation eg zero hours contract, low pay			
					Noise – operations and vehicles				
					Accidents				
					Non-reusable packaging (and taxes)				
									Inefficient back door systems
Absent	There is a need... / ...but we fail to deliver it					Temporary lack of labour/materials			
				Packaging does not biodegrade					
						Limited learning and development			
						Limited career prospects (~ demotivation/high staff turnover)			
						Inconsistent service level			
Surplus	We create this... / ...but it's not needed					Low productivity / idle time			
						Next-day delivery for three-day lead time			
						Labour overcapacity			
						Excess packaging			
						Selling less than we could			

System condition key

1 scarce materials taken from the earth
2 man made toxic and persistent materials
3 destruction and pollution of nature
4 work and/or use conditions
M multiple/monetary

SOURCE: C Weetman, after Vladimirova (2015) (see endnote 12)

FIGURE 13.6   System conditions for a sustainable society

A sustainable society:

 Cycles finite resources infinitely, avoiding the need for new extraction (eg urban mining)

 Ensures **man-made substances are safe and biodegradable or recyclable**: in production, use and end-of-life

 Regenerates living systems to provide abundant natural resources and healthy ecosystems (air, atmosphere, soil, water, biodiversity)

 Business creates **meaningful jobs, supports communities** along its supply chain and pays for its externalized costs

SOURCE: Adapted from the Future-Fit Foundation (2019)[13]

its multi-stakeholder approach in my circular economy workshops, examining products from a range of viewpoints to identify the value missed and lost, and uncover new value opportunities.

Shared value, created by Michael Porter and Mark Kramer, is 'a management strategy focused on companies creating measurable business value by identifying and addressing social problems that intersect with their business'.[14] The Shared Value Initiative website describes three ways of creating shared value:

- reconceiving products and markets;
- redefining productivity in the value chain;
- local cluster development.

In Chapter 5, we noted the Future-Fit Foundation arguing that in shared value approaches, business still comes first, as 'negative impacts are not sufficiently internalized, or are justified by "doing good" elsewhere.' Instead, the Future-Fit Foundation advocates **system value**, in which business 'in no way hinders – and ideally contributes to – society's progress toward future-fitness'. It offers a free, open-source benchmarking system to allow companies to 'align their success with that of society'.[15] The benchmark uses four system conditions, based on the *Natural Step* (mentioned earlier in the book). I've adapted those, rewording them to focus on what we should do, rather than what we should not (see Figure 13.6).

For a broader approach, companies can sign up to the United Nations Global Compact (UNGC) commitments (2010),[16] with 10 principles covering human rights, labour, environment and anti-corruption. By early 2016, the UNGC reported that 8,600 companies in 163 countries had filed over

FIGURE 13.7   The doughnut of social and planetary boundaries

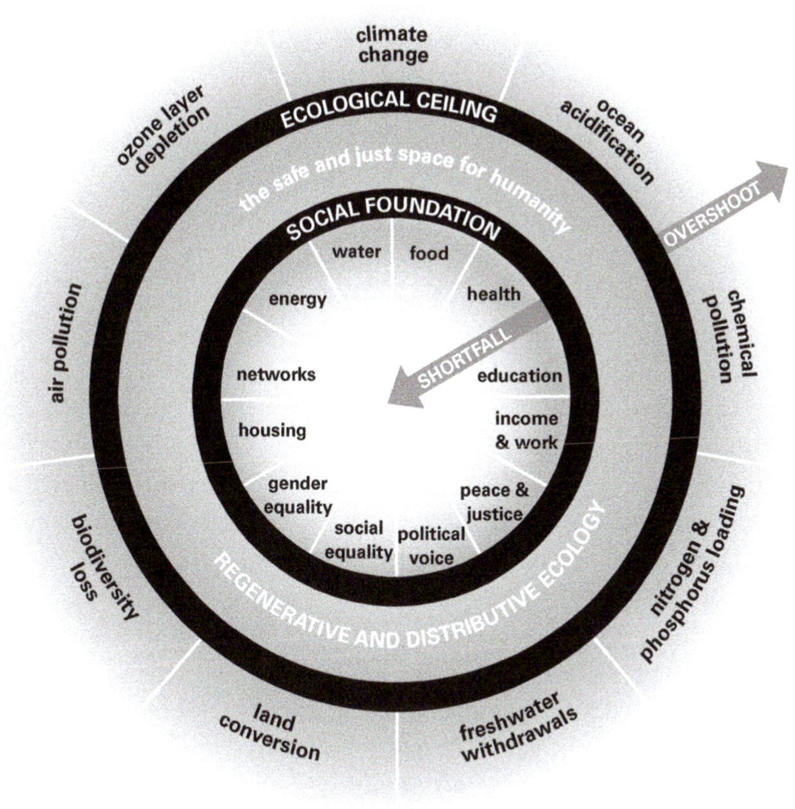

SOURCE: © Kate Raworth (2017)

37,000 public reports, explaining how their companies had performed against these commitments.

An alternative model is Kate Raworth's concept of **Doughnut Economics** (see Figure 13.7). Raworth uses the nine planetary boundaries (set out by Rockstrom et al) together with 12 dimensions of a social foundation (derived from internationally agreed minimum social standards, identified in the Sustainable Development Goals in 2015). Raworth says that 'between social and planetary boundaries lies an environmentally safe and socially just space in which humanity can thrive.'[17]

Risks and opportunities

Successful business strategy evaluates the likely impact of relevant external drivers. Are new technologies threatening to disrupt your sector? Are you at risk from an established competitor? Are there new threats from startups, whether focused on your sector (for example, Airbnb for hotels, Uber for taxis) or from an established company moving into your space (eg Amazon moving into food and grocery deliveries)?

Using tools like **SWOT** analysis (strengths, weaknesses, opportunities and threats) is useful to combine both internal and external factors, looking at the business purpose and 'unique selling point' whilst looking externally at likely changes and competitor activities. **PEST** (political, economic, social and technological) analysis can help to focus on the changes, risks and opportunities that already exist, or are likely to arise during implementation of the strategy. PEST is often expanded to include environmental and legal factors, becoming **PESTLE**. Although these factors will differ for each business, common threads will appear across several of the PESTLE headings, many of which we covered in Chapter 5.

Political factors, including governmental interventions at regional, national and local levels, include trade agreements and fiscal and economic policies, for example taxing waste sent to landfill. There are global political drivers too, such as the declarations of climate and biodiversity emergencies. We mentioned geopolitical factors in Chapter 5, affecting trade agreements and resource security.

Economic factors include inflation, economic growth or recession, and interest rates. Forecasting future price trends is complex, and does not necessarily depend on historic patterns – however, it is worth regularly reviewing the outlook for prices of key **resources**. Long-term patterns are shown in the Global Commodity Index, created by McKinsey Global Institute, which is included in many of the Ellen MacArthur Foundation reports – or you can search the McKinsey consulting website for the MGI Commodity Price Index.[18]

Social and demographic factors include population growth and demographic changes such as the age of consumers, availability of labour, health factors, fashion trends, attitudes to education, career, politics and so on. Cultural factors may be important – millennials are favouring 'use' models in preference to 'ownership', and research is showing that people feel good about buying eco- or ethically-conscious products, and many prefer to buy fewer, but higher-quality products. Trends towards buying experiences instead of products, the expanding use of the internet and social media can all support circular strategies.[19]

Technological factors include the developments we have covered earlier in the book, with digital, 3D printing, the Internet of Things, big data and more. The accelerating rate of dissemination means more rapid adoption of recent innovations, as they become cheaper and perform better – digital technology transformed the music and photography sectors in just a few years. Might your competitors be looking at how to 'virtualize' your product, offering it as a digital service – or compete by offering 'pay per use' through mobile technologies?

Legal and regulatory factors may overlap with political agendas (eg taxes on sugar to support improved national health, reduce healthcare costs and welfare budgets). There may be disruptive innovations that challenge existing laws, such as the Uber model clashing with licensed taxi drivers in London and other cities, or Airbnb hosts contravening local legislation on sub-letting. Existing or new standards may be important, whether compulsory (eg EU Ecodesign) or voluntary, such as organic or sustainable sourcing standards. A law on Ecocide would drive more sustainable behaviour, and the campaign is gaining attention around the world, with governments taking an interest.[20] Governments (via taxation) fund the cleaning up of **business externalities**, and many are looking to redirect these costs back to those responsible. Product stewardship legislation already applies to certain products in the European Union, and some sectors are looking at collaborative agreements to head off legislation. The issues include chronic, expensive health conditions caused by diet, air pollution, waste disposal and so on – and of course the need to fulfil the Paris Agreement commitments on reducing GHG emissions.[21]

We have mentioned **environmental** factors throughout the book. Again, many of these overlap with other areas – climate and weather changes may affect communities, causing migration and civil unrest, which in turn creates geopolitical pressures and economic risks. Our overarching aim should be to regenerate, not deplete or destroy, the living systems that we all depend on to survive, and thrive.

Overcoming barriers

A report from the Ellen MacArthur Foundation (2012),[22] challenging the viability and business case for circular approaches, outlines a number of common concerns, with their circular solutions:

- **Shifting to performance models will increase the 'total cost of ownership'.** Durable products could discourage customers from replacing older models with newer, more efficient versions. Lease or rental models can easily overcome this issue, and performance or results contracts encourage both the provider and the user to opt for the most efficient products.

Models like these also encourage modular designs to enable easy repairs and upgrades.

- **Making longer-lasting products means fewer sales in the longer term.** This is likely to affect poorer-performing and less durable products, and manufacturers and retailers may have to adapt their offers to include refurbishment, repair and resale to replace profits from those lost sales.

- **Customers prefer to own rather than rent or pay-per-use.** Studies show that millennials are preferring use instead of ownership, and the accelerating development of technology is encouraging more people to set up pay-per-use and subscription contracts. Business customers will evaluate the balance sheet and cash-flow benefits of ownership compared with other ways to access the product.

- **Switching away from a sales-based business model reduces cash flow.** Financing the initial reduction in cash flow may be challenging and risky for companies, but banks such as DLL are recognizing commercial opportunities from supporting circular models, and are developing financial services to help with rental and pay-per-use models. Startups like TurnToo are linking manufacturers and users, for example partnering with Philips to offer the 'pay per lux' lighting service to businesses.[23]

Markus Zils, alumni of McKinsey, speaks of the need to 'rethink the business case' for the circular economy, and looks at how to counter objections:[24]

- **If resource prices fall, the business case doesn't work.** Resource price trends declined gradually throughout the 20th century, as we improved techniques for finding, extracting, farming and processing resources. The trend has now reversed, with a steep upward trend in the 21st century. Demand is now outstripping supply, and for finite resources, we have now found (and used) all the easy-to-get-at sources.

- **The business model does not work for low-cost products.** It is easier to envisage the business case for B2B and higher-value products, but there are plenty of opportunities for lower-value products too. Options include using recycled materials, making the product and the packaging more durable, moving to refill and refurbishment models, or delivering direct to consumer.

- **Customers are not ready for this – they demand the lowest-cost products.** Ownership is becoming less relevant for some products and some demographic groups. People are becoming more open to responsible consumption and 'sharing' models, and consumer activism is growing, fuelled by NGO campaigns such as Oxfam's 'behind the brands' scorecard.[25]

We might hear other objections: perhaps that the manufacturing and supply chain footprint is too complex to understand and change. In a white paper on the circular economy, McKinsey highlights the multi-tier supply and manufacturing networks that many companies have developed.[26] Examples include a B&Q cordless drill, with up to 80 components using 14 different raw materials from around seven countries. We can envisage many more products with hundreds of components, materials and sources. This makes closing the loop challenging, potentially requiring complex reverse networks and additional logistics costs. McKinsey advocates partnership approaches, such as allowing suppliers to deal with used components and make decisions on what to reuse or recycle. Tracking location and condition of products and components can improve the effectiveness of reverse supply chains, potentially directing products to the appropriate recovery process without the need for centralized collation and inspection.

Beginning the journey

The journey and 'road map' will be unique to each business and the scope and scale of early initiatives will depend on the level of knowledge and buy-in for circular economy approaches. Senior stakeholders may already be well informed and enthusiastic, with less awareness across functional groups of managers and other colleagues. Alternatively, it may be a handful of people, perhaps in design or supply chain roles, seeing the opportunities and needing to convince a wider group about the benefits. In each scenario, spending time translating the broader vision into something more tangible for each group of stakeholders is beneficial. Avoid using jargon, focus on the value opportunities and reduced risks, and provide examples of innovations from similar sectors, sizes of business, target customer groups and so on.

Having generated interest and enthusiasm, you can look at low-risk ideas, focusing on a few specific priorities. Ensuring that the first few initiatives are relatively simple and can become learning opportunities will help maintain enthusiasm and momentum for bigger-scale initiatives in the next phases. Communicating progress and learnings (positive and negative) will maintain enthusiasm. Encouraging ideas and feedback from all groups of stakeholders, both internal and external, can highlight potential problems early and elicit new ideas, adjustments and enhancements. Communicating the benefits – 'towards pleasure and away from pain' – helps people feel proud to be involved, pursuing 'future-proof' goals.

Generating early ideas

Researching issues and market opportunities will help define the strategy and build a business case. The potential 'landscape' of ideas and initiatives could be wide, so it can be useful to start with a rough plan and highlight what you **do not know**. I use an approach based on the *permaculture* whole-system design model, with three stages:

- **Define** – aims and purpose; scope and boundaries; resources and information; early ideas;
- **Plan** – a project plan; risks, mitigation and contingencies; designs, structures and resources;
- **Do** – implement; evaluate; tweak and improve.

For your aims and purpose, do you want to start with slow and small steps or a major strategic leap? Or perhaps move forward on both simultaneously? The scale of risks and opportunities might mean a startup takes a different approach from an established, larger-scale business.

Resources and information starts with what you know and can see. How much do you and your team know about the circular economy and the issues of the linear economy? Can you see circular ideas – in the same sector, or triggered by innovations in other sectors? What misconceptions might you need to deal with – such as 'the circular economy is just a fancy name for recycling', or 'it's just going to cost us money for some green PR'? Who are your stakeholders, and what is the 'ecosystem' supporting your business (organizations, rules, resources, etc)? Use systems thinking to understand this and all the connections and feedback loops.

This approach aims to work in a more evolutionary way, recognizing that the original purpose and ideas may change when more information emerges, after reflecting on risks, and when the costs and timescales for the project become clearer. The 'do' phase benefits from regular reviews, or 'feedback loops', helping to 'tweak and improve' the project scope, boundaries, resources and so on.

Supply chain stakeholders

Each business will face unique challenges in moving to a circular model. Engaging stakeholders, both inside and outside the business, is a key priority, helping generate ideas as well as support for change. Finding information about current practices, materials and impacts can be a challenge, particularly if the current supply chain involves multiple tiers of suppliers spread across different regions and countries. In the early stages, there is a danger of aiming to include too much in the project scope, meaning that data collection is onerous and time-consuming. Suppliers especially may be reluctant to share data, worrying that it gives away their expertise, or might be used to negotiate new prices.

Which materials are priorities for your business? You may decide to rank on cost, disruption, or the ease of recovery. These days, many products lack transparency on the materials and formulation. **Chemicals and materials** are becoming ever-more complex, and circular economy approaches aim to simplify the bill of materials, both at the design stage and from regular reviews to examine whether materials can now be simplified or substituted. The McDonough Braungart Design Chemistry (MBDC) Cradle to Cradle® Design Framework evaluates new product designs against three sets of criteria:[27]

- **Materials chemistry:** what chemicals are in the materials specified for the product, and are these the safest chemicals available?
- **Disassembly:** can we take the product apart easily at the end of its useful life, and recycle the materials?
- **Recyclability:** do the materials contain recycled content? Can these materials be recycled again at the end of the product's useful life?

The MBDC Design Framework classifies each material, using a hazard assessment of the chemicals used to manufacture the material. It looks at criteria for human health, including carcinogenicity, endocrine disruption, various toxicities and others, and for environmental health, such as heavy metal content, toxicities, and persistence or biodegradation.

Mapping the benefits

To decide where to start, it is useful to 'map' the benefits of the initial ideas. Sketching a simple X-Y graph or four-box chart can help your team evaluate competing factors: such as level of risk versus impact on the business, the scale of change (strategic versus operational), cost versus future revenue, and so on. It is worth repeating the exercise for different time horizons, as short-term risks and opportunities can look very different from longer-term perspectives, looking 15 to 30 years ahead. What ideas do you have for reducing risk, reducing costs, evolving products, expanding markets and sales channels? How can you improve business capabilities and resilience? From this exercise, you can prioritize some quick wins, and some longer-term ideas, and then look to see what further information you would need to better explore and evaluate these.

The business case is likely to feature a range of 'soft' as well as quantifiable benefits, as we saw earlier in this chapter.

Your business may already have processes for planning and implementing major projects, which can be adapted to fit the complexities and 'whole system design' approach needed for circular models.

From ideas to action

How can you transfer your ideas into action? Can you identify early adopters, and involve them in the product or service design? Are there willing partners in your existing network of suppliers, or have your found potential new collaborative partners in your research? Could you try a frugal innovation approach, seeking to develop a minimum viable product (MVP) and test it quickly and cheaply? Beginning with lower-risk and lower-capital initiatives, such as resource-efficiency and waste-reduction, can build a 'circular investment fund' for more adventurous, longer-term projects whilst highlighting the benefits to the 'unconvinced' or 'sceptics'. Thinking about the 'soft benefits', such as stronger relationships and word-of-mouth marketing, could help you decide how to evaluate these to create a more holistic business case and check for 'unintended consequences'.

Toolkits and resources

We have looked at both internal and external factors, and the importance of involving a wider range of stakeholders. We can also see from the circular economy framework (see Figure 13.8) that external factors play into our circular aims – resource availability, legislation, acceptance of new approaches to design or business models, finding suitable collaboration partners.

FIGURE 13.8   Circular Economy Framework 2.0

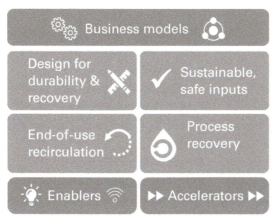

SOURCE: © Catherine Weetman

The 'design and supply chain' components provide a useful checklist:

- How will you secure **safe, sustainable inputs** from local and diverse upstream supply chains?
- Can you **design** products, services and circular **business models** to slow, narrow and close the loop?
- How can you create more value from **process inputs**, for reuse, or for new by-products and co-products?
- How will you **recover** and **regenerate** resources at **end-of-use**?

There are several free resources and toolkits to help you get started. Circle Economy, an employee cooperative consultancy, hosts **Circle Lab,** an open-source database of tools, reports and case studies. It has several thousand examples (including many from my database) and searching this might spark ideas for your own business or products.[28]

The **Circular Economy Toolkit,** from the Institute for Manufacturing (IfM) at the University of Cambridge, is a free resource for businesses, including assessment tools, best practice and a DIY workshop guide.[29]

The **Circular Design Guide** is a collaboration between the Ellen MacArthur Foundation and design consultancy IDEO.[30] The Ellen MacArthur Foundation also has a toolkit for policymakers, which identifies eight key insights, details policy options, opportunities and barriers.[31] This includes the McKinsey ReSolve framework we mentioned in Chapter 3.

There are tools for cities, for procurement teams, and for designers. **The Great Recovery Project** (2012–16) saw the RSA working with Innovate UK, looking at the challenges of waste and circular economy opportunities through the lens of design: setting out the position that 'waste is a design flaw'. There is a website archive with videos, reports and case studies 'to inform and inspire the design of products and services for a circular economy'.[32]

At a strategic level, **Osterwalder's Business Model Canvas**[33] is a useful tool, and for startups, the **Lean Canvas** can help you think differently. Consultancy Wiithaa developed the **Circulab Canvas**, and has a range of other tools on its Circulab website.[34]

Resource exchanges and platforms could help you identify sources of materials, or find partners to use your excess materials. We have mentioned International Synergies, with teams around the world, and there are other material and resource exchange platforms, some for specific sectors or products.

Throughout the book, we have emphasized the importance of using a holistic, whole-system approach to look at potential innovations and strategies (see Chapter 4). Here, we look at a tool providing a cross-functional approach to whole-system design, for businesses aiming to develop circular models:

CARD TOOL FOR WHOLE-SYSTEM DESIGN AND BUSINESS MODEL DEVELOPMENT IN A CIRCULAR ECONOMY
Contribution by Barry Waddilove

How can we help established corporate organizations with complex global supply chains to make the transition from linear to circular business models? Many sustainable design projects tend to maximize benefits within specific areas of the business, without properly accounting for the subsequent consequences elsewhere. Product teams include specialists from many fields, who must collaborate effectively to achieve a successful circular business model. How can we persuade everyone to rally behind the next 'big idea'?

A system design approach emphasizes the value of all flows in material, energy and people. However, typical approaches to ecodesign require the details of materials, energy, assembly process and production capability to be defined before an effective sustainability assessment can be carried out. This is somewhat impractical when environmental impacts are best minimized at the front end of eco-innovation.[35] Current design evaluation tools such as life-cycle assessment are acknowledged as being complex, requiring sophisticated software and specialist jargon.[36] Engineers find it challenging to implement rigorous lean or SixSigma processes, which guarantee quality based upon an early estimation of product life, long before market success or failure has been understood.

The challenges are not limited to the field of design development. A successful transition to a circular economy requires both product and business model innovation. It requires input from all business functions, because whilst we work to adapt the materials and energy that come into the factory, we are also potentially changing the relationship with our customer in how the product or service is delivered. Businesses adapting products and supply chains for a circular economy should seek to develop an enduring brand relationship built on personal service and maintenance, instead of one where the relationship is severed as soon as the product breaks.

Whole-system design provides this rigour by helping to view an entire system 'as a whole from multiple perspectives to understand how its parts can work together as a system to create synergies and solve multiple design problems simultaneously. It is an interdisciplinary, collaborative and iterative process.'[37] How do we make this process approachable for teams working in a complex corporate organization with a diverse workforce and varying degrees of technical knowledge? This question generated significant debate during a week-long Ellen MacArthur Foundation summer school I attended in 2014. Initial inspiration suggested the idea of a circularity challenge or game, which people could play to explore new ideas. Further research revealed 'gamification' as an emergent field with significant potential for engagement and behaviour change. Ultimately, I settled upon the idea of designing a simple card game so that system design could be explored by anyone in the company, from the CEO to the sales teams to the engineers in the factory – everyone can play cards.

I created my 'Circular Innovation Card Deck' and then looked for companies to evaluate early versions of the tool. Beginning with a relatively simple business, I then moved towards deeper evaluation by a variety of more complex international businesses. The final card game emerged after significant testing with over a dozen international companies, many of whom were actively involved in development of circular products and services. Card designs are shown in Figure 13.9.

Introduction to the card game

The game has a three-stage process:

- **Stage one** aims to summarize a basic system map of the existing business
  – with activities of the company and its supply and distribution network,

FIGURE 13.9 Whole-system design game – card designs

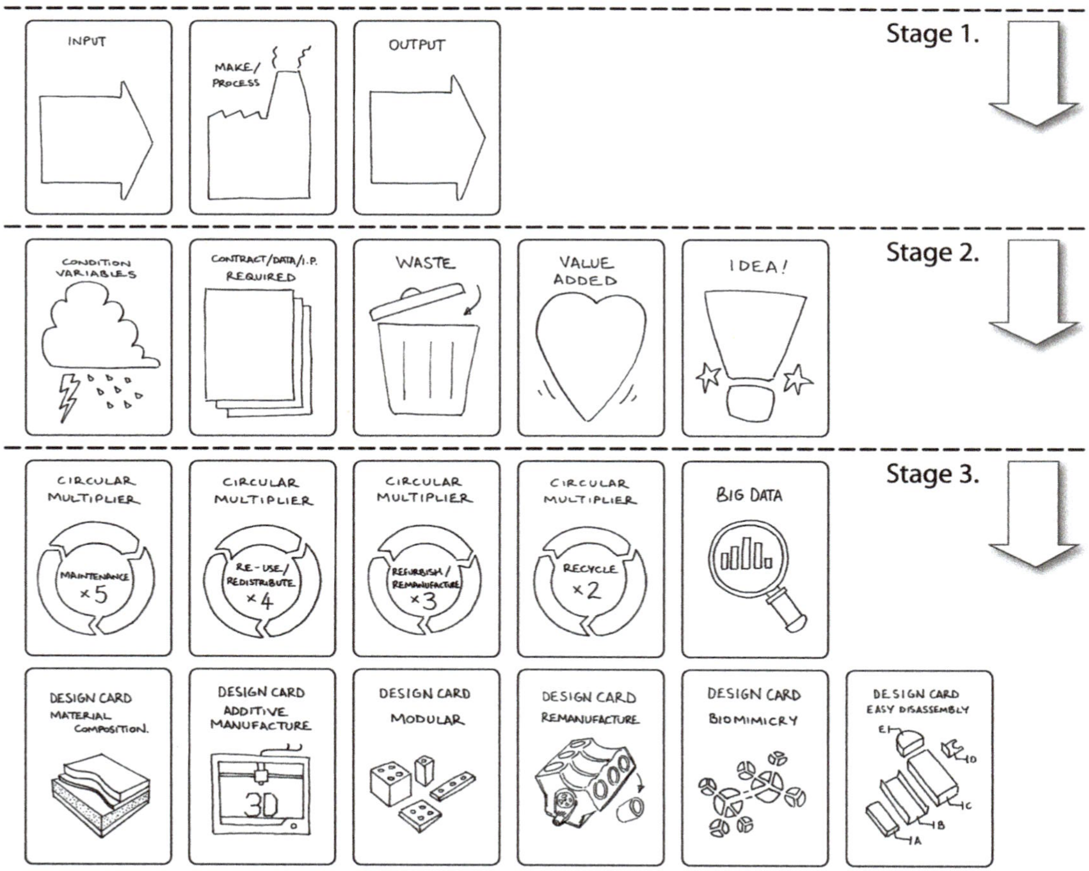
Stage 1.
INPUT
MAKE/ PROCESS
OUTPUT
Stage 2.
CONDITION VARIABLES
CONTRACT/DATA/I.P. REQUIRED
WASTE
VALUE ADDED
IDEA!
Stage 3.
CIRCULAR MULTIPLIER
MAINTENANCE ×5
CIRCULAR MULTIPLIER
RE-USE/ REDISTRIBUTE ×4
CIRCULAR MULTIPLIER
REFURBISH/ REMANUFACTURE ×3
CIRCULAR MULTIPLIER
RECYCLE ×2
BIG DATA
DESIGN CARD MATERIAL COMPOSITION.
DESIGN CARD ADDITIVE MANUFACTURE
3D
DESIGN CARD MODULAR
DESIGN CARD REMANUFACTURE
DESIGN CARD BIOMIMICRY
DESIGN CARD EASY DISASSEMBLY
E
D
C
B
A

SOURCE: © Waddilove (2014)

summarized as either inputs, internal processes or outputs. This helps people explain the 'main activities' of the current business from their own perspective whilst highlighting key external stakeholders such as suppliers or important customers.

- **Stage two** is 'hazards and opportunities' for the existing business, described from the perspective of the interviewees' current position and their circle of influence within the company. These cards are placed on top of any relevant stage one cards.

- **Stage three** reviews the potential circular projects. The choices are again made from the players' perspective and often circular projects are potential solutions to some of the challenges identified during stage two. Again, these cards are placed on top of relevant existing cards.

At the end of the game, players review the potential circular economy projects by lifting each 'project stack' from the card table. Each stack of cards includes a circular idea with clear links to an existing business challenge, and potentially to a raw material, process or customer. This connected approach to problem-solving helps gain buy-in for a new project proposal from the wider business organization. Ideally, the game is best played one-on-one with a variety of different individuals or functional teams, compiling the results to identify key challenges and value-adding circular projects.

Card game procedure in detail

Players are shown the diagram in Figure 13.10, which summarizes themes and card subjects revealed during the game. Each interviewee is asked to describe their personal view of the company system as it relates to their role and the product in question.

Players follow the 'game instructions' shown in Figure 13.11, adding sticky notes to each input card placed on the table. Stage one clarifies the underlying system of the current business. Stage two highlights hazards and opportunities; stage three identifies circular economy design ideas and business models. Typically, gameplay and discussion take between 90 minutes and two hours.

During the game design phase, I recorded feedback from the players. Figure 13.12 summarizes many of these insights and highlights a selection of participants' feedback received during the research project.

Insights from the research

The system innovation cards were originally created as an approachable tool for businesses to evaluate circular innovation projects. Many companies that

FIGURE 13.10   Introduction to the theme for the game

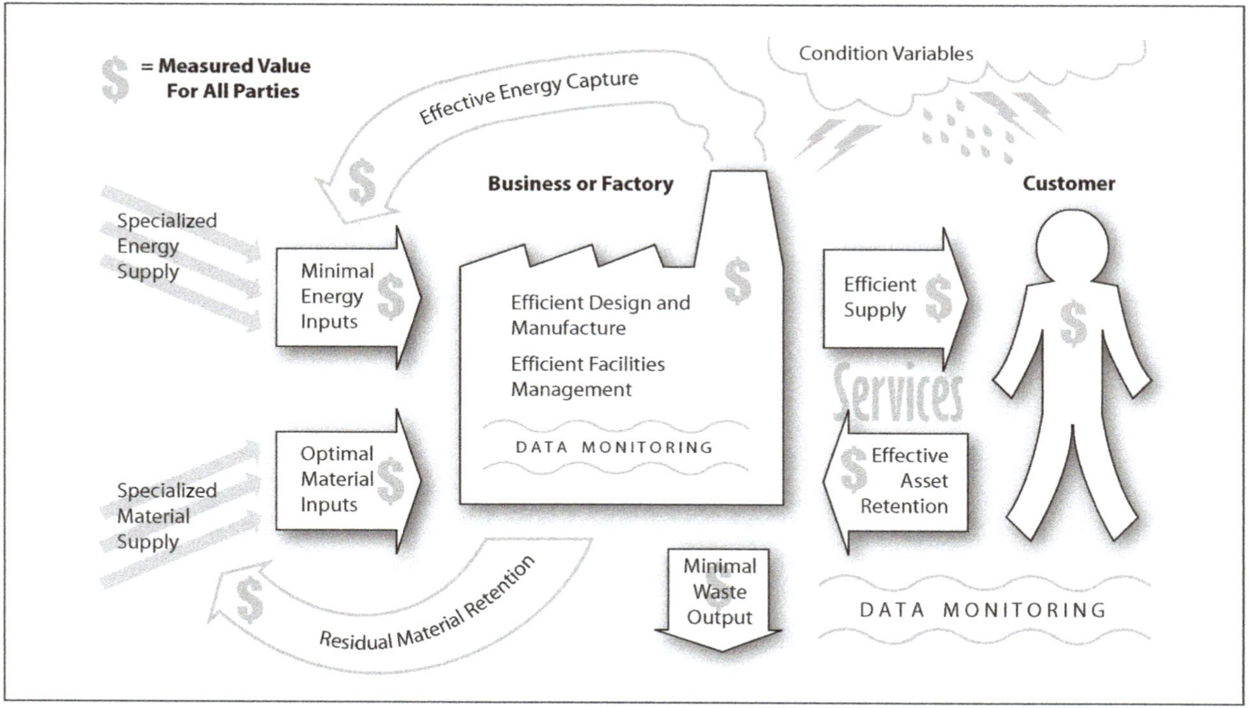

$ = Measured Value For All Parties

Condition Variables

Customer

Efficient Supply

Services

Effective Asset Retention

DATA MONITORING

Effective Energy Capture

Business or Factory

Efficient Design and Manufacture

Efficient Facilities Management

DATA MONITORING

Minimal Waste Output

Minimal Energy Inputs

Optimal Material Inputs

Specialized Energy Supply

Specialized Material Supply

Residual Material Retention

SOURCE: © Waddilove (2013)

FIGURE 13.11 Game instructions

Stage / Card Type	Required Equipment: Card Pack, Memo Notes (various colours), Marker Pen, Video Camera, Tripod
Pre-Interview	Request: Please select a product offered by your company which we will use as the focus for research questions during this activity
Stage One	**Question Prompt**
Input	Please use the memo pad provided to describe all inputs to your business (eg Raw Materials, Components, Energy, Labour)
Make/Process	Describe all processes that occur within your business to create the product (eg Design, Assembly, Testing, QA, Packaging)
Output	Describe outputs: What leaves the factory, what is your brand/service offering (eg Product, Differentiation, Sales Route, Online Service)
Stage Two	**Question Prompt**
Condition Variables	Review your system map. Highlight condition variables affecting your business (eg Price Variation, Material Availability)
Contract/Data/I.P.	Highlight areas of the business where legal documents may be required (eg Design Patents, Supplier/Customer Contracts, Warranty)
Waste	Describe any waste that currently exists within your system (eg Material Offcuts, Energy, Human Activity, End-of-Life Packaging)
Value Added	Describe the value added for your external clients/suppliers/customer and internal employees (eg Brand, Design, Reliability)
Ideal	Pause and review your whole system including stage two cards - Add any new ideas that have come to mind during the process
Stage Three	**Question Prompt**
Circular Multiplier: Maintenance ×5 Reuse ×4 Refurbishment ×3 Recycling ×2	These are your Circular Multiplier Cards. They allow you to add value to areas of your business using the Circular Economy approach highlighted in our introduction. You will notice the cards include a multiplication value, this is based upon published research demonstrating that higher value can be achieved through 'inner circle' activities such as maintenance. Try to use more than one multiplier card and also identify projects in different areas of your map (eg Input, Process, Output)
Big Data	Now identify areas of your business which could benefit from I.T. Infrastructure with a focus on Big Data
Design Cards: Remanufacture Biomimicry Active Disassembly Easy Disassembly Modular	These are your Design Cards. They help you to identify design activities which may help with the execution of innovation projects defined during this process. Please select any cards which you think will be useful and place them next to the area of the system map where they would apply. Use multiple cards if required and also aim to identify projects in different areas of your map which may benefit (eg Input, Process, Output)
Conclusion	Your system map is now complete. Please take time to review and identify which projects have the most value for your business.

SOURCE: © Waddilove (2013)

FIGURE 13.12 Whole-system design game – key criteria

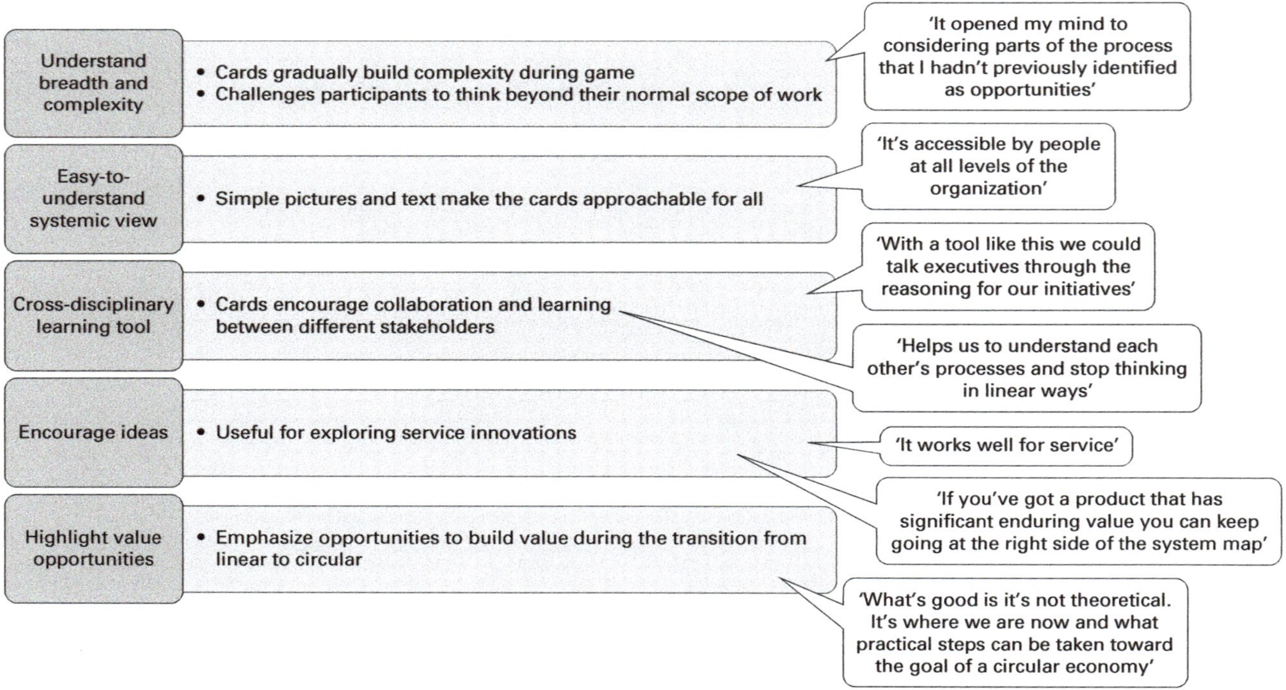

Understand breadth and complexity	• Cards gradually build complexity during game • Challenges participants to think beyond their normal scope of work
Easy-to-understand systemic view	• Simple pictures and text make the cards approachable for all
Cross-disciplinary learning tool	• Cards encourage collaboration and learning between different stakeholders
Encourage ideas	• Useful for exploring service innovations
Highlight value opportunities	• Emphasize opportunities to build value during the transition from linear to circular

'It opened my mind to considering parts of the process that I hadn't previously identified as opportunities'

'It's accessible by people at all levels of the organization'

'With a tool like this we could talk executives through the reasoning for our initiatives'

'Helps us to understand each other's processes and stop thinking in linear ways'

'It works well for service'

'If you've got a product that has significant enduring value you can keep going at the right side of the system map'

'What's good is it's not theoretical. It's where we are now and what practical steps can be taken toward the goal of a circular economy'

SOURCE: Barry Waddilove

have used the cards are inspired to identify 'test projects' targeted at specific problems in their current system. Working this way enables a small team of circular economy advocates (who may include stakeholders from both inside and outside the business) to demonstrate 'early wins' and gradually build the company's appetite for larger and more ambitious projects. This method is analogous with the approach taken by many larger corporations to sell key initiatives to a multifaceted organization or stakeholder group.

Enabling a clear systemic view is challenging, as business models within the circular economy will potentially be more complex. However, teams must acknowledge and accept this complexity; to discover the full value of materials and energy flows throughout a product's serviceable life, it is essential to work through the system map in detail. Fine filtering of systemic business value is becoming easier to measure using digital technologies. Manufacturers are investigating new approaches to *servitization*, which enable measurement of 'total value throughout life' for each product created. In a circular economy, the accurate measurement and tracking of enduring value throughout service life is an essential counterpoint in highlighting the lost value of waste.

Reflecting on successful card sessions, it is clear that the three stages play an important role in identifying opportunities for change. Innovations identified during stage three were often grouped around business challenges identified in stage two. This observation links to studies around the diffusion of innovations by Geels (2004),[38] where opportunity niches play a vital role as the seeds for business transformation.

Research interviews highlighted the value of the system innovation cards for international business models. Companies with significant influence over their whole supply and service system are likely to benefit most from the circular economy. The leading companies in a new circular economy will demonstrate perseverance and genuine ambition to create a symbiotic stakeholder network, which uses technology in all stages of a product life-cycle to focus on the needs and ambitions of their individual customers. This persistent attention to user satisfaction will create enduring brand relationships, which respect the true value of resources in an increasingly complex and competitive global market.

Measurement and assessment tools

How should we measure progress and success? **Risk assessments** will differ for each business, and looking at the short-term versus long-term risks may

FIGURE 13.13   Natural Step scorecard – fashion example

Natural Step criteria	Supply chain stage				
	Raw materials	Manufacture	Logistics and sales	Use	End-of-life
Scarce materials taken from the earth	⬇	⬊	⬇	⬊	⬆
Man-made toxic and persistent chemicals	⬊	⬇	⬊	⬊	⬊
Destruction and pollution of nature	⬈	⬇	⬊	⬊	⬇
Work and/or use conditions	⬊	⬊	⬈	⬊	⬇

Key:	Good	Quite good	Quite bad	Bad	Don't know
	Positive impacts, no concerns	Positive or neutral impacts, few concerns	Negative or neutral impacts, many concerns	Negative impacts, widespread /major concerns	Not enough information
	⬆	⬈	⬊	⬇	?

SOURCE: Adapted from Streamlined Life Cycle Assessment (based on Natural Step System Conditions), Sustainable Wealth Creation, 2007, with kind permission of Forum for the Future

give different outcomes. Key criteria may include costs, disruption to the business, non-availability (eg drought affecting crop production), or whether the material is sustainable. A 'quick-scan' approach, for example using the *Natural Step* scorecard approach (mentioned earlier and in Chapter 5), shown in Figure 13.13, would highlight the areas with the worst impact, and act as a discussion tool for business priorities. For a more detailed approach, you could use the open-source Future-Fit Business Benchmark, inspired by the Natural Step.[39]

The **Material Circularity Indicators** tool from the Ellen MacArthur Foundation and Granta (2015) aims to help companies estimate the effectiveness of the transition towards circular products.[40] The tool uses material flows to provide a 'material circularity indicator' from zero to one and requires a range of information inputs, including:

- **Production inputs:** looking at levels of virgin materials, recycled materials and reused components.

- **Use phase 'utility':** can the product be used more intensely, eg in a shared-use model? This compares the intensity of product use versus a similar 'industry average' product. This examines durability, together with maintenance and repair and shared-use models.

- **Post-use destination:** measuring how much material goes to landfill; how much goes for energy recovery; how much is collected for recycling or reuse.

- **Recycling efficiency:** examining the efficiency of the processes producing recycling input and recycling post-use materials.

The Ellen MacArthur Foundation is now working on the **Circularity Score**, a company-level assessment tool due to be launched in 2020, which 'allows companies to:

- highlight the proactive efforts they make to capture circular economy business opportunities through strategic prioritization and innovation;

- provide a "snapshot" of the circularity of their material flows and service models as they are today;

- understand the most important development areas to concentrate on with the guidance of an analyst commentary.'[41]

Summary

Global trends and drivers create a landscape of opportunity for companies beginning the transition to a circular, sustainable approach. Taking a broad perspective and involving a wider range of stakeholders to maximize the enthusiasm, ideas and momentum delivers more robust outcomes. This broad perspective is fundamental in the business context too, using a 'whole-system design' approach to assess the potential impact of external forces, consequences of change, and so on. We can see that the journey is likely to be a 'long and winding road' – the important thing is to begin, then build experience and momentum, and look for disruptive opportunities.

You could approach the exercise as if you were a potential competitor – if you were starting from scratch, what would you design? How would you meet the needs of the market whilst future-proofing your supplies, and avoiding externalities (that might be penalized by future legislation)? How would you regenerate living systems to ensure they continue to provide those services we depend on – pure air, clean water, healthy soils, pollination, waste to food or energy, and more?

> Leading companies can do something magical. They can create the future ... They can inspire changes much greater than they could make alone, and they can act as catalysts for a wider movement of people that want to change direction but can't always see how to do it.
>
> Paul Polman, former CEO, Unilever and Chairman of the World Business Council for Sustainable Development[42]

Further resources

Braungart, M and McDonough, W (2008) *Cradle to Cradle: Remaking the way we make things*, Vintage Books, London

Ellen MacArthur Foundation [Online] www.ellenmacarthurfoundation.org/ (archived at https://perma.cc/HS26-8LZL)

Future-Fit Foundation (2019) [online] futurefitbusiness.org/companies/ (archived at https://perma.cc/V49C-FK6T)

Lovins, AB et al (2013) *A New Dynamic: Effective business in a circular economy*, Ellen MacArthur Foundation Publishing

Meadows, DH (2008) *Thinking in Systems: A primer*, ed Diana Wright, Sustainability Institute, Chelsea Green Publishing, United States

Permaculture Association UK [Online] https://www.permaculture.org.uk/ (archived at https://perma.cc/ZM5R-G5JA)

Sweeney, LB and Meadows, D (1995) *The Systems Thinking Playbook*, Chelsea Green Publishing

Notes

1   Cheshire, I (January 2014) [accessed 15 May 2016] Press release: Comment: A New Spur to Innovation, Writes Sir Ian Cheshire, Kingfisher plc [Online] http://www.kingfisher.com/index.asp?pageid=55&newsid=1038 (archived at https://perma.cc/CC8D-BPBT)

2   De Wit, M et al (2018) [accessed 27 November 2019] *The Circularity Gap Report*, 22 January [Online] https://www.circle-economy.com/the-circularity-gap-report-our-world-is-only-9-circular/ (archived at https://perma.cc/T2EX-VJ2E)

3 European Commission (2019) [accessed 27 November 2019] *Towards a Circular Economy* [Online] ec.europa.eu/commission/priorities/jobs-growth-and-investment/towards-circular-economy_en (archived at https://perma.cc/5PJB-AL2Q)

4 World Economic Forum (2014) [accessed 27 November 2019] *Towards the Circular Economy: Accelerating the scale-up across global supply chains* [Online] reports.weforum.org/toward-the-circular-economy-accelerating-the-scale-up-across-global-supply-chains/ (archived at https://perma.cc/2MVF-PTXV)

5 Accenture Newsroom (28 September 2015) [accessed 27 November 2019] *The Circular Economy Could Unlock $4.5 trillion of Economic Growth, Finds New Book by Accenture* [Online] newsroom.accenture.com/news/the-circular-economy-could-unlock-4-5-trillion-of-economic-growth-finds-new-book-by-accenture.htm (archived at https://perma.cc/7L9P-XUEK)

6 Ellen MacArthur Foundation (20 June 2015) [accessed 27 November 2019] Circular economy would increase European competitiveness and deliver better societal outcomes, new study reveals [Online] www.ellenmacarthurfoundation.org/news/circular-economy-would-increase-european-competitiveness-and-deliver-better-societal-outcomes-new-study-reveals (archived at https://perma.cc/4PFW-E22D)

7 Continental Tyre Group Ltd, Taraxagum [accessed 27 November 2019] [Online] www.continental-tyres.co.uk/truck/company/sustainability/taraxagum (archived at https://perma.cc/H2SW-W9N5)

8 Circular Economy Podcast, Episode 3 (3 June 2019) [accessed 27 November 2019] [Online] https://www.rethinkglobal.info/tom-harper-circular-asset-management/ (archived at https://perma.cc/YWU8-85UW)

9 Circular Economy Podcast, Episode 6 (14 July 2019) [accessed 27 November 2019] [Online] https://www.rethinkglobal.info/adam-fairweather-reimagine-waste/ (archived at https://perma.cc/EXC3-9WZ6)

10 Vladimirova, D (2014) [accessed 23 May 2016] New business models for a sustainable future, *Institute for Manufacturing Review*, University of Cambridge, pp 16–17 [Online] www.ifm.eng.cam.ac.uk/research/ifm-review/issue-2/new-business-models-for-a-sustainable-future/ (archived at https://perma.cc/KJ2V-P7R5)

11 Bocken, N, Short, S, Rana, P and Evans, S (2013) A value mapping tool for sustainable business modelling, *Corporate Governance*, **13** (5), 482–497

12 Vladimirova, D (2015) The Cambridge Value Mapping Tool, *Institute for Manufacturing Review*, Issue 5 [Online] https://www.ifm.eng.cam.ac.uk/research/industrial-sustainability/sustainable-business-models/tools/cambridge-value-mapping-tool/ (archived at https://perma.cc/KJ2V-P7R5)

13 Future-Fit Foundation (2019) [Online] http://futurefitbusiness.org/what-is-a-future-fit-business/ (archived at https://perma.cc/N6Z2-73V8)

14 Shared Value Initiative (2016) [accessed 3 June 2016] [Online] https://www.sharedvalue.org/about-shared-value (archived at https://perma.cc/W9RC-KCE8)

15 Future-Fit Foundation (2019) [accessed 28 November 2019] [Online] futurefitbusiness.org/companies/ (archived at https://perma.cc/V49C-FK6T)

16 United Nations Global Compact (2010) *Supply Chain Sustainability: A Practical Guide for Continuous Improvement*

17 Raworth, K (2017) [accessed 28 November 2019] *What on Earth is the Doughnut?* [Online] www.kateraworth.com/doughnut/ (archived at https://perma.cc/LA5E-BSYG)

18 McKinsey (2016) [accessed 3 June 2016] *MGI's Commodity Price Index: An Interactive Tool* [Online] www.mckinsey.com/tools/wrappers/redesign/interactivewrapper.aspx?sc_itemid={0237e967-a10a-489f-b428-c5aa3437d98f} (archived at https://perma.cc/R898-UJFR)

19 Euromonitor International (2019) [accessed 28 November 2019] *2019 Megatrends: State of Play* [Online] go.euromonitor.com/white-paper-consumers-2019-megatrends-state-of-play.html (archived at https://perma.cc/64W6-YVNR)

20 End Ecocide [accessed 15 May 2016] [Online] www.endecocide.org/ (archived at https://perma.cc/455N-99R6)

21 UNFCCC (2016) [accessed 15 May 2016] Paris Agreement [Online] unfccc.int/paris_agreement/items/9485.php (archived at https://perma.cc/A6KQ-N83H)

22 Ellen MacArthur Foundation (2012) [accessed 23 May 2016] News, *But Does it Actually Work?* [Online] www.ellenmacarthurfoundation.org/news/but-does-it-actually-work (archived at https://perma.cc/YF89-XDS8)

23 Ellen MacArthur Foundation (2016) [accessed 18 May 2016] *Case Study: Selling Light as a Service* [Online] www.ellenmacarthurfoundation.org/case-studies/selling-light-as-a-service (archived at https://perma.cc/6QLK-FWPH)

24 Zils, M (2015) *Re-Thinking the Business Case for a Circular Economy*, presentation at Ellen MacArthur Foundation Re-thinking Progress, Bradford University, 14 April 2015

25 Behind the Brands [accessed 10 December 2019] [Online] https://www.behindthebrands.org/ (archived at https://perma.cc/V7EG-Z6YW)

26 Nguyen, H, Stuchtey M and Zils, M (2014) [accessed 23 May 2016] Remaking the industrial economy, *McKinsey Quarterly*, February, p 11 [Online] www.mckinsey.com/business-functions/sustainability-and-resource-productivity/our-insights/remaking-the-industrial-economy (archived at https://perma.cc/2X98-874K)

27 Rossi, M et al (2005) [accessed 23 May 2016] *Herman Miller's Design for Environment Program* [Online] chemicalspolicy.org/downloads/HermanMillerDardenCaseStudy8Nov05.pdf (archived at https://perma.cc/2XBE-44ZY) p 2–3

28 Circle Lab (2019) [accessed 27 November 2019] [Online] www.circle-lab.com/knowledge-hub/circular-economy-strategies (archived at https://perma.cc/33LJ-4SDD)

29 Circular Economy Toolkit [accessed 27 November 2019] [Online] www.circulareconomytoolkit.org (archived at https://perma.cc/YN6P-HWKX)

30 Circular Design Guide [accessed 27 November 2019] [Online] www.circulardesignguide.com/ (archived at https://perma.cc/CAP8-HP5V)

31 Ellen MacArthur Foundation (26 June 2015) [accessed 27 November 2019] *Toolkit for Policymakers* [Online] www.ellenmacarthurfoundation.org/publications/delivering-the-circular-economy-a-toolkit-for-policymakers (archived at https://perma.cc/GU8T-V9DC)

32 The Great Recovery [accessed 27 November 2019] [Online] www.greatrecovery.org.uk/ (archived at https://perma.cc/V975-8GMJ)

33 Strategzyer (2019) [accessed 27 November 2019] *Business Model Canvas* [Online] www.strategyzer.com/canvas/business-model-canvas (archived at https://perma.cc/6J7Z-WNUY)

34 Circulab (2019) [accessed 27 November 2019] [Online] https://circulab.com/ (archived at https://perma.cc/8ZPX-AQ7Y)

35 Bocken, N, Farracho, M, Bosworth R and Kemp R (2014) The front-end of eco-innovation for eco-innovative small and medium sized companies, *Journal of Engineering and Technology Management*, **31**, pp 43–57

36 Vogtländer, J (2010) *A Practical Guide to LCA for Students, Designers and Business Managers*, VSSD, Delft

37 Blizzard, J and Klotz, L (2012) A framework for sustainable whole systems design, *Design Studies*, **33**, pp 456–79

38 Geels, F (2004) From sectoral systems of innovation to socio-technical systems: insights about dynamics and change from sociology and institutional theory, *Research Policy*, **33** (6/7), pp 897–920

39 Future-Fit Foundation (2019) [accessed 28 November 2019] [Online] futurefitbusiness.org/companies/ (archived at https://perma.cc/V49C-FK6T)

40 Ellen MacArthur Foundation and Granta (2015) [accessed 23 May 2016] *Circularity Indicators: An approach to measuring circularity*, Project Overview [Online] www.ellenmacarthurfoundation.org/assets/downloads/insight/Circularity-Indicators_Project-Overview_May2015.pdf (archived at https://perma.cc/S4DU-CCG4)

41 Ellen MacArthur Foundation (2019) [accessed 27 November 2019] *Circularity Score* [Online] www.ellenmacarthurfoundation.org/resources/apply/measuring-circularity (archived at https://perma.cc/838E-99MN)

42 Polman, P (2013) [accessed 15 May 2016] Why UN climate talks must deliver a brighter future for us all, Blog, *Huffington Post* [Online] www.huffingtonpost.com/paul-polman/un-climate-talks_b_4177721.html (archived at https://perma.cc/LB36-B6TH)

GLOSSARY

Note: In each chapter, glossary terms are highlighted in italics, generally the first time they appear in each main section within a chapter.

3D printing (3DP) 3D printing, also known as additive manufacturing (AM), refers to various processes used to synthesize a three-dimensional object. In 3D printing, successive layers of material are formed under computer control to create an object of almost any shape or geometry. Objects are produced from a 3D model, CAD or other electronic data source. A 3D printer is a type of industrial robot.

accelerators External factors that encourage circularity by influencing choices or promoting circulation. These include collaborations, independent assessments and certification, financial support, government policy and legislation.

additive manufacturing *3D printing* in the term's original sense refers to processes that sequentially deposit material on to a powder bed with inkjet printer heads. More recently, the meaning of the term has expanded to encompass a wider variety of techniques such as extrusion and sintering-based processes. Technical standards generally use the term *additive manufacturing* for this broader sense. See also 3D printing.

aquaponics Aquaponics systems combine conventional aquaculture (raising aquatic animals such as fish, shellfish, crustaceans or molluscs in tanks) with hydroponics (cultivating plants in water) in a symbiotic environment. In normal aquaculture, excretions from the fish can accumulate in the water, increasing toxicity and compromising the health of the fish. In an aquaponics system, water from an aquaculture system is fed into a hydroponic system where bacteria break down the excretions into by-products, including nitrates and nitrites. These by-products are then available to provide nutrition to plants, and the cleaned water recirculates back into the aquaculture system.

arbitrage The simultaneous buying and selling of securities, currency or commodities in different markets or in derivative forms in order to take advantage of differing prices for the same asset.

artificial intelligence (AI) AI is the broader concept of machines being able to carry out tasks in a way that we would consider 'smart': performing cognitive functions in a similar way to humans – for example, finding information, reasoning and decision making.

big data Large, complex data sets, with challenges for analysis, capture, data curation, search, sharing, storage, transfer, visualization, querying, updating and information privacy. The term may also refer to the use of predictive analytics or certain other advanced methods to extract value from data, and seldom to a particular size of data set.

bill of materials (BoM) A list of materials, components and sub-assemblies required to make the product.

biocapacity The capacity of a given biologically productive area to generate an ongoing supply of renewable resources and to absorb its spillover wastes. Unsustainability occurs if the area's ecological footprint exceeds its biocapacity.

biological nutrients Materials from the biosphere that are/have been living things, eg food, fibres, timber.

biomass Organic matter derived from living, or recently living, organisms. It includes components such as lignin, cellulose, hemicellulose, extractives, etc.

biomimicry 'An approach to innovation that seeks sustainable solutions to human challenges by emulating nature's time-tested patterns and strategies.' Biomimicry is design that works like nature, rather than merely looking like nature. It asks the question 'how can we fit on earth as elegantly as the living systems around us?' Its aim is to create new ways of living, including products, processes and systems that are sustainable over the long term. (Definition by Biomimicry Institute – see biomimicry.org/what-is-biomimicry/#.VsW6dOahOkV (archived at https://perma.cc/U68G-N9FX))

biorefining The processing of biomass into a range of bio-based products such as food, feed, chemicals, plastics, heat and fuels.

biosphere The regions of the surface and atmosphere of the earth or another planet occupied by living organisms.

business-to-business (B2B) Transactions between businesses.

business-to-consumer (B2C) Businesses selling or transacting with consumers.

butterfly diagram Popular name for the Ellen MacArthur Foundation diagram illustrating the biological and technical flows, and the four types of loop in the circular economy. (See Figure 1.4 on page 24 of this book.)

by-product An incidental or secondary product made in the manufacture or synthesis of something else: eg zinc is a by-product of steel manufacture.

cascaded materials, or cascading This refers to the way resources are used for different (lower-value) purposes over multiple cycles. For example, solid wood is first used to make furniture. It may then be recovered for recycling into particleboard, followed by fibre-based products, then bio-chemicals might be extracted, with the last resort being burning it for energy and heat.

circular economy (CE) A circular economy is an alternative to a traditional linear economy (make, use, dispose) in which we keep resources in use for as long as possible, extract the maximum value from them whilst in use, then recover and regenerate products and materials at the end of each service life. (Definition by WRAP – see www.wrap.org.uk/content/wrap-and-circular-economy (archived at https://perma.cc/SV96-VRPZ))

circular service provider An organization that provides circular economy services to a range of customers, processing and recirculating materials originally produced by another manufacturer or brand. Examples include a specialist recycler, independent remanufacturer or reseller.

closed loop Product or materials retained or recovered for use again by the same company – whether for use in the same product or process, or for a different product or process.

cloud computing Cloud computing, also known as on-demand computing, is a kind of internet-based computing that provides shared processing resources and data to computers and other devices on demand.

collaborative consumption The reinvention of traditional market behaviours – renting, lending, swapping, sharing, bartering, gifting – through technology, taking place in ways and on a scale not possible before the internet. (Definition by Rachel Botsman – see rachelbotsman.com/thinking/)

component Parts, assemblies or sub-assemblies included in the finished product. They are usually removable in one piece, and have unique identifiers in the bill of materials. Examples include a sauce used in a recipe for a takeaway or 'ready meal', an electric motor used in a vacuum cleaner, or a circuit board in a laptop computer.

compound Two or more ingredients, or elements, chemically united in fixed proportions. Some further processing is involved, perhaps using heat or water, or a chemical agent to create the reaction. Examples are metal alloys such as steel or brass, smokeless fuel (based on coal), or a blended fruit-juice drink.

conflict minerals Natural resources extracted in a conflict zone and sold to fund the fighting.

consumer-to-business (C2B) Consumers selling products or services to businesses.

co-product Production of a main product can also create co-products (which involve similar revenues to the main product), by-products (which result in smaller revenues) and waste products (which provide little or no revenue).

corporate social responsibility (CSR) A form of corporate self-regulation integrated into a business model. The aim is to increase long-term profits and shareholder trust through positive public relations and high ethical standards to reduce business and legal risk by taking responsibility for corporate actions. CSR strategies encourage the company to make a positive impact on the environment and stakeholders including consumers, employees, investors, communities and others.

Cradle to Cradle® (C2C) (Or regenerative design) is a biomimetic approach to the design of products and systems. It models human industry on nature's processes, viewing materials as nutrients circulating in healthy, safe metabolisms. (Definition by Braungart, M and McDonough, W (2002) *Cradle to Cradle: Remaking the way we make things*.)

dematerialization The dematerialization of a product literally means less, or better yet, no material is used to deliver the same level of functionality to the user. Sharing, borrowing and the organization of group services that facilitate and cater for communities' needs could alleviate the requirement of ownership of many products.

design and supply chain The central section of the circular economy framework used in this book, covering circular inputs, product design, process design and circular flows.

design for disassembly (D4D) The process of designing products so that they can easily, cost-effectively and rapidly be taken apart at the end of the product's life, enabling components to be reused and/or recycled.

distributed manufacturing (redistributed manufacturing) A form of decentralized, local manufacturing using a network of geographically dispersed manufacturing facilities, coordinated using information technology.

downcycle (downcycling, downcycled) Converting end-of-use products or materials into new products or materials, which are of poorer quality and reduced functionality, eg plastic recycling: converting mixed plastics (of one or more different compositions) into lower-grade materials.

e-waste (electronic waste) Electrical or electronic devices discarded at end-of-use.

ecodesign An approach that aims to minimize the overall environmental impact of a product or service. Ecodesign encourages innovative design solutions that consider the entire life-cycle, from extraction or harvesting of raw materials, through production, distribution and use, all the way to end-of-use recycling, 'repair-ability' and disposal.

ecological economics Academic research that aims to address the interdependence and co-evolution of human economies and natural ecosystems over time and space. It is distinguished from environmental economics by its treatment of the economy as a subsystem of the ecosystem and its emphasis upon preserving natural capital.

ecological footprint The productive area required to provide the renewable resources humanity is using and to absorb its waste. The productive area currently occupied by human infrastructure is also included in this calculation, since built-up land is not available for resource regeneration. (Definition by Global Footprint Network – see www.footprintnetwork.org/en/index.php/GFN/page/footprint_basics_overview/ (archived at https://perma.cc/FT7T-HYUM))

ecosystems A community of living organisms in conjunction with the non-living components of their environment (eg air, water, mineral, soil) interacting as a system. These biotic and abiotic components are regarded as linked together through nutrient cycles and energy flows.

ecosystem services The benefits people obtain from ecosystems. These include provisioning services such as food and water; regulating services such as flood and disease control; cultural services such as spiritual, recreational and cultural benefits; and supporting services such as nutrient cycling that maintain the conditions for life on earth.

Electrical and Electronic Equipment Sustainability Action Plan (esap) UK initiative for WEEE recovery, managed by WRAP.

embedded resources The sum of all the resources (materials, energy and water) required to produce any goods or services, as if that resource was incorporated or 'embodied' in the product itself.

enablers Enablers can be deployed to help circularity; including thinking differently with new approaches to design, systems thinking, and green chemistry; using new materials to replace finite sources with renewable or recycled alternatives, to avoid toxic chemicals, and to improve product functionality. Enablers include adopting new technology, including the internet of things, artificial intelligence, platforms and sharing apps, etc.

end-of-life (EoL) The point at which a product is destroyed at the end of its useful life. This term is used to highlight lost opportunities for reuse, repair, remanufacture, recycling, etc.

end-of-use The point at which a product reaches the end of a 'use cycle', and is exchanged or returned for reuse (eg reselling or renting), repair, remanufacture, recovery of resources, etc.

enterprise resource planning (ERP) A category of business management software – typically a suite of integrated applications – that an organization can use to collect, store, manage and interpret data from many business activities, including product planning, purchase, manufacturing or service delivery, marketing and sales, inventory management, shipping and payment.

environmental profit and loss accounting (EP&L) EP&L places a financial value on environmental impacts along the entire value chain of a business to help companies combine sustainability metrics with traditional business management. (Definition by Trucost – see www.trucost.com/environmental-profit-and-loss-accounting (archived at https://perma.cc/H3TL-2MFW))

eutrophication The increase in additions of nutrients (especially nitrogen and phosphorus) to freshwater or marine systems, which leads to increases in plant growth and often to undesirable changes in ecosystem structure and function.

extended producer responsibility (EPR) A mandatory type of product stewardship that includes, at a minimum, the requirement that the manufacturer's responsibility for its product extends to post-consumer management of that product and its packaging. (Definition by Product Stewardship Institute – see www.productstewardship.us/?55 (archived at https://perma.cc/QND7-BEWR))

externalities (externalizing) Defined by the OECD as 'the economic concept of uncompensated environmental effects of production and consumption that affect consumer utility and enterprise cost outside the market mechanism ... causing private costs of production to tend to be lower than its "social" cost. NB the "polluter pays" principle aims to prompt households and organizations to internalize (pay the true cost of remedies for) externalities in their plans and budgets.'

fast-moving consumer goods (FMCG) Fast-moving consumer goods (FMCG) or consumer-packaged goods (CPG) are products that are sold quickly and at relatively low cost. Examples include non-durable goods such as soft drinks, toiletries, over-the-counter medicines, processed foods and many other consumables. In contrast, durable goods or major appliances such as kitchen appliances are generally replaced over a period of several years.

feedstock Anything used to make a new product. This includes raw materials and components, and can be from virgin sources or recycled. (Definition by the Ellen MacArthur Foundation.)

Forest Stewardship Council (FSC) An international, non-governmental organization dedicated to promoting responsible management of the world's forests. FSC runs a global forest certification system with two key components: Forest Management and Chain of Custody certification. See www.fsc-uk.org/en-uk/about-fsc (archived at https://perma.cc/W367-TD84).

gig economy The trading of individual tasks or 'gigs' between individuals and organizations, often associated with freelance work, either part-time or full-time.

Global Reporting Initiative (GRI) An international independent organization that helps businesses, governments and other organizations to understand and communicate the impact of business on critical sustainability issues such as climate change, human rights, corruption and many others. (Definition by the Global Reporting Initiative – see www.globalreporting.org/Information/about-gri/Pages/default.aspx (archived at https://perma.cc/VZ4F-XMAJ))

green chemistry The design of chemical products and processes that reduce or eliminate the use or generation of hazardous substances. (Definition by the United States EPA – see www.epa.gov/greenchemistry/basics-green-chemistry (archived at https://perma.cc/M6UV-A22H).)

greenhouse gas (GHG) Some gases in the earth's atmosphere act a bit like the glass in a greenhouse, trapping the sun's heat and stopping it from leaking back into space. Many of these gases occur naturally, but human activity is increasing the concentrations of some of them in the atmosphere, in particular: carbon dioxide (CO_2); methane; nitrous oxide; fluorinated gases. (Definition from European Commission – see ec.europa.eu/clima/change/causes/index_en.htm)

gross domestic product (GDP) The monetary value of all the finished goods and services produced within a country's borders in a specific time period.

industrial ecology (IE) The study of material and energy flows through industrial systems. The global industrial economy can be modelled as a network of industrial processes that extract resources from the earth and transform those resources into commodities, which can be bought and sold to meet the needs of humanity. Industrial ecology seeks to quantify the material flows and document the industrial processes that make modern society function. Industrial ecologists are often concerned with the impacts that industrial activities have on the environment, with use of the planet's supply of natural resources, and with problems of waste disposal.

industrial symbiosis Industrial symbiosis engages traditionally separate industries in a collective approach to competitive advantage involving physical exchange of materials, energy, water and/or by-products. The keys to industrial symbiosis are collaboration and the synergistic possibilities offered by geographic proximity. (Definition by M Chertow (2012) Industrial symbiosis – see www.eoearth.org/view/article/153824 (archived at https://perma.cc/VW2U-GNBK))

intelligent assets Physical objects that can sense, record and send information about their status, condition, their surroundings and so on. These objects may be connected in the internet of things, or not part of a network: instead holding their information for interrogation, downloads, etc, on request, or when triggered.

internet of things (IoT) Interrelated computing devices (machines, sensors, wearable objects etc) that have unique identifiers (UIDs) and are able to transfer data over a network without needing human interaction.

life-cycle assessment (LCA) A cradle-to-grave approach for assessing industrial systems that evaluates all stages of a product's life. It provides a comprehensive view of the environmental aspects of the product or process.

massive online open courses (MOOC) An online educational course, generally free of charge, aimed at unlimited participation and open access via the internet.

materials 'Raw' forms of biological or technical nutrients, extracted or mined, or harvested from nature, including any processing to refine or clean them ready for use. If combined with other materials, they become compounds. Technical examples are iron, coal and granite, and biological examples are timber, fish or skimmed milk ('refined' by separating out some of the original milk fat).

mobile apps (apps) A computer program designed to operate on mobile devices such as smartphones and tablet computers.

mobile internet (mobile broadband) Marketing term for wireless internet access through a portable modem, mobile phone, USB wireless modem, tablet or other mobile devices.

natural capitalism The productive use and reinvestment in not just physical and financial (goods and money), but also natural and human capital (nature and people, including individuals, communities and cultures). (Definition by Hawken, P, Lovins, AB, Lovins, LH (2010) *Natural Capitalism: The next industrial revolution*, Earthscan, London.)

Natural Step The Natural Step, founded in Sweden in 1989 by scientist Karl-Henrik Robèrt, is a global network of non-profit organizations, focusing on sustainable development using a science-based framework. Its mission is to accelerate the transition to a sustainable society: 'in which individuals, communities, businesses and institutions thrive within nature's limits'. It defines four system conditions for a sustainable society, covering material extraction, man-made substances, degradation of nature and providing capacity for everyone to meet his or her basic needs.

non-government organizations (NGOs) A non-profit, voluntary citizens' group organized on a local, national or international level. NGOs perform a variety of service and humanitarian functions, bring citizen concerns to governments, advocate and monitor policies and encourage political participation through provision of information.

nutrients In the circular economy there are two types as described by McDonough and Braungart (*Cradle to Cradle: Remaking the way we make things*): biological nutrients, designed to re-enter the biosphere safely and build natural capital, and technical nutrients, which are designed to circulate at high quality without entering the biosphere. (Definition from Ellen MacArthur Foundation – see kumu.io/ellenmacarthurfoundation/educational-resources#circular-economy-general-resources-map/key-for-general-resources-map/intro-to-the-circular-economy (archived at https://perma.cc/4P6D-LR6Y))

open loop Used product or materials are reused by a company *other than the original producer* – whether for use in the same kind of product or process, or for a different product or process.

open loop – cross-sector Used materials or products flow across to one or more *different industry sectors*. An example is plastic recycling, where specialist processors deal with mixed plastic waste streams, such as packaging from household waste collections.

open loop – same sector Used materials and products flow back to a different company, but in the same industry sector, eg a specialist metals recycler involved in processing steel and aluminium from end-of-life cars, or a company that resells or remanufactures products originally made by another company.

open source (open sourcing) A collaborative method for developing software, hardware and design, based on transparent (and often distributed) development, and the open sharing of files and solutions.

original equipment manufacturer (OEM) A company that makes a part or component that is used in another company's end product. For example, if Acme Manufacturing Co makes power cords that are used on IBM computers, Acme is the OEM. OEM also refers to parts available on the open market, eg bearings with standard part numbers suitable for multiple products.

pay per use Payment of a fee for each use of a product or service, such as a bicycle from a city fleet.

peer-to-peer (consumer-to-consumer) (P2P) Transactions between individual consumers (citizens), or 'peers'.

permaculture Permaculture design uses systems thinking to create sustainable, self-supporting outcomes for a wide range of projects. Its origins are in agroforestry, and increasingly people are using it to design housing, communities, farms, smallholdings and gardens. It aims to develop efficient, productive systems that are ecologically sound. Permaculture designers aim to get more out of life by using less, minimizing inputs and maximizing outputs, so reaping benefits for the earth and wider society.

platforms An online 'meeting place' or exchange, allowing parties to communicate or transact with each other, eg as buyers and sellers. Examples include Uber, eBay, Preloved, Gumtree, Amazon Marketplace and Zipcar.

portable appliance testing (PAT) Examination of electrical appliances and equipment to ensure they are safe to use. Most electrical safety defects can be found by visual examination but some types of defect can only be found by testing.

process inputs Energy, water, cleaning products or chemicals to enable, speed up or slow down the manufacturing process, transit packaging, etc. All are used in the supply chain or manufacturing process, but do not form part of the final product.

product The outcome of the production process, consisting of one, several or many materials, compounds and components. This is the item used or consumed by the end user. We need to consider the context, eg an orange is a product, and if the orange is processed into orange juice, it becomes a different product. The distinction depends on whether further processing occurs, and helps differentiate between the different parts of the supply chain process.

product life-cycle management (PLM) In industry, product life-cycle management (PLM) is the process of managing the entire life-cycle of a product from inception, through engineering design and manufacture, to service and disposal of manufactured products. PLM integrates people, data, processes and business systems and provides a product information backbone for companies and their extended enterprise.

product stewardship The act of minimizing the health, safety, environmental and social impacts of a product and its packaging throughout all life-cycle stages, while also maximizing economic benefits. (Definition by Product Stewardship Institute – see www.productstewardship.us/?55 (archived at https://perma.cc/QND7-BEWR))

product-service systems (PSS) An integrated product and service offering that delivers value in use. (Definition by Neely, A (2013), Cranfield University – see andyneely.blogspot.co.uk/2013/11/what-is-servitization.html (archived at https://perma.cc/JPX4-W9QD))

Programme for the Endorsement of Forest Certification (PEFC) An international non-profit, non-governmental organization dedicated to promoting sustainable forest management; the PEFC is the certification system of choice for small forest owners.

prosumer A person who combines the economic roles of producer and consumer.

rare earth elements (REE) Rare earth elements, sometimes referred to as 'rare earth minerals' or 'rare earth metals', are a group of 17 chemically similar metallic elements, including the non-lanthanides scandium and yttrium, that have a diverse range of specific applications in a wide range of consumer electronics, in environmental technologies and in military applications.

rebound effect The reduction in expected efficiency gains from new technologies, due to behavioural or other systemic responses. For example, cheaper energy may mean people will buy more energy-consuming products.

recondition Potential adjustment to components bringing an item back to working order, although not necessarily to an as-new state. (Definition by the All-Party Parliamentary Sustainable Resource Group – see www.policyconnect.org.uk/apsrg/research/report-remanufacturing-towards-resource-efficient-economy-0 (archived at https://perma.cc/THM5-LK28))

recycling Extraction of a product's raw materials for use in new products. This is a good option for products that are easily constructed and have minimal numbers of components. (Definition by the All-Party Parliamentary Sustainable Resource Group – see www.policyconnect.org.uk/apsrg/research/report-remanufacturing-towards-resource-efficient-economy-0 (archived at https://perma.cc/THM5-LK28))

redistribute Redistribution markets move items from where they are not needed to somewhere they are needed.

refurbish To return a product to a satisfactory working condition, which may involve rebuilding or repairing components close to failure, even if no faults are apparent.

remanufacturing A series of manufacturing steps acting on an end-of-life part or product in order to return it to like-new or better performance, with a warranty to match. (Definition by Centre for Remanufacturing and Reuse – see www.remanufacturing.org.uk/what-is-remanufacturing.php (archived at https://perma.cc/2YYW-6B7U))

repair To return a faulty or broken product or component to a usable state.

repurposing Transforming an object (product, component or materials) from its original intended use or purpose to an alternative use or purpose.

resource efficiency Using the Earth's limited resources in a sustainable manner while minimizing impacts on the environment. It allows us to create more with less and to deliver greater value with less input.

reuse Simple reuse of a product, component or material, for the same purpose, with no modifications.

secondary raw material (or secondary material) Material recovered from existing products or processes and recycled to be used again (in contrast to primary, virgin material).

servitization The innovation of an organization's capabilities and processes to better create mutual value through a shift from selling product to selling product-service systems. (Definition by Neely, A, Cranfield University – see andyneely.blogspot.co.uk/2013/11/what-is-servitization.html (archived at https://perma.cc/JPX4-W9QD))

shared value Shared value is a management strategy focused on companies creating measurable business value by identifying and addressing social problems that intersect with their business. The concept was defined by Professor Michael E Porter and Mark R Kramer – see www.sharedvalue.org/about-shared-value (archived at https://perma.cc/R4XH-AFRZ).

sink (natural capital context) The capacity of the environment to absorb the unwanted by-products of production and consumption: exhaust gases from combustion or chemical processing, water used to clean products or people, discarded packaging and goods no longer wanted. (Definition by the OECD – see stats.oecd.org/glossary/detail.asp?ID=6569 (archived at https://perma.cc/N4ZH-TK3P))

source In the context of natural capital, the supply of resources and services provided by or taken from nature. Resources include forests, mineral deposits, fisheries and fertile soil. Services include pollination, purification of air and water.

stock-keeping units (SKUs) An item of stock (product, component, material) that is unique because of some characteristic (such as brand, size, colour, model). Each SKU is assigned a unique identification number.

supply chain operations reference model (SCOR) The world's leading supply chain framework, linking business processes, performance metrics, practices and people skills into a unified structure. The SCOR six distinct management processes are: Plan, Source, Make, Deliver, Return and Enable. (Definition by APICS Supply Chain Council – see www.apics.org/sites/apics-supply-chain-council/frameworks/scor (archived at https://perma.cc/2ECQ-CE4K))

sustainable development The United Nations Report of the World Commission on Environment and Development: Our Common Future in 1987 (the 'Brundtland report') defined sustainable development as 'development which meets the needs of current generations without compromising the ability of future generations to meet their own needs'.

systems thinking The process of understanding how things influence one another within a complete entity, or larger system. In nature, examples include ecosystems in which various elements such as air, water, movement, plants and animals work together to survive or perish. In organizations, systems consist of people, structures and processes that work together.

technical nutrients Materials extracted from the earth's crust (eg metals, minerals, fossil fuels) or man-made (eg polymers, alloys and other man-made materials).

triple bottom line (TBL) Used to focus corporations (companies) on the environmental, social and economic value they add – and destroy. 'At its broadest, the term captures the whole set of values, issues and processes that companies must address in order to minimize any harm resulting from their activities and to create economic, social and environmental value.' (Definition by John Elkington – see www.sustainability.com/library/the-power-to-change#.V0pxxeSK2kV (archived at https://perma.cc/ML8J-C9YB))

upcycle (upcycling, upcycled) A process of converting materials into new materials or products of higher quality or increased functionality. (Definition by the Ellen MacArthur Foundation.)

urban mines The process of reclaiming compounds and elements from products, buildings and waste, may also refer to the facilities for reclamation, eg recycling plants/processing facilities.

value chain The full range of activities undertaken to bring a product or service from its conception to its end use and beyond.

virgin material Material that has not been previously used or consumed, or processed other than for its original intended function.

volatile organic compounds (VOC) One of a number of chemicals, including acetone, benzene and formaldehyde, that evaporate or vaporize readily and are harmful to human health and the environment.

Waste Resources Action Programme (WRAP) UK charity, publishing research, delivering consumer campaigns, grants and financial support.

Numbering system used in this book

One million = 1,000,000
One billion = 1,000,000,000 = 1,000 million
One trillion = 1,000,000,000,000 = 1,000,000 million

INDEX

Note: Numbers in headings are filed as spelt out; acronyms and 'Mc' are filed as presented; '#' is ignored for filing purposes. Locators in *italics* denote information within figures or tables.

CPSIA information can be obtained
at www.ICGtesting.com
Printed in the USA
BVHW071935221222
654846BV00001B/1